AF848446

Globalization and the Decline of American Power

This book explores America's decline as a global power, arguing that the implosion of Pax Americana was initiated by the process of globalization, preceding the collapse of the Soviet Union by nearly a decade. The era of Pax Americana, and with it American hegemony, is conclusively passed, and will not return in current global conditions.

There is a stark contrast between the present epoch and the postwar era of American hegemony (1945–1979) in which the United States, at least outside of the Soviet sphere of influence, largely managed the international economy and reigned over international politics and relations. Drawing on both theoretical and empirical evidence, this book shows that the era of globalization unleashed forces—social, political, and economic—which broke down the status quo of American hegemony. Author Cyrus Bina also establishes that since the Iranian Revolution (1979), US involvement throughout the Middle East, in Iraq, Afghanistan, Libya, Syria, Yemen, and now notably in Ukraine has been motivated by the freefall of American hegemony and an attempt to get it back by direct or indirect military force. Bina utilizes these contexts for wider analysis and critique of a number of theories commonly used to analyze economy, polity, geopolitical, and dynamics of crisis and social change in capitalism.

This book will be of great interest to students, academics, and policymakers on subjects of Economics, International Relations, Global Studies, International Political Economy, Political Geography, Sociology, and postwar History.

Cyrus Bina is Distinguished Research Professor of Economics at the University of Minnesota (Morris Campus), USA. He was formerly a fellow and associate at the Center for Middle Eastern Studies, Harvard University (1990–1995). He is a pioneering theorist of globalization of oil and the unification of energy sector, globalization of world economy and decline of the Pax Americana, and a specialist on modern Iran and the contemporary in the Middle East. His work is also published in Chinese, German, Japanese, Italian, Persian, and Spanish, among others. He is a Fellow of Economists for Peace and Security and an editor for the Journal of Critical Studies in Business and Society.

Routledge Frontiers of Political Economy

Economics and Art Theory
Edited by Stratos Myrogiannis and Constantinos Repapis

Capitalism and Agrarian Change
Production and Reproduction in Indonesia
Muchtar Habibi

Capitalist Agriculture and the Global Bee Crisis
Rebecca Ellis

China, Trust and Digital Supply Chains
Dynamics of a Zero Trust World
Warwick Powell

Macroeconomic Modelling, Economic Policy and Methodology
Economics at the Edge
Edited by Mikael Randrup Byrialsen, Hamid Raza and Finn Olesen

Economics, Anthropology and the Origin of Money as a Bargaining Counter
Patrick Spread

Bernard Schmitt's Quantum Macroeconomic Analysis
Alvaro Cencini

Blockchain and the Commons
Vangelis Papadimitropoulos

Globalization and the Decline of American Power
The Political Economy of the American Fall
Cyrus Bina

For more information about this series, please visit: www.routledge.com/Routledge-Frontiers-of-Political-Economy/book-series/SE0345

Globalization and the Decline of American Power

The Political Economy of the American Fall

Cyrus Bina

Routledge
Taylor & Francis Group
LONDON AND NEW YORK

First published 2023
by Routledge
4 Park Square, Milton Park, Abingdon, Oxon OX14 4RN

and by Routledge
605 Third Avenue, New York, NY 10158

Routledge is an imprint of the Taylor & Francis Group, an informa business

© 2023 Cyrus Bina

The right of Cyrus Bina to be identified as author of this work has been asserted in accordance with sections 77 and 78 of the Copyright, Designs and Patents Act 1988.

All rights reserved. No part of this book may be reprinted or reproduced or utilised in any form or by any electronic, mechanical, or other means, now known or hereafter invented, including photocopying and recording, or in any information storage or retrieval system, without permission in writing from the publishers.

Trademark notice: Product or corporate names may be trademarks or registered trademarks, and are used only for identification and explanation without intent to infringe.

British Library Cataloguing-in-Publication Data
A catalogue record for this book is available from the British Library

Library of Congress Cataloging-in-Publication Data
Names: Bina, Cyrus, 1946– author.
Title: Globalization and the decline of American power : the political economy of the American fall / Cyrus Bina.
Description: Milton Park, Abingdon, Oxon ; New York, NY : Routledge, 2023. | Includes bibliographical references and index.
Identifiers: LCCN 2022024765 | ISBN 9780815353317 (hardback) | ISBN 9781032380032 (paperback) | ISBN 9781351136785 (ebook)
Subjects: LCSH: Power (Social sciences)—United States. | Hegemony—United States.
Classification: LCC HN90.P6 B529 2023 | DDC 303.30973—dc23/eng/20220609
LC record available at https://lccn.loc.gov/2022024765

ISBN: 978-0-8153-5331-7 (hbk)
ISBN: 978-1-032-38003-2 (pbk)
ISBN: 978-1-351-13678-5 (ebk)

DOI: 10.4324/9781351136785

Typeset in Bembo
by Apex CoVantage, LLC

Contents

Notes on Sources

Concerning published materials, the author (Cyrus Bina) is the copyright holder of the following work with the expressed permission of the publishers. The inventory of sources used (either wholly or in part) in this volume is as follows:

"Internationalization of the Oil Industry: Simple Oil Shocks or Structural Crisis?" *Review: Journal of Fernand Braudel Center* 11 (3), 1988, by *The Fernand Braudel Center* at Binghamton University, Binghamton, New York; "Some Controversies in the Development of Rent Theory: The Nature of Oil Rent," *Capital & Class* 39, 1989, by Sage Publishers, Thousand Oaks, California; "Limits to OPEC Pricing: OPEC Profits and the Nature of Global Oil Accumulation," *OPEC Review* 14 (1), 1990, by Wiley, UK; "Oil, Japan, and Globalization," *Challenge: A Magazine of Economic Affairs* 37 (3), 1994, and "The Globalization of Oil: A Prelude to a Critical Political Economy," *International Journal of Political Economy, International Journal of Political Economy* 35 (2), 2006, by M. E. Sharpe, Armonk, New York, Taylor & France; "OPEC in the Epoch of Globalization: An Event Study of Global Oil Prices," *Global Economy Journal* 7 (1), 2007, by Berkeley Electronic Press, California; "Competition, Control and Price Formation in the International Energy Industry," *Energy Economics* 11 (3), 1989, by Elsevier, New York; "The Rhetoric of Oil and the Dilemma of War and American Hegemony," *Arab Studies Quarterly* 15 (3), 1993 and "On Sand Castles and Sand-Castle Conjectures: A Rejoinder," *Arab Studies Quarterly* 17 (1 & 2), 1995, by the editor; "Is It the Oil, Stupid?" *The URPE Newsletter* 35 (3), 2004, by Union for Radical Political Economics; "The American Tragedy: The Quagmire of War, Rhetoric of Oil and the Conundrum of Hegemony," *Journal of Iranian Research and Analysis* 20 (2), 2004 and "Crossroads of History and a Critique of Prevailing Political Perspectives," *Journal of Iranian Research and Analysis* 26 (2), by the editor; *Oil: A Time Machine*. Linus Books, 2012; "Synthetic Competition, Global Oil, and the Cult of Monopoly," in *Alternative Theories of Competition*. Routledge, 2013; "Specter of Globalization: Marx, Gramsci and Disjointed Time," *World Review of Political Economy* 10 (4), Winter 2019 (open source), published by Pluto Press; "Oil, COVID-19, and the Global Economy," published electronically on *New Cold War* website, April 28, 2020 (open source); "Corona's Bio-Economic Crisis and the Post-Corona World," *International Critical Thought* 10 (4), January 21, 2021 (open source) Taylor & Francis online.

Acknowledgments

The idea of this book goes all the way back to when the Pax Americana was very much alive, and the Soviet Union was at its peak. It was the question of tendency by both observation and sensible reasoning about the world then that prompted me to take this idea seriously against the many who were still thinking that both the Pax Americana and the Soviet bloc are the permanent fixtures of our universe. Though the intense work on this volume started about 5 years ago when I was participating in the Allied Social Science Association (ASSA) meetings, in January 2017, in Chicago, and at Hyatt Regency, I stepped into the publisher's exhibition hall at Routledge Both for a promising conversation with Andy Humphries, the publisher, and the rest is history. Of course, the background of this commitment goes back to the ASSA meetings, in January 2014, in Philadelphia, where I was a speaker at a roundtable on economic security, organized by Economists for Peace and Security (EPS), and was kindly approached by Andy to do a volume on global security.

The last 5 years have been like the mother of all turbulence in my both personal and professional life while the keen sense of posterity, on the one hand, and unnecessary irritation, isolation, and immense fine-tuning owing to this godforsaken pandemic and its aftereffects, on the other, created an exceptional atmosphere of evanescence and aura of universal uncertainty beyond belief. Yet, hope for completion of this book and my articulation of definite apprehension toward uncritical progressives and dilapidated views of so many on the radical left on the very planet on which we live kept me going. This book is simply a glimpse of a half-century of critical observation which intensely has to do with the transmogrification of today's economy, polity, and social relations across the globe, with no iota of apology.

Over the span of the last 5 years, I owed a debt of gratitude to too many colleagues and friends whose inclusion exceeds, which is not possible in this little note. They know who they are, and I am eternally grateful to them. Among those that in one way or the other inspired this project, several names come to mind. These are the individuals whose presence or action made a tangible impact on the completion of this volume. Among my students, I wish to thank John W. Barber, Sierra Brown, Matthew Ebaugh, Duan Liu, Bingyuan Yan, and Zahng Yang who contributed immensely to the discussions while in my political economy and transnational enterprise classes at the University of Minnesota (Morris Campus). My dear colleagues Arne Kildegaard and James Wojtaszeh, both of UMM, knew what is at stake when one teaches a heavy load of upper-division classes together with twice as much research that receives little more than lip service from the central administration and top leadership. They were my source of encouragement when I felt not unlike an alien from outer space in the movie, Starman.

There are other colleagues and friends in both academic and other professional capacities that were supportive of my work on this and other theoretical and empirical work in and out of the United States who inspired me with their own writings and professional activities. The late Eugenia Correa, Alicia Giron, Natasha Hernández, Jesus Sosa from the National Autonomous University of Mexico; Mario Seccareccia of the University of Ottawa; Anwar Shaikh and Sanjay Reddy of the New School for Social Research; Jamee Moudud of Sarah Lawrence College; and of course, the late John Weeks of SOAS, University of London. I profusely thank James K. Galbraith and Thea Harvey Barratt of Economists for Peace and Security for their continuous support of my work and its political impact on the cause of global peace. Catherine Davies should be praised for setting off the idea of writing a piece on COVID and the negative price of oil in 2020. Frances Boys should be applauded for her frequent invitations to write when she was the editor of the URPE Newsletter. I wish to thank Gao Jingyu and Wang Zhen of the Chinese Academy of Social Sciences and respective editors of *International Critical Thought* and *World Review of Political Economy*, for the primary materials that were revised and updated in this volume. Pezhman Rahimi deserves special thanks for several years of dedication to my work, among others, of the production of three separate lecture series (in Persian) on a critical look at imperialism, critical political economy, and oil: from cartelization to competitive globalization, available on YouTube; I owe Afarin Moezzi for carrying out a series of painstaking interviews with me, on pertinent issues of our time, for the Persian speaking world.

Back to UMM, I am grateful to LeAnn Dean (director), Peter Bremer, and Naomi Skulan of Rodney A. Briggs Library, and to Lawrence Godwin of information technology support, for their dedicated service beyond the call of duty.

Last but certainly not least, I wish to express utmost appreciation to Andy Humphries for his trust in me and for being patient in the completion of the book. My thanks also go to Emma Morley and Jake Millicheap who took care of the manuscript toward publication. For any probable errors of omission or commission, I alone am responsible.

May not an ass know when the cart draws the horse?

King Lear
Act I, scene 4
William Shakespeare

1 Introduction

The American World Order Is Passé

I wish you to be the leader of the free world.

—Volodymyr Zelensky (from his bunker in Kiev pleading for WWIII)
Address at the joint session of US Congress, March 16, 2022[1]

China understands its economic future is much more closely tied to the West than it is to Russia.

—President Biden (following the NATO Summit on Ukraine Crisis)
Press Conference on Russia's invasion of Ukraine—March 24, 2022[2]

I

The cat is out of the bag, and the tooth-and-nail struggle of the United States against its irrevocable global decline is wide in the open. The free fall of the American hegemony, whose deep wounds could be tracked and traced through Afghanistan, Iraq, Libya, Syria, and Yemen, to name a handful of brutal and barbaric devastation entwined with subsequent humiliating and predictable defeat after defeat by the United States, is now visibly in the middle of Europe, a continent that gave us the two most devastating world wars of the twentieth century. This time, Ukraine, a patch of divided land and holdover of Tsarist Russia and then the fragment of the now-defunct USSR, on the one hand, and between the encroaching of post-Soviet NATO toward the eastern borders of the newly formed Russian Federation, on the other, is the target of the "new" world order that has since the fall of the Soviet Union *fancied* by the United States. The US freefall, together with the irrelevance of NATO, is incontestable, even by those deprived of theoretical analysis who often think with their eyes. The Russian invasion of Ukraine was not inevitable but the United States, together with the sheepish stance of the European fragments of now-defunct Pax Americana, made it so.[3] The Russian invasion of Ukraine was not unprovoked either, as the prehistory of this very conflict, and similar provocations by the United States, goes all the way back to day one, right after the collapse of the Berlin Wall in 1989; the preamble was the US illusory vision for another "American century" (and worse, the myth of unipolarity) in a political

DOI: 10.4324/9781351136785-1

atmosphere in which dust was not yet settled and the skyline of the post-American polity was not yet resembled a post-American world in the making.[4] The prediction of this conflict turning into a possible full-scale war was made by William Burns—the former US ambassador to the Russian Federation, and presently the CIA director in the Biden administration—in 2008.[5] The orthodox geopolitical scholars too, such as John Mearsheimer, although mistakenly captivated by the whimsy of the "unipolar" thesis, as early as 2014 had predicted that the redline of Russia in Ukraine would not let NATO stretch its military grip aiming to encircle the Russian territory.[6] These facts are not in dispute by anyone with a modicum of intelligence, including the submissive leaders of the present fragments of the Pax Americana in Western Europe. There is also no dispute on the reality of post-American Europe, a scenario within the grasp of more pragmatic leaders of France and Germany in Europe, aside from mini-states that would rather float fatalistically within post-Soviet NATO[7] way beyond its original charter in the Pax Americana. What is in dispute is owing to the myopic vision of the many on the left and the right in Europe, North America, Latin America, Africa, and Asia is whereabouts as to the utter force of epochal change and impossibility of the second American century or something looks like the American world.[8] Yet, within all this, particularly the nonsense of American centrality, a quick comparison of Emmanuel Macron's image of the existing situation in the world and that of Alex Callinicos, a self-styled Marxist, is not only interesting but also mindboggling. This sadly shows that on occasion, when it comes to critical issues, right-wing liberals are light years ahead of loads of oblivious and out-to-lunch leftists.[9] To this end, the scores upon scores within the radical left are not only cluelessly muddied the issues surrounding geopolitics but also divested themselves of deeper theoretical vision unblemished by Hobsonite and neo-Hobsonite view of the world as to the epochal-making and all-encompassing transformations that within the span of two decades underpinned and facilitated the collapse of the postwar Pax Americana (1945–1979) and that of the Soviet Union (1922–1990) in sequential efficacy of a one-two punch. However, the quality, character, and differing political effects of these two sequential breakdowns, on the one hand, and visibility of dust and debris in the falling-out of the latter, on the other, had immediately gave off a whiff of invincibility to the latter, particularly its defunct hegemon—the United States. And this was *inter alia* the beginning of an illusion for a sizable and varied spectrum, from the right of the right to the left of the left, on the ideological and political scale, in one single mission: to propagate the American-centered view of the world around by misidentifying it with the epoch of globalization. As has been shown in this book, the dogmatic and fragmented view of the traditional left and eclectic vision of self-styled radicals are equally injurious as the right-wing orthodoxy in deterring truth and in the obfuscation of today's reality. Indeed, in methodological terms, the former predictably act and contribute as an appendage of the latter to the misidentification of our era, the mystification of our economy, the misperception of power, and obscuring of "world order" in our polity, in both war and peace.

Finally, a variety of nationalistic (and nation-state centered) analyses include those of the left and the right in the middle of the Ukraine conflict when it comes to oil, gas, and other vital resources from both the European and global view at large. Again, the clueless and theory-less left mimics the right by obfuscating the context and production of oil, natural gas, energy, and other vital resources, and by dubbing them "Russian," "American," etc., in this crisis. Here, Achille's heel of the orthodox theory of international relations (geopolitics?) and imperialism (counterpart of nationalism), an impression portrayed in the works of the many neo-Hobsonites within radical leftists find consonance. They both believe in ad hoc manipulation and monopoly, without knowing or interested to know the undercurrents of change that have already taken place, say, in the oil and energy sector since the oil crisis of the early 1970s. They both treat not only oil, energy, and other such resources through the prism of the nation-state per se but also everything else that habitually comes to view uncritically and in a fetishistic manner. And sadly, the globalization of oil (and energy), a reality that was proven by this author more than four decades ago, has no meaning to both orthodoxy in geopolitics and the traditional left other than a trifling metaphor even today. The two chapters on oil in this book are intended to particularly refresh the memories of those progressives who drive toward Marx (and Marx's theory of value) in their daydreams but bizarrely shunt the vehicle of analysis head-on to right-wing orthodoxy.[10] This gives the impression that with these chest-beating and impulsive friends within the overwhelming radical left (even self-styled Marxists) the struggling masses and working class across the globe need no enemies. It is within the larger context of this book that theory, policy, and praxis go hand in hand and why in reality, despite the manifestation of long intranational and international class polarization, sharpened contradictions, and worldwide multifaceted struggles, the radical left is so universally ineffectual.

II

It is first and foremost demonstrated in the book that periodization of capitalism is internal to overcoming of barriers and thus expansion of capital itself and that such dynamics occur deep and wide across the geography of production, the ultimate manifestation of which is globalization. This theoretical context is then concretized again theoretically to assess the various alternatives, particularly those inaugurated by the advent of monopoly capitalism, a mainstay of the overwhelming majority of radical left across the world since Hilferding and Lenin. Here, it is vigorously argued that neither the categorical quash of Marx's value theory à la Paul Sweezy (and Monthly Review School) nor other a bit more bashful variety, say, Ernest Mandel's has any methodological or factual room for the analysis of contemporary capitalism.[11] Along the same lines, it is reminded that "monopoly capitalism" itself is a mode of appearance and thus a cause of deception by those who offhandedly utilized it as a point of departure in the periodization of capitalism.[12] Contrary to the traditional left mesmerized, secondhand through Lenin via Hobson's, it is also demonstrated that imperialism is not a perpetual concept and that it must be identified as a historical period whose corporeality validates the pre-globalized conditions of capitalism displayed in concrete geopolitics and polity in general, and thus any ad hoc conflicts or full-scale war beyond it need not be couched in such anachronistic mode. In other words, in the epoch of globalization actions among nations that may lead to the lack of resolution and consequently toward war need not be grounded on a bygone era of imperialism and *dogmatically* branded as "inter-imperialist rivalry."

More specifically, it is shown that the collapse of the postwar Pax Americana (1945–1979) is none other than the loss of American hegemony to which the United States was suspended in the balance and the fall of American power is but a quintessential *effect* of globalization, a punishing irony of capitalism itself.[13] Thus, the immensity of these invasions and participation in bloodshed in Iraq (1990–1991), Yugoslavia (1999),[14] Afghanistan (2001), Iraq (2003), Libya (2011), Syria (2011),[15] Ukraine (2014), and Yemen (2014), *inter alia*, by the United States is motivated by the freefall of American hegemony and an attempt to get it back by sheer military force. This is also a kernel of an *impossibility* theorem articulated in this book.

The aforementioned context provides a footing for wider analysis and radical critique of a handful of perspectives that pretend to explicate economy, polity, geopolitical, and dynamics of crisis and social change in capitalism. One of these perspectives is World-Systems theory à la Geovanni Arrighi (and similarly Emmanuel Wallerstein's) whose setting comprises *transhistorical* inquiry imposed on specific history and the misuse of hegemony in such circumstances. World-Systems theory, a school of thought primarily in sociology that seemingly overstretches the multifaceted field of global transformation, is exemplified as a non-starter in this book. Another perspective envelops Hardt and Negri's *Empire*, a provocative yet revealing project that points to an imaginary place (without time) counterfeited out of the years of misreading and then deliberate misplacement of Marx's methodology, theories of class, value, competition, exploitation, with the imagery of postmodernism and attitude on the scramble and assemblage of *multitude*.[16] As has been shown, the rhetoric of globalization based on *Empire* is but a pseudo-analysis that maligns the transnationalization of capital as a social relation and obfuscates the (epochal) manifestation of globalization. A wrong turn of digital, the so-called virtual technology, on the one hand, and of hyper-subjectivity running haywire, on the other, is perhaps the set-off of such fiasco.

Finally, there are other critiques on issues surrounding the substitution of neoliberalism for globalization, as a measure of periodization and an index of capital's overcoming and prevailing over the barrier of geography and confusion over monopoly and competition in contemporary capitalism. Implicit in this volume is also a stark contrast between the theory of globalization offered in this book and the Uno School (with or without embellishment and amplification through transhistorical method of "critical realism") in which the dichotomy of abstract and concrete is so visibly noticeable through the artifice of preset (and superimposed) stages, and which—unlike Marx's method of abstraction—Uno's theory of value arbitrarily built upon the erroneous perception of money.[17] The details of all this and more are critically presented in the volume. The origins of globalization in this book are initiated by the inner dynamics of social capital itself in which the stages of development are themselves internally grounded upon overcoming the surmountable barriers external to capital, including the barrier of geography across the global landscape.[18] The emergence of globalization and the universality of capitalist social relations inaugurated the highest stage of capitalism, and as thoroughly established in the book the eclipse of the postwar Pax Americana (1945–1979) is the very consequence of this universality.[19] The tectonic plates, so to speak, had already moved, and when it comes to geopolitics the world is now in the middle of political disorder, excruciating aftereffects, and long reverberations.

III

The contour of the US descent from the pinnacle of postwar international hegemony today is now conspicuously perceptible from the dilapidated surface of physical, social, and political underpinnings across the United States where the regression of inside enjoins the degeneration of outside. However, posturing as "leader of the free world" and claiming the "seat" at the "head" of the proverbial table has remained an alarming habit that could not be worn off easily, particularly in a turbulent transition to the post-Pax Americana world.[20] Thus, the Biden administration—after 4 years of political and ideological striptease on both the domestic and global stages—has its hands full in grappling with the deep economic and political polarization at home and the resuscitation of failed and flopped pre-Trump foreign policies that had already sunk the United States further into the abyss of antiquated and decaying American order. To be sure, this intervening disorder is but a deliberate creation by the United States alone since the end of the Cold War.

To those hesitating to accept this conclusion, that is, the vast majority of unsuspecting observers who are constantly bombarded by the war of ideology through other means, namely, by the tsunami of press and propaganda, we must insist to look into the original sin of George H.W. Bush's massive invasion and permanent military expedition across the Persian Gulf, in 1991, although the fall of the Soviet Union was not settled yet, and direct involvement of the Clinton administration in the breakup of former Yugoslavia that predictably led to the bloody civil war that followed in the late 1990s. These are not short of a collection of committed original sins according to which the United States' appeal to the "rule of international law" conveniently reverberates since the post-Soviet world.

One must remember the deliberate circumvention of international law through arm-twisting, bribery, and wiretapping of the UN General Assembly by the (George H.W.) Bush administration (1990–1991)[21] engaged in flat-out disregard for the United Nations which was in due time followed by a series of illegal invasions by the Bush-Cheney administration. Therefore, any appeal to international law by any American official is none other a sham. The context (and pre-contexts) of these illegal acts by the United States should set the acquisitive reader on the accurate course of nearly all conflicts that while tragic nevertheless point to the mother of all mischief-making, namely, the United States, also having to do with the current dreadful war in Ukraine. In the meantime, parallel with the actual combatants inside Ukraine and war of misinformation and disinformation across the Western media, the fog of a larger war hovers over Europe and beyond.[22] There are three major measures that may illustrate the fragility, instability, and anachronistic nature of America's post-Pax American/post-hegemonic reality when it comes to foreign policy across the board at this juncture.

First is the difference between the real and imaginary views of the post-Cold War, the latter transpires the hallmark of not only the US foreign policy apparatus and apparatchiks but also their dutiful broadcasts through the promoting arm of US mainstream media amplified and editorialized across the political landscape.[23] This includes an exaggerated characterization of the United States as "leader of the free world," hurly-burly juxtaposition of "democracy" and "authoritarianism," and weaponization and transposition and of every subject, pertinent or not, into an arsenal of defying the epoch (and order) of globalization in this dangerously wrecking disorder across the world.[24] The impulsive, indelicate, and reactionary motto "you're either with us or against us" is not just a specific signature for the likes of George W. Bush (the crudest of US presidents running neck-and-neck, say, with Donald Trump) when it comes to foreign policy; this peculiar mindset is the very symptom of the undercurrent of loss of hegemony and decline of the United States as a global power, thus a permanent feature of self-flagellating policymaking in Washington since the fall of the Pax Americana.

The collapse of the Soviet Union appears to have refurbished the threadbare ideology of American "exceptionalism" that was long force-fed the domestic civil society and, at the same time, brandish as a triumphal badge of invincibility in the foreign adventures and misadventures. The peddling of this deep-seated creed has been so widespread through the educational institutions of the West beyond the geographical boundary of the United States. It is within this context that the two intertwined relics of the yesteryears, namely, "US leadership" and "free world," are weaponized against real and imaginary enemies as a standard strategy in foreign policy. The deceptiveness of this illusion thus affected the misbelief of "the end of history" along with the impulse of yet another "American century." We now know that Fukuyama's *The End of History* was a shameful self-deception; the real history that was long ended is the Pax Americana (1945–1979). Within the same context, there are overstated claims vis-à-vis the resuscitation of the purported US postwar alliance out of a patchwork of Western countries that once belonged to the imperial domain of the now-defunct Pax Americana. That is why the US decline, precipitated by the breakdown of postwar economic and political institutions, prompts a zero-sum game in today's geopolitics. Therefore, the illusion of *alliance* and the rhetoric of *unity* are not supported by the reality (of globalization) on the ground and material conditions that are many times more potent and much more imposing than the United States and its superfluous and wobbly alliance with Europe; the same sweeping changes that splintered the old postwar polity would not allow another world (in terms of both economy and polity) in the alleged American vintage. The fall of the United States from the pinnacle of global power is neither accidental nor revocable as the American elite, particularly the fossilized political class in Washington, attempted to restore by any means necessary. This is but a daydream for the cold warriors who won the battle but lost the war in their retirement. And in this pitiful state of unrest, neither American political party is up to the historic and necessary task of cutting down to size and quitting the boastful mission of gunrunning, and, provoking, meddling, and fueling the bloody wars around the world.[25]

The second is the adversity of 9/11 (September 11, 2001), utilized rather ironically by those who believed that the world stage is unoccupied and that the United States can quickly establish its supremacy across the globe and spread Washington's agenda in the nook and cranny of the planet in short order. This was motivated by the myopic intellect and mechanical mindset of those at the top and at the center of the policymaking system who saw the façade of geopolitics and passed over the larger dynamics and deeper underside of change. They defrauded both themselves and the world with the daydream of "unipolarity" and the whimsy of "liberal order," a worldview that is none other than a badly written fairy tale with horrendous consequences. The consequences (in West Asia and North Africa) have been perpetual war, torrents of blood, the genocide of biblical proportion, and ultimate defeat after defeat for the United States, which furthered the velocity of decline and sunk the latter further into the abyss. Aside from the message and motivation of those in the US leadership involved, the repercussion of all this is none other than the reality that the "America century" was long over. This means that—after the collapse of the bipolar world of the Pax Americana—speaking and striving for a "unipolar" leadership by any means necessary are both bloody costly and mightily humiliating for the United States. In this context, the doctrine of the "war on terror," displayed in Afghanistan, Iraq, Libya, Syria, and Yemen, to name a handful, just like an X-ray machine reveals every bone in the skeleton of American anachronistic imperialism, not unlike the latter days the British colonial empire. Just as the Trump presidency revealed the real face of the Confederacy, despite a flurry of post-Confederate institutions, a burst of constitutional amendments, and struggles for civil rights in the United States, the latter's global erosion is now fused with domestic degeneration. And, to the extent that this translates to power in a global sense, America's inside and outside would certainly be subject to mutual reinforcement toward further decline.[26]

The third is the American intrinsic vision against global change and a foreign policy essentially grounded on nostalgia and by any means necessary. This of course comes at the expense of an economy and polity that are not compatible with America's nostalgic vision of sitting at the head of the table, so to speak. In other words, despite the American popular psyche in Wall Street and Main Street, this "table" and its "head" do not constitute a part of the corporeality of international relations (and geopolitics) today. First, the table has turned; second, the "head" was figuratively mummified and patently relegated to the annals of history; in other words, the United States is no longer hegemonic or exceptional, particularly in the global polity in the making that already is the living negation of the Pax Americana. However, just as the tectonic plates of the new polity pressed against one another and the forces of globalization devastated the institutions and vestiges of the past era, the United States (and what is known as the "West") is slow to realize that the new order runs by much deeper and more pivotal forces far beyond defunct postwar hierarchies.[27] Nevertheless, this interlude in geopolitics and international relations is needlessly replete with rancor, deliberate obstruction, and downright nostalgia, defining the United States (an alienated and defunct hegemon) in an increasingly less and lesser-acknowledged than in the bygone era and accustomed world.

The war in Ukraine is the latest example of a tragedy that was repeated more than once since the fall of the Soviet Union interweaved by the illusion of another American century. The Ukrainians are the latest casualties of this impulsive and bogus strategy that was tried a dozen or more times in different reincarnations elsewhere with overall failure and incalculable devastation in blood and treasure, and with bitterness in the mouth of millions upon millions, both the ones that took the brunt of it head-on and those in billions who observed it with much agony since 1991. This time Ukrainians are both the mercenaries and victims of the American (and NATO) proxy war against the Russian Federation. And this war is literally a trigger away from a full-scale war that may bring the world to a nuclear exchange either on purpose or by mistake. In the Cold War era, the United States countered the Soviet Union and fought against what was known as communism; today, the United States is countering China and Russia against global capitalism, or more correctly, global capitalism fought the United States through the disruption of the Pax Americana, and thus cut the United States down to size, so to speak. In other words, the hang-up of the United States is the epochal change that was brought to bear by globalization (globalized capitalism) as fully explicated in this book.

The geopolitics here are the tip of the epochal change, and without the latter, the former may never be understood in isolation and by itself as a standalone discipline. This war between the unschooled and semi-schooled appears to be Putin's war, but those who can see clearly beyond the surface on the battlefield and penetrating the depth and profundity of dynamics that led to this conflict would recognize that neither labeling it as Putin's war nor insulating it from the task of the United States and NATO expansion, the very cause of this bloody mess, carries no credibility. The pretentious justification for the "nuclear umbrella" across Europe, after the Cold War, notwithstanding the rejection of Russia's inclusion in NATO earlier, on the one hand, and the deliberate eastward expansion of NATO, on the other, speak for themselves and for the dubious political position of the United States in the world, the manifestation of which is not pretty for Europe either.[28] Yet, there is no shortage of Orwellian posturing and chicanery over this war. The example of what President Biden mouthed on March 25, 2022, on "democracy" and "freedom," while visiting the members of the US Army's 82nd Airborne Division in Poland, is among many that both reveal and obfuscate the profundity of American constraint and state of precarity. Yet the diatribes and theatrics are the same both in attending to quandaries abroad or at home.[29]

In the meantime, the "Doomsday Clock,"[30] which was set on January 20, 2022, at 100 seconds to midnight, is now much closer, alerting us precisely to the *ultimate cause* of the post-Soviet collapse and in this emerging world that may not have a palpable connection with the collapse of the Pax Americana and the inevitability of fall of the American hegemony. Yet, the fall of American hegemony, and more importantly the irreversibility of this fall, is the mother of all conflicts in today's world. This, of course, combined with the collapse of the Soviet Union, created an incendiary condition unparalleled in recent history, a situation that breeds conflict after conflict in the post-American world. The train of globalization has long departed from the proverbial station, but nostalgic America is still running rather frantically toward the rear cars to reach the *familiar* point of departure, and in so doing bumping into and knocking off other passengers that are standing on the way. This includes both economics and politics, as for instance the monotonous sanctions and their intended, as well as unintended consequences (see the backfire of sanctions and countersanctions in Ukraine's case), come full circle at the doorsteps of the United States. Neither is babbling about "human rights" working as a *weapon* anymore. Why? Because the United States contemporaneously (never mind historically at its inception) is a notorious violator of human rights. This should be added to the shameful and hypocritical stance and conduct of the US government toward documented war crimes that the United States, in collaboration with NATO, has perpetrated in Afghanistan, Iraq, Libya, Syria, Yemen, and elsewhere in the world in broad daylight.[31] The crucial problem in all this is that this defunct hegemon tooth-and-nail refuses to admit its fall from power and amicably accept its real place in the present epoch. One may look at the pugnacious posturing and audacious oration of the despairing US president (Joe Biden) in his recent 4-day trip to Europe (notably the last day of his visit to Poland—next door to the war zone) and see the profundity of frustration toward the world beyond the American diktat.[32] The underpinnings of this and the many more issues of theoretical, historical, and empirical import are the in-debt subjects of the chapters that follow.

Notes

1 This is a part of the plea by Zelensky facilitated by the EU and Canada earlier, and on March 16, 2022, by the United States to fight the choreographed war words against Vladimir Putin and the Russian invasion of Ukraine on February 24, 2022. A disturbing part of all these arrangements is that Zelensky has been repeatedly asking for the

so-called *NO-Fly Zone* over Ukraine's air space by the US and NATO forces, which would likely set off World War III and nuclear Armageddon. Nonetheless, short of the no-fly zone, the United States directly (and indirectly via NATO) continues to pour gasoline on the fire by a massive transfer of advanced defensive and offensive weapons to Ukraine and by stage-managing Zelensky's daily claims and demand, and the unceasing barrage of propaganda across the world. See Wolf, Zachary B. Curt Merrill, and Ji Min Lee 2022. "Zelensky's Address to Congress" (annotated), *CNN* March 16, 2022; retrieved: March 18, 2020: www.cnn.com/interactive/2022/03/politics/ukraine-zelensky-congress-speech-annotated/. For an example of a no-fly zone, see Cole, Juan 2022. "Ukraine: What the Libya War Tells Us About Why We Really Don't Want a NATO No-Fly Zone," *Informed Comment* March 9; retrieved: March 23, 2022: www.juancole.com/2022/03/ukraine-libya-really.html and Bennis, Phyllis 2022. "Say No to a No-Fly Zone in Ukraine," *The Progressive Magazine* March 24; retrieved: March 25, 2022: https://progressive.org/op-eds/no-to-a-no-fly-zone-in-ukraine-bennis-220324/?emci=b826efc6-4fac-ec11-997e-281878b83d8a&emdi=570acc8b-67ac-ec11-997e-281878b83d8a&ceid=3882723.

2 President Biden speaks following the NATO Emergency Summit on Russia's Invasion of Ukraine, March 24, 2022. CNBC (Live Broadcast from Brussels) on YouTube channel; retrieved: March 24, 2022: www.youtube.com/watch?v=iOgxfstkBvk. Biden's comment on China is of utmost relevance to the central thesis of this book where he unwisely imagines that the United States is the epicenter of the global economy; listen to this clip from minute 6:27 till 6: 40. Biden's inept US-China and Russia-China trade comparison is a sign of incompetence, if not sleepwalking unconsciously toward the distant past. He forgets that the tectonic plates of epochal change reverberated throughout the globe and blaming Putin by no means sufficient to conceal the real cause of war in Ukraine and decouple the broadening of NATO toward deliberate destabilization of Europe and faking the need for "American leadership." The Russian invasion of Ukraine, on February 24, 2022, was unnecessary had it not been for America's latest bloody mischief-making in the middle of Europe. And, identifying this war as Putin's war is but pitifully disingenuous in the first place; it is also utterly dangerous to submerge the world in economic crisis and put it on brink of WWIII and possible nuclear exchange, at the same time. This is what American leadership means today, that is, obstruction, devastation, and barricade to progress at the threshold of the new polity.

3 To be sure, the war that led to the fragmentation of former Yugoslavia was first instigated by the United States in the late 1990s. This war was deliberately conducted at the time the world was still recovering from the collapse of the Soviet bloc and the United States (and the Clinton administration) fancying itself, however asinine, in fantastic terms as a "unipolar" global order to do as it please in this misperceiving political atmosphere, thus engendering civil war and forceful militarization of these fragments into NATO.

4 The pre-history of conflict that led to the Russian invasion of Ukraine points to a consistent pattern of US culpability as the former US diplomat and Assistant Secretary of Defense in the Clinton administration (1993–1994) discloses in this lengthy interview: Freeman, Chas W. 2022. "The US fighting Russia 'to the Last Ukrainian': Veteran US Diplomat," *The Grayzone* (Pushback with Aaron Maté) March 22; retrieved: March 2022: www.youtube.com/watch?v=0vxufUeqnuc.

5 See Burns, William J. 2019. "How the U.S.-Russian Relationship Went Bad," *The Atlantic* April; retrieved: March 15, 2022: www.theatlantic.com/magazine/archive/2019/04/william-j-burns-putin-russia/583255/. This is the confession of someone who understands the balance of power in his own de facto sense of the term. It was long known to US political leadership that Ukraine is a *serious redline* for Russia under Putin or anyone else at the helm.

6 Chotiner, Isaac 2022. "Why John Mearsheimer Blames the U.S. for the Crisis in Ukraine" (an Interview), *The New Yorker* March 1; retrieved: March 15, 2022:

www.newyorker.com/news/q-and-a/why-john-mearsheimer-blames-the-us-for-the-crisis-in-ukraine; and Mearsheimer, John 2022. "Intervention d'un géopolitologue très apprécié d'Emmanuel Todd, John Mearsheimer, au sujet de la crise ukrainienne," *YouTube* March 13, 2022; retrieved: March 21, 2022: www.youtube.com/watch?v=w5qSO1BbXsU. Given the facts on the ground, I arrest unequivocally that the United States (and NATO) has since the late 1990s been methodically instigating a premeditated strategy of provocation toward the Russian Federation, a preamble of which was the 2014 coup in Ukraine. The war in Ukraine could have been prevented if the United States had accepted its declining status in the world and thus acknowledged that Ukraine must be a buffer state. Instead, the US—and the US alone—provoked this war in a premeditated fashion to fancifully restore its bygone hegemonic past. The corpus of this volume is about theoretical as well as the institutional decline of American power and a palpable demonstration that a falling power that does not recognize its limits is much more dangerous for world peace than a rising one. Therefore, the hysteria about the *unprovoked* Russian invasion of Ukraine is both disinformation and misinformation.

7 To perceive the tenuous function of NATO, one may remember the inclusion of the Russian Federation in G8 (G7 plus Russia) in 1997 and return to G7 in 2014, after the US coup in Ukraine and subsequent annexation of Crimea by Russia. This shows the caricature of NATO and its use at the service of idiosyncrasies of the former hegemon, a loose cannon that not only jeopardizes European security but also endangers peace and tranquility across the world.

8 For a seminal summary of kneejerk reactions to this war by the political class in the West, and their reverberation in political and cultural spheres in the captivated media, including the right and the left, see Zevin, Alexander 2022. "The Normal War," *New Left Review* (Sidecar, NLR blogpost: Politics) March 31; retrieved: April 2, 2022: https://newleftreview.org/sidecar/posts/a-normal-war?pc=1432. Here, warmongering attitude (laced with a heavy dose of Russophobia) on the part of liberals and the nature of liberalism had become crystal clear. This also casts a long show upon the sorrowful state of the radical left, including self-styled Marxists, that failed to grasp the underlying dynamics of *epochal change* and the real cause of this conflict.

9 See Macron, Emmanuel 2019. "French President Emmanuel Macron Lays Out France's Foreign Policy Priorities," *French Public Broadcast Service* (YouTube Video) August 27, 2019; retrieved: March 20, 2022: www.youtube.com/watch?v=4t75eVvLnn8; also Associated Press (AP) 2019. "Macron Calls for a New Global Economic Order," *Courthouse News Service* August 27; retrieved: March 20, 2022: www.courthousenews.com/macron-calls-for-a-new-global-economic-order/. As AP reported: "Macron said '*we are living the end of Western hegemony*' in the world" (emphasis added). To be sure, Macron's assessment is shallow, transhistorical, and long overdue, yet embraces a grain of truth in the direction of undercurrents of historic changes that had already occurred, and since the 1990s resurfacing time to time on the global scene owing to the collapse of postwar Pax Americana (1945–1979). Callinicos's verdict on the polity in which we currently live, on the other hand, is hollow, inconsistent, deceptive, and indeed an affront to the teachings of Karl Marx and genuine Marxism. See Callinicos, Alex 2022. "Why the Ukraine Crisis has Dragged On," *Socialist Worker* February 21; retrieved: March 11, 2022: https://socialistworker.co.uk/alex-callinicos/why-the-ukraine-crisis-has-dragged-on/.

10 The theory of oil rent in the context of Marx's theory of value, in conjunction with the *competitive* globalization of petroleum, was introduced by the present author in the late 1970s and early 1980s. See *inter alia* Bina, Cyrus 1985. *The Economics of the Oil Crisis*. New York: St. Martin's (London: Merlin Press); Bina, Cyrus 1989. "Some Controversies in the Development of Rent Theory: The Nature of Oil Rent," *Capital and Class* 39: 82–112; Bina, Cyrus 2006. "The Globalization of Oil: A Prelude to a Critical Political Economy," *International Journal of Political Economy* 35 (2): 4–34. It is significant

within the context of, say, Nord Stream 1 (and when or if it comes to fruition Nord Stream 2), the pipeline that carries natural gas from Russia to Germany, to note that the globalization of petroleum (oil and gas) leaves no room for speaking of a national (or regional) identity for these commodities at all. Thus, speaking of "Russian oil" or boycotting "Russian gas," for that matter has little meaning in the skim of things surrounding the Ukraine conflict and US sanctions. The global oil (and gas), including that of the United States, is an indivisible and unified market across the globe.

11 This goes for the alleged new approach, namely, "geopolitical economy," a crafty extension of traditional imperialism/nationalism (binary), repacked recently in a new format, critiqued in the volume.

12 There are scholars who justifiably argue that Marx's *Capital* was written beyond the context of national (or nation-state) boundaries and that Marx was keen on colonialist expansion and "primitive accumulation" across the periphery of capitalism at large. Yet, they tend to overlook the methodology of Marx's *Capital*, a potential global vision that would turn into an actuality across the world via the theory of value. Some of the scholars in this category, although critical of, say, Lenin or Hilferding concerning imperialism, they nevertheless do not properly (that is, methodologically) differentiate between "primitive accumulation" and "accumulation of capital," thus obfuscating the meaning of globalization as capitalist imperialism. A quintessential example of this—an approach that inter alia continues to speak of as "global north/global south"—can be found in Predella, Lucia 2013. "Imperialism and Capitalist Development in Marx's Capital," *Historical Materialism* 21 (2): 117–147. Here in this article, despite certain advances, neither Hilferding, Lenin, or Luxemburg, nor others in the contemporary period, such as Bukharin, are critiqued for their misperceived and misleading notion of competition in conjunction with the materiality of concentration and centralization of capital at the present age.

13 Consistent with the theoretical underpinning of this book, it must be reminded that contentions that liken the present juncture to the pre-1914 or any such episode in the past concerning the global sea-change in geopolitics are devoid of the essence in that they erroneously cling to the artifice of appearance of events rather than the underpinning of globalization of capitalism across the world; they tend to compare apples and oranges, so to speak, and by doing so comparing a fully developed world of capitalism with the colonial (and undeveloped) world of the yesteryears, and thus unwisely and misleadingly resurrecting the lapidated conceptualizations of the past (such as monopoly, imperialism, and direct plunder) by means of anachronism. In this context, the self-styled Marxists are the worst among these writers. Why? These ideologues appear to have little clue as to the operation of Marx's law of value as opposed to the recipe of Hobsonite "monopoly capitalism."

14 Deliberate intervention in the civil war in Yugoslavia, first preplanning to weaken what is perceived as an obstacle to American domination in Europe and then absorbing the fragments into NATO. The familiar "humanitarian intervention" in this conflict was the weapon of choice and Western media dutifully excreted a distorting touch and playacted rather remarkably as cavalry to the rescue. All this come to fruition in the second period of the Clinton administration and under the first woman to serve as the secretary of state (1997–2001), Madeleine Albright.

15 The colonial mindset and criminally unlawful engagement of Israel in the protracted war in Syria should not be discounted. Not to mention the occupation of part of this country (Golan region) since 1967. The apartheid Israel is a holdover from the time that the Pax Americana was in the business of eradicating formal colonies and establishing a sphere of influence across the world. Producing yet another colony in the middle of the Middle East was quite a monkey wrench in the system that has not been subsided in more than 70 years since the colonization of Palestine and some 40 years beyond the collapse of the Pax Americana. For a remarkable and lucid volume on the

origins of colonization of Palestine see Gendzier, Irene L. 2015. *Dying To Forget: Oil, Power, Palestine & the Foundation of U.S. Policy in the Middle East*. New York: Columbia University Press. For further information, see Khalidi, Rashid 2020. *A Hundred Years' War on Palestine: A History of Settler Colonialism and Resistance, 1917–2017*. New York: Metropolitan Books.

16 For recent postmodernist manipulates of political economy literature, see Mavroudeas, Stavros D. 2006. "A History of Contemporary Political Economy and Postmodernism," *Review of Radical Political Economics* 38 (4), Fall: 499–518.

17 Michael Heinrich has made the same slip-up on concept and place of money in value theory by circumventing Marx's method of abstraction and by plunging into a "monetary theory of value," thus playacting a "Milton Friedman" in Marxian debates.

18 This includes all barriers except the barrier of capital (as a social relation) itself. The only insurmountable barrier to capital is capital itself. This is the key for those who wonder about the instability and crisis-ridden characteristic of capitalism.

19 The collapse of the Soviet Union, at the end of the 1980s, was a hefty catalyst that compounded the world disorder and ironically concealed the downfall of the American era from the many unsuspecting observers around the world, including oblivious (and arrogant) political class in Washington; so, the illusion of "unipolarity" splashed onto the political discourse, particularly in the international relations schools across the West, without an iota of foundation, except (1) in pure ideological propaganda, such as Fukuyama's *The End of History*, and (2) thru either unprovoked military intervention or the consequential interventions in civil wars that followed. To be sure, as history suggests, such actions were entwined with blowbacks of the incalculable political cost that over time sunk the United States further into the abyss; any such reference to "unipolarity" or a "moment of unipolarity" is contradiction-in-terms, tautological nonsense, and a chimera bereft of value.

20 To simply decipher the background of the havoc in a protracted war that ignited since the 2014 US collaborated coup in Ukraine, which has now found a culmination and predictable blowback in Russian full-scale invasion, listen to Sergey Lavrov, the Russian foreign minister; this exclusive interview was published on April 19, 2022, on YouTube: www.youtube.com/watch?v=_syI2X-ZD8o.

21 For a glimpse of George H.W. Bush's role in the context of militarization of the Persian Gulf vis-à-vis the UN General Assembly, see Khan, Nasir 1994. "US Abuse of UN in Gulf War," *Economic and Political Weekly* 29 (35), August 27: 2277–2282; retrieved: April 5, 2022: www.jstor.org/stable/4401680. The rhotic of "international law" and appealing to it at this juncture and in this context has little meaning.

22 From Britain's left vista, the tip of kneejerk reaction to the war in Ukraine is ably portrayed in Seymour, Richard 2022. "The Belligerati," *New Left Review* (Sidecar blogpost—Politics) March 22; retrieved: March 25, 2022: https://newleftreview.org/sidecar/posts/the-belligerati?pc=1431.

23 The ferocity of such modus operandi reaches its peak out and in the open during international conflicts where straightforward demonizing, character assassination of foreign leaders, and both misinformation and disinformation take center stage to molest and insult the intelligence of the public at large. Those who hesitate to accept this conclusion should be kind enough to inspect the record during the Pax Americana (1945–1979), say, in the case of Premier Mossadegh in Iran or President Allende of Chile, and the post-Pax Americana in case of Saddam Hussein of Iraq, Moammar Gaddafi of Libya, and presently barefaced demonization of Vladimir Putin of Russia in the recent crisis in Ukraine. The US mainstream media had played not only as foot soldiers but also as commanding generals in the perpetual war of American exceptionalism.

24 The current conflict in Ukraine is inter alia a universal laboratory for the war of rhetoric that is not only choreographed with intermittent falsity but also sprinkled with enough fakery in order to obliterate the other side. Here, the lion's share of all this comes from

the United States, the beleaguered Ukrainian government, and the scores of journalists that by and large conditioned by the grand narrative of "democracy versus autocracy" divide, assiduously if inescapably doing the bidding of the former hegemon, namely, the United States. Never mind that Ukraine is not more than an oligarchic parliamentary regime since its inception in the aftermath of the Soviet fall. Even the revered Jane Ferguson of PBS (see the NewsHour, March 17, 2022) is sadly affected by such rhetoric and dutifully practicing it in her report from the battlefield in Ukraine. See www.pbs.org/video/russian-invasion-tape-jane-1647552338/; retrieved: March 18, 2022. The thin *veneer of liberalism*, a wonderful cover for warmongering and the systematic slaughter and devastation of countries that wish not to submit, on the one hand, and weaponizing anything and everything from A to Z to justify them, on the other, is the last gasp of the defunct hegemony by the United States today. And when it comes to geopolitics, this same attitude is already expressed in Francis Fukuyama's filtered scenario, namely, *The End of History*, in the aftermath of the fall of the Soviet Union. "Democracy vs. Autocracy" is the new "iron curtain," a *narrative* that is invented and pressed by the United States (and its known collaborators) on the public at large across the globe. The clumsiness of this devious taxonomy is immediately revealed when authoritarian Poland suddenly turns into the darling of the Biden administration in NATO for staging war against autocracy in Russia. This hyper-Orwellian war of words over Ukraine also turned the seemingly independent journalists into the yellow ones. Here, anchor of the NBC News, Lester Holt, is yet another incredible victim of this ploy, a mouthpiece that echoes White House political positions verbatim to unsuspecting audiences on a nightly basis.

25 A remarkable example inter alia is the Biden administration's fight against Russia by the Ukrainians in Europe, in which sadly the average Ukrainian dies for US bleeding objective and *unattainable* American hegemony. The US choreography of this war in coordination with the multimedia propaganda, including numerous TV programs with Volodymyr Zelensky, is a reminder of blatant "reality shows" on American TV, a war of information and misinformation toward obfuscation and changing the *context* of the conflict. Yet the most dangerously alarming aspect of the manipulation of social media in this war is a deliberate mixture of real and invented facts that could purposefully ignite some sort of "humanitarian intervention," like what was choreographed by US planners (and NATO) in the case of the no-fly zone in Libya (2011) or by the George H.W. Bush administration prior to the US invasion of Iraq (1991), against Saddam Hussein in Kuwait. This time and this technique is a guarantor of WWIII, as nuclear-armed Russia is no Libya or Iraq. The innermost foundation of such scenarios is of course predicted in this book, a volume that has to do with the epoch of globalization and the fall of American power; for the immediate reflection of the present conflict in Ukraine and the outright and intrinsic role in the United States, see Mearsheimer, John 2020. "Why Can't Ukraine Decide Its Own Future," *YouTube Channel* April 8; retrieved: April 9, 2022: www.youtube.com/watch?v=oR-yS6kULXw. My dispute, in this case, with Mearsheimer is on the assumed unipolarity; I think the "unipolarity" was merely a mirage, which alone appeared as real to those who saw the fall of the Soviet Union but emphatically closed their eyes (and minds) to the collapse of Pax Americana and US decline.

26 For a glimpse of palpable political instability and domestic social fragility in the United States, see PBS Broadcast, March 29, 2020. "Plot to Overturn the Election," *Frontline* (54-minute Video); retrieved: March 29, 2022: www.pbs.org/wgbh/frontline/film/plot-to-overturn-the-election/.

27 As demonstrated in this book, both right-wing orthodoxy in international relations theory and scores of traditional leftists speak of globalization as if it is an article of evolution. Nearly all ubiquitous narratives that attempted to prop up the United States and identify it under the rubric of globalization are blindsided as to the theoretical import and contradictory application of the latter against US hegemony and the ultimate fall of

American power. All the orthodoxy on geopolitics does is to focus on China's rise and tautologically speak of global "competition" (that is, between the US and China) rather than search for the very basis that led to such disorder.

28 See Putin, Vladimir President of the Russian Federation: "Speech at the Munich on Security Policy," February 10, 2007, Munich, Germany; retrieved: March 15, 2022: http://en.kremlin.ru/events/president/transcripts/24034/print. This is the first open and formal retort to the seemingly unipolar ambition of the United States by Russia, and as such it must be carefully studied and treated as a baseline for the events and years to come. Furthermore, let there be no doubt whatsoever that NATO, an instrument of the Cold War, has since the late 1990s been an offensive military alliance throughout.

29 As domestic and foreign affairs are bound to be dialectically on the same page, so to speak, one needs to take one's cues from what is going on in the inside. Thus, a serious study of international relations (and geopolitics) cannot be indifferent to organic fusion and the mutual impact of these two integrated dimensions. For a relevant source on the impact of US foreign interventions and wars on the authoritarian quality of American society, see Belew, Kathleen 2018. *Bring the War Home: The White Power Movement and Paramilitary America*. Cambridge, MA: Harvard University Press.

30 For the cause and extent of this provocation, see Starkey, Sara 2022. "Putin Reminds Everyone that Ukraine Joining NATO Could Lead to Nuclear War," *Bulletin of the Atomic Scientists* February 11; retrieved: March 28, 2022: https://thebulletin.org/2022/02/putin-says-ukraine-membership-in-nato-would-make-nuclear-war-more-likely/.

31 A brief reminder can be viewed on Democracy Now: "Vijay Prashad on the War in Ukraine & the West's 'Open, Rank Hypocrisy' in Condemning War Crimes," *Democracy Now* April 15, 2022; retrieved: April 16, 2022: www.youtube.com/watch?v=TloP2RdHVPw.

32 Borger, Julian 2022. "Joe Biden Arrives in Europe for Summits . . .," *The Guardian* March 23; retrieved: March 29, 2022: www.theguardian.com/us-news/2022/mar/23/joe-biden-europe-russia-ukraine-nato-g7-european-council; Pettypiece, Shannon 2022. "Takeaways From Biden's Trip to Europe: Unity, Reassurance and a Memorable Gaffe," *NBC News* March 27; retrieved: March 29, 2022: www.nbcnews.com/politics/white-house/takeaways-bidens-trip-europe-rcna21718. As can be seen in the previous two journalistic coverages, the moment is the essence and not the underlying forces that brought the world to the brink of this disaster.

2 Road to Perdition

The American Debacle in Afghanistan

We will get on our way to a new record of expansion . . . that will carry us into the next American Century.

—George H.W. Bush
State of the Union Message to the Nation
(January 29, 1991)[1]

Our war on terror begins with al Qaeda, but it does not end there. It will not end until every terrorist group of global reach has been found, stopped and defeated.

—George W. Bush
Address to Joint Session of the Congress
(September 20, 2001)[2]

I sometimes wonder what use there is in trying to protect the West against fancied external threats when the signs of disintegration within are so striking.

—George Kennan[3]
The Architect of Cold War

Preface

The anticipated American fall in Afghanistan is the tip of the iceberg, exemplifying the manifold debacles of the post-9/11 period. It is the opposite of what the US leadership attempts to brandish to the world as a "unipolar" hegemony. As demonstrated throughout this volume, the American *hegemony* eclipsed along with the breakdown of the *Pax American* (1945–1979), some four decades ago. That is why the war in Afghanistan was lost even before its inception. The American era resembles a "black hole" that had collapsed onto itself by the force of globalization. The Pax Americana (1945–1979) had long gone; the postwar American institutions, the paraphernalia, the comportments, and the doctrines and policies of the postwar era are all negated by the transformation of the world toward globalization. Yet the American leadership, fooled by the collapse of the Soviet Union, tended to opt for another "American Century." Thus, Saddam Hussein's invasion of Kuwait was used as a pretext by

DOI: 10.4324/9781351136785-2

the Bush (H.W.) administration to engage in a wholesale militarization of the Middle East and to send a massive (and permanent) military expedition to the Persian Gulf toward the fortification of this dream.

The corollary of the Reagan administration, and the Bush administration's back-to-back involvement in the Afghan war against the Soviets, resulted in one hell of a payback on 9/11, just when the Bush-Cheney administration was ready to take the helm. Cheney (the real president) and his fellow Cold Warriors welcomed and embraced 9/11; it was a godsend for doubling down on "unipolarity" toward another "American Century." Dick Cheney and Donald Rumsfeld prepared to invade seven nations in the greater Middle East, starting with Afghanistan (2001). As the ploy of al-Qaeda and Saddam Hussein proved inadequate for the pressing invasion of Iraq, the Bush-Cheney administration doubled down to concoct yet another motive—the WMD. In the meantime, the "Axis of Evil" was born in order to broaden the scope of the American rampage toward the illusory cause of "unipolarity." This chapter is a glimpse of a defunct hegemon that grossly overestimated its power and mistaken its predictable fall for its imaginary rise.

Introduction

During forced and disorderly US (and NATO) evacuation from Afghanistan, in dreadful and desperate conditions of multitudes of men, women, and children, wedged between barbed wire, and the advancing Taliban at Kabul airport in agony and desperation, the flashbang of the initial rampage by Neocons (and the multifarious Cold Warriors)—party to a 20-year nightmare—was all-over mainstream media. At the head of this dog-and-pony show of resentment at departure (and evacuation) was George W. Bush—the original sinner with an I.Q. of a cucumber—who deliberately confuses the *cause* of this ordeal with its *effect*.

George W. Bush rebukes the Biden administration, not for pitiable planning of this evacuation, but for bringing this delinquent, depleting, and drifting war to an end.[4] He sheds crocodile tears for women of Afghanistan[5] vis-à-vis the Taliban, yet his imbecility does not allow him to comprehend that these monsters are the handiwork of his own father (as vice president and president, 1981–1992), having to do with deterring the Russian "infidels" in Afghanistan some 40-year earlier, thus instigating the start of "perpetual war" long before 9/11.

The Biden administration followed the Trump administration concerning a complete withdrawal of remaining US military and civilian forces from Afghanistan by August 31, 2021, after two elongated decades of occupation. It is significant that the Trump team had completely written off the participation of the puppet regime in Afghanistan and opted to "negotiate" exclusively with the Taliban.[6] This would tell us two significant things: (1) that the Taliban held all the cards in these negotiations while the American side had naught and (2) that the US team was fully mindful of the fragility and feebleness of the puppet regime and knew all too well the susceptibility of the Afghan military to breakdown. These points were also translucent to the Biden administration which exhibits more experience in foreign policy in the quagmire of Afghanistan than its predecessor does.[7] All this is aside from the fraudulent and aimless American mission in this 20-year occupation, hence an inevitability of unconditional surrender by Americans, just in Vietnam.[8]

As it turns out, the Taliban too were keenly aware of the rickety nucleus of the puppet regime and regime change in Afghanistan. This was a remarkable submission to a horde of long-bearded fanatics who seemed to have time-traveled via the wormholes of history and impulsively landed in this century. Incidentally, those of us who may have a long memory should be able to recall and identify the very hand that had fed and shaped these monsters (the cohorts of Osama bin Laden) as the fighting force during the entire decade of the 1980s, against the Soviet "infidels," in the ill-famed Soviet invasion of Afghanistan.[9]

"Original Sin" and the Lingering Aftermath

Some of us who're old enough to recall the fall of Saigon and remember the mortifying images on that faithful day, in April (1975), at the rooftop of the American Embassy in Saigon, the images at Kabul airport, and a desperate crowd of Afghans clinging to the exterior of the US Air Force C17 transport aircraft is a déjà vu. Forty-six years hence, the reverberation of that crushing defeat is so clearly in tandem with today's images at Kabul airport where the transport planes full of human cargo fly out of Kabul every 45-minute or so, while a sea of people striving to get onboard. This illustrates an aftereffect of yet another lost war by the United States in the post-9/11 period. Yet, if the American downfall in Vietnam overlapped with the beginning of the end of *Pax Americana* (1945–1979)[10]—a *tragedy*, this shattering defeat in Afghanistan is a *farce*. Since this time, the defeat is owing to America's own incarnated monsters. At any rate, by sheer design (i.e., the choreography of duplicity and disinformation), nostalgia for power is much more devious and addicting than the real power itself.[11]

Unlike the bleeding-heart liberals and heartless conservatives, one does not think that American and NATO forces should stay in Afghanistan or for that matter anywhere else. Instead, a judicious mind questions the very morality, legality, and legitimacy of the "War on Terror" doctrine—chicanery of monumental proportion and a power-grab by a debased, disgraced, and defunct ex-hegemon. The doctrine of "war on terror"[12] rather clumsily warrants, in disguise, the old colonial and semi-colonial decrees, and verdicts that once upon a time sanctioned by the likes of Winston Churchill (the ill-famed white supremacist) in the colonial, corrupt, and long-demolished *Pax Britannica*. American invasion (and a 20-year occupation) of Afghanistan is the *firstborn* of this doctrine that was long kept on a *military* respirator until recently.[13]

"War on Terror" also stands rather euphemistically for *another* "American century," in neoconservatives' lexicon. Neoconservatives (neocons) saw in their fantasy a "unipolar" polity in the making just after the breakdown of the Soviet Union. The neocon aphorism, "Mr. Gorbachev: bring down that wall," by Ronald Reagan, a second-rate Hollywood actor, who held the US presidency (1981–1989), was a harbinger of the extreme euphoria; this led to the successful infiltration of this extremist worldview in the US foreign policy circles since the 1990s. The liberals and liberal hawks too within the US foreign policy establishment were not far behind.

Having been in the academy and visiting Harvard at the time, this writer was privy to so many pertinent presentations, debates, and public and private nuances in the aftermath of the Soviet fall on the perception and attitude of American academics and their counterparts, particularly in NATO member countries. The present writer, however, was suspicious of the propaganda and euphoria and their consequence with respect to the newly emerging (global) polity. The collapse of the Soviet Union gave a false impression to the American leadership at the time, intimating that the sky is a limit and that a "unipolar order" should be at hand. This reflection and the echo of elation are particularly prominent in the address to the joint session of the Congress, declaring a "new order," by President George H.W. Bush. This address was justifiably choreographed along with the decimation of Iraq by the US forces and the speedy launch and spread of massive military and naval bases, including the HQ of the US Fifth Fleet, in the Persian Gulf.[14]

As we already know, the chickens of the anti-Soviet warfare and strategy in Afghanistan came to roost finally in the homeland on September 11, 2001,[15] and it finally turned out that the "unipolarity" is fanciful self-aggrandizement. Nevertheless, the neocon-infested Bush-Cheney administration missed this opportunity and doubled down on their groundless pipedream. The US leadership neither understood that, by the late 1970s, American hegemony—along with the underlying postwar institutions—had come apart[16] nor realized that 9/11[17] is but a tangible occurrence caused by (1) collapse of the postwar American order and (2) the "new order," concocted a decade earlier by George H.W. Bush, is but the pie in the sky. Incidentally, the Orwellian quality of the American political class and the way in which it views the world and perceives the order or disorder is quite mindboggling.

The usual ideologues and cheerleaders of the orthodoxy (liberals and conservatives alike) in the academy too were either unconcerned or mute as to the meaning of hegemony, hegemonic power, and loss of hegemony in the absence of hegemonic institutions. The ruling authorities in the United States and their dutiful followers here and abroad were nevertheless mesmerized, if not completely stoned, by the fragility of the Soviet economy and the sudden implosion and disintegration of the Soviet Union. They also stopped thinking about the massive and permanent transfer and relocation of major sectors and industries from the United States, via extensive outsourcing, known as the *plant closing* in the mid-1980s.[18] The US governing class was slow to realize that these changes would be essentially irreversible and that such gigantic displacements could extricate the United States from the epicenter of world production for good.

More importantly, the peculiar petty bourgeois "can-do" attitude in America was not a match for the formidable global forces that virtually made many evitable matters, suddenly inevitable.[19]

These Pax American ideologues failed to appreciate that *globalization*, as an epochal social relation, had by this time ascended from the wreckage of mummified institutions of the Pax Americana, namely, World Bank, IMF, NATO, and G7—onetime paraphernalia of the defunct postwar order.[20] Similarly, they were blindsided by the universality of globalization that axed and abolished the status of American hegemony in short order. Meanwhile, the United States—between the "festive" fall of the Soviet Union and the stinging jolt of 9/11[21]—slumbered in the bubble of "unipolar" order.[22]

More amazing, however, is why the traditional Left had not been able to decode the epic vicissitudes that subtly foreshadowed the onset of the present epoch and stage, *globalization*.[23] It is also puzzling that radical scholars, even Marxists, routinely danced around issues and postulates, such as neoliberalism[24] (a doctrine mistook for stage), "new" imperialism[25] (alluding to monopoly capitalism and bygone political era), imperialist globalization[26] (an eclectic misnomer), American globalization[27] (first half of the story and half-truth), geopolitics[28] (a skin-deep vision and appraisal), monopoly-finance capital[29] (the usual story of *Monthly Review*), or a flat-out mixture thereof. The majority of the Left (so-called heterodoxy in and out of the academy) essentially missed the deep *essence* of epochal change and decidedly engaged in the petty-bourgeois habit of holding to the impressions and surfing on the *appearance*. This in a nutshell is the story of the intellectual weapon and ostentatious radicalism of those on the other side, who have long been barking, so to speak, without an actual bite.

Incidentally, a number of liberals and pseudo-leftists, oblivious to the collapse of oil monopoly and ignorant of the universally competitive oil since the 1970s, took to the scavenger hunt to find a cause of the American invasions of Afghanistan and Iraq in oil. They absorbed by possible foreign contracts on oil pipelines that could go through Afghanistan and focused on Iraqi oilfields, and then triumphantly deduced that the access to oil must be the motivation of these invasions. Sometimes in traditional leftist activist circles, this declaration unveils itself as "blood for oil." Such diagnostician is a hoax; it is a distraction, which dangerously obfuscates the cause; besides, in methodological terms, it is no more than a vulgar tautology. This view is quite ignorant of the larger context of this collision course; it misreads the corollary of the US offensive as a cause and obfuscates the manifold effects of worldwide globalization, revealed vividly in these invasions.[30]

Nostalgia Is a Seductive Liar[31]

In 1991, George H.W. Bush pontificated: "We will get on our way to a new record of expansion . . . that will carry us into the next American Century." He was unaware of *small detail* that low and behold the first "American Century" (the *Pax Americana*, 1945–1979) too by this time had fallen apart, and that the breakdown of the Pax Americana dates a decade earlier than the downfall of the Soviet Union. This oversight is a reminder of Mark Twain's delightful axiom: "You cannot depend on your eyes when your imagination is out of focus." George Bush (H.W.) apparently has been suffering from a seductive ailment in straight thinking, known as the presumption of "vacuum," according to which breakdowns in socioeconomic systems are essential without embedded reasons, and thus they generate a vacuum. To fill such "vacuums" without external forces is a welcome opportunity.

Hence, the worldview in Washington was to expedite the demolition of the Soviet Union after the implosion, on the one hand, and to occupy the international space (and familiar international polity) that was in spare of moment interrupted and disordered by the chaos of implosion, on the other.[32] The 1991 George H.W. Bush military expedition to the Persian Gulf, therefore, was a cunning and calculated move not so much for discord with Saddam Hussein (or solidarity with Kuwait) but essentially for the filling of presumed "vacuum" and unveiling of the purported *new order*.

Conjecture of vacuum, which has plentiful academic followers, particularly in orthodox circles of political science and international relations, is silent about the dynamics of collapse and the centrality of epochal context in the case of the Soviet Union. The dialectic of underlying cause in a larger context is an *academic* matter in the eyes of those who were waiting for 70 years to discard the content and to stuff it with something else. The off-the-cuff orientation of this view will have to become crystal clear in some 20 years hence when on the face of it a defiant Russian Federation on the one hand and a half-dozen lost wars in central and west Asia, not to mention North Africa, on the other, are at the doorsteps of beleaguered America, hence the story of US foreign policy and attitude toward "collapse," "vacuum," and the need for filling (nicknamed, American leadership), just like the filling of potholes on the street.

This perfunctory attitude and positivistic approach are also trendy among clueless leftists and pseudo-radicals who speak of the American power in such terms as if the absence of the Soviet Union has made the United States more hegemonic. They tend to misidentify *rabidity* with *hegemony*, and worse, these pseudo-radicals are completely oblivious to the worldwide socioeconomic underpinning, value-theoretic undercurrents, and subtleties of our epoch. Incidentally, it is remarkable that in modern astrophysics (and cutting-edge astronomy), unlike its Newtonian counterpart, reference to *void* (vacuum) is neither accepted nor necessary for proof of what is keeping the universe together or apart. Here, a vacuum, just as the collapse of the Soviet Union—irrespective of its critical cause—is but a mirage that tautologically grips the observer.

The illusion of power and US nostalgic vision, however, are inseparable from so many American misadventures in Afghanistan,[33] Iraq,[34] Syria,[35] Libya,[36] Yemen,[37] and other parts of the globe, since the fall of the Soviet Union. The analog of this is defeat after defeat, political suicide after political suicide, and humiliation after humiliation unparalleled in recent memory. On the other hand, having had the habit of weaponizing anything and everything in the bombastic language of the Cold War, the United States turned human rights, democracy, freedom, free world into a weapon, and disguised itself as the "leader of the free world" for perpetuity. Hence, a fraudulent 20-year-old invasion/occupation of Afghanistan is now officially ending with further humiliation.

Yet, such invasion/occupation bears an ironic signature of the pre-Pax Americana era when the specter of colonial *Pax Britannica* had been hovering above the bloody horizon. This explains in stark and clear-cut terms the nature of this retrograde enterprise and where the United States stands today. There was no legitimate reason for a full-scale invasion of Afghanistan. Yet, the search for Osama bin Laden—the presumed cause of this invasion—took the backseat reportedly for the purpose of invasion and occupation for unlimited time. However, the fundamental strategic decision upon which this particular invasion—other than the aimless deception of "war on terror"—was deliberately left ambiguous and for public imagination. This speaks volumes about not only *illegality* but also the sheer *criminality* and *immorality* of American conduct in this invasion.[38]

As implied earlier, the collapse of the "American Century" (1945–1979) and the fall of the Soviet Union deep down are the epoch-making effects of globalization, which among others effectively clipped the wings of American hegemony and similarly disrupted the mess of Soviet bureaucracy—a force much greater than both combined—in short order. Therefore, the American worldview (and foreign policy associated with it) is guilty of double jeopardy, namely, (1) seductive nostalgia and (2) an illusory vision of a "unipolar" world. Thus, today's American predicament is the cumulative outcome of the past conduct that unsurprisingly carries the mother lode of inevitability (and predictability) akin to Greek tragedy.

As has been argued in this chapter, the invasion of Afghanistan, and subsequent invasion of Iraq by the Bush-Cheney administration, was essentially at the service of power projection across the Soviet-less world, far beyond Afghanistan. This project, however, is but building upon the fortifications that were underwritten and established by George H.W. Bush early on toward another "American Century" by means of "unipolarity" via the bloody expedition and full-scale war of 1991 across the Persian Gulf. Yet, it had fallen to the Bush-Cheney administration to finalize this imaginary mission by embracing 9/11, in order to operationalize the doctrine of "War on Terror" and engage in an open-ended war against everyone and everywhere. Nevertheless, the universality of the blowback in this addictive and predictive stratagem is but translucent. The brunt of defeat after defeat, calamity after calamity, disgrace after disgrace, might not have yet caught up with a *defunct* and *bruised* hegemon that had lost its relevance markedly on the global stage.

The Bush-Cheney doctrine of "war on terror"[39] (to date a tacit standard for US foreign policy) is an open-ended tiptoeing on the edge of the abyss,[40] as a flurry of disgrace upon disgrace, caused by all these intrusion and incursions, appears to have little ethical, legal, and logical repercussion on profound nostalgia and the runaway self-destruction of the United States.[41] Unless somehow US *deep state* (for the lack of better terms) may convince itself in the interim that America had not only been successively defeated in these wars (the effect) but also lost its *age* and precisely cut down to size by epochal forces (the cause) that are much more omnipresent and omnipotent than America, China, the EU, and Russia combined.

In this context, *globalization* is the very constitution of the whole—the fabric of epochal change; whereas *geopolitics* stands for the playground of conflicting constituent parts acting in concert within this fabric since, by definition, no *part* can be independent of the identity of the *whole*. In other words, geopolitics in its *genuine* definition has no universality of its own. Here, the hand of the epoch is a critical arbiter. Therefore, resorting to geopolitics in this epochal change is neither methodologically sound (smacking a tautology) nor historically accurate since *geopolitics* is but a skin-deep account of much deeper epoch-making changes that had arisen from shifts of the tectonic plates.[42] For instance, the so-called *realist* approach to geopolitics, among others, suffers from the lack of (1) depth and (2) specificity when the protagonists anchor their argument to the mode of appearance (i.e., the sheer balance of power) and fruitless axiomatic factors toward transhistorical analysis.

Puppetry, Pretense, and Pandemic Terror

While the chaotic American evacuation was in progress, Jens Stoltenberg (Secretary General of NATO—the paraphernalia of Cold War and a "brain dead" entity[43]) surmised why the puppet regime in Kabul collapsed without any resistance and at no time. He quickly turns around rather triumphantly and puts the blame at the doorsteps of the Afghan army, the victim of a 20-year-long American dog-and-pony show, and the quintessential corollary of puppetry, deception, and pandemic corruption in "American" Afghanistan. Stoltenberg wonders about the finale that has long been obvious to the multitudes of unschooled and semi-schooled around the world (including the Taliban themselves) who saw in advance cataclysmic and devastating signs all over the proverbial wall of Afghanistan.

These multitudes have always been more judicious, much more adept, and a good deal more realistic than the likes of Mr. Stoltenberg in NATO (or for that matter, Dr. Faustus in Washington). Deciphering this quandary, for Stoltenberg and his NATO co-defendants, is both straightforward and complicated.[44]

An overwhelming majority of Afghans abhor both the American occupation and return of the Taliban; yet this resilient, self-conscious, and long interrupted nation has a long memory and impeccable experience certainly was able to validate which one is worse (and more dangerous, in the ballpark) than the two. They know that colonial occupation (euphemized rather unkindly, as "nation-building") in this time and age is anachronistic and feels strongly that this cruel and open-ended imposition had demolished the flesh and soul of their nation. They also recognize, by experience, the hands that fed and shaped the beginning and development of the Taliban some four decades ago, in the 1980s anti-Soviet war in Afghanistan.

The people of Afghanistan know very well who had thrown the secular nation of Afghanistan to the proverbial dogs of the Taliban. Therefore, they had no choice but the spare the moment in this chaotic changeover, to defer to the *monster* rather than the *monster*-maker—for now. In another word, the groundswell of multitudes in Afghanistan has had no stomach for this monster-maker-cum-puppet-master, any longer. The tyranny of the Taliban (Washington's creation, aided by Pakistan ISA and Saudi[45] finance), in this *Sophie's choice* scenario, seemed less of a hazard than 20-year cumulative devastation by the occupying puppet masters and perpetual terror mongers, those in charge of Frankenstein's foreign policy—as "war on terror"—in Washington. To sum up: the swift breakdown of the American house-of-cards in Afghanistan is not a surprise, but the culpability is squarely at the doorsteps of those in NATO (an outfit devoid of licit jurisdiction in Afghanistan)—like Jen Stoltenberg—who illicitly and eagerly played a critical part in it.

As for those who sidetrack the calamity of this cruel and rancorous occupation by allusion to "nation-building"—pro and con—I must say that the US foreign policy machine from the outset had not been interested in building anything in the emerging global polity since the 1990s, akin to the post-American era. Indeed, in recent decades, Washington operated like a runaway train and wrecking crew toward self-destruction and destruction of other nations. The post-hegemonic America is not interested in *construction* but in *destruction* as long as the hand of Time fails to move back to the good old days of American pomp and hegemony.

As a result, Afghanistan, Iraq, Syria, Libya, and Yemen are all remarkable examples of this prearranged and predestined deportment. The so-called *pivot to Asia*, Russophobia, and any attempt to demolish the *buffer* of Ukraine, to encircle the Russian Federation, by the United States, are all quintessential *variants* of this unpeaceable, nostalgic, and hysterical foreign policy, not unlike the tantrum of a tough guy who had misplaced his favorite neighborhood for good. This style in foreign policy is a warning sign of a declining power in free-fall which is a hell of a lot more dangerous than a power on the rise. Thus, the tactics of American unilateralism, with or without the dog-and-pony show of NATO, only fit the similes of the "unipolar" dream, despite the incontestable realities on the ground. Therefore, those who speak of the US intervention (and occupations), with a hint of "nation-building," in Afghanistan or elsewhere, must educate themselves on the history of post-9/11 tumult, particularly the US terror mongering of the "war on terror," and think again. Given the insurrection of January 6, 2021, and the specter of wrecking crew at the heart of Washington, one may ask, is it not strange to expect nation-building in Afghanistan by a belligerent power, when the latter's own nation is in need of refurbishing?

In retrospect, the parody of nation-building is an afterthought conceived by those who choreographed the invasion of Afghanistan as a launching platform for the perpetual "war on terror," an agenda that demanded territory, proximity, and absolute authority to operate with impunity.[46] That is why the initial search for Osama bin Laden[47] suddenly took a backseat and Donald Rumsfeld (then Secretary of Defense) impatiently turned into *regime change* in Afghanistan.[48] Therefore, those in the media who casually allude to (American) "nation-building" in Afghanistan are either unfamiliar with the notion of open-ended war (i.e., "war on terror") or frankly do the betting of Rumsfeld's long-lasting concealment.[49] Incidentally, there is a common assertion, alleging that the 2003 invasion of Iraq had prevented the United States from full attention to the quagmire of Afghanistan. Yet, given the aimless and perpetual nature of the "war on terror" by the Bush-Cheney administration and, more importantly, the quagmire of Iraq—one more remarkable setback—such allegation is claptrap. To be sure, the United States had no plan for nation-building in Afghanistan or Iraq.

Now, the reverberations of this chaotic evacuation start to proliferate and then recycle in the next stage-managed US election by the demagogues, war profiteers, mercenaries,[50] Cold Warriors, and war criminals across the US domestic political landscape, that is to say, within oligarchic corporate anarchy that utterly failed to keep the *republic*.[51] Yet Orwellian quality of the politics in the United States does not allow a smidgen of accountability, let alone the prosecution of planners and choreographers of this colossal calamity, just like years past in Vietnam where the pattern of deception is the word for word.

The American political class is neither able nor willing to strike at the heart of the "war on terror." The governing elite prefers to avoid the rotten core and stick to the margin where populist politics is rambling and raw. Exposing the original cause of all this needs fortitude in both domestic and foreign policies, which ultimately would expose the Achilles' heel of the American decline and thus a lampoon of another "American Century," which in turn requires an immediate foreign policy U-turn suitable to the tenor of our present epoch. In the aftermath of such catastrophes, therefore, there are foreign policy debates on the caricature of the problem between those who wish not to bog down in such misadventures (and yet blushing and susceptible to the "leader-of-the-free-world" *virus*) and those who are longing for fearmongering and perpetual war anytime and anywhere on the planet.[52] The recent George W. Bush spectacle of shedding crocodile tears for Afghan women in this evacuation is a remarkable illustration of the latter.

Concluding Remarks

The United States lost the war in Afghanistan on the drawing board and at inception, prior to its commencement on Sunday, October 7, 2001.[53] The neocon architects were not interested in Afghanistan *per se*; they planned for the invasion of some seven countries in central and west Asia—known in the colonial lexicon as the greater Middle East. The code word, the "Axis of Evil," included two of them—Iran and Syria—plus North Korea.[54] Soon after the 9/11, Donald Rumsfeld was looking for al-Qaeda in the person of Saddam Hussein in Iraq.[55] "Rumsfeld was saying we needed to bomb Iraq," according to Richard Clarke, the counterterrorism chief at the White House.[56] Dick Cheney and George W. Bush convinced him that he should wait a little longer for the invasion of Iraq, which requires a bit more incredible and grander deception, namely, Weapons of Mass Destruction (WMD).[57]

The US war in Iraq was initiated and lost in a jumble of jockeying for "unipolar" supremacy the second time around—the first time, in 1991, under George H.W. Bush—just a fortnight after 9/11. The US war in Syria was lost too. The US war in Libya produced a wall-to-wall pile of rubble submerged in torrents of blood in the territory that is now a sanctuary and breeding ground for terrorists in North Africa. Incidentally, the post-Qadhafi Libya is a remarkable accomplishment of Hilary Clinton (Secretary of State in the Obama administration), aided by the artful touch of NATO.[58] Finally, the 2014 impulsive US coup in Ukraine against President Viktor Yanukovych—remember Victoria Nuland[59] in the mix—conceived and executed by the Obama administration caused a blowback that led to the annexation of Crimea by the Russian Federation for good.

These are just a handful of foreseeable blowbacks by a defunct hegemon whose self-destructive behavior allows no limit. The fall of Afghanistan is an incongruity since this fall is reflective of not only the dream of a "unipolar" America turned into a self-evident nightmare but a head-on testament also to the collapse of American hegemony attached to the defunct *Pax Americana* (1945–1979). Given all this, one could only hope that the political class in Washington (and the coattails in NATO member countries) would turn around and seriously think about the newly emerging world and new polity, and newly emerging balance of power, amicably toward the world peace.

Finally, it would be crucial to look at the chaotic scenes of the American evacuation in Kabul airport on August 15, 2021, with an eye upon the stormy and roaring American mob, on January 6, 2021, on the grounds of the US Capitol in Washington.[60] These two sets of events are organically related. These separate images in time and place are the two sides of the same coin. These images jointly speak on the dialectic of US foreign and domestic policies, and economically, politically, and strategically interwoven within an organic whole. These images emphatically point to a punishing passage, euphemized as a *road to perdition*. These images do not lie; they tell us something that any inquisitive mind can grasp. These images tell us plenty about the unsettled US (domestic) history,[61] the melancholy of American exceptionalism, implosive foreign policy, and a declining power that cannot walk the earth straight in its own shoes. These pictures are a synopsis of the in-and-out of America as we speak.

Notes

1 The 41st president of the United States, George H.W. Bush, gave the 1991 State of the Union Address on Tuesday, January 29, 1991, at 9 p.m. EST, in the chamber of the United States House of Representatives to the 102nd United States Congress. The transcripts are available at The American Presidency Project—UC-Santa Barbara: www.presidency.ucsb.edu/documents/address-before-joint-session-the-congress-the-state-the-union-1. Retrieved: August 20, 2021.

2 President George W. Bush's address to a joint session of Congress following 9/11 — September 20, 2001: The White House: https://georgewbush-whitehouse.archives.gov/news/releases/2001/09/20010920-8.html; On YouTube: September 3, 2021 (PBS NewsHour): www.youtube.com/watch?v=ZF7cPvaKFXM. Retrieved: September 3, 2021.

3 George Kennan (in *Friendly Fascism: The New Face of Power in America* [1980] by Bertram Gross).

4 See Quint Forgey, "Bush Slams Biden's Afghanistan Withdrawal," *Politico*, July 14, 2021. Retrieved: August 20, 2021: www.politico.com/news/2021/07/14/bush-bidens-afghanistan-withdrawal-499598; Virginia Chamlee, "George W. Bush Says Afghanistan Withdrawal is a Mistake: 'Breaks My Heart'," *People*, July 14, 2021. Retrieved: August 20, 2021: https://people.com/politics/george-w-bush-says-afghanistan-withdrawal-is-a-mistake-unbelievably-bad/.

5 Heather Digby Parton, "No, George W. Bush doesn't Deserve a Pass on Afghanistan," *Salon*, August 18, 2021. Retrieved: August 20, 2021: www.salon.com/2021/08/18/no-george-w-bush-doesnt-deserve-a-pass-on-afghanistan/. A serious treatment of this issue can be found in Kim Berry, "The Symbolic Use of Afghan Women in the War on Terror," *Humboldt Journal of Social Relations*, Vol. 27, No. 2 (2003), pp. 137–160.

6 For a history of this group, see Ahmad Rashid, *Taliban: Militant Islam, Oil, and Fundamentalism in Central Asia*, Second Edition, New Haven: Yale University Press, 2010. The reader, however, should be cognizant of the author's view of oil (pipeline), a subject arbitrarily tossed in the hopper, as a purported motivation for the American presence in Afghanistan. As for *access* (i.e., monopoly retrieval) to oil, it has been rendered pointless with *decartelization* and *globalization* of petroleum and energy since the oil crisis of the 1970s. See Cyrus Bina, "War Over Access to Cheap Oil, or the Reassertion of U.S. Hegemony—Debunking a Popular Myth," in *Mobilizing Democracy: Changing the U.S. Role in the Middle East*. Greg Bates (ed.), Monroe, Maine: Common Courage Press, 1991, pp. 71–81.

7 To be sure, since the fall of the Soviet Union the strategic aim of US foreign policy has been to engage and overwhelm the post-Soviet world with both the *soft* and *hard* offensive in the mix. The claim is that the US won the Cold War without firing a shot. This whimsy of course would dovetail rather aptly with grandstanding ideology of both wings of the elite in the United States who are still living in a dreamlike post-Soviet world yet have no clue as to the larger devastating sea-change of post-Pax Americana, which cut down the United States to size, so to speak. In this context, withdrawal of the troops from Afghanistan by the Biden administration is but a *forced* withdrawal due to the strategic defeat, not only in Afghanistan but also everywhere else across the Middle East.

8 See Daniel Ellsberg, *The Pentagon Papers* (As published by The New York Times), New York: Bantam Books, 1971; *The Pentagon Papers* at 50: A Special Report, *New York Time*. Retrieved: August 20, 2021: www.nytimes.com/spotlight/the-pentagon-papers; National Archives, *Pentagon Papers*. Retrieved: August 20, 2021: www.archives.gov/research/pentagon-papers; Floyd Abrams, "Daniel Ellsberg's 'Heroic Conduct' in Leaking the Pentagon Papers—Opinion Letter," *The New York Times*, August 14, 2021. Retrieved: August 20, 2021: www.nytimes.com/2021/06/14/opinion/letters/pentagon-papers-daniel-ellsberg.html.

9 See Alan Taylor "The Soviet War in Afghanistan, 1979–1989," *The Atlantic*, August 4, 2014. Retrieved: August 20, 2021: www.theatlantic.com/photo/2014/08/the-soviet-war-in-afghanistan-1979-1989/100786/; New World Encyclopedia, *Soviet-Afghan War*. Retrieved: August 20, 2021: www.newworldencyclopedia.org/entry/Soviet-Afghan_War.

10 Ronald Steel. *Pax Americana*. New York: The Viking Press, 1967; Cyrus Bina, "Farewell to the Pax Americana," in *Islam, Iran, and World Stability*. H. Zangeneh (ed.), 41–74, New York: St. Martin's Press, 1994.

11 See this very point in James Risen, "A War's Epitaph," *The Intercept*, August 28, 2021. Retrieved: August 30, 2021: https://readersupportednews.org/opinion2/277-75/71214-a-wars-epitaph-for-two-decades-americans-told-one-lie-after-another-about-what-they-were-doing-in-afghanistan.

12 See White House, *The National Security Strategy of the United States of America*. Washington, DC: Government Printing Office, September 17, 2002.

13 Hannah Bloch, "A Look at Afghanistan's 40 Years of Crisis—From the Soviet War To Taliban Recapture," *NPR*, August 31, 2021. Retrieved: September 1, 2021: www.npr.org/2021/08/19/1028472005/afghanistan-conflict-timeline.

14 See Cyrus Bina, *A Prelude to the Foundation of Political Economy: Oil, War, and Global Polity*, New York: Palgrave Macmillan, 2013, Chapter 7, for pertinent issues and the context.

15 See FRONTLINE, "America After 9/11. PBS—*A Two-Hour Documentary Special*," September 7, 2021, YouTube. Retrieved: September 7, 2021: www.youtube.com/watch?v=Q5iBxva_pm8.

16 Cyrus Bina, "The American Tragedy: The Quagmire of War, Rhetoric of Oil, and the Conundrum of Hegemony," *Journal of Iranian Research and Analysis*, Vol. 20, No. 2 (November 2004), pp. 7–22.

17 As I specified long ago:

> [The] perpetrators of 9/11, aside from foreign policy considerations, have accomplished a more sinister mission. . . . In Gramsci's terms, they pitted "political society" against "civil society" in America, by promoting the former to outdo the latter by the agony of constant surveillance across the homeland. They tossed the Trojan horse of blanket suspicion right in the middle of America's civil society . . . in an atmosphere of fear and intrigue unleashed and utilized by the state. Hence the birth of a full-blown *paranoiac state*.
>
> (emphasis in original)

Cyrus Bina, *A Prelude to the Foundation of Political Economy: Oil, War, and Global Polity*, New York: Palgrave Macmillan, 2013, p. 3. In light of this point, it is important to look at the dragnet pattern of surveillance and its utilization to conceal and cover up the US atrocities and war crimes from the public. In this regard, the remarkable story and courageous act of Edward Snowden—probably equivalent to Daniel Ellsberg's—is worth reading. See Luke Harding, *The Snowden Files*. New York: Vintage, 2014; Shoshana Zuboff, *The Age of Surveillance Capitalism: The Fight for Human Future at the New Frontier of Power*. New York: Public Affairs, 2019.

18 See Cyrus Bina, Lauri M. Clement, and Chuck Davis (eds.), *Beyond Survival: Wage Labor and Capital in the Late Twentieth Century*. New York: Routledge eBook Edition, 2016, DOI: https://doi.org/10.4324/9781315482415; the first chapter is by Bina and Davis on "wage labor and global capital" and the process of universalization. Here, "outsourcing" eludes its original meaning as global competition displaced and dismantles the birthplace of world production. This has been a predicament, among many, of the United States since the mid-1980s.

19 The attitude at the *Council on Foreign Relations*—a government think-tank—can be sampled in I. H. Daalder and J. M. Lindsay, "The Committee to Save the World," *Foreign Affairs*, November–December 2018, pp. 72–83.

20 For a comprehensive assessment of epochal change and the loss of American hegemony, see Cyrus Bina, "Specter of Globalization: Marx, Gramsci and Disjointed Time," *World Review of Political Economy*, Vol. 10, No. 4 (Winter 2019), pp. 484–518.

21 See *The 9/11 Commission Report*. New York: W.W. Norton & Company, 2004.

22 One should note that soon after the fall of the Soviet Union, Neocons in the academy were looking for a *new enemy* and new conflict in order to justify the US incursion into the foreign lands. Huntington (at the time at Harvard) was the first among them; see Samuel Huntington, "The Clash of Civilizations," *Foreign Affairs*, Summer 1993.

23 Cyrus Bina, "Globalization: The Epochal Imperatives and Developmental Tendencies," in *The Political Economy of Globalization*. S. D. Gupta (ed.), Boston: Kluwer Press, 1997, pp. 41–58.

24 A typical protagonist in this category is David Harvey, author of *A Brief History of Neoliberalism*, New York: Oxford University Press, 2005. He mingles *neoliberalism* with *globalization* and mangles Marx's *synthetic* competition with monopoly, among other things. Ben Fine and Alfredo Saad-Filho are also among the protagonists who tried to *periodize* contemporary capitalism by allusion to neoliberalism (a doctrine) rather than through the negation and overcoming of national boundaries by the three essential forms of capital, stage by stage. See Ben Fine and Alfredo Saad-Filho, "Thirteen Things You Need to Know About Neoliberalism," *Critical Sociology*, Vol. 43, No. 4–5 (2016), pp. 685–706. My critique can be found in "Specter of Globalization: Marx, Gramsci and Disjointed Time," *WRPE*, Vol. 10, No. 4 (Winter 2019), pp. 484–518, and "Corona's Bio-Economic Crisis and the Post-Corona World," *International Critical Thought*, Vol. 10, No. 4 (January 2021), pp. 566–574.

25 This is a point about David Harvey, *The 'New' Imperialism*, New York: Oxford University Press, 2003. Here, Harvey is on a fishing expedition on the subject of oil and OPEC, and the touchy-feely semblance of "monopoly," which compelled him to write this book. He neither has adequate knowledge about oil and energy nor is equipped with a watertight theoretical analysis of Marx's competition and my own longstanding study of the globalization of oil and energy. For a critique, see Cyrus Bina, *A Prelude to the Foundation of Political Economy: Oil, War, and Global Polity*, New York: Palgrave Macmillan, 2013, Chapter 5: "Oil and Capital: 'Logic' of History and 'Logic' of Territory," pp. 129–158.

26 This phrase is blending "imperialism"—an epoch surrounded by cartels and monopolies—and "globalization"—an expression purported as monopoly capitalism—in an eclectic mix. This extends Lenin's *Imperialism* to *globalization*, the contemporary phase of capitalism. For a critique of Lenin's *Imperialism* see Cyrus Bina, *A Prelude to the Foundation of Political Economy: Oil, War, and Global Polity*, New York: Palgrave Macmillan, 2013, Chapter 5: "Oil and Capital: 'Logic' of History and 'Logic' of Territory," pp. 129–158.

27 See Leo Panitch and Sam Gindin, *The Making of Global Capitalism: The Political Economy of American Empire*, New York: Verso, 2012. Despite the valuable efforts and painstaking research, which has gone through this important book, nevertheless, an imperative half of the story, i.e., *global capitalism*—an entity much grander than the United States, the EU, China, and Russia combined—is left out. Global capitalism is not the same as "American capitalism"; global capitalism already contradicted and quashed the American hegemony and all the paraphernalia and power of the postwar *Pax Americana*. For a critique, see Cyrus Bina, "Specter of Globalization: Marx, Gramsci and Disjointed Time," *WRPE*, Vol. 10, No. 4 (Winter 2019), pp. 484–518.

28 It is self-evident from this buzzword (i.e., geopolitics) that concern here has two aspects: (1) geography and (2) politics, which runs in the confines of international relations. Such a framework only registers the effects of deeper changes according to the stage-by-stage transformation of *capital* (i.e., the social relation), particularly in the contemporary epoch of *globalization*. Therefore, (1) *geopolitics* alone (e.g., the rise of China vs. the United States) cannot explain the origin of the conflict that is embedded deep in the changing world, and (2) every epoch necessitates its own geopolitics and thus the

geopolitics under the Pax Americana should differ from the one applicable to the post-American world of *globalization*. Sometimes in such frameworks, a somewhat propped-up version of politics, dubbed political economy, is utilized to nuance the field as the geopolitical economy. A popular version of this position, in my view, is Radhika Desai, *Geopolitical Economy: After U.S Hegemony, Globalization and Empire,* London: Pluto Press, 2013. As I will attempt to explicate later in this book, it is an attempt to give credence to an alternative that is neither cohesive nor composed of a solid foundation—this is simply not the way to approach "the future of world capitalism."

29 This view, known as Monthly Review School, does substitute *monopoly capitalism* for Marx's value-theoretic analysis and the thesis of "stagnation" for technological change and fast-paced accumulation of capital in late capitalism. For a glimpse of this "alternative" to Marx's, see John Bellamy Foster and Robert W. McChesney, *The Endless Crisis: How Monopoly-Finance Capital Produces Stagnation and Upheaval from the USA to China*, New York: Monthly Review, 2012.

30 I have spent some three decades quashing any claim to the effect that oil was the motivation in both the massive 1991 American military expedition by the George H.W. Bush administration and post-9/11 invasions by the Bush-Cheney administration. See Cyrus Bina, "The Rhetoric of Oil and the Dilemma of War and American Hegemony," *Arab Studies Quarterly*, Vol. 15, No. 3 (Summer 1993), pp. 1–20. Yet this popular myth dies hard. See Michael T. Klare, *Blood and Oil: The Dangers and Consequences of America's Growing Dependency on Imported Petroleum,* New York: Metropolitan Books, 2004, Michael T. Klare, "It's the Oil, Stupid," *The Nation*, April 24, 2003, and my retort: Cyrus Bina, "Is It the Oil, Stupid?" *URPE Newsletter*, Spring 2004. Retrieved: August 20, 2021: www.academia.edu/33487296/BinaArticlePages_URPENewsletter_Spr2004_pdf.

31 An apt phrase by George W. Ball, Under Secretary of State for Economic Affairs under both President Kennedy and President Johnson, and Under Secretary of State under President Johnson. He was probably one the most credible diplomats of his time. The context which I present here couples with the two highly combustible features, namely, the *nostalgia* and the *defeat*, a product of which may lead to *fascism*. This phenomenon is an observable tendency in the United States today.

32 There is interesting prehistory to all this. It is worth remembering Brzezinski's "doctrine"—a favorite US strategy by Zbigniew Brzezinski, National Security Adviser during the Carter administration—setting up the *green belt of Islam* across the southern borders of the Soviet Union in the west and central Asia. This strategy took center stage in February 1979 *Revolution* in Iran and the United States supported the counterrevolution in Iran, headed by Ruhollah Khomeini; the authorization of this strategy was officiated at the Guadeloupe conference (January 4, 1979–January 7, 1979), thus the US literally obliterated a popular and progressive revolution that overthrew the Shah's regime in Iran. Ironically, as I demonstrated fully elsewhere, this was also the historic end of the postwar Pax Americana and the collapse of American hegemony. On the issue of the US role in the *counterrevolution* in Iran, see the interview with Cyrus Bina, "What's at Stake for Iran in Syria?" *The Real News Network*, October 30, 2015. Retrieved: September 3, 2021: www.youtube.com/watch?v=9g4sV8GXWCc; Cyrus Bina, *The 1979 Revolution and Counterrevolution in Iran* (in Persian), Process Publisher, 2021b. Retrieved: September 3, 2021: https://newprocess2010.files.wordpress.com/2021/05/cyrus-bina-57-new-1.pdf. For struggle inside in Iran and a sample of political uprisings, see Cyrus Bina, "Post-Election in Iran: Crossroads of History and a Critique of Prevailing Political Perspectives," *Journal of Iranian Research and Analysis*, 26 (2). Fall 2009. Retrieved: January 15, 2022: http://www.iran-echo.com/echo_pdf/bina-post-election_iran.pdf.

33 See Craig Whitlock, *The Afghanistan Papers*, New York: Simon & Shuster, 2021.

34 See Seymour M. Hersh, *Chain of Command: The Road from 9/11 to Abu Ghraib*, New York: HarperCollins, 2004; Cyrus Bina, "America's Bleeding 'Cakewalk'," *EPS Quarterly*, Vol. 19, No. 4 (2007).

35 See Seymour M. Hersh, "Whose Sarine?" *London Review of Books*, Vol. 35, No. 24 (December 19, 2013); Seymour M. Hersh, "The Red Line and the Rat Line: Erdoğan and the Syrian Rebels," *London Review of Books*, Vol. 36, No. 8 (April 17, 2014).
36 See Dan Glazebrook, "The Lessons of Libya," *CounterPunch*, November 12, 2014. Retrieved: August 20, 2021: www.counterpunch.org/2014/11/12/the-lessons-of-libya/.
37 See Helen Lackner, *Yemen in Crisis: The Road to War*, London: Verso, 2019.
38 It is disheartening to note how the New York Times was conspiring with the Bush-Cheney administration's dirty tricks on the invasion of Iraq in its various reporting and its *editorial* endorsed the war. For more information, see Howard Friel and Richard Falk, *The Record of the Paper: How the New York Times Misreports US Foreign Policy*, New York: Verso, 2004.
39 The Cheney-Rumsfeld unruly method of dealing with alleged terrorism is also described as "a 1% doctrine"; for further information, see Ron Suskind, *The One Percent Doctrine*, New York: Simon & Shuster, 2006.
40 See Jane Mayer, *The Dark Side*, New York: Doubleday, 2008.
41 The Bush-Cheney administration abrogated the various Geneva conventions against torture and engaged in the torture of detainees across the board. See Philippe Sands, *Torture Team: Rumsfeld's Memo and the Betrayal of American Values*, New York: Palgrave Macmillan, 2008.
42 A notable example in orthodox international relations theory and geopolitics is Henry Kissinger, *World Order*, New York: Penguin, 2015. This book is a compendium of positivism, an ad hoc view of the balance of power, and superficial view of change, particular to mainstream political science.
43 *The Economist*, "Emmanuel Macron Warns Europe: NATO is Becoming Brain-Dead," November 7, 2019. Retrieved: September 3, 2021: www.economist.com/europe/2019/11/07/emmanuel-macron-warns-europe-nato-is-becoming-brain-dead.
44 See Michael Skinner, "Twenty Years of the Afghanistan Occupation Ends: A New Phase of Struggle Begins," *The Bullet*, September 2, 2021. Retrieved: September 2, 2021: https://socialistproject.ca/2021/09/twenty-year-afghanistan-occupation-ends/#more.
45 It is also critical to note in this arrangement that a peculiar sect of Islam, known as Wahhabism/Salafism—observed in Saudi Arabia—stood as a prime political ideology in religious schools (i.e., *madrasas*) under Pakistani ISA where the Taliban tutored and obtained their worldview.
46 The following is a sample of a slipup on nation-building by a progressive historian: Alan Singer, "'Nation Building' Fails in Afghanistan," *Daily Kos*, August 22, 2021. Retrieved: August 24, 2021: www.dailykos.com/stories/2021/8/22/2047578/-Nation-Building-Fails-in-Afghanistan?_=2021-08-22T17:06:20.000-07:00. A difficulty with such an analysis is that it takes words of those at the helm, like Bush, Rumsfeld, or Cheney, at face value, rather than searching for what these people are up to.
47 See Seymour M. Hirsh, "The Killing of Osama bin Laden," *London Review of Books*, Vol. 37, No. 10 (May 21, 2015).
48 For a fascinating story of this character, see Andrew Cockburn, *Rumsfeld: His Rise, Fall, and Catastrophic Legacy*. New York: Scribner, 2007.
49 Concerning the invasion of Iraq Donald Rumsfeld, a barefaced arch-neocon, notably stated, "I don't do quagmires." As it turned out, he *himself* was a *quagmire*.
50 See Jeremy Scahill, *Blackwater: The Rise of the World's Most Powerful Mercenary Army*, New York: Nation Books, 2007.
51 Right after the 1787 Constitutional Convention, in Philadelphia, Benjamin Franklin's coherent and qualified reply: "The Republic, if you can keep it," in a good measure anticipated the adversity of time and the contradictory evolution of the United States of America. His doubt is certainly perceptible today more than ever in every nook and cranny of this country. James K. Galbraith calls it a "Corporate Republic"; see James K. Galbraith, *The Predator State*, New York: The Free Press, 2008.

52 See this recent piece: "Preparations for the 'Next Afghanistan' have already begun," OP-ED by Thomas Palley, August 19, 2021. Retrieved: August 20, 2021.

53 The CIA and Special Forces were on the ground in Afghanistan as early as September 26, 2001. The bombing of Afghanistan also started early on.

54 George W. Bush reference to the "Axis of Evil," among others, see President George W. Bush *State of the Union Address*, January 29, 2002. Retrieved: August 20, 2021: https://georgewbush-whitehouse.archives.gov/news/releases/2002/01/20020129-11.html.

55 See Ted Bridis, "Rumsfeld 'Wanted to Bomb Iraq' After 9/11," *Independent*, March 21, 2004. *Archived from the original on July 11, 2020.* Retrieved: August 20, 2021: www.independent.co.uk/news/world/americas/rumsfeld-wanted-to-bomb-iraq-after-9-11-65340.html. In this report, "Rumsfeld Was Saying We Needed to Bomb Iraq," according to Clarke. Clarke then stated, "We all said, 'No, no, al-Qa'ida is in Afghanistan.'" Clarke also revealed that Rumsfeld complained in the meeting, "there aren't any good targets in Afghanistan and there are lots of good targets in Iraq."

56 See Richard A. Clarke, *Against All Enemies: Inside America's War on Terror*, New York: Free Press, 2004.

57 See Hans Blix, *Disarming Iraq*, New York: Pantheon Books, 2004.

58 See Andrew Quinn, "Clinton says Gaddafi Must Go," *Reuters*, February 27, 2011. Retrieved: August 20, 2021: www.reuters.com/article/us-libya-usa-clinton/clinton-says-gaddafi-must-go-idUSTRE71Q1JA20110228; Democracy Now: *The Libya Gamble: Inside Hillary Clinton's Push for War & the Making of a Failed State Guests: Scott Shane and Jo Becker* (co-wrote a two-part recent exposé for the Times called "The Libya Gamble.")—"Hillary Clinton, 'Smart Power' and a Dictators Fall" (NYT) and "A New Libya, With 'Very Little Time Left'," *New York Times*, March 3, 2016. Retrieved: August 20, 2021: www.democracynow.org/2016/3/3/the_libya_gamble_inside_hillary_clinton.

59 BBC diplomatic correspondent Jonathan Marcus, Ukraine Crisis: Transcript of leaked Victoria Nuland-Geoffrey Pyatt call about the plot. Here is a transcript, February 7, 2014. Retrieved: August 20, 21: www.bbc.com/news/world-europe-26079957.

60 For the horrifying side effects of war on the home front see Kathleen Belew, *Bring the War Home*, Cambridge, MA: Harvard University Press, 2019.

61 For an early origin of the history of the United States, see Howard Zinn, *A People's History of the United States*, New York: HarperCollins, 2015.

3 Specter of Globalization

The Rise and Fall of the Pax Americana

And still your fingers on your lips, I pray. The time is out of joint.

—William Shakespeare
Hamlet, Act 1, Scene 5

Foreword

This chapter aims to combine a critique of political economy with that of transnational polity in a united theoretical foundation. It begins by (1) exploring the development of capitalism into stages, (2) showing that this should necessarily lead to globalization, and (3) validating that in the epoch of globalization no hierarchical interstate (hegemonic or not) political order may stand a chance for survival. These highly abstract theoretical queries, on the one hand, follow Karl Marx's critique of capitalism, and on the other hand obtain further theoretical and historical concretization in Antonio Gramsci's hegemony, before their realization at observables levels via the rise and fall of the postwar Pax Americana (1945–1979). The periodization of capitalism—a clue embedded in Marx's *Capital*—underpins how the postwar Pax Americana, Marx's "conquest of the mode of production," and Gramsci's hegemony set the context for a synthetic approach to the rise and fall of American power. Finally, it is argued in this chapter and throughout this book that the force of globalization is the arbiter of time, despite the *declining power syndrome*, in this disjointed polity.

Introduction

After the sesquicentennial of the first volume of *Capital* (Marx [1867] 1977) and the bicentenary of Marx's birth (see Bina 2018),[1] Karl Marx's monumental work on the critique of political economy, his vision, foresight, and method on the *differentia specifica* of capitalism have yet to find equivalence in richness and far-reaching influence in nearly every nook and cranny of the world now (see Liedman 2018 for Marx's life and work). Those versed in critical scholarship and immersed in political praxis should be confidently in a position able

DOI: 10.4324/9781351136785-3

to assess the contemporary world in which we live. They should be able to perceive the cumulative transformation of capitalism, say, from the nineteenth to the twenty-first centuries and examine the contours of the evolutionary as well as revolutionary changes that have taken place across this small planet.[2] They should be able to see the unity and the contradiction across the modes of production and appropriation. They are expected to appreciate the necessity of continuity and change in all aspects of life, including economy, polity, and social relations, thus the truth about the indispensability of *crisis*. And those versed in critical scholarship and immersed in political praxis should be terrified when the limits of both social systems[3] and natural systems[4]—and the dialectical interaction of the two—are inescapably reached.

This chapter intends to uncover (1) that there is an insufficient appreciation for Marx's value theory as it may relate to our contemporary epoch,[5] (2) that there is substantial confusion over Antonio Gramsci's concept of hegemony, particularly as it may relate to the Pax Americana in its rise and challenging fall, (3) that there is a qualitative difference between globalization and neoliberalism, and (4) that this blunder may have larger implications for the identity of our epoch. The latter differentiation is critical against the widespread obfuscation of the two among traditional leftists and many self-styled Marxists across the world.[6] Periodization of capitalism essentially resides in the *capital* itself and its inherent self-expansion.[7] In both epochal and methodological terms, globalization is none other than the potentiality turned into a sweeping actuality displayed across the nook and cranny of the planet. At the more concrete level of abstraction, the collapse of the Pax Americana (1945–1979)[8] has a far-reaching implication for the polity, American hegemony, the future of the interstate system, and thus the global balance and distribution of power.

Globalization is none other than the operation of Marx's law of value on the global scale, precisely reaffirming the universality of capitalist social relations across the world. This law[9] (or theory) is manifesting the proliferation of all three circuits of commodity, money, and productive capital worldwide, interwoven and dovetailed in the inharmonious process of global accumulation. These circuits display the dialectical workings of the sphere of production, the sphere of exchange, and the sphere of distribution both within and without the conventional boundaries of nation-states. Capital accumulation on a global scale adheres to the law of value, which leads to uneven development both within and between national boundaries, and which eventually cut across the worldwide geography of production. The unevenness of capital, therefore, is inherent in the process of accumulation, just as capitalist competition, as an inner nature of capital, leads to further concentration and centralization of capital. This of course is contrary to the cult of monopoly (à la Hobson [1902] 1961; Hilferding [1910] 1981; Baran and Sweezy 1966,[10] or Braverman 1974),[11] prevalent and popular in the neo-Marxian literature, New Left, and the leftist's lexicon in general, particularly the Anglo-American school of *monopoly capitalism*, which also takes its cue ostensibly from Lenin's theory and the era of *Imperialism*.[12] Today, contrary to this, Marx's law of value is the kernel of the universality of capitalist social relations—an era that I have long called and identified as the epoch of globalization (Marx [1847] 1973, [1939] 1973, [1867] 1977, [1885] 1981, [1894] 1981).

The monopoly capital school (Baran and Sweezy 1966), while on the surface paying lip service to Marx, nevertheless offers its deaf ear to Marx's theory of competition and unwisely throws his value theory under the proverbial bus (see Marx [1847] 1973, Ch. II, sec. 3; Cypher 1979; Moudud et al. 2013). Contrary to those leftists (like Samir Amin), who tend to subordinate globalization to "global north"/"global south" (by resuscitating the threadbare center/periphery thesis), thus recklessly defacing Marx's theory of value (Amin 1974, 2013a, 2013b),[13] this chapter is an attempt in bringing Marx's unrealized potentiality (in the nineteenth century) to a realized and unclouded actuality in the twenty-first century. Globalization (an unbroken and elucidated entity, as a structure and an epoch, reflecting the social relation of capital worldwide) vindicates Marx's original vision after some 150 years. Marx's law of value uniquely illuminates the universal conquest of the capitalist mode of production in today's globalization. That is why, the (methodological) reduction of this epoch to what is now fashionable as "neoliberalism"[14]—a term suitable for the policy or economic strategy—is unbefitting to periodization, and for the same reason, in methodological terms, divorced from Marx's method of analysis and theory of value. Much ado about "financialization," too, is a lure for a detour from the very context of this worldwide crisis.[15] Finally, this is one of the hallmarks of this chapter: while the Pax Americana played the crucial role of expecting mother in the course of maturation of the fetus, midwife of the new era and arbiter of mutual exclusion had to cut the umbilical cord of this historic pregnancy to save the newborn, and let the ailing mother step into the sunset of history. This too speaks rather pointedly of another critical sunset, the breakdown of American hegemony.

In what follows, we would only deal with a bit more manageable subset of these larger issues, focusing on the notion of hegemony, while also showing that the separation between the "metropolitan center" and "periphery"[16] need not be perpetual and that the presumption of such dichotomy, both theoretically and empirically, is flawed (see Weeks 1981; Bina and Yaghmaian 1988, 1991). This point is implicit here in the section on global conquest of the mode of production.

The first section sketches the contours of post-hegemonic chaos and disorder and sets out to identify the misuse of power in US foreign policy based on capricious deduction and unilateral action. In the following section, the meaning of hegemony and the nature of hegemonic power will be deciphered. The transformation of developing regions of the world is then addressed in conjunction with the speedy development of technology toward cheapening of labor power in advanced industrialized countries. This was the essential ingredient for the transnationalization of capital in the postwar period. The next section imparts the exposition of the ascent and descent of the Pax Americana (American Order). Here, globalization of capital (as a social relation) exceeded the structural constraint, institutional wherewithal, and the historical capacity of the American Order and by the same token the threshold of leadership that had since the World War II been handed over to the United States (Steel [1967] 1970). Fittingly, though, a defunct order begets a defunct hegemon.

Disjointed and Disordered Interlude

In the aftermath of the massive capital flight (in the form of both money and productive capital) and "plants closing" in the 1980s, particularly in the aftermath of the 1991 US intervention in the Persian Gulf, we were alarmed over the consequence and sadly the predictable backlash of the US global decline. This was just before the US celebrated attitude toward the collapse of the Soviet Union and Eastern Europe, which left a bit of ideological sweet taste in the mouth of those who quickly took their cue from "the end of history" and wished another "American century" in the seemingly composed and tranquil period before the eventual storm. Francis Fukuyama, the imperial wizard of American neoconservatism, was among the first to be bamboozled by this transitory episode, amid the dog-and-pony sideshows in the media early by the Reagan administration and later by the George H.W. Bush and the Clinton administrations (see Fukuyama 1992). The events surrounding 9/11 (that is, September 11, 2001) were a shocking revelation for those who had overlooked the gleaming indications that transmitted the breakdown of the postwar Pax Americana (see Wallerstein 2002; Bina 2013b, 2–3). The American officials (of both political parties) either did not see or did not want to see that the new global polity in the making and the American hegemony do not mix and that the balance of power has already changed. The scores of American academics in and out of the US government had little clue as to the dynamics of the new era. Their counterparts in the West—the so-called partners or allies in the old system—also did little more than lip service to elucidate that the new balance of power is in the making and that nostalgic American leadership echoing the Pax Americana is inconsequential. However, among the standing ideological institutions of Pax Americana, higher education in social sciences sustained the greatest harm. The academy in the West (that is, the fragmented bits of the now-defunct Pax Americana), particularly in the discipline of international relations (and geopolitics) suffered the brunt of the ideological blunder associated with the claim of "unipolarity," "liberal order" (an aphorism for fallacious liberalism and furtive control), and the Orwellian concept of freedom.

The collapse of the Soviet Union (followed by unmitigated humiliation of Russian leadership) made Washington overconfident, even upbeat (see Nye 1991). The blindsided US policymakers overlooked the unraveling of the postwar international system: the collapse of the Bretton Woods system (1944–1971), globalization of oil and energy via the oil crisis of the 1970s, and the transnationalization of production, outsourcing, and finally global hypercompetition and rampant deindustrialization of the once captain of the industry and innovation. The record of a substantial exodus of companies in nearly all industries from the United States in the 1980s is common knowledge (see Bina et al. [1996] 2015). Aside from the rusty hulks of the IMF and the World Bank, one may also investigate the status of the North Atlantic Treaty Organization (NATO), a Cold War relic, dragged injudiciously into the twenty-first century from the vagaries of yesteryears belonging to the now-defunct Pax Americana.

By sheer incredulity, the US leadership (of both political parties) thought that there is something "exceptional" about the United States that may turn the wheel of history the other way. They thought that such an "exception" is in the DNA of American power. Many sanguinely underestimated the unavoidability of this historical fall. Some shuffled desperately between "hard power" and "soft power," and rather tautologically made the case for the necessity of American (global) leadership (see Nye 1991, 2004). Others palpably decided to intervene and devastate country after country, region after region, by resorting to real or imaginary "allies" misusing and violating the new polity in the making. The reality of course proved tougher (and more overpowering) than nostalgia or the ideology had gone mad. Consequently, the world is now much closer to nuclear war than ever.

A quarter of a century ago, following the first US intervention in Iraq, we made the following observation:

> In the past [i.e., the era of Pax Americana], the United States had sufficient [epochal] hegemony to maintain the world [according to its historical mission.] Now, it is striving to maintain [the nostalgic impression of] that hegemony. Hence, we now see the type of military intervention that neither serves American interests nor substitutes for political [and economic] weaknesses. Thus, at this historical juncture, attempting hegemonic reassertion through aggression proves contradictory and self-limiting, thereby bringing to the open the most critical aspects of U.S. participation in [escalating] the present global disorder.
>
> (Bina 1993, 4)

This chapter also attempts, in both tenor and theory, to show the ever-increasing gap between reality and the mentality of those in charge of US foreign policy, particularly the Cold War attitude of ideologues and diehard neocons, given the mindboggling changes that have taken place against the US rule in the global economy and polity. For instance, the rhetoric of "our world order" (a camouflage for the denial of changing world), recycled frequently as a conceited distraction, typically coupled with bouts of nostalgic self-glory, is still the defining way of thinking within the foreign policy circles in the United States (see Anderson 2013, 113–167). The addiction to power and its diminished base appears to be the biggest conundrum for the United States as well as a huge political burden in the emerging world today. The so-called pivot to Asia (read China) or expansion of NATO inching toward the borders of the

Russian Federation or strangulation of Venezuela is now among American extraordinary activities, not to mention the past misadventures in Afghanistan, Iraq, Libya, Syria, and Yemen, that so far boomeranged big time.

Consequently, irreconcilable differences between persistent realities on the ground and Washington's relentless denial hardly allow for an orderly transition toward the post-American global polity anytime soon. The question of war and peace, therefore, does not only hinge on the settlement of disputes on a daily basis in this transition but also the very transition to new world order is hostage to this nostalgic attitude and unconstructive engagements. Hence, one should expect continued chaotic patterns of conflict in this disordered and disjointed period.[17] As one can anticipate, the mixture of prolonged *defeat* and compulsive *nostalgia* is the stuff of which *fascism* could be a by-product. The world has not yet forgotten the experience of the Third Reich and the rise of Nazis in Germany in the interwar period. There the humiliating defeat in the World War I, the toll of hefty war reparations imposed rather underhandedly by the victors, and the enduring nostalgia in Germany itself, had in the end led to the unthinkable (see Keynes 1920).[18] Nevertheless, the United States appears to be a bit far from an orientation toward such fascistic circumstances; yet given the experience so far, the distance toward this possibility is fast shrinking. For a commentary on the inauguration of Donald J. Trump as the forty-fifth president of the United States, see Bina (2017).[19]

Hegemony: Synthesis of Consent and Force

Hegemony, whether intended for domestic class relations (à la Gramsci) or the relation of power across the international polity (among the nations), denotes a set of concrete, historically determined, and indivisible institutions that ultimately confirms the faith of a particular power structure and identifies the character of a hegemon. Hence, hegemony—utilized in Gramsci's contemporary discourse—signifies a relation first, and hinges on a structure that binds the subject and object of power together. At the same time, being a subject in Hegelian subtext, a hegemon is an active agent whose autonomy is contingent upon (1) the dynamics of consent and force and (2) the capacity and scope of the mediating and underpinning institutions. In this manner, it is possible to theorize the notion of hegemony both historically and specifically.

The indivisibility embedded in the very meaning of hegemony is also the consequence of indivisibility and organic unity of economy, polity, and society in the capitalist mode of production. Marx's method of abstraction (i.e., an attempt at theorizing) primarily starts with concrete observation of real social phenomena in capitalism that have not yet been stripped of their encumbered layers and incidental characteristics that would make them appear chaotic and contradictory aggregate (Rosdolsky 1977). The task of abstraction is to set aside any contingently chaotic elements (the task of *undressing* in the jargon of dialectic) in order to uncover the bare unity of the subject. This step consists of the point of departure according to Marx's methodology. Yet this is only a half of the story. The other half of conceptualization, according to Marx, is to concretize this abstracted entity systematically in order to reach the point of concrete return (Bina 2013b, 130–133). The latter completes the circle of conceptualization via the mediation of historical facts and empirical reality at one's disposal at the time. Marx's theorization is neither idealist (i.e., it does not start with an idea as a point of departure) nor empiricist (i.e., empirical data are not a point of departure in Marx's theory), nor axiomatic (i.e., unexamined assumptions have no role in Marx's theory), nor speculative. Here, empirical data, as such, are no more than abstract entities and thus do not represent the concrete reality. Moreover, the data used in empirical testing may not meet the requirements of the point of return, i.e., as a concretized abstract. Therefore, except by chance or coincidence, virtually all hypotheses testing, built on axiomatic constructs, especially in the social sciences, are essentially speculative and devoid of a solid theoretical foundation.

To put it in methodological terms, hegemony is the reference to a specific epistemology drawn from the mediating relations that inform the nature (i.e., ontology) of power and power relations in capitalism. Therefore, hegemony is not synonymous with a set of circumstances that, for instance, would translate to direct force, domination, or military occupation, including colonial domination. In other words, hegemony is a kind of power (and power relation) that is governed by mediation and mediating institutions which themselves are subject to definite dynamics that regulate sociopolitical tendencies and the social relations in capitalism. Such dynamics, for instance, are present in Gramsci's notion of hegemony in the context of class struggle and class interest, mediated by the institutions of civil society and thus the realm of politics in both Gramsci's and Marx's frameworks.

Therefore, despite the etymology of hegemony since ancient Greece or premodern China, the main ingredients of hegemony (i.e., consent and force), as related to power relation in contemporary capitalism, do not (and should not) operate in a manner of zero/one switch in our everyday digital communication. For consent and force in hegemony so defined, neither express a particular *state of affairs* in contemporary capitalism nor invoke independent existence from one another. The notion of consent and force in Gramsci is a part of an organic whole, a dialectic, that represents a synthesis that is neither force nor consent in the pre-synthetic (i.e., crude and mechanical) interpretation of many Gramsci scholars in the Anglo-American tradition, exemplified by Perry Anderson (2017).[20] Hegemony so defined also embodies the undivided whole, contrary to the fragmented views (on the left and on the right) that arbitrarily consign it to standalone components of the system, such as economic, political, or military facets of the system. Moreover, the reader should realize that these facets themselves have no autonomous presence without the organic and undivided domain of power in a holistic manner.

The internal dynamics of consent and force are parts of the intrinsic ideological power of the whole, which in turn provide the impetus for leadership in a hegemonic system; this *power* is far from any aggressive power projection by *unmediated* means. This, in a broad measure, reflects Gramsci's hegemony related to the direction of class struggle within the framework of civil society and nation-state. This also applies to the broader arena of international economy and polity, particularly the rise and fall of the Pax Americana. As indicated earlier, consent and force are necessary and sufficient for defining the hegemonic power. Yet, just as the indivisibility of time and space in modern cosmology, the dynamics of consent and force form an *inseparable* potency. To see the point here clearly, one may draw an analogy parallel with "spacetime," a powerful theoretical discovery in modern cosmology and astrophysics. Here just as *spacetime* is indivisible, consent and force are forming a synthesis toward the expression of hegemony. Another parallel is the notion of competition in Marx, which relies on the concentration and centralization of capital (far from the illusory spectrum of perfect competition/perfect monopoly in contemporary neoclassical economics) and thus presents capitalist competition in its synthetic form (Shaikh 1977, 1980, 2016; Shaikh and Antonopoulos 2013; Clifton 1977; Bina 2013a; Weeks 2013).[21]

Thus, a synthetic theory of hegemony has nothing to do with shuffling between consent and force along the artifice of language and within an imagined spectrum with no end in sight. If hegemony (in modern capitalism) does not operate as a switchboard between a detached *consent* and a standalone *force* at the discretion of a supposed hegemon, then one wonders about the proliferation of literature on the subject that treats it transhistorically and the status of Gramsci's unique organic concept. Gramsci is rather explicit about the antithetical coexistence of hegemony and military force in the following passage:

> As soon as the dominant social group [i.e., the hegemon] has exhausted its function, the ideological bloc tends to crumble away; then 'spontaneity' may be replaced by 'constraint' in ever less disguised and indirect forms, culminating in outright police [i.e., military] measures.
>
> (Gramsci 1971, 60–61)

To uncover the reasons behind the fall of American hegemony, one must look at the underpinning (hegemonic) institutions that mediated within the Pax Americana and held the American power together for just a little over three decades in the postwar period. Today's diffusion of power and the tendency toward a multipolar global polity reflect the fall of the American power as the underpinnings of postwar polity (along the multifaceted economic, political, social, and ideological dimensions) have been melted away since the early 1980s. In political terms, *globalization* is a definite term for (1) the undoing of the old order, (2) the dismantling of the American hegemonic power (based on the time-honored hierarchy of nation-state that once was the backbone of the postwar polity), and (3) the transitioning toward a full-fledged multipolar world. Gramsci focused on the "organic intellectuals" and complex intricacies of "civil society" and "political society" in modern civil society and the "world of production" (Gramsci 1971, 12). In this chapter, our task is to focus on the rise and demise of the postwar order via the ascent and descent of American hegemony owing to the globalization of capitalist social relations anticipated by Marx's theory of value. This volume is also an undertaking consisting of the various levels of analysis, from proximate and concrete to hidden and abstract toward a critical analysis of our time.

The pervasive notion of hegemony popularized in the orthodox International Relations literature justifies the *unmediated* impositions that more often than not capitalize on the direct antagonistic force and interactions among the opposing counterparts in the polity, particularly the international polity. Simply put, "hegemony" so defined is not significantly different from *domination*. Indeed, a remarkable journalistic replication of such an interpretation is so widespread in the academy and the media that, despite the lack of critical justification, it is nevertheless appealing to popular culture everywhere across the global divide. Therefore, it is often painstakingly difficult to get through an intelligent discussion without a great deal of digression and considerable shift of focus when, for instance, it comes to the question of hegemonic rise and demise of the Pax Americana.[22] Hegemony, so perceived, remains an ad hoc, ahistorical, tautological, and imprecise buzzword used not only by the majority of public but also by many specialists across all social sciences (be it the left or the right) today. The common understanding of the hegemonic position in popular expression is the deployment of force from without in order to dominate the opponent, rather than relying on the mediating institutions, i.e., institutions that sanction the mission of hegemony. On the contrary, US interventions in all three Persian Gulf wars, namely, the 1980–1988 Iran–Iraq war, the 1991 US invasion of Iraq, and the 2003 US invasion and occupation of Iraq, should not be identified as hegemonic (see Senate Committee on Foreign Relations 1987; House Committee on Foreign Relations 1990; Bina 1993, 2004b; Huntington 1993; Adelman 2002; Battle 2003). These encounters by any account were aggressive acts of domination in desperation.

Thus, any forceful domination by military means is indeed a nullification of hegemony and in the context of the defunct Pax Americana an exemplary sign of America's hegemonic decline. To put it simply and bluntly, one does not burn the house in which one shares in its hegemonic ownership with a material interest in the neighborhood—even the Cosa Nostra appreciates this simple principle. White House (2002) reveals a newly embraced doctrine in foreign policy (i.e., Doctrine of Preemption), which is indeed a remarkable manifestation of the fact that the United States lost the world that in whose construction it had once a great part (see Hersh 2004; Bina 2007). And this is more than the proof in the pudding not only on America's diminished capacity and inconsequential leadership in the world today but also on America's destructive measures toward the transition to the new global polity in the making.

A tangible example of hegemony is discernable in the case of employment (of wage labor in both manual and mental manifolds) in capitalism. Given the everyday struggles of the majority of people in the world for survival—and entirely aside from Marxian theory of employment—there is little doubt that working for a wage is not without exploitation. Yet despite such contemptible acknowledgments, people are looking for a job, any job, all the time. People even beg to have a job; they beg to be so exploited by capitalism. This shows the embedded power of capitalism and the very stuff that hegemony is all about. Consent is thus inherent deep within the structure of capitalist relations in a hegemonic fashion.

Hegemony must have several interlaced features as follows. It should be (1) spontaneously consensual, (2) internally determined, (3) historically sanctioned, (4) holistically undivided, (5) structurally synthetic, and (6) institutionally mediating. In our view, these characteristics are inseparable and must be simultaneously present for hegemony to take hold. In other words, these elements are the vital signs of hegemony as opposed to, say, domination, colonial control, or forced invasion. The story of hegemony is the mutuality of the whole, albeit with its internal contradictions, and thus the echo and exercise of reconciliation within the system as a whole. The focus here in this chapter is chiefly on the rise and the fall of hegemonic Pax Americana, a historically specific interstate system that was erected after the World War II (1945) and collapsed in the late 1970s. Hegemony is also a mutual characteristic of the system as a whole—not a detached property of the hegemon. American hegemony, therefore, was as good as the postwar mediating institutions that once upon a time shouldered the epoch of Pax Americana (Bina 1991, 1993, 2004b; Anderson 2002). Hence, hegemony thrives through the reflection of the whole, not the exertion of the parts. Otherwise, any claim to hegemony turns into an algebraic sum of its constituent parts and predictably diminishes to the fallacy of composition. For that reason, in our case, the United States undertook hegemonic power by the virtue of postwar Pax Americana, not by some mystical properties intrinsic to "American exceptionalism."[23] Aside from its circularity (i.e., its tautological trait), deriving the notion of hegemonic power from "American exceptionalism" is to stand hegemony on its head. In the absence of hegemonic Pax Americana, therefore, speaking of American hegemony is meaningless, it has neither relevance nor consequence (Bina 1993, 2004a, 2004b).

Global Conquest of the Mode of Production

The issue of propagation and the conquest of the mode of production are critically important for the *periodization* of capitalism and for our argument in this chapter. Here, we have essentially relied on Marx's *Capital* and *Grundrisse*, which theoretically anticipated all these massive changes in the next century, including those of the postwar period under the Pax Americana. Marx's insights are also essential for the identification of the sequence of events that have led to transnationalization and globalization of capital (i.e., the disappearance of "national capital"), which—as we have shown elsewhere—forcefully countered the very foundations of the now-defunct Pax Americana.

Marx argued:

> Within a single society . . . the mode of production of capital develops in one branch of industry. . . . Nevertheless, it is (1) its necessary *tendency to conquer the mode of production in all respects*, to bring them under the rule of capital. Within a given national society this already necessarily arises from the transformation . . . of all labor into wage labor; (2) as to the external markets, capital imposes this propagation of its mode of production through international competition. Competition is the mode generally in which capital secures the victory of its mode of production.
>
> (Marx [1939] 1973, 729–730; emphasis added)

Globalization of capital is *prima facie* a point of departure from past measures that capitalized on international trade, export of financial capital, piecemeal transfer of physical capital, or bilateral transmission of technology from location to location. Globalization of capital refers to a systematic transformation in which the unit of analysis no longer centers on the habitual conception of the nation-state prevailing in both the orthodox and heterodox literature in economics and political economy (Bina 1994a, 1997, 2011). Following Marx, we argue that capital in its highest epochal realization (i.e., as a universal social relation) must operate transnationally with little concern about geographical, juridical, or national boundaries. Far from being a fetish (i.e., an object), capital as a global social relation roams and rambles in all its essentially conceivable forms—commodity, money, productive—across the nook and cranny of the contemporary world. Therefore, the epoch of globalization, often incorrectly categorized as "neoliberalism" or "neoliberal policy," is essentially a manifestation of the universalization of social relations at the highest stage of capitalism. Today's contention over the epoch of globalization is not unlike the quarrel by Vladimir Ilyich Lenin against Karl Kautsky (an influential leader of the Second International) in the first decades of the twentieth century on the theoretical import of *imperialism* as a historical era in capitalism—as opposed to a mandate, conviction, strategy, or a policy, proposed by the latter (Lenin [1916] 1970a, [1916] 1970b).[24] Neoliberalism, in its present vernacular by the traditional left, is no more than a set of policies. Globalization is simply an epoch, not a policy.[25] Moreover, globalization is a universalized and sustained epoch and, despite speculative and hotheaded claims in both business and social media, cannot be abrogated by any authority through adverse policy, adverse decree, adverse protocol, adverse natural calamity (e.g., COVID-19), or other seemingly adverse means, such as an economic boycott in the peacetime or otherwise. One simply cannot amputate a social relation of such a monumental proportion through such a flimsy measure.

This stage in the development of capitalism also mirrors the universal status of labor and capital in class terms as de facto global categories that should constitute the class struggle across the globe, on the one hand, and the fast-changing technology and universal cheapening of labor power, on the other. This is what pertains to Marx's vision in *Capital* (vol. 1), having to do with his studious value theory as the first principle for a theory of periodization in the capitalist mode of production. Thus, one must simply avoid originating one's analysis with features or historical circumstances that are transient, contingent, and conditional in capitalism; the level of analysis matters and, at the highest level of abstraction, Marx's value-theoretic framework is centered on capital in general as a potential embryonic form through to the actual universalization of social relation. The embryonic possibility then under definite conditions turned into an actuality of social relations diffused through all barriers, including the barrier of international geography. Thus, the domain of capital (as a social relation) expanded stage by stage through the circuits and threefold moments of capital, anticipated in Marx's theory of value. This presents a (highly abstract) theoretical foundation for the periodization of capitalism as a mode of production. What is well known as the laissez-faire stage of capitalism, in the lexicon of mainstream economics, is when the circuit of capital in commodity surpasses the boundary of the nation-state. At this stage, "primitive accumulation"[26] of capital was significant (e.g., the enclosures of commons in Britain), and there was merely a rudimentary structure in the banking system, while the joint-stock companies (i.e., the primacy of corporate form in the capitalist mode of production) began to bloom. The inauguration of finance capital set the second stage known as a monopoly. This is known also as "managerial capitalism," the symptomatic of a dichotomy between the ownership and control over property, a separation that decidedly led to the nearly unlimited access to money capital without the barrier of individual private property.[27]

Global conquest of the capitalist mode of production is often portrayed in terms of regional trading blocs or in what has long been a practice for the traditional left as a dichotomy of center-periphery. The geographical expansion of social capital (i.e., capital in aggregate) has always been disruptive and at an *uneven* pace. The uneven nature of economic development in capitalism has had its counterpart both *intra*nationally and *inter*nationally across the advanced capitalist countries (ACCs) and less developed countries (LDCs), as the accumulation of capital has taken place globally.[28] One advantage of starting with the analysis of capitalist social relations, rather than capital as a national, physical, or a monetary entity, is to acknowledge the historical departure of developing nations from their pre-capitalist past in conjunction with a widespread infusion of manifold technological change that had already occurred in the advanced industrialized countries. The context and complexity of this *conjunction*, then, may be able to offer a glimpse of larger transformations that occurred across the world economy, especially since the postwar Pax Americana.

First, many post-colonial states have emerged from the colonial division of labor and "primitive accumulation" of capital since the end of the World War II. Import-substitution industrialization and, its sequel, export-oriented industrialization were universal economic strategies that largely prepared these countries to overcome their internal barriers to capitalist development and facilitated their entry into the postwar international capitalist market. These strategies in turn led to the *internal* propagation of capitalism in many of these social formations and paved the way for embracing the *external* penetration of what is to be evolved as transnational capital. For instance, a careful glance at the postwar land-reform programs in the "Third World" would point to the widespread separation of the immediate producer from the means of production across the board. This provided us with a vantage point to observe a transfer of the massive supply of potential wage labor from the countryside to the urban centers to be utilized for the import-substitution and export-led industries in many of these LDCs. Here, in their Twentieth-Century scenario, the postwar land-reform programs had decisively facilitated the creation of the *home* market hand-in-hand with decidedly the potential (organic) penetration of the world market in the LDCs in question (Bina and Yaghmaian 1988, 1991).

Here, the internationalization of circuits of capital, particularly its productive form, reinforced the production of relative surplus value through the technology transfers and their application in the emerging labor processes in many of these LDCs. This was an initial attempt to proliferate the circuit of social capital toward the transnationalization via concordance between spheres of circulation, on the one hand, and to facilitate the requirements across the spheres of production, on the other hand, beyond the boundaries of the nation-states (Brenner 1977; Fine 1978; Palloix 1975, 1977). In the meantime, there emerged a series of organizational and technological innovations, leading to further transformation of production processes in advanced capitalist countries (Rosenberg [1982] 1995). The motivation for these changes expanded and intensified the *real* subsumption of labor under capital—as opposed to the *formal* subsumption of labor under capital (see Marx [1867] 1977, 1019–1038). These transformations, and motivation toward the "conquest of the mode of production" (to put it in Marx's persistent adage), have had only one universal purpose: to *cheapen* the value of labor power (the mother of all commodities) both intranationally and internationally across the globe.[29] Concisely, the fundamental underlying motivation of the capitalist production, whether expressed through neo-Taylorism, self-directed work teams, Fordism, neo-Fordism, flexible-and-lean production systems, or the computerization of production through computer-aided design/computer-aided manufacture, or robotics and virtually fully automated manufacturing, has universally been the cheapening of labor power across the board (Shaiken 1986; Freeman 1994; Bina and Davis 2000; Bina 2012e).

Globalization of capital is a phenomenon that is universally contingent upon the reduction of the value of labor power via incessant changes in technology. The progressive cheapening of labor power across every production unit, every industry and sector, across nearly every geographical location is in tandem with the universal proliferation of technically advanced labor processes immersed in fast-paced and persistent technological change. Here, several decades of intense, per unit of output, devaluation of labor power, and massive technological displacement of workers—in the advanced capitalist countries—had suddenly found their *cumulative* application in the labor processes within LDCs.

A by-product of this universally qualitative advance has so far been a massive surplus population—a gigantic and bulging reserve army of unemployment—at the global level (see Bina 2005). The rise of this reserve army, the simultaneous intensification of labor processes via an equally amplified capitalist competition, together with the astonishing speed of technological transformation, exerted substantial downward pressure on the value of labor power and comparatively on the level of wages for the overwhelming majority of workers globally. In recent decades, global production, hyper-competition, and fast-paced technological change have also created a broad response from workers far and wide with multilayered and multidimensional effects across the world.

The Rise and Fall of the American Order

To appreciate the concrete display of hegemony in the then ascendant Pax Americana (Steel [1967] 1970),[30] we simply need to focus on the application of the (tripartite) American Doctrine of Containment after the World War II. This doctrine was an embodiment of (1) the containment of the Soviet Union; (2) the suppression of democratic/nationalist movements across the "Third World"; and (3) the control, co-option, and constriction of domestic "civil society" within the United States (Draper 1991). This three-pronged strategy has not yet been adequately theorized in an integrated fashion and without prejudice in the literature on international relations. Holistically, contrary to the paucity of systematic theorization, the latter two categories provide a broader and stronger ideological framework for the containment of the Soviet bloc (and the subsequent 1949 Chinese Revolution and containment of the Peoples Republic of China). In other words, an overemphasis on anti-communism alone is not sufficient to express the ideological substance and organic consequence of the postwar American hegemony. The architect of the American containment against the Soviet Union was George Kennan (see Kennan 1947), who had prudently salvaged the US foreign policy from wholesale bellicosity, hasty ambition in taking over the entire postwar world, and the reckless application of nuclear bombs the likes of which was unleashed pitilessly on Japan in the very last days of the World War II.

The first containment crystalizes the placing of the Soviet Union behind the ideological divider of the Iron Curtain, and the initiation of material and ideological enforcement of the Cold War from the outset (Fleming 1961; Leffler 1984). Hence, Cold War was indeed a manifold hegemonic phenomenon, spanning the economy, polity, and realm of ideology and culture, from the race for space, the research and development, weaponizing the proliferation of consumer goods, the fetish of openness and democracy, to Hollywood,[31] Mickey Mouse, Rock 'n' Roll, Hula-Hoop, and the deployment of Christian Mega Churches as a weapon of mass propaganda. The US propaganda machine also doubled down on the fairy tale of American exceptionalism to glue all these pieces together in order to be able to project hegemonic power in the postwar era. In popular terms, this was a "cherry on the top," by simply portraying the façade of power, when all the while the (real) power in effect was enforced by the postwar economic and political institutions which underpinned the American hegemony. In other words, it was not "American exceptionalism" that had run the course of postwar hegemony but hegemonic institutions that carried the United States to the throne of hegemony so far as they persisted in the postwar period. Thus, the reasons for the rise and fall of the postwar institutions (of Pax Americana) are the same reasons for the rise and fall of the American world and American (hegemonic) power.

The second containment doctrine emerged from the time of the declaration of anti-colonial policy by the United States, on the one hand, and the subsequent destabilization of the democratic and independent movements throughout the "Third World," on the other. This doctrine is illustrative of, for instance, the 1953 CIA coup d'état against Mossadegh in Iran or the 1954 CIA coup d'état against Arbenz in Guatemala. The deliberate and widespread subversion against independent governments and democratic movements and installment of numerous handpicked dictatorships and politically corrupt regimes in the then "Third World" was by no means exception but a rule under the Pax Americana, yet the world then and now wonders why the doublespeak of "freedom" and "democracy" obtained so much popularity in the United States and the West in general. At any rate, this was a par of contradictory outlook, archaic political attitude, and an embodiment of Pax Americana itself (Green 1971; Galeano [1973] 1977; Blum [1986] 2003; Kinzer 2003, 2013). Moreover, the US attempt at the transformation of pre-capitalist social formations in the aforementioned part of the globe—for instance, via the cookie-cutter with respect to land-reform programs—had led to hasty, paradoxical, and undemocratic transformation in the international capitalist orbit under the Pax Americana (Bina and Yaghmaian 1988).

Finally, the third containment strategy was duly implemented through American domestic thought control and the deliberate expulsion of independent institutions and organizations that had been a part of the US domestic "civil society"—such as militant labor unions and progressive political institutions of the real or imaginary left. This, in turn, had given rise to devising a "hegemonic model" for wide-ranging ideological emulation that had predictably and permanently shifted the direction and scope of American popular politics to the far right of the political spectrum for good, and categorically marginalized a massive number of progressive intellectuals, generation after generation. McCarthyism is but the tip of this iceberg which unleashed the potency of conservatism in liberal disguise while propelling and normalizing the right in the newly formed political spectrum.[32] When it comes to the assessment of this containment strategy, its insidious effects are somewhat permanently imprinted on the American psyche (Levin 1971). As we have maintained elsewhere, "America itself has become a prime casualty [of this doctrine] that has yet to recover from its prolonged [intellectual] timidity, its chronic insecurity, and above all, the injuries sustained to its collective consciousness" (Bina 1993, 6).

In the economic arena, the institutionalization of hegemony was accomplished through the rule of the US dollar as a universal currency, conjoined with the newly devised international monetary system, known as the Bretton Woods system (1944–1971). This arrangement—coupled with the Marshall Plan for the postwar reconstruction of Europe and the Agency for International Development for the "Third World"—exponentially increased US hegemonic power during the formative years of the Pax Americana. Institutionally, the powerful US-sanctioned international institutions, such as the International Monetary Fund (IMF) and the World Bank, came to lead and influence the modus operandi of quintessential development strategies that paved the way for a hegemonic ascent of the entire system. Indeed, the socioeconomic restructuring of the Pax Americana was preconditioned upon the eventual *absorption* of the lion's share of the earth's inhabitants across the vast geography of production and exchange, known as the Third World. Such absorption was, of course, contingent upon what Gramsci called "passive revolution," in which the separation of the immediate producer from land created an internal market for the propagation of capitalist accumulation and overarching penetration of transnational capital (Bina and Yaghmaian 1991).

On the contrary, the colonial system of Pax Britannica literally lived and died by the sword: first, by the predominance of *direct* colonial administration; second, by means of *direct* plunder of raw materials and natural resources; third, by the way of *direct* and unmediated repatriation of surplus (and wealth) from the colonies; fourth, by means of foreign policy grounded upon *gunboat* diplomacy; and fifth, by espousing explicit (and official) racial, physical, and cultural segregation *across the empire* (see Cable 1971).[33] These features should carry no hint of hegemony whatsoever; they are the stuff of bullying in the schoolyard, albeit on much larger scale and scope. Thus, from the standpoint of international relations and the identity of our epoch, those who ascribe *hegemony* to colonialism in general, and to the British Empire in particular, are among the most superficial and misleading observers of a comparison between the Pax Britannica and postwar Pax Americana.

Given the depiction of Pax Americana earlier, the scope of hegemony can be measured by focusing on the socioeconomic forces that formed the foundation of this international order at the time. In this context, the postwar system of Pax Americana enjoyed a variety of mediating economic, political, and ideological institutions that laid its cornerstone. During the height of its hegemony, postwar Pax Americana led to the progression of capital in its full-fledged transnational structure. American hegemony so acquired was by no means secure. From time to time, it suffered from contradictory challenges that visibly disclosed its fragility. The self-induced conduct and aftereffects of a series of CIA coups d'état and covert interventions stand as a grand testament to internal contradictions (for instance, America's counterfeiting democracy) and America's hegemonic fragility. To be sure, these and other political and ideological US atrocities were unbecoming of hegemony and thus showed the open-endedness and instability concerning the US leadership in its different periods of time. These coup d'états, therefore, expressed a state of suspended animation, if you like, between "war of movement" and "war of position" in Gramsci's manner of speaking (see Anderson 1976–1977, 2017; Sassoon 1982; Bocock 1986; Thomas 2009; Bina 2013b, Ch. 7).

Nevertheless, the United States survived all these impulsive political conducts through to the end of the Pax Americana. It was the maturity of capitalist social relations and the punishing force of capital's globalization that eventually caught up with the American hegemony, American polity, and the American era. In other words, the contained (in this case, forces much, much larger than America) broke the container, the vessel, the outmoded shell. This should speak loud and clear on the cause of the closing of the American hegemony and the conclusion of the quintessential US leadership in the world. Indeed, once the "conquest of the mode of production"—to put it in Marx's ripe catchphrase—crossed the Rubicon of globalization, neither the external crutch of hegemony nor the seeming exceptionality of America's real or imaginary leadership could have a useful place in the universe of globalized capital. In other words, the spread-out geography of production, distribution, and exchange, and above all capital's social relation did not need this particular and indeed dilapidated external crutch to lean on. Incidentally, this should have a strong implication for the flimsy foundation of orthodoxy in international relations (and geopolitics) that seemingly rotates around the parable of nationalism, the fairy tale of transhistory, or worse, American exceptionalism. To put it succinctly, in the emerging world of today, the hegemony of capital (in the sense of Marx) should trump all hegemonies. To peek at the angle of individual sectors, though, the transnationalization of capital posits the oil and energy sector as an *avant-garde* of globalization (Bina 1989, 1991, 1995, 2006; Bina and Vo 2007). The oil crisis of the early 1970s was but a crisis of decartelization of oil and its competitive restructuring, which accordingly led to globalization and worldwide pricing of oil (Bina 1985, 1988, 1990, 1992, 2004a).[34]

As we have seen, the overriding reason for the implosion of Pax Americana was a series of cumulative changes that eventually led to an epochal and vast qualitative change across the global socioeconomic structure in the 1970s. The enormity of this grand sea change also displaced the constituent parts of the system, particularly the hegemonic position of the United States which once was at the apex of the "old" international system.[35] Therefore, the claim of "unipolarity" (euphemism for another American century) made by the neoconservatives, Cold Warriors, and many more jubilant observers of the fall of the Soviet Union within the orthodox international relations literature is but superficial at best, and misleading indoctrination at worst.[36] To be sure, postwar Pax Americana was befittingly collapsed nearly a decade before the fall of the Soviets. At a more fundamental level, globalization is reflective of the mobility of capital across the boundaries of the nation-states, which *inter alia* led to the devastation of the pre-existing national hierarchies, including the international division of labor, the time-honored locations of technology, technological development, and the boundaries of nearly all markets in goods, services, and labor power since the 1970s. In the meantime, on the conception of the nation-state as a recent reconstruction, Benedict Anderson (1991) offers a lively perspective that fits quite well with the arguments presented in this chapter and in this volume.

The plants closing across the United States constitute the story of the grand sweep toward the rationalization of manufacturing and other related industries across the board and across the global divide in swiftness and velocity unparalleled in our recent memory (see Bina and Davis [1996] 2015). The rise of worldwide inequality is also deeply rooted in this very transformation that the world exhibits both intranationally and internationally (see Galbraith 2012; Piketty 2014). The so-called outsourcing cut across and bared deeply to the bone the industrial base of once prosperous and promising postwar America. This was happening in the 1980s when Ronald Reagan was riding high toward the "Shining City on the Hill," and on the surface, all seemed triumphant on the Western front. Nevertheless, in reality, the world was already slipping from the outmoded grasp of the United States, and the plants' closing was merely a mop-up operation that demonstrably spelled out the end of the American hegemony (see Bina et al. [1996] 2015). All this was of course amid hyper-competition and fast-paced technological change across nearly all industries and throughout the worldwide geography of production (Bina and Davis 2008). In economic, political, and institutional terms, the European unification, leading up to the European Union (EU), the designation of the euro as a contending world currency, and other cataclysmic political and ideological occurrences, since the late 1970s and mid-1980s, that devastated and distanced the patchy and disjointed former client states within the now-defunct Pax Americana, are all manifestly the tendencies that also measure the contours of this grand epochal change.

Concluding Remarks

As has been explicated earlier, hegemony is a deliberate concurrence of consent and force in a historically specific and politically explicit setting in which spontaneity tend to underlie the fabric of power. Consent and force are not two separate entities but constitute a part of a synthetic whole, thus negating any unduly reduction to either of these constituent parts. Therefore, force, particularly *dominating* force, has little to do with hegemony. At the same time, such synthesis does not lend to partitioning into the economy, polity, ideology, culture, and social relation, for the identification of hegemonic power. In other words, hegemony represents every single facet of these multiplicities in organic unity. Thus, military superiority by itself, aside from those aspects, is not a sign of hegemony. Indeed, the popular phrase, "military hegemony," is but a contradiction in terms. In light of all this, it would be appropriate to say a few words in passing on the claim of the "inevitability" of US global leadership, via the *bound-to-lead* perception of the US power by other means, dabbed "soft power," as a proper substitute for the so-called hard power by certain American protagonists who wish to extend America's hegemonic life (see Nye 1991, 2004).

Soft power though seems to work along the line of power by persuasion (and indeed cooption) and in a way tends to mimic "spontaneity," which is among the differentiating aspects of hegemony. Yet global hegemony is not a matter of choice, and thus hegemonic power cannot be obtained by mere persuasion, cooption, sugarcoating, cunning, fictitious "partnership," joint military exercise, "special relationship," "preferred trade," and, in a nutshell, by deliberate willpower—hegemony is not voluntary. In this context, hegemony is (historically) unique, and just like virginity, when you lost it, it is lost forever. This has little to do with intention and a lot to do with the obtainability of objective conditions that would delineate and pair off a historical period and polity in unison. The proposition, such as "soft power," sums up to icing on the cake where there is no cake—which then amounts to mere fictitious leadership. Hence, the United States is bound to neither lead nor bound to be a hegemonic power any longer via mimicking the rendition of "soft power." The thesis of "soft power" by Nye appears to have been placing the cart before the horse, so to speak; and by invoking the premise of "soft power" and pledge of "bound to lead" toward the rekindling of US global leadership, Nye appears unmindful of the internal dynamics and, more important, transitory nature of (mediating) institutions under postwar Pax Americana that tightly held the American hegemonic power intact. He has forgotten that the world has now entered the tumultuous post-American global polity in the making and that there is no going back. That is to say, the old balance of power is neither possible nor desirable. Yet, there are those who, not unlike Don Quixote, struggle both faithfully and fancifully to resuscitate the world order that belonged to the not-so-distant past (see Daalder and Lindsay 2018).[37] While the orthodoxy in international relations grasps at straws on every occasion to restore the US leadership, the clueless heterodoxy, too, in order to justify the rise of American power, goes to any length to obfuscate (and minimize) the diminished status of the United States vis-à-vis the rise of the globalized world as it stands today (see Panitch and Gindin 2012). The orthodoxy though does not quite get it that "what's done cannot be undone."[38]

Globalization of capital is the manifestation of the "conquest of the mode of production" across the world. It aims toward the universalization of capital's social relation against nearly all barriers, including the borders of the nation-state across the board. Contrary to Lenin's popular thesis, *Imperialism: The Highest Stage of Capitalism* ([1916] 1970), the capitalist mode of production proper is neither monopoly nor stagnating, nor ends up at the "imperialist stage," where and when nearly four-fifths of the world's population had neither known nor ever lived under capitalism. Long before Lenin takes his cue from Hobson, in *Imperialism*, globalization of capital was anticipated in Marx's magnum opus, *Capital*, and the theory of value erected upon synthetic competition, not despite, but because of concentration and centralization of capital, the lifeblood of capitalist accumulation. According to Marx, capital is not a "thing" but a *social relation* that would almost universally turn all objects of utility, quintessentially labor power (the mother of all commodities) into the object of capital. Speaking of transnationalization of capital (i.e., capital on the global stage) is thus none other than the universalization of this social relation, which also amounts to the conquest of the mode of production across the planet. Therefore, it is useful to note that, from the standpoint of methodology, casual references, say, to "imperialist globalization," would set the status and stage of the contemporary globalized world of capitalism back to a period in which neither the law of value had a possibility to operate universally nor synthetic competition, given the limited concentration and centralization of capital, had been strong enough to operate beyond the boundaries of a handful of capitalist states. Imperialist globalization is but an oxymoron frequently uttered by those on the left who appear bashfully twirling around the dilapidated notion of "monopoly capitalism," the very core of imperialism. This is also a whisper that takes refuge in the presence of imperialists (read American imperialism) and miserably misses the boat, so to speak, on much deeper issues that underpin globalization, including contrary and countering forces of globalization against the American wherewithal and power. In this chapter, we presented the notion of globalization in separate but organic undertones, namely, (1) globalization,[39] a gauge for "conquest of the mode of production"; (2) globalization, a yardstick for identity of the newest stage of capitalism; and (3) globalization, a criterion for universalization of the law of value.

To sum up, the critical corollary of all this for today's corporeality is the appreciation of both observable and unobservable facts on the ground. First, the acknowledgment that the Pax Americana has long been displaced and that the loss of hegemony on the part of the United States is irretrievable. Second, the recognition of new *international norms* worthy of this post-American era is not only desirable but also of absolute necessity, particularly in the current transitory watershed. Third, the necessity of handling setbacks arising from disruption, unilateralism, unauthorized use of force, de facto violation of international law, and prevention of international conflict by fresh institution building, including invigoration of the Geneva Conventions, and universal condemnation of protracted wars, directly engaged or indirectly provoked by the defunct hegemon. Fourth, the removal of causes of poverty and the catastrophic conflicts in the world. Fifth, the safeguard against the possibility of nuclear war, particularly during the present watershed and this tempestuous historic crossroads. Sixth is the recognition that climate change itself is a major source of polarization and conflict, and thus should be identified as the universal source of instability. Finally, if history can be of any consolation, the acknowledgment of the fact that declining powers inflict more damage and pose more danger to peace and stability than the rising ones; thus, safeguarding the security of the ongoing transition in which today's global polity has one foot in the past and another in the future. Today, the scope and scale of *universal* uncertainty instigated by globalization are limitless. Expected calamities due to the human-induced climate change, on the one hand, and the widening inequality in global income and wealth distribution, the accelerating worldwide class polarization, global poverty, and the massive global unemployment, on the other, are a recipe for deliberate and eventual self-destruction of life as we know it. Thus, speaking of geopolitics, particularly in an orthodox international relations variation, is not only inadequate but also quite misleading in a provisional polity where "The time is out of joint" (*Hamlet*, act 1, scene 5). Today, profound class polarization that had led to the "planet of slums"[40] and a glimpse of the "sixth extinction"[41] have both tested the limits of our planet. As for the specter of globalization, similarly, COVID-19 traced, measured, and ironically (and tragically) identified the presence and contour of *globalization* in one colossal sweep across the globe.

Notes

1 *"Bicentenary of Marx's Birth, His Legacy, and His Last Laugh (1818–2018)"* is a concise piece published in *People's Daily* (China) on the bicentenary of Karl Marx's birth, celebrated along with the Second World Congress on Marxism, held on May 5–6, 2018, at Peking University, Beijing, China. Here is the link as published to its Chinese translation on May 5, 2018: http://paper.people.com.cn/rmrb/html/2018-05/08/nw.D110000renmrb_20180508_2-21.htm. The original in English can be found on URPE's link: https://urpe.wordpress.com/2018/05/05/bicentenary-of-marxs-birth-his-legacy-and-his-last-laugh-1818-2018/.

2 In the letter of March 25, 1852, to Joseph Weydemeyer in New York, Marx remarked, "There is no more splendid time to enter this world than the present. Come the day when people can travel from London to Calcutta in a week, both our heads will long since have rolled or started to roll. And Australia and California and the Pacific Ocean! The new world citizens will be unable to comprehend how small our world once was" (Marx to Joseph Weydemeyer), Karl Marx Frederick Engels *Collected Works* (Marx and Engels Letters, 1852–1855) vol. 39, p. 70.

3 In addition to a profound class polarization and insurmountable income and wealth inequality, we now are on the verge of breaching the threshold of climate cataclysm and the natural limits of the ecosystem. We live in a social system that predictably threatens the well-being of the planet and the existence of all species, including ourselves. Although theoretically and empirically silent on the nature of capitalist production, Piketty (2014) is a fitting and alarming source for a demonstration of the deepest division yet in the world's wealth distribution, particularly in the United States, since the 1970s. Yet there are also two very critical volumes, one on the deep disparity (titled, *Inequality*) and another on the contemporary worldwide crisis (titled, *The End of Normal*), by James K. Galbraith, ably sketching our present predicaments (see Galbraith 2012, 2014).

4 For issues surrounding climate change and incontrovertible threats to our planet, see Christophe Bonneuil and Jean-Baptiste Fressoz (2017). The Shock of the Anthropocene (London: Verso, 2017). This is a magnificent source of investigation and indeed a wake-up call.

5 The periodization of capitalism is one of the most obscured and least understood subjects in Marxian literature to date. In Fine, Ben and Laurence Harris (1979). *Rereading Capital* (New York: Columbia University Press, 1979), Fine and Harris dealt with so many crucial issues in Marx's *Capital* and this has since inspired a large spectrum of scholars interested in Marx. Yet in this work, Fine and Harris also introduced a peculiar framework for the periodization of capitalism. The authors divided the capitalist mode of production into three distinct phases: (1) laissez-faire capitalism, (2) monopoly capitalism, and (3) state monopoly capitalism (see Fine and Harris 1979, Ch. 7 and Ch. 8). The authors state that they wish to follow Marx's method of periodization of feudalism, thus focusing on the transformation of rent. This provides a key to the periodization of capitalism. This rationalization appears to be based on symmetry between the internal

collapse of feudalism and that of capitalism. There is also an implication that the transition from capitalism to socialism may have similar or parallel patterns. This appeal could in turn open the door, perhaps inadvertently, for an unnecessary question that as if socialism is a "mode of production." Here, I must remind the reader of Lenin's "transition from capitalist to a higher socio-economic order" in Vladimir I. Lenin, *Imperialism: The Highest Stage of Capitalism* (Peking: Foreign Language Press, [1916] 1970a, 148), and the red flag it raises on the critical connotation of the capitalist mode of production as such (see Bina 2013b, Ch. 5, 130–140, for a critique of Lenin's view).

Fine and Harris introduce yet another measure of periodization as they move to the "world economy" in Chapter 9. They embrace the internationalization of capital in its three forms, namely, commodity capital, money capital, and productive capital. Here, the authors appear to have resorted to a dual (or parallel) periodization to comply with the demand of the geography of production. The authors knew fully well that a periodization based on the three forms of capital should constitute the highest level of abstraction and thus all-encompassing. Nevertheless, the duality of two separate periodization they promoted here would generate confusion, to say the least. This dichotomy poses a methodological problem between national and transnational domains, and thus obfuscates the propensity toward the universalization of social relations and further obscures the globalization of capital, for instance, along the mental constructs, such as the *logic* of history and *logic* of territory, proposed by David Harvey (see Harvey 2003; and Bina 2013b, Ch. 5, for a critique).

The essential ingredients for a genuine theory of periodization in capitalism are already available in *Capital* (vol. 1). Here, Marx reveals that capital in its highest abstract form stands as an embryo of social relations, which potentially transforms into an actuality—an eventual body of social relations universally. In this transformation, based on the law of value, the tendency for the conquest of the mode of production necessitates an incessant overcoming of the barriers of all sorts under capitalism. The barriers of the working day, skill formation, time and motion, private ownership (corporate form), present and future (credit system), inter-industry, scale, and scope are the familiar ones. "The *true barrier* to capitalist production," Marx contends, "is *capital itself*" (Marx [1894] 1981, 358, emphasis in the original). All barriers, other than capital itself, are detectable at lower (i.e., concrete) levels of abstraction and thus incompatible with a highly abstract and universal theory of periodization. Therefore, the only option is to return right back to *capital* itself in its self-expansion in pursuit of the "conquest of the mode of production." This abstract framework is also concisely inferred by Marx in *Grundrisse* (Marx [1939] 1973, 729–730).

It is within this context *alone* that capital in its *tripartite forms* constitutes both a point of departure and a point of return. Similarly, it is within this context *alone* that the question of geography and internationalization of capital find a mutual ground form-by-form, circuit by circuit, and stage by stage toward globalization. Thus, a periodization built on the laissez-faire/monopoly/state monopoly footing is neither consistent with an expected level of abstraction nor compatible with Marx's theory of synthetic competition (see Marx [1847] 1973), nor abiding by Marx's dictum that capital has no nation. Likewise, in this regard, falling back on the leftist tradition that long follows Hobson ([1902] 1961), Hilferding ([1910] 1981), Luxemburg ([1913] 1951), and Lenin ([1916] 1970) is indeed a risky business. Hence, eclecticism in method, the duality of vision, and a trace of monopoly appear to have obstructed a genuine notion of periodization among the traditional left today. For instance, Samir Amin also follows the same theme and scheme when it comes to the periodization of capitalism (see Amin 2013a).

6 Nearly four decades fast forward, co-authored with Alfredo Saad-Filho, Ben Fine enters into a new debate again on stages in capitalism. This time he converges on neoliberalism. In a paper, co-authored with Alfredo-Saad-Filho, Fine put forth a laundry list of 13 points for neoliberalism to be a new stage in capitalism (see Fine and Saad-Filho 2016).

Many of the points on this list are but the essential ingredients and conditions that reflect features of globalization. Nevertheless, the authors insist on their "thirteen things you need to know about neoliberalism," as the title of the paper suggests. One of the obsessions in this paper is an overemphasis on "financialization," a crowd-pleasing catchword that since the 2008 financial crash has obtained explosive popularity. The authors' usage of "financialization" here has to do with neoliberalism, the target of their stage theory. As we know, the 2008 crisis within and across the financial markets metastasized speedily and quickly spread through non-financial firms and circuits of global capital across the world. I consistently argue in the book that all this was because of the globalization of social relations of capital at the present stage. And neoliberalism, as such, is a stage neither by itself nor by the grace of "financialization." Globalization, on the other hand, is a stage in which capital completes its conquest of the mode of production worldwide, a theme foreseen in Marx's *Capital* some 150 years ago.

7 A quick mention of *Empire* (2000) by Michael Hardt and Antonio Negri might be appropriate here, before attending to more pressing issues. I had shared with Negri the keynote podium in November of 2008 at a conference on *Cognitive Capital and Spaces of Mobility* (www.kurrents.org/arkiv/conf2008/index.html) at the University of Gothenburg, Sweden. This led to an opportunity for me to speak with Negri candidly about issues surrounding globalization and his work. The political stance and attitude presented by Negri (and Hardt) can be characterized in a nutshell: (1) devoid of class and class struggle, (2) obsessed with "cognitive capital," (3) bewildered on the role of technology in capitalism, (4) detached from the reality of the labor process, and (5) mystifying, to say the least, on America's role and the global order.

8 The postwar Pax Americana (1945–1979) is both methodologically and historically a concrete vehicle for tracking the social relations of capitalism in transition. It was essentially this inter-state system that was a conduit for internationalizing capital in both commodity and finance forms, while in the latter part of its existence, also promoted the internationalization of productive capital. From the perspective of the *moment* of finance capital, Pax Americana was a setting for the depiction of control and promotion of cartels (including International Petroleum Cartel, 1928–1972). Yet, from the stance of burgeoning productive capital, it stood as a transitory vehicle for transnationalization of capital in all its three forms. At the end of this contradictory evolution, *synthetic competition* (see Marx [1847] 1973, Ch. II, section 3) gained the upper hand and in due course, the wherewithal of the system came to a halt via globalization. This complex, conflicting, and contradictory system collapsed under its own weight late in the 1970s. At the more concrete level of abstraction, the collapse of the Pax Americana was due to the failure and eventual collapse of its hegemonic institutions in succession. The content (i.e., the forces of globalization) simply outlived the outmoded vessel (i.e., the hulk of the Pax Americana). The first crack in the core of this prodigious and intervening structure was the breakdown of Bretton Woods (1944–1971), and the second in the following was the thunderbolt of the crisis of globalization of oil in the early 1970s (see Bina 1985, 1992, 1995, 2006; Bina and Vo 2007). The collapse of the Pax Americana was a display of dialectic and dynamics of unity and contradiction within the economy, polity, and social relations, which culminated in a multifaceted crisis as an aftereffect. One can follow a simple rule to track the rise and fall of the Pax Americana: it is through the transformation of oil, as a *time machine* (see Bina 2012a).

9 "All laws" in Marx's work are "tendencies." This shows that, unlike the mainstream economic theory, subjects are *not* treated as a state of affairs but as transforming entities from *potential* to *actual*. In this manner, Marx's theory of value at the highest abstract level (1) embodies the whole economy (in today's lexicon, macroeconomics), (2) enunciates the foundation of class and class struggle, and (3) appeals to ubiquity of capital as a social relation. In embryonic form, the origins of these characteristics are all rooted in *Capital* (vol. 1).

10 Paul Sweezy in a daring tone endorsed the phrase "monopoly capitalism" as he approvingly attributed it first to Thorstein Veblen, an American institutionalist economist, and a critic of "conspicuous consumption." Sweezy's motive of change of heart toward Marx is a sad story that could be identified by interrelated blunders in methodology. First, Sweezy's confidence in the conformist method of "successive approximation," i.e., the idealization of the subject and arrangement of reality to replicate it. Second, Sweezy's lack of sufficient knowledge about the nature and origin of *synthetic* competition in Marx. Third, Sweezy's slip-up on Marx's commentary on the joint-stock companies and his reliance on Engel's flawed interpretation of capitalist competition (see Sweezy 1981 and *Capital*, Vol. 3, Ch. 27). It is heartbreaking that such a remarkable figure and wonderful mentor to my own generation could fall for "monopoly capitalism," a little gawky tautology of a phrase.

11 Harry Braverman, *Labor and Monopoly Capital* (New York: Monthly Review Press, [1974] 1998) has emerged as a quintessential volume on deskilling of labor yet having grounded on monopoly capitalism; it precisely (although gingerly!) negates Marx's theory of synthetic competition and, by implication, Marx's theory of value. Braverman treats concentration and centralization of capital as a monopoly, and by assuming monopoly, he turns his rather useful (empirical) investigation into a tautological report. The lumpiness of capital here does not sit well with those faithful to the thesis of monopoly capitalism. In addition, Braverman's deskilling of the *crafts* (a pre-capitalist activity) is not a substitute for a well-developed theory of skill formation in capitalism. It is interesting to note that Sweezy (1981), quarreling over the competition with Marx, recites a full paragraph from Braverman in order to show that Marx's theory of value is passé and "monopoly capitalism" is in the vogue (see Sweezy 1981, 11). For a critique of Braverman's notion of skill, see Bina (2012c, 2020b).

12 Written in 1916, in the middle of the war, *Imperialism: The Highest Stage of Capitalism* is perhaps the most popular outline in the radical left literature as had been so fittingly anticipated by the author himself. *Imperialism* portrays capitalism *inter alia* as (1) a decomposing and stagnating system and (2) a "monopoly" system in the early twentieth century in which nearly the four-fifths of the world had not yet seen let alone experienced the very meaning of capitalism, and which the pre-capitalist stage of "primitive accumulation" was still in full swing. This judgment (of the capitalist mode of production) proved very costly for Lenin and his comrades, as early as 1919, following the Russian Revolution. Contrary to Marx's view, this stagnationist thesis is on the mind of very many traditional leftists around the world today.

13 *Empire of Chaos* is a catchphrase used by Samir Amin in reference to the display of unilateralism by Washington in the aftermath of the fall of the Soviet Union in the 1990s. This assessment is at best a skin-deep rendition of present-day global realities and at worst an untidy proposition devoid of a systematic assessment that drives the United States to such catastrophic undertakings toward self-destruction and the destruction of what is still standing from the edifice of the past. To be sure, this type of reasoning is not without circularity (see Amin 1992).

14 The literature on political economy is replete with the phrases, such as "neoliberalism," "neoliberal era," or "global neoliberalism," referring to the present phase of capitalism since the 1970s. Here there is a divide among several subgroups of radical economists. An example of radical scholarship on this subject can be seen in Kotz (2015). The author argues "neoliberalism is the most useful concept for understanding the current form of capitalism." He characterizes the neoliberal era with "two related developments that have stirred much debate, globalization, and financialization" (Kotz 2015, 4). This book is both theoretically and empirically within the *social structure of accumulation* (the SSA thesis)—a version of the French regulation school popularized among radical scholars in the United States. I contend that the analysis of global capitalism and the dynamics of

capitalist social relation is much deeper and way beyond this mid-level approach, known as the SSA thesis.

15 The coinage of "financialization," as an equivalent to globalization or even neoliberalism, is a ploy; it reveals naught and conceals a lot. It is misleading politically and distracting methodologically. First, the very context of the 2008 financial crisis is globalization, without which one could not even imagine such a worldwide contagion in terms of speed, scale, and the scope of proliferation in recent memory. Second, capital is not a thing but a social relation. Thus, by putting stress upon a stand-alone *form* (or moment) of capital in isolation, i.e., by fetish mongering, one could not appreciate the nature of this crisis fully. The authenticity of this new obsessive/compulsive catchphrase in my view is suspect. Concerning the 2008 financial crash, I find Durand's *Fictitious Capital* (2017) to be delightfully useful on the cause of the crisis. Yet, the cloud of accepted wisdom often obscures the author's outlook on globalization. For a quick backdrop on the 2008 crisis, see Bina (2010).

16 Viewing "center" and "periphery," at face value, may not be always immune from tautology. Since, methodologically, in such a context, the point of departure in the analysis could not obtain a possibility of independence from the point of return. The quintessential examples of tautological reasoning are plenty in both orthodox and heterodox economics literature, particularly in economic development (see Amin 1974; Emmanuel 1972; Frank 1969).

17 There are numerous examples of unilateralism and lawlessness on the part of US leadership, be it under the Republicans or the Democrats. The case in point is the wholesale destruction and devastation of Libya under the Obama administration. In 2011, the US government assured China and Russia (the two permanent members of the UN Security Council with veto power) that it had no intention of regime change in Libya and the removal of Col. Gadhafi and asked for their cooperation to withhold their veto with respect to vote on a "no-fly zone" over Libya. China and Russia agreed. After the vote and adoption of the Security Council Resolution 1973 in March of 2011, the United States cunningly changed the course and did what it had long been on its agenda since the Reagan administration. The United States, France, and Britain then (under the façade of NATO) bombed Libya to bits in support of Jihadists and other like-minded terror groups concealed as political opposition in Libya. This rather predictably caused the slaughter of Gadhafi in broad daylight by the latter and turned the country into the piles upon piles of ashes, town after town, neighborhood by neighborhood, border to border, and limb to limb, soaked in torrents of blood across the provinces. The US Secretary of State Hillary Clinton had been in Libya several weeks earlier and devotedly showed up in picture-taking with signs of victory alongside some of these criminal "liberators" at Benghazi airport. It is interesting to note that upon Gadhafi's gruesome murder, Hilary Clinton, in a well-publicized interview, triumphantly declares, "we came, we saw, he died," showing once again the irony and true colors of US foreign policy. The UN Security Council Resolution 1973 (March 17, 2011, www.un.org/press/en/2011/sc10200.doc.htm); the story of this tragedy can be found in Glazebrook (2014).

18 *The Economic Consequences of the Peace* (http://oll.libertyfund.org/titles/keynes-the-economic-consequences-of-the-peace) is one of the most thought-provoking writings of John Maynard Keynes, written in defiance against Britain concerning the Paris Peace Conference of 1919, at whose behest he served as the chief representative of the British Treasury. Article 231 of the Versailles Treaty was primarily the point of contention. Keynes's sharp intuition, foresight, and aptitude for anticipation of what was to come in the interwar period in Germany had come through this gem of a nearly overlooked book. Fromkin's *A Peace to End All Peace* ([1989] 2009) is another appropriate read as a backdrop to the original sin in which the Ottoman Empire was carved by the victors in the First World War.

19 The reports on Donald Trump's mendacities and his pugnacious conduct abound since his inauguration. Yet, in the scheme of things and scale of objectivity, we should not distract ourselves from the focal point of crumbling American postwar institutions, deep socioeconomic divisions, and the limited political options here since the 1970s. To this one may add the reactionary political/cultural/ideological values that were kept under the surface that, not unlike the return of the specter of Hamlet's father in the tragedy of *Hamlet*, are a reminder of the assassination of Abraham Lincoln on that fateful evening of April 15, 1865, in Ford's Theatre, Washington, DC. At this crossroads where the anxieties are soaring in America, there is plenty of allusion to civil discourse and civil war in this fragmented, thumped, and Trumped social (dis)order domestically. Here is the link to an example: https://foreignpolicy.com/2017/03/10/will-we-have-a-civil-war-a-sf-officer-turned-diplomat-estimates-chances-at-60-percent/. For a closer look at Donald Trump's presidency, see the trilogy Woodward (2018, 2020), and Woodward and Costa (2021).

20 Perry Anderson is a well-known historian with a long and distinguished career that includes teaching at UCLA, where I was also served as a visiting scholar in two separate intervals in the first decade of this century. He also deserves praise for his earlier books in history that made a positive impression in shaping my thought about the past. In the instance of hegemony, i.e., hegemony as relates to Gramsci, however, he is mistaken (read Anderson 1976–1977, side-by-side Anderson 2017). In his latest work (2017), Anderson attempts to unravel the treatment of hegemony and power trans-historically; that is, he stresses the genealogy and history of hegemony from time immemorial to the present. This is an ingenious method for generalization, but it is also negating the specificity of the concept in Gramsci's and its specific context in the social relations and the mediating capitalist institutions. In other words, Anderson's method of analysis is transhistorical. The casual use of this expression that once upon the time (ancient, medieval, and colonial times) proved trendy, suddenly (inadvertently or not) here finds its way into the power structure of *differentia specifica* of capitalist social relations. To provide an example, money in the ancient times, say, during the Achaemenid Empire in Persia (550 BCE—330 BCE), had certainly not yet taken on the systematic burden of the social relations; it had not yet assumed the mantle of an equivalent form (of value) and it had not yet stood for *abstract labor.* The currency in ancient Persia was the *daric*, which, in the lexicon of social relations, is incommensurable with the currency in modern Persia (Iran), the *rial.* The fact that in conventional language we identify them as "money," should not have bearing on the stark differences in the *purpose* for which they were utilized. As I understand it, the context of hegemony in Gramsci is specific to capitalism as it uniquely parallels the previous analogy. Furthermore, Marx's methodology (and Gramsci's) demands specificity. Similar drawbacks also bedevil the trans-historical characteristic of World-Systems School, which treats hegemony panoramically. For instance, see Arrighi (1990 and 1994).

21 These are a few leading sources that proved to be at the forefront of the theory of competition and capitalist competition a' la Marx. Among these, the reader should pay close attention to Shaikh (2016), *Capitalism: Competition, Conflict, Crises*, a magnum opus on competition and a goldmine for the exploration of larger and pertinent issues surrounding the political economy of turbulence in capitalism.

22 I find it obligatory to touch on the work of neo-Gramscian scholars, notably Robert W. Cox, in the international relations literature (see Cox 1987; Cox and Sinclair 1996; Cox and Schechter 2002). Alison J. Ayers also edited a critical volume (Ayers 2008) that I find useful for examination of the views and methodology of these scholars, particularly Cox's. There is a chapter in this book by Alfredo Saad-Filho and Alison Ayers in the first part of which the authors lucidly show the inconsistency and eclectic methodology employed by Robert Cox and his neo-Gramscian colleagues concerning the world order. Yet, despite their sharp angle and position—which is identical to

my own criticism of Cox's scholarship—Saad-Filho and Ayers stop short of offering a genuine alternative to Cox's. Their conclusion, after a sophomoric glance at the postwar economy, is but a focus on the policies and strategies that had led to the termination of "Keynesianism" and the advent of neoliberalism cobbled together and erroneously presented as a new stage in capitalism (see Ayers 2008, Ch. 5, 109–132). On a different note, there is a tendency in the international relations literature lately that calls itself neo-neo-Gramscian (NNG), exemplified by Jonathan Pass (2019). This book is the latest illustration of the use (and misuse) of Gramsci's hegemony, which ironically sets forth that twenty-first-century America is hegemonic.

23 The so-called American exceptionalism has appalling prehistory that to this date still haunts this nation and still demands answers other than appealing to external adventures—from Monroe Doctrine to Iraq's Abu Ghraib—long interlaced with American history. Appealing to "manifest destiny" is but one of these outlandish original sins. A glimpse of turbulent pre-history, inauguration, and the maturity of the United States is articulated carefully in Howard Zinn ([1999] 2015).

24 It is critical to note that this analogy is limited to a distinction of policy or doctrine from the category of history, which Lenin correctly invoked against Karl Kautsky. However, invoking a historical period is one thing, and the necessity of mediation of such history toward erecting a theory of periodization for capitalism is quite another. Alluding to the export of capital (a moment of capital in money form), detached from the capital in its three moments in accumulation, plus adopting Hobson's view of monopoly capitalism (as the highest stage), is far from a theory of periodization grounded in Marx's theory of value.

25 Despite his longstanding scholarship, David Harvey turned out to be somewhat controversial on not only the question of "New Imperialism," periodization of capitalism, and globalization but also on Marx's theory of competition, theory of rent, and Marx's value theory (see Harvey [1982] 1999, 2003, 2011); for my critique (see Bina 2013b, 114–118, 144–149).

26 In *Capital* vol. 1, Ch. 26, under "The Secret of Primitive Accumulation," Marx challenged the classical economists on theoretical and historical grounds. He blasted Smith's "previous accumulation" as too passive and too peaceful. Marx defined the concept by its modifier, "an accumulation which is not the result of the capitalist mode of production but its point of departure." Then after a brief discussion about "complete separation between the workers and the ownership of the conditions for the realization of their labor," Marx turned to identify "two transformations, whereby the social means of subsistence and production are turned into capital, and the immediate producers are turned into wage-laborers." Conclusion: "So-called primitive accumulation . . . is nothing else than the historical process of divorcing the producer from the means of production. It appears 'primitive' because it forms the pre-history of capital and the mode of production corresponding to capital" (Marx [1867] 1977, 873–875). The postwar land-reform programs designed by the World Bank and implemented throughout the "Third World" (countries in the American orbit) in the 1950s and 1960s are the quintessential examples of "primitive accumulation."

27 In their recent book, Duménil and Lévy—contrary to all evidence to date on Marx's monumental work—contend that corporate capitalism, i.e., managerial capitalism, is a *sui generis* mode of production (see Duménil and Lévy 2018). The authors' emphasis appears to be on the lack of apparent commensurability between this and the early phase of capitalism and the alleged departure of what they term "Marx's law of history." As an academic, no stranger to this perplexing subject and someone fully familiar with practical details within the field of management, corporate structure, and corporate strategy, who taught these very subjects for nearly three decades, I am quite astounded by this latest revelation. In *Capital*, Vol. 3, Ch. 27, on the subject of credit and joint-stock companies, Marx merely dropped a single line, "the abolition of the capitalist mode of production within the capitalist mode of production itself," which was predicated upon

"the abolition of capital as private property within the confines of the capitalist mode of production itself" (Marx [1867] 1977, 567–569). Here, I wish to register a strong difference with the view that *managerial capitalism* is a new mode of production. Besides being blindsided by the organizational form of accumulation, this view appears to consign Marx's theory of value to the so-called laissez-faire capitalism which essentially consists of mom-and-pop stores and petty merchants, and reserves something else for what's known as managerial capitalism. Did Marx really have to agonize for so many years over the law of capitalist accumulation in order to identify mom-and-pop stores as one mode of production and corporate capitalism as another mode of production allegedly belonging to two different universes? To call managerial capitalism a *new mode* (rather than a new phase) is perhaps a symptom of confusion by the authors over the "mode of production" and the lack of appreciation of the various levels of abstraction in Marx's methodology.

28 There is a tendency on the left, particularly the Anglo-American left, to foist the piggyback of "combined development" on Marx's theory of uneven development. This supposed invention could turn into a nuisance, particularly concerning the subtleties of the stages of economic development and, in methodological terms, the distinction of where and when Marx's value theory operates in full swing. At any rate, there is no credible reference to this arbitrary and needlessly politicized phrase in the entire Marx's writings. For further critique of this pseudo-concept, see the pertinent chapters in this volume.

29 It is profoundly critical to make a distinction between *cheap labor* and *cheapening labor power* from the standpoint of Marx's value theory. The first refers to the availability of labor with substandard wages. For example, the attraction and movement of individual capital (i.e., a transnational corporation) toward such regions as south and Southeast Asia, Latin America, and Africa, for cost-cutting purposes. In such cases, when and where cheap labor dissipates, there is little incentive for cutting costs in this manner across those regions. Hence, one cannot define the capitalist mode of production by the availability of already existing cheap labor. Whereas, the cheapening of labor power emanates from the very nature of capital (capital in general), displayed through constant technological change (see Bina 2012d). This hinges on an inner means (of capital), not an external source, through internal self-regulation and the incessant competition based on the law of value. This stands in stark contrast to the stagnationist thesis promulgated in Lenin's *Imperialism*, a quintessential feature of monopoly capital. Similarly, contrary to Luxemburg ([1913] 1951), capitalism is not defined by *external* material sources, including cheap labor. Cheapening of *labor power* is an internalized foundation (i.e., an inner force) and thus the defining characteristic of capitalism.

30 To my knowledge, Ronald Steel first coined the term *Pax Americana* in the first edition of his book with the same title in 1967. He then published a revised version of the same in 1970.

31 For masterful imagery on the US propaganda and profound ideological indoctrination on cultural fronts by the American movie industry (see Dorfman and Mattelart [1971] 2018).

32 This political episode should be placed squarely within the context of Jim Crew laws in the south and the blemish of ongoing rampant racism across the United States at this time. One wonders how such a country as this could speak of democracy and boastfully lecture other nations on the virtues of freedom.

33 To peek into the soul of the British Empire (and the so-called Commonwealth), one should carefully read through Winston Churchill's speech—known as the "Iron Curtain speech—delivered on March 5, 1946, at Westminster College, Fulton, Missouri" (Churchill 1946). In a collage of bombastic assemblage of word and ambition, Churchill attempted to convince the then-American leadership and the world that the reeking corpse of the British Empire deserved a station in the postwar polity in the making. He brashly boasted that the United States and Britain (and Canada!) were the only nuclear

powers in the world. Churchill preached on the preeminence of the "English-speaking peoples" and "Christian civilization," and the duty of safeguarding their "way of life." He then in a mixture of desperate utterance and anxious affection pleaded the fate of the British Empire, cunningly fudging the divergence of the *old* and the *new*; and finally in a barrage of rancor in his sardonic phrase, "Iron Curtain," set the stage for the division of the world and the future isolation of the Soviet Union. Churchill's homily and his infantile attraction to ethnic, racial, cultural, and religious identity in an insolvent and segregated colonial world stood alone and echoed as a parody. Yet his historic utterance of the "Iron Curtain" on that fateful afternoon in this little sleepy town in rural America sowed the seeds of the Cold War. Here is the link to the speech: www.cia.gov/library/readingroom/docs/1946-03-05.pdf.

34 An ardent reader must realize that the decartelization of oil was prompted by a worldwide crisis that led to the collapse of the International Petroleum Cartel (1928–1972), which subsequently restructured and rationalized the entire industry across the world. This is known as decartelization and competitive globalization of oil in the early 1970s. Bina (1985) is a groundbreaking study of this transformation founded on Marx's theory of value, a value-theoretic analysis for all energy sources (including major fossil fuels), the hallmark of which is inspired by synthetic competition spelled out in *The Poverty of Philosophy* (Marx [1847] 1973). Marx's *Capital*, Vol. 3, utilizes the same notion of competition, as he records, "*In competition . . . everything appears upside down*" (Marx [1894] 1981, 311; emphasis in original). This is a stark contrast with mainstream economics methodology and fiction of "pure competition" as a routine point of departure. In this fallacious worldview, the contagion of fakery is always possible in all branches of economics (see Frankfurt 2005; Bina 2012a, Ch. 14, Weeks 2011, 2014, for diagnosis and critique). Here, considerable numbers of (self-styled) heterodox economists (including many faculty and students in well-known heterodox economics programs) have fallen victim to this borrowed fakery. Radical Marxists too were not immune from this methodological blunder, as the specter of Hobson's (via Lenin's) cartels and ghosts of the defunct monopolies of the yesteryears appear to be haunting their imagination. It is instructive why Ben Fine, a world's finest Marxist scholar, tends to fumble on a distinction between a *surreal* world of oil cartel that "[binds] the majors and non-majors together in a cartel that now includes both" and a *real* decartelized/globalized world of competing oil that had materialized since the 1970s (see Fine and Harris 1985, 86–87). A short answer may lie in an illusory view of the periodization of capitalism and a slipup on Marx's theory competition, both of which are potentially symptomatic of the very tradition that harkens back to the early part of the last century to Hobson, Hilferding, Lenin or Luxemburg. For a longer answer, see other chapters in this volume.

35 This poses a formidable challenge to those on the left who may claim that not only the American power (i.e., hegemony) is essentially intact but also contend—even at this stage—that global capitalism is somewhat analogous to American capitalism. I find *The Making of Global Capitalism: The Political Economy of American Empire* by Panitch and Gindin (2012) an emblematic of this group in political science, international relations, and related subjects. The authors are correct in questioning those who made a cottage industry of the "Iron Law" of history but are mistaken on the *reduction* of global capitalism to the American Empire, thus backing themselves into a corner on some thorny methodological and political issues the least of which concern the nature of globalization and the future of America power. Hence, this potentially promising volume stumbles on three key questions at once: (1) the rise and fall of the Pax Americana—what the authors call the "American Empire," (2) the rise and fall of American hegemony, and (3) the epoch of globalization, an era antithetical to the "American Empire." For a critical review of Panitch and Gindin (2012) see Robinson (2014).

36 Both the sequence and interval of the collapse between the fall of the Pax Americana and that of the Soviet Union would tell us that the declining United States could not

be the cause for the fall of the Soviets. To be sure, the collapse of the Soviet Union was an implosion with internal cause, just as the breakdown of the Pax Americana was an internal failure. In retrospect, a brief period of the post-Soviet euphoria in the 1990s was a lost decade for the United States. The impulsive allusions to "unipolarity," on the one hand, and the injudicious desire for another "American century," on the other, were a pointless exercise. Soon after the euphoria was subsided and the Cold War machine decelerated, the foreign policymakers in the United States invented the Doctrine of Preemption (following the artifice of "terrorism") after 9/11 (see White House 2002), and subsequently the Bush-Cheney administration adopted an all-or-nothing strategy by pouring tons of proverbial gasoline on the burning Rome, prompting further degeneration of US power. When the dust had finally settled, there was no winner in this protracted Cold War tragedy, as if one has sat through an original play by Shakespeare's own choreography in *Julius Caesar.*

37 To be sure, Trump's election (and the Trump administration's agenda on foreign policy) is merely a belated symptom (not the cause) of the collapse of the postwar system. In this article, the authors plead rather desperately with "the United States' friends and allies" to act "more ambitiously" toward 70 years of "shared commitment to democracy, freedom, and human rights and a belief that advancing them globally was an essential contribution to international peace and prosperity" (Daalder and Lindsay 2018, 81). Well, Orwell himself could not have put it better in this doublespeak. This tragedy reminds me of Macbeth who, in Shakespeare's words, is repeating to himself and pleading with a handful of soldiers in the compound: "Fear not, till Birnam Wood do come to Dunsinane!" (Act 5, scene 5).

38 *Macbeth*, Act 5, scene 1.

39 Contrary to conventional economic wisdom, globalization is not a repeated phenomenon that allegedly had occurred late in the nineteenth century (via the international trade), the middle of the twentieth century (via the Pax Americana), and again late in the twentieth century (see Palley 2018). This eclectic vision *inter alia* adds more fuel to the confusion over the concept itself and further obscures the distinctive meaning of globalization as a stage theory. To be sure, the linear treatment of trade and for that matter, the period of postwar Pax Americana, as "globalization," has long been the subject of mainstream economics and orthodox international trade theory. Calling them *globalization*, as Palley (2018) does, is a travesty. The upside-down Hobsonite view of competition, combined with the Heckscher–Ohlin model of axiomatic international trade, in the formative years of the neoclassical theory of trade, precluded the orthodoxy from perceiving the significance of stages and thus the qualitative change toward globalization. Such an ad hoc comparison is routine in mainstream trade theory. Unfortunately, many in the heterodox tradition exhibit little insight on this very delicate point. There are also similar examples outside economics. Panitch and Gindin (2003), for instance, refer to the early decades of the twentieth century as an instance of "earlier failure of globalization" (see Panitch and Gindin 2003, 4–5).

40 Referring to a gem of a book by Mike Davis (2017).

41 This refers to an eye-opening volume, with the same title, in accord with what I (as an energy and environmental economist) had also in mind in this chapter (see Kolbert 2014).

4 Globalization of Oil

Cartel, Cult of Monopoly, and Synthetic Competition

> Imagination, is, from a utilitarian point of view, the opposite of realistic perception, seeing things that are not.
>
> — **Don Gifford**
>
> The Farther Shore (1990)

Introduction

This chapter is an attempt to provide a theoretical foundation for the evolution of world oil from cartelization to its eventual competitive globalization. This groundwork parallels historically and politically with the globalization of capital at large and pivotal consequences that eventually led to the collapse of the Pax Americana (1945–1979). Such an intimate correspondence and congruence could not be a coincidence when the vital relationship between cartelized oil and power politics comes into the view and the attachment of Pax Americana's umbilical cord to cheap (i.e., colonized, and cartelized) oil from the Middle East was the norm, at its very inception. Therefore, a theoretical investigation into the root cause of cartelization and the subsequent decartelization (and globalization) of oil must be considered as an intimate part of the exploration that attends to the rise and fall of the Pax Americana. Decartelization of oil in the early 1970s has not only had a profound implication for the transformation of oil and energy itself but the collapse of the International Petroleum Cartel (IPC) and the absence of cartelized oil also removed one of the formidable instruments of US foreign policy, which was a significant feature under the postwar Pax Americana. Indeed, the significance of the globalization of oil against the backdrop of many years of intricate US political ties with IPC is a key component of the fall of the American power. That is why cartelization and decartelization of oil to all intents and purposes fit together with materials in this volume.

Competition in modern capitalism manifests in the mutual interaction of capital and the forces that regulate the formation of value and market prices across the economy; these forces reflect the wholesale commoditization of material life and class polarization. The law of value operates through the inner

DOI: 10.4324/9781351136785-4

dynamics of competition. Likewise, capitalist competition is as pervasive in modern capitalism as the law of gravity upon the falling bodies on earth. As the law of gravity in cosmology is not caused by the effect of gravitational pull on heavenly bodies, the law of value in capitalism is not produced by capitalist competition. It is competition that reveals the law of value. In this issue, Karl Marx alerts us that "In competition . . . everything appears upside down" (Marx, *Capital*, vol. 3, [1894] 1981, 311). Therefore, competition is not simply a state of affairs, assumed in mainstream economics, but a turbulent process that reveals the dynamics of the accumulation of wealth through the formation of value and the prices in capitalist economies. The same analogy relates to rent proper in mature capitalist economies. Capitalist competition, unlike the ideal type of "perfect competition" (a point of departure in the mainstream economics competition), necessitates the concentration and centralization of capital across the board and rather eloquently conforms to the integration of capitalism in its colossal corporate form across the boundary of the nation-states today. In this chapter one of the most integrated sectors of the global economy is the subject of scrutiny and thus a demonstration of capitalist competition; and if this will prove the point that the characterization of today's oil sector, along the line of "imperfect competition," "oligopoly," or "monopoly," is little more than a mental construct, then all other sectors with lower concentration and centralization of capital are in the ballpark of real competition. This also goes for the neo-Marxian theory of "monopoly capital," the neo-Ricardian/Sraffian theory (see Shaikh 1982 for a critique), and the post-Keynesian/Kaleckian theory, among others, whose delineation either implicitly or explicitly assumes departure from "pure competition." On the other hand, for the Classical School, Schumpeterian School, Austrian School, and the economists associated with the Oxford Economists' Research Group competition, far from being "perfect" or "imperfect," is a process by which capitalism propels itself rather dynamically.

As indicated earlier, the neoclassical theory of market structure—an arbitrary spectrum of "perfect competition" and "perfect monopoly"—obfuscates the reality of competition that is so universally geared toward concentration and centralization of capital. This obfuscation, i.e., *faking* the very accumulation of capital as a departure from capitalist competition, would conceal the very dynamics of contemporary capitalism. Yet, someone who produces this kind of research by means of this bizarre framework does not necessarily lie, since fakery and falsity are not the same. Here the intention is "neither to report the truth nor to conceal it." Nevertheless, by doing so, someone who fakes the truth necessarily conceals their own intent at "misrepresentation." As shall be explored further in this chapter, there is an astronomical distance between seeking a (specific) truth and faking it. Here, a perfectly (i.e., fictionalized) competitive model and its imperfectly competitive counterpart are like the Siamese twins. Thus market-perfect and market-imperfect views within neoclassical economics operate on the same plane despite the differences.

Cartels, although concentrated, are protected entities that aim at substituting competition for direct control for a while and under certain historical circumstances; yet these entities fall prey to eventual internal and external pressures that are brought to bear because of competition. A universal example of this is the International Petroleum Cartel (1928–1972) in which the entire oil industry (including US oil) was subject to vertical control. Yet, this mother of all cartels was disrupted from within and eventually squeezed from without by the "independent" oil companies, among others, before a complete annihilation at the threshold of the new era that began with the oil crisis of the early 1970s across the globe. In other words, the regulating forces in the budding era of de-cartelization and global competition brought the least and the most productive oil regions of the world together in one undivided industry and led to the formation of (competitive) spot and futures markets across the globe. Finally, it is argued in this chapter that OPEC is not a cartel but a rent-collecting agency compatible with worldwide capitalist competition across the industry (Bina 2012c).

The oil sector—in its evolutionary change toward globalization—is a quintessential case that perceptibly depicts the departure from a monopoly (cartel) toward worldwide competition. Today, *crude oil* is by far the most concentrated industry in the history of capitalism. Yet, as this chapter demonstrates, it is among the most competitive sectors of the world economy. As shall be argued here, such competitiveness emerged through the evolutionary transformation of the oil sector during the 1950s and 1960s, with the eventual display of differential profits turning into differential oil rents and the tendential equalization of profit rates across industries. This means that differential rents associated with oil are the consequence of competition rather than market "imperfection" or "monopoly," inundated in both orthodox and heterodox economic theories. This is also contrary to certain self-styled, anti-neoliberal Marxists, such as David Harvey (2010, 2012), whose eclectic methodology allows for blending the longstanding differentiated status of land as capital, as opposed to landed property (Marx [1847] 1973, 143–144),[1] and carrying "monopoly rent" (a provisional category unrelated to the theory of value) into the mix of competitively driven differential rents. Competition in modern capitalism is neither perfect nor imperfect but *real*; and it is *not despite* the universality of concentration (and centralization) of capital but, quite the contrary, *because of it*. Consequently, an arbitrary division of capitalism into "competitive" and "monopoly" phases that, among others, paves the way for the ejection of *value* categories in much of the neo-Marxian literature is but falling victim to the parody of competition in mainstream economics.

A Note on Methodology

It is often stated that explanations that are used for the understanding of the real world are hardly axiomatic but driven synthetically from the existing phenomena at hand. Such explanation, of course, hinges on the systematic study of the subject in its proper context and historical specificity. This is true for all scientific inquiries, from modern astrophysics, which thrives on the cosmic expansion of the universe, to political economy, which carries its context within the evolutionary history of capitalism. In both cases, context and distinctiveness are the driving force behind an explanation that is synthetic—not axiomatic. Therefore, capitalizing merely on the criterion of logical necessity, associated with axiomatic statements, is not only misleading but also distracts us from the object of explanation.[2]

Successful analyses often rely on relevant, consistent, and transparent methodologies. In this chapter, care has been taken to avoid the axiomatic, speculative, mechanical approach that typically characterizes the orthodox economic analysis. We also try to steer clear of the *ideal* spectrum of the so-called market-structure theory that circularly furnishes the tautology of "pure" competition and "pure" monopoly, a common and popular approach by today's orthodox and overwhelming majority of heterodox economists. A typical investigation begins with the observation of a given concrete fact as a point of departure. But a concrete observable fact itself is a unity of diverse and complex determinations that consist of an outcome, and, hence, constitutes a point of arrival. Thus, we need to abstract from the complexity of this concrete "chaotic whole," in order to discover the presupposed, simpler (abstract) categories that have secured its ultimate determination. This, of course, is a familiar process of conceptualization (i.e., abstraction) in any scientific inquiry. Yet, the process remains incomplete if one does not attempt to reproduce this given concrete (in thought) by way of such abstractions.

These abstractions are not *axiomatic* but *real*, precisely by virtue of being themselves derived from observable facts or concrete phenomena. Thus, the relationship between the theory (abstract) and observable reality (the concrete)—that is, systematic theorization—involves a round-trip (dialectical) movement: (1) departing from an observable (concrete) phenomenon in order to detect its presupposed abstract determinations (categories) and (2) returning to reconstruct the original concrete via these abstract determinations once again. This two-way journey (i.e., from the point of departure to the point of arrival) thus completes the *appropriation* of concrete (the phenomena) by thought—which is the very essence of *real* abstraction, the very prerequisite of theorization without speculation and speculative reasoning.

As Marx put it, by entering into this (dialectical) journey, "the chaotic conception of a whole" would turn into "a rich totality of many [ordered] determinations and relations."[3] Marx also criticized Hegel for not realizing that reconstruction of the *real* subject in thought is not the cause of its existence, but rather—by presupposing the existence of the subject matter—turns it into a concept, a thought category within the grasp of mind for appropriation.

Such a concept—as a category—need not be imaginary, axiomatic, or dependent upon arbitrary and ad hoc assumptions. The assumptions—and their possible role in theorizing—are thus the potential effects of the concepts themselves. In other words, in this (materialist) methodology all pre-givens (i.e., the points of departure) are the real subjects that persist to be perceived by the mind, not the very products of the perceiving mind in the embodiment of axioms or *idealized* truths that would consciously or unconsciously blemish the investigation with tautology.[4] There are a number of interpretations of Marx's remark that "all science would be superfluous if the form of appearance of things directly coincided with their essence"[5]; yet the very implication of this frequently cited phrase reveals the fact that as soon as *tautology* enters into the explanation, science, that is the search for meaning, is thrown out of the window.

A pertinent issue in this chapter is the question surrounding the connotation, historical necessity, and dynamics of competition in the oil sector; and whether the evolution, and observable concentration and centralization of capital in the global oil industry—particularly with respect to the determination of oil rents—can be measured by the axiomatic spectrum of competition/monopoly. This, of course, would have an immense implication for the formation of market prices either directly in terms of perceived (market) power relations among the loosely defined *inter*national entities as "multinational oil" or by means of the *theory of value* mediated through the concentration and centralization of capital in today's unified *trans*national oil sector. It goes without saying that if we were to start with "power" and "power relations" as a premise and, at the same time, wish to prove the existence of power and power relations, our conclusions would be devoid of any analytical value regardless of whether this tautology is made implicitly or explicitly.[6] Therefore, the theorization of any concrete subject must take the latter as its starting point. In other words, to be true to itself, *theory* (as an attribute of the thinking head) must be derived from *reality*, and not the reverse; theory should not be superimposed on the subject matter for the purpose of evaluating and measuring the reality, for instance, in the manner of the orthodox spectrum of pure competition/pure monopoly. In theorizing, the point of departure must never be the thinking—or unthinking (!)—head.

Another methodological issue is the *evolution* of oil production through the specific historical stages, leading to this sector's *trans*formation from international cartelization to transnational (i.e., global) competition. The real abstraction in general, and within this sector must necessarily reflect the evolutionary transformation of the real subject matter within the historical time.

The observable present as the concrete and complex *outcome* of this evolution, however, is always entangled with the residue of the historical past. Hence the issue of independent validity of abstract categories comes to predate the present observable concrete. In other words, is this method of categorization a legitimate measure for the periodization of history into the various modes of production (*à la* Marx's); and, by the same token, is our own periodization of oil production into distinct stages of development a sound theoretical undertaking? Is this historical division a product of ad hoc impression of the periods under investigation without adequate abstraction?

The following passage sheds some light on the question of epochal abstraction and historical categorization in Marx's critique of political economy:

> Bourgeois society is the most advanced and the most complex historical organization of production. The categories which express its relations, and an understanding of its structure, therefore, provide an insight into the structure and the relations of production of all formerly existing social formations the ruins and component elements of which were used in the creation of bourgeois society. Some of these unassimilated remains are still carried on within bourgeois society, others, however, which previously existed only in rudimentary form, have been further developed and [thus] attained their full significance, etc. . .. Bourgeois economy thus provides a key to the economy of antiquity, etc. But it is quite impossible [to gain insight] in the manner of those economists who obliterate all historical differences and who see in all social phenomena only bourgeois phenomena. . . . In all [societal] forms in which landed property is the decisive factor, natural relations still predominate; in the forms in which the decisive factor is capital, social, historically evolved elements pre-dominate. Rent cannot be understood without capital, but capital can be understood without rent. Capital is the economic power that dominates everything in bourgeois society. . . . It would be inexpedient and wrong therefore to present the economic categories successively [i.e., in sequence of their historical presence] in the order in which they played a dominant role in history.
>
> (Marx [1859] 1970, 210–213)[7]

The observer who attempts to examine the present (i.e., the contemporary society) must proceed from the presupposition of the capitalist economy, both in reality and in mind, in order to identify the *specific* categories involved, which in turn allows for simpler categories to reflect both the complex and intensified relations of the developed concrete and the undeveloped and slight relations of immature concrete. Money, for instance, made its presence prior to capital, wage labor, and modern landed property in the historical time. Yet, money did not become a full-fledged category (i.e., an equivalent form or *subordinate relation* in capitalism) until the development of the capitalist mode of production.[8] Finally, in the context of real abstraction and epochal categorization, the development of ground rents (including oil rent) parallels the development of specific forms of modern landed property valorized by capital in the context of capitalist social relations.[9]

Mutating Oil: From Actual Monopoly to Real Competition

The story of Middle Eastern oil, including its turbulent maturity into a modern industry, can be identified in three distinct stages of historical significance: (1) the era of worldwide cartelization, 1901–1950; (2) the period 1950–1972 transition; and (3) the epoch of competitive globalization since the mid-1970s. A slightly longer but overlapping division may identify the evolution of oil in the rest of the world—including the US domestic oil industry: (1) the era of classical cartels and oil trusts of 1870–1910; (2) the period of regulated neo-cartelization, and control of 1911–1950; (3) the period of nascent 1950–1972 competition; (4) the epoch of competitive globalization since mid-1970s.[10] This is a story of capital in one of the most integrated industries of our time and the way in which it had come to its own. When capital (as a social relation) was weak it needed crutches—formidable crutches: monopoly and cartel—to lean on and limp along; as soon as it had become strong (i.e., self-sufficiently competitive), it threw the crutches and walked on its own.

A careful examination of a century of worldwide oil production, between 1870 and 1970 would bring to light the predominance of administered pricing and cartelized practices that ruled the entire oil business. These practices were often supported, if not instigated, by colonial powers in the hinterlands and to some extent by the governments of major industrial countries in the heartlands of capitalism. Yet, there is a great deal of resistance on the part of the popular masses against these monopolies and manipulating practices in the United States, particularly toward John D. Rockefeller's oil empire. The public pressure eventually provoked the Sherman Antitrust Act of 1890 (a measure on the books against predatory practices), which subsequently led to the breakdown of Rockefeller's Standard Oil Trust in 1911. Nonetheless, some of the separate fragments—such as Standard Oil of New Jersey, Standard Oil of New York, Standard Oil of California, Standard Oil of Ohio, etc.—had become so huge, so vertically and horizontally integrated, and so syndicate-like that they had decided to renew their worldwide union (in terms of "As-Is Agreement") in the Achnacarry Castle, Scotland, and to form the International Petroleum Cartel in 1928.[11] This consolidation is particularly important for the fact that, according to the As-Is Agreement, the wellhead cost of US oil (at the Gulf of Mexico) had turned into the primary basing point in the calculation of the administered prices across the worldwide networks of the cartel.[12] However, this singular (universal) mechanism was accompanied by adding another basing point in the Persian Gulf, as new and bountiful oil deposits were discovered in the region.

The administered pricing of oil under the cartelized oil was an accounting scheme that ought not to be confused with market prices in the ordinary economic sense and placed arbitrarily on the footing with competitive oil prices of today. Yet, the linear view of neoclassical economic competition identifies any concentration and centralization of capital as a monopoly (and cartel) and treats the two as part of the same continuum with respect to allocating rules of production and pricing of oil. The neoclassical economic methodology gives the impression that such differences are merely mechanical (not epochal) and thus treats them contemporaneously. This reveals the futility of all axiomatic theories that are devoid of real subjects and deprived of definite history or tangible reality. The IPC was the market onto itself across the board and the only game in town, so to speak; it was the very essence of administrated pricing without mediating institutions (for the financial arrangements in this period see Mikdashi 1966). The IPC literally owned the international oil market as the cartel and had total control over both the demand and supply of the international market according to the principles of the Achnacarry Agreement. And despite the façade of multiple accounting schemes at the basing point of the Gulf of Mexico or that of the Persian Gulf, this charade was not even mimicking the law of one price. The formation of IPC was the result of the collusion of national cartels that operated across the world at the time. This period overlapped with what Lenin defined as the epoch of imperialism in which the world, among others, was divided among monopolies and national cartels.

During this epoch, known as the period of the internationalization of finance capital, money as capital began to germinate and hold roots across boundaries of the nation-states; but the circuit of social capital had yet to be completed with the internationalization of productive capital—an essential condition for unbroken valorization across the transnational geography of production. In the period identified by Lenin (and observed earlier by J.A. Hobson),[13] nearly four-fifths of humanity in the world neither lived in capitalist societies nor had ever known what living under social relations of capitalism would really look like. This is a specific period with precise features as unique as the unmitigated cartelization and the full-blown sway of the IPC across the geography of world oil production. And, as for the regulating mechanism (i.e., a scheme for production and pricing), this cartel (a worldwide industry comprising many firms, not a single enterprise) hung in the balance for decades by controlling supply according to the forecast of demand region by region and together by the basing point accounting. This of course, in practice, was sanctioned by the United States as it was tacitly a significant component of the Marshall Plan and an integral part of postwar Pax Americana (1945–1979).

These practices, however, began to lose their considerable command and effectiveness in the 1950s and 1960s. Proliferating market forces that permeated and challenged the administrative control of the IPC and gradually loosened the domain of control and arbitrary pricing of oil.

The second stage in the development of Middle Eastern oil constitutes a transition to transnationalization and a tendency toward unified global pricing of oil (1950–1972). This stage saw a transitory coexistence of the declining cartelized institutions and the proliferation of market relations, which were conducive to competitive global pricing. Here, it can be demonstrated that the cartelization of oil belongs to a historical stage in which the internal transformation and corresponding institutional framework of global capitalism have not yet been fully advanced.

The basic identifying features of this period are: (1) the dominance of long-term oil contracts (the colonial concession system)[14]; (2) the establishment of "basing-point" oil pricing in the Persian Gulf similar (but with lesser magnitude) to the basing point at the Gulf of Mexico; (3) the utilization of "posted prices"[15] for calculating oil revenues due to be paid to exporting countries; and

(4) the formation of OPEC.[16] During this period, given the desire for *stabilizing* the "basing-point" price of oil in the Gulf of Mexico, US domestic oil had been the subject of cartelized control with further scrutiny.[17] This basing point system, which was founded on the wellhead price of US oil in the Gulf of Mexico, had long been used as an administrative yardstick for the pricing of oil anywhere in the world (see Keysen 1949; Machlup 1949).[18]

Given the new and bountiful discoveries of cheaper oil in the Persian Gulf, oil produced from the Middle Eastern region had gradually displaced US oil, moving to the regional markets close to the Western Hemisphere.[19] This prompted the IPC to cut the Persian Gulf posted prices in order to control the interregional flow of oil vis-à-vis the US oil region. The rationale was that since the "posted price" was also a mechanism for the internal transfer of oil within the cartel's worldwide network, cutting the posted price of Persian Gulf oil would reduce the supply from this region, thus mitigating the flow of oil to Western markets.[20] This was precisely according to the principles of As-Is Agreement which prohibited the movement of oil from one producing region (the Persian Gulf) to another (Gulf of Mexico), thus keeping the apple cart of monopoly control from disturbance (see Blair 1976; Engler 1977). But the very fact that the companies were able to do just that proves how huge the profits of their Middle East Oil operations must have been. It also shows how tight, in the absence of valorized oil and a fully developed global oil market, the cartel's grip was over the control of both US domestic and international oil. At this time, the role of the Eisenhower administration (and Dulles Brothers, John Foster at the State Department, and Allen at the CIA) should not be discounted for being hand-in-glove with the IPC vis-à-vis safeguarding of the cartelized oil. This clearly reveals the attachment of the umbilical cord of US foreign policy to the IPC for both economic and political objectives. This transitional period also saw the formation of OPEC, which embodied the major rent-collecting oil producers and thus created a potential for the recognition of *oil rent* as a price-determined economic category in the modern oil industry.[21] As a result, the struggle over the magnitude of the "posted prices" became the focal point of contention between the IPC and members of OPEC for the years to come.

From the 1950s through the end of the 1960s, there emerged three major developments, which forcefully undermined the cartelized character of the industry and helped unify the pricing of oil globally. First, there appeared a sweeping macroeconomic change in OPEC's relationship with the IPC[22]; this had to do with further integration of these oil-exporting countries into the world economy (Bina 1990, 2012c). Second, there was a steady stream of entry by a group of oil companies, known as the "independents" into the international oil market. These companies were either excluded from the network of IPC or newly formed to partake in the incipient market that was evolving, thus undoing the grip of the cartel vis-à-vis the economic and political circumstances. This was a grand experiment on the so-called barriers to entry, and in retrospect, it was settled unilaterally by the eventual collapse of the IPC in 1972. To identify some of these "independents," names such as Ashland Oil, Atlantic-Richfield, Occidental Petroleum, Amerada Hess, Marathon Oil, Continental Oil, City Service, Sun Oil, Union Oil, Philips Petroleum, and Getty Oil will come to mind (see Blair 1976; Bina 2012b).

Third, there was a considerable increase in the exploration and development costs of US domestic oil (already among the highest costs in the world). This was due, in part, to the highly fragmented domestic oil leases connected to the new oil exploration activities and, in part, to the exorbitant cost of additional capital investments made by the US domestic producers (under IPC) in the existing and, certainly, aging US oilfields.[23]

At the present, contrary to previous historical stages, oil pricing is the outcome of global competition among the existing oil regions of the world. These oil regions exhibit cost structures of varying magnitudes; however, in competition, the leaseholders must obtain at least an average rate of profit, in the long run, in order to stay in business. Given the persistence of differential costs (reflecting differential productivity) among these regions, any low-cost oil region would thus show profits that are above the industry's average. In other words, the low-cost oil regions, in addition to competitive profit, would show additional profits that are commensurate with their own differential cost advantage. These excess profits belong to the distinct category of (differential) oil rent, which, the lessor, the owner of oil-in-place can appropriate accordingly. The size of the oil rents, therefore, is simply dependent upon the magnitude of differential productivity (and, by implication, that of the differential profitability) of all competing oil regions globally. Hence, differential profits turn into differential oil rents; and all differential oil rents are price-determined.[24] This universal rule applies equally to both OPEC and non-OPEC producers. This explains, for instance, why OPEC prices are no longer insulated from the determining (and often, undermining) impact of spot (and futures) prices in the global oil market.

The development of global spot (and futures) markets in the oil industry is not the cause but the consequence of (1) the extent of globalization of the oil industry and, in turn, the profundity of the integration of the oil-producing nation-states within the global economy; (2) the critical importance of US oil cost structure in valorization and setting the price of oil worldwide; (3) the competition of all oil regions under a unified value and worldwide pricing rule; (4) the replacement of the cartelized arrangements and hands-on administered pricing by inherently turbulent and uncertain forces within the global oil market; and, by implication, (5) the restoration of OPEC merely as a rent-collecting association, entwined with valorized oil, with no predisposed protection from the resilient market forces and inherent turbulence associated with regulating the process of accumulation (Bina and Vo 2007).

The onset of these post-monopoly adaptations found its *creative* action in the wholesale *destruction* of the IPC in the biggest crisis of restructuring that this industry had ever known in the oil crisis of the early 1970s. This was the crisis of valorization of oil beyond a single oil region, including the US oil, which we identified as globalization and valorization of oil deposits across the geography of production. Valorization that, to put it in Marx's precise expression, accomplished an organic union between global capital and the landed property across the board.[25] Like any other valorization in capitalism, this valorization too is not free of contradiction and conflict. But the capital and landed property are not two different entities in the case of oil; they now reside in one valorized body, and it would be misleading, as Harvey (2003, 2010) insists, to speak of two different "logics" for their worldwide dynamics (see Bina 1985, 2012a). The consequence of all this was the emergence of worldwide competitive prices founded on the costliest oil region (namely, US domestic oil) and the formation of worldwide differential oil rents corresponding with the more productive oil regions outside the continental United States. And contrary to popular belief, given the global valorization of oil, it is not OPEC oil, but US domestic oil, that governs the production price of oil worldwide. The policy issues on this and other pertinent points will be taken in the next section.

Oil: Competition, Global Valorization, and Public Policy

Indeed, if the economic theory were to follow concrete economic events and occurrences, the oil sector has proved to be a fertile ground for theorization. For instance, oil, its cartelization, and its eventual transformation into a fully competitive global industry should be a goldmine for theorists and a godsend for experimentalists in all social sciences.

Yet, while contingencies matter, identification of the regulating mechanisms that belong to continuity and break in a particular history is paramount. That is why the periodization of oil in definite historical stages, from a virtual monopoly under the IPC to a global industry immersed in competition, is a prerequisite for any viable theory of oil. As explained earlier, the globalization of oil united nearly all producing oilfields across the globe under a single value and pricing system in competition. Let us elucidate what it means along with four overlapping yet well-defined points: (1) the highest cost (least productive) oil region has to regulate the limit of the price of production if this region were to remain in production; (2) the less costly (more productive) oil regions may collect a differential rent calibrated by the differential productivity of oilfields located in their geographical limit; (3) every oil region in the world would exhibit universal tendency to receive a competitive rate of profit in the long run; (4) in step with the globalization of oil, OPEC producers too would take their cue from the competitive global oil market—similar to non-OPEC producers—and collect differential oil rents commensurate with the productivity of oil produced within their border. This also gives credence to the concept of *regulating capital* in Marx (*Capital*, vol. 3, [1894] 1981, Ch. 10)—as opposed to marginal capital in neoclassical economics—which in the oil sector is always entwined with the least productive oilfields.[26] These oilfields might be the least productive originally or may have been made least productive by the successive application of capital. Therefore, in addition to natural fertility, the question of capital deepening is of theoretical as well as practical importance for a consistent theory of rent in the oil industry (see Bina 1985, Ch. 5; Bina 1989a; Bina 2012a, Ch. 2 and Ch. 4).

The size of these oil rents is also dependent upon the magnitude of oil prices in the long run, subject to the production price of the costliest and most explored oil region, the lower-48 states oil region in the United States. This oil region also was controlled and cartelized by the IPC, both prior to and after the Achnacarry Agreement of 1928. In the early 1970s, the crisis of decartelization (and globalization) of oil led to and displayed the restructuring and rationalization of all oil regions in terms of competitive pricing according to the law of value (and prices of production), grounded in Marx's value theory and centered on US oil—the costliest in the world. In other words, it is the costliest oil located in the US that governs the value, price of production, and the oscillating world oil market prices across the board and on a daily basis, not OPEC nor any other imagined authority or country (see Bina 1985).

Oil is a commodity that at its point of origin has no significance once it enters the unified pool of the global oil market. Notwithstanding the regional differential costs of production, the market price of oil is the same across the globe, as the short-run market prices are governed by the spot and futures oil markets. These competitive prices are in stark contrast with the "posted prices" which were instituted by fiat and administered under the command of the IPC. Moreover, the existence of "posted prices" is a symptom of colonial oil concessions in the Middle East, Africa, and Latin America, which in turn provided justification for recognition of "cheap oil" as opposed to "expensive oil." This implies that, from the standpoint of competitive pricing across the board, there is virtually no distinction between "cheap oil" and "expensive oil" anymore. Indeed, any concisely persistent allusion to "cheap oil" in this day and age is not but a sneaky sign of craving for colonialism—the age of pre-valorization of oil deposits in the Middle East, Africa, and Latin America. "Cheap oil" from faraway places can also be a sign of longing for the defunct and bygone era of Pax Americana.[27] Therefore, it is no longer justified, if not downright silly, to speak of "cheap oil" from the oil producers in the Middle East, North Africa, or Latin America.[28] Because, given the differential rents, roughly similar prices hold across the board. To be sure, since our crossing of the Rubicon in the mid-1970s, it is not only silly to contemplate that the Middle East oil is "cheap oil," but also incredibly romantic to contend for far-reaching projects, such as "energy independence" by means of further exploration in the US Outer Continental Shelf and/or Alaska's Arctic National Wildlife Refuge (ANWR). The fact is that such alternatives neither reduce the overall production cost of US oil—given that the production price in the lower-48 states' oil region regulates the long-run price of oil—nor will add enough oil long enough to lower the price in the near term. Besides, given the 2010 BP blow-up and massive oil spill in the Gulf of Mexico, these haphazard and uncertain projects are not prize-worthy in the view of direct and indirect exorbitant social and environmental costs associated with them. This goes for the $7 billion

Keystone XL project, a 2,763-kilometer pipeline from tar sands in Alberta, Canada all the way across the US continent to oil refineries in Houston and Port Arthur, Texas, that is planned to add 700,000 barrels of oil daily to the US market. This toxic project is the potential for unforeseen accidents that would make the Exxon Valdez oil spill across the shoreline in Prince William Sound, Alaska, in 1969, and the 2010 Deepwater Horizon-BP oil spill in the Gulf of Mexico combined, look like a minor accident. As can be seen, the burden of the tar sand project in Canada itself, the biggest source of pollution (and "public bad") and the nastiest method of physical destruction of the environment in the world, and the carrying of 700,000 barrels of "dirty oil" (nicknamed by industry watchers) daily across the pristine and vulnerable midst of the United States is a hypocritical tactic to achieve "energy independence." It goes without saying that the allusion to energy independence is a pure ideology that has no basis in today's realities, given the ubiquity of the globalization of oil (the core of value formation in energy) and the omnipresence of global spot and futures markets under which "independence" is practically impossible in the US, or anyplace else, other than the deletion of all sources of fossil fuels altogether.

As for the impact of additional domestic supply on the price, the anticipated production price of oil (per barrel) from ANWR should be considerably below that of the existing US oilfields in the lower-48 state region. These newer oilfields are potentially much more productive and upon production would potentially generate substantial differential oil rents. This is in contrast with the older *regulating*[29] oilfields that have long been under successive application of capital and no oil rent tied to their output in the lower-48 states' region (see Bina 1985, Ch. 5; 2006, 2021a, Ch. 4). Hence, in this case, the desire for self-sufficiency, following the policy of "drill, baby, drill," does not necessarily get rid of the least productive oilfields by pressing down the center of gravity of value (and price of production) for the US and global oil. Consequently, those who rely on Ricardo's *unidirectional* "order of cultivation" to the land of inferior quality cannot be more wrong. This also goes for this mental analogy (and flimsy metaphor) in mainstream (resource) economics that "the fruit hanging lower on the tree is harvested first."

On the other hand, a glance at recent US natural gas production by "fracking"—otherwise known as hydraulic fracturing—while it may add to the supply of hydrocarbon, is a practice that involves production costs (private and social) that are high, hidden, and exceedingly uncertain to be sustainable in the long run. Besides, the globalization of oil is a concrete example of an interdependent world that progressively advances toward further fusion and mutuality. Therefore, the penchant for "energy independence" is not something that is dependable or maintainable in today's globalized world. The appeal to such idealized alternatives, though a populist one, is inundated with xenophobic overtones and an inexplicable sense of nostalgia. The sore point is that the alleged reliance on the Middle East oil and OPEC "monopoly" embraced by popular media always finds a dramatic rationalization via the fable energy independence or mental construct of "perfect competition."[30] As can be seen, our argument is not limited to esoteric academic issues; the framework presented here very much concerns the two very critical areas of public life, namely, the US environmental policy and the US foreign policy. The present conflict in Ukraine and the tenor and tone of the Biden administration's reaction to it vis-à-vis the acceleration of US oil and gas production should be critically and carefully put in the aforementioned context.

Orthodoxy and the Euthanasia of Capitalist Competition

It is no exaggeration to declare that competition is among a handful of concepts that ravaged both orthodox and heterodox economics. Within the orthodoxy, "perfect competition," while it obtained the status of an axiomatic model (logical and timeless), nevertheless stood against the evolution and particularity of capitalism. An axiomatic spectrum of competition/monopoly became a standard model for the calibration of real capitalist enterprises which are placed nearer or further from these two imaginary poles. This method (with respect to calibration of competition) holds an uncanny resemblance to the Procrustean bed—an iron bed used by Procrustes ("The Stretcher") for modification of the human body consistent with the size of a chosen benchmark. Yet, at least in this mythological story, Procrustes used a real bed as a measure, not an imaginary one.

This parable is useful for the identification of orthodoxy, and some of its counterparts within heterodoxy, from the standpoint of dealing with capitalist competition. The spectrum of competition/monopoly is said to be a heuristic device for calibration of real competition in capitalism. Yet, a departure from the (illusory) "perfect competition" is a demarcation that also grants concrete identity to the departed, that is, "imperfectly" competitive firms—an identity that is other than competition.[31] In other words, the door had already been closed to the possibility of competition in capitalism by such an embrace. And no amount of departure from "perfect competition"—displayed through "appreciation" of realism ever—disentangles the subject from the grip of orthodoxy. Consequently, our criticism does not end with neoclassical economics, a bastion of orthodoxy, but extends widely to all self-styled heterodox economists who survive on this or any other stratagem in denial of competition in mature capitalism, particularly on its global stage.[32]

At this juncture, let us switch gears and take up the question of competition from Marx's standpoint, in the presence of concentration and centralization of capital.[33] The emphasis on the presence of the latter render competition genuine and germane to the accumulation of capital. Thus, capital widens and deepens further, first within a single production unit, then within a multi-plant enterprise, and in due time beyond an industry, a collection of industries, a national economy, a region composed of many nations, and finally across the world, where competition gains overwhelming momentum and breathtaking intensity like the wildfire in a dried-up forest which spreads in every direction. According to Marx, competition is not passive, it is not a bundle of harmony;

competition is not a state of affairs but a contentious and contending process arising from the inner mutuality of capital in aggregate, which is manifested by individual capital's interface and interaction. In other words, capitalist competition is a synthetic enterprise. Aside from the genesis of Marx's observation in *The Poverty of Philosophy* (published in 1847), a treatise on the method and vision of capitalism and a reply to Proudhon's *The Philosophy of Poverty*, it is imperative to note that competition in Marx is the process (and inner force) by which capitalism renovates and restores itself toward maturity. Therefore, the maturity of capitalism, particularly on its global stage, is but an insignia of competition, not a monopoly (Bina 1997). But the indoctrinating vision of neoclassical competition, reinforced by the anachronism of Lenin's *Imperialism*, created a fertile ground for this false and contrary impression across the board in nearly all social sciences, including economics. For Marx, capitalist competition is historically advancing, not retreating. How historically? The following passage is instructive:

> What competition brings about, first of all-in-one sphere, is the establishment of a uniform market value and market price out of the various individual values of commodities. But it is only the competition of capital in different spheres that brings forth the production price that equalizes the rates of profit between those spheres. The latter process requires a higher development of the capitalist mode of production than the former.
>
> (*Capital*, vol. 3, [1894] 1981, 281)[34]

In a not so recent issue of the *Socialist Register*, David Harvey writes:

> When demand and supply are in equilibrium, he [i.e., Marx] argued, they cease to explain anything while the coercive law of competition functions as the enforcer rather than the determinant of the general laws of motion of capital. This immediately provokes the thought of what happens when the enforcement mechanism is lacking, as happens under conditions of monopolization, and what happens when we include spatial competition in our thinking, which is, as has long been known, always a form *monopolistic competition* (as in the case of interurban competition).
>
> (Harvey 2012, 7, emphasis added.)

Let us identify several problems in this tiny passage. First is the question of market demand and supply and their accidental equilibrium in a disaggregate economy such as the capitalist one. Even central planning cannot run a tight ship to equilibrate the demand and supply of the commodities on a daily basis. And this is crystal clear for Marx who describes:

> If demand and supply cancel one another out, they cease to explain anything, have no effect on market value and leave us completely in the dark

> as to why this market value is expressed in precisely such a sum of money and no other.
>
> (*Capital*, vol. 3, [1894] 1981, 291)

The context of this statement is the contention that relying on equalization of demand and supply—the fact that more and more economists lived in this self-delusion ever since—is no more than a tautology and that the "inner laws of capitalist production clearly cannot be explained in terms of the intersection of demand and supply" but by the value (or, in more developed capitalism, prices of production) as the center of gravity of fluctuating market prices. Harvey does not appear to grasp this elementary point that short-run market prices are only accidentally identical to the magnitude of value in commodities.

Second, Harvey appears confused about the role of competition between "enforcer" and "determinant" with respect to "the general laws of motion of capital." Marx is very explicit about what capitalist competition does or does not do. He observes: "Competition executes the inner laws of capital; makes them into laws toward the individual capital but does not invent them. It realizes them" ([1939] 1973, 752). Marx maintains consistently:

> Competition generally, this essential locomotive force of the bourgeois economy, does not establish its law, but is rather the executor. Unlimited competition is therefore not the presupposition for the truth of the economic laws but rather the consequence—the form of appearance in which their necessity realizes itself. . . . Competition, therefore, does not *explain* these laws; rather lets them be *seen*.
>
> (Marx [1939] 1973) ibid., 552, emphasis in original)

Again, Marx declares: "Conceptually, *competition* is nothing other than the inner *nature of capital* . . . the inner tendency as external necessity" (ibid., 414, emphasis in original). Marx continues:

> [T]his much is clear: a scientific analysis of competition is possible only if we can grasp the inner nature of capital, just as the apparent motion of the heavenly bodies are intelligible only to someone who is acquainted with their real motion, which are not perceptible to the senses.
>
> ([1867] 1977, 433)

Third, there is little chance of misunderstanding the aforementioned statements if one appreciates the intricate process of value formation in mature capitalism. Such appreciation is contingent upon a meaningful critique of neoclassical theory, which sometimes lost on the left, particularly the radical left. Therefore, Harvey's confusion in the preceding passage is not an exception. He focuses exclusively on the meaning of "executer" as "enforcer" and with an anticipation that a particular state of affairs, namely, capitalist competition needs execution. Harvey's deduction then tells him that the absence of such enforcement is because of "conditions of monopolization," and by blending "spatial competition" in the mix as a radical geographer, he reaches a conclusion that has been known to him via the mainstream theory—"monopolistic competition" (or "imperfect completion" in Joan Robinson's lexicon). That is how Harvey throws his impressionable audience swirls of neoclassical economics fakery in the name of Marxism. As Ben Fine documented,

> Harvey's contradictions are not always as dialectical as they might be. For internal contradictions, at the economic level, Harvey presents the three volumes of *Capital* as successive models rather than as the reproduction in [the] thought of simple categories at more concrete and complex levels. This means that the unity of his treatment is flawed.
>
> (Fine 2006, 138)

The implication of such methodology is probably not more damaging than in Harvey's *The 'New' Imperialism*.[35]

As can be seen, Harvey has shown little appreciation for the subject of capital accumulation, which is tied to the dynamics of the inner nature of capital captured by Marx's value theory and displayed through synthetic competition in capitalism proper. And while, for instance in *Monopoly Capital* (1966), Baran and Sweezy directly shot down Marx's theory of value (and theory of competition) in a swift, straightforward, and painless strike, Harvey has taken his time by several decades of on-the-one-hand and on-the-other-hand hesitation, before he artfully entombs the value theory for good.

Now, let us shift gears and focus on Milios and Sotiropoulos' *Rethinking Imperialism* (2009) in which competition in Marx's sense is appreciated by critiquing Monopoly Capitalism in many of its trappings and manifestations, yet remains unsatisfactory from the standpoint of the historical materialism. This volume speaks of "historical transformation of power balance," yet it fails to recognize that the theory of value is a materialist theory, which comes to be further realized with the development of capitalism from potential to actual. Hence, it succumbs to Althusserian idealism in contradistinction with Marx's real abstraction and concretized theoretical framework. Milios and Sotiropoulos inform us rather tautologically that the transformation in the capitalist mode of production (CMP) has already happened from the production of the absolute surplus value to that of the relative surplus value; all we must worry about is to attend to the question of balance of power. They write:

> The transformations we have described . . . distinguish the form of capitalist domination even in the first period after [the] industrial revolution in the nineteenth century (capitalism of absolute surplus-value) from the later form of this domination (capitalism of relative surplus-value). That which was transformed is not the "laws" of capital accumulation corresponding to the CMP, or in other words the structural characteristics of capitalist relations at all social levels, *but the conditions and forms of appearance of capitalist*

> *relations in the historical perspective*. In other words, it is *a question of* [the] *historical transformation of power balance* and accordingly of the organizational forms of power in developed capitalist social formations.
>
> (2009, 129, emphasis added)

This passage is indeed a smoking gun, that is, a quintessential admission of the Althusserian propensity to mental construction and idealism advocated by the authors. Here is why: (1) by invoking the form of "domination," the authors insinuate authenticity and obfuscate the centrality of capital's overcoming of all its "natural" limits (including the limitation of "working day") in concrete historical reality; (2) by ignoring the limitation of the working day, they miss the opportunity to see the battle over cheapening of labor power, the essential meaning of technological change in CMP proper—this would obscure the real meaning of intrasectoral and intersectoral competition at the level of the theory and across the global divide; (3) by introducing "a theory of modification of competition" (Chapter 8), the authors do not realize that all these *modifications* are but the very weapons of capitalist competition—they appear to mimic the orthodoxy's view of imperfect competition; (4) by presenting the notion of "imperialist chain" (an idealized generality), they negate the period characterized as era of *imperialism* (e.g., by Lenin and others) and undermine the significance of transnationalization and contemporary globalization of capital; (5) by idealizing Marx's theory of value, they overlook the concretization at the level of the theory (with respect to both accumulation and class polarization), and neglectfully relegate nearly all the attributes of transforming capitalism to "social formation," and then dismissively label them as "historicism."

To be sure, *Rethinking Imperialism* is very much justified in critiquing monopoly capitalism theory, center/periphery thesis, "new imperialism," and Imperialism, as the "latest" stage of capitalism.

The authors attempt to demonstrate that competition is a necessity in capitalism, despite the denial of a "stage theory," and the alleged inapplicability of a theory of periodization. Milios and Sotiropoulos also resolutely point to the shortcomings in Harvey's (and Callinicos') notion of "geopolitical competition" and its implication for today's globalized world. But they misinterpret Schumpeter's theory of innovation via "creative destruction" (for instance, by lumping it together with Hilferding's)—and Schumpeter's theory of competition—by the unnecessary cherry-picking and focusing on his theory of imperialism alone (see pp. 62–69, pp. 70–77, p. 143). *Rethinking Imperialism* still is antithetical to the many monopoly theories that come to contrast with the notion of competition in contemporary capitalism. Yet, it succumbs to an ideal type, not quite dissimilar to the neoclassical view, by diminishing Marx's *synthetic* theory to an Althusserian idealist method and lexicon (see Marx 1969, 126–134; on method see Marx [1939] 1973, 100–108). In a way, "successive approximation"—a method of mimicking the ideal by the concrete—is remarkably at work in this book due to the shaky foundation of Althusserian Marxism. Notwithstanding a good deal of justified criticism of the Sweezy-type approaches, the authors caught on their own self-inflicted methodological dead end on the alleged imperialist chains and proto-orthodox theory of competition.

Synthetic Competition: Authenticity, Fakery, and Falsity[36]

Since the events that led to the oil crisis of the early 1970s, it is rather transparent that the applicability of orthodox economic theory to oil, energy, and perhaps life as we know it under capitalism must be questionable. It is also crystal clear that orthodoxy has had a pernicious, if only surreptitiously, influence on the methodological underpinnings of many self-styled heterodoxies in economics. And this damaging influence is so embedded in certain heterodox views that it cannot be masked by refurbishing the orthodoxy through revised assumptions (while keeping the framework); nor can it be cloaked any longer in "radical" rhetoric dished out to the public with straight face. The brunt of our criticism here is directed against the notion of competition (and monopoly) in neoclassical economics, where the point of departure originates from the illusory characterization of real competition. By introducing a deceptive category of "pure competition," the so-called mainstream economics attempts to show how much the real world is apart from this ideal type, as the latter measures the real competition how to be. "Pure" or "perfect" competition preaches harmony to real competition—the latter being the very glimmer of the struggle between individual capitals and within capital in aggregate. It preaches a picture-perfect harmony from the pulpit of neoclassical orthodoxy and emphatically asks, "Can't we all get along?" Pure competition instructs real competition on how to be unreal and how to be a counterfeit—a fake so that it would be qualified as "competition" in the idealized methodology of mainstream economics. Perfect competition threatens to revoke the identity of real competition by retitling it as "imperfect competition," "monopolistic competition," "oligopoly," or "monopoly." Yet all these fantastic demands are fallen upon the deaf ears of competition in the everyday reality of acrimonious capitalism. The authenticity of real competition would not submit to the counterfeit of pure competition, except in the imagination of a typical mainstream economist.

Indeed, contrary to the faulty description in mainstream economics textbooks, no single instance in the history of capitalism would ever support production under "pure competition." Cavalier references to small farmers in the elementary-level economics textbooks, as "purely competitive" producers, are begging the basic knowledge of production and pricing on small farms and, at the same time, betraying the susceptibility and response of these (small) farmers to competitively driven technology and fluctuating market demand across the industry. Misplacing the actual identity of these producers, as perfectly competitive, is not short of "misrepresentational intent,"[37] a cardinal sin that decidedly harms the exposition of truth. Such producers are not only struggling along the trajectory of concentration and centralization of capital on a daily basis but also themselves are the very product of such dynamics. The tragedy is that capitalism under pure competition is no more than a counterfeit, an imposter. Consequently, intended, or unintended, this is a source of methodological deception on the part of mainstream economics.

On the empirical grounds, neither the resilience of capital accumulation nor the violence of ongoing bankruptcies appears to have had any tangible consequence on the modality of perfect competition and its overriding effect on the core of mainstream theory or the minds of its advocates. This ideal imposter continues to hold sway over the axiomatic spectrum of competition/monopoly, where the calibrating ideal keeps wreaking havoc with the reality of competition in the everyday life of enterprises. In this idealized spectrum, the distinction between competition and non-competition is first along a qualitative and then along with a quantitative dimension: (1) by substituting fake for genuine (i.e., "perfect" for synthetic competition) and (2) by traveling (quantitatively) along an imaginary spectrum, from "competition" to "monopoly." This, in part, explains why the neoclassical theory of competition carries with it a label of "quantitative theory of competition" in the literature (see Weeks 1981a, Ch. 6, 2011). Yet, it would be more helpful to pay attention to its qualitative dimension—a dimension that disqualifies this hypothesis right on the drawing board. Finally, the reader must be reminded that the rejection of "perfectly competitive" models, and the acceptance of the "imperfectly competitive" ones (a modified version of the same), may not absolve the theorist from the fakery embedded in its original form. In other words, no amount of "successive approximation" (or in this case, "successive deviation") may rescue a theory that derives from counterfeit.[38]

The idealized notion of "pure competition" (and its corollary: "pure monopoly") has not been so vigorously discredited as in the case of globalization oil, where the *real competition* goes hand in hand with concentration and centralization of capital. Indeed, even no tiny industry of modest structure that pretends to operate on a capitalistic basis and thus abides by concentration and centralization of capital can be found to behave according to "pure competition" anywhere on the planet today. Therefore, one cannot separate competition from the realm of persistent technological change, a universal medium for the accumulation of capital. Hence the process of concentration and centralization of capital should be seen as the initiator of competition—not its demolisher—in a sufficiently long run. Our deepest concern with respect to the neoclassical notion of competition, however, is over its intrinsic fakery—not falsity—carried through "pure competition," a crippling birth defect that does not leave every model of imperfect competition along the spectrum unruffled. To be precise, we have no dispute over the *logical* consistency of axiomatic statements that define pure competition. Our point of contention, however, is that these statements, aside from their consistency, are completely detached from the object of their analysis and thus utterly devoid of meaning with respect to the reality of the capitalist competition. Consequently, they measure competition as a fable only in the imagination of neoclassical economists (for influences beyond this school see Shaikh 1980).

Classical political economy, particularly the works of Smith, taught us that capitalist competition has a crucial history that ascended from crumbling vestiges of the feudal monopoly. Therefore, competition in capitalism, far from being an "axiom," is a self-evident portrayal of antagonism against economic, political, and traditional institutions that were not submissive to the emerging institutions of capitalism. And if the idea of capitalism is inseparable from its concrete material birth and its particular history, then reducing it to an axiom (1) would obfuscate the distinction between pre-capitalist monopoly and the process of concentration and centralization under capitalism and (2) would open the door for speculation on considering capitalism as an eternal (and natural) system. Marx developed his critique of the classical school by taking a cue from these historical observations and produced an articulate and robust theoretical framework for capitalist competition in the presence of concentration and centralization of capital. Moreover, Marx decoupled capitalism from the shackles of the "natural law"—espoused by the classical school. Capitalist competition for Marx is uniquely discernible for a specific period of history, thus pertains to capitalism proper, and is neither needful of "axiom" nor revolving around axiomatic speculation—competition is simply an antithesis of feudal monopoly. And integration is seen neither as "imperfection" (of competition) nor as evidence of monopoly (or oligopoly) in capitalism. Smith and Ricardo too had scarcely put up with such mischaracterization as the classical school had no stomach for methodological blunders that are now the signature of the neoclassical economics of today (see Semmler 1984). It has been shown, first by Marx ([1847] 1969, [1867] 1977, [1894] 1981), and then by Schumpeter (1928, 1942), that the integration of capital is none other than the mutuality of production in competition.

In a little gem of a book, titled *On Bullshit*, Frankfurt (2005) presents us with the distinction between falsity—which depends on downright lying—and fakery—which rests on "misrepresentational intent," expressed by "bullshit." Here are two remarkable passages:

> [A] person who undertakes to bullshit his way through has much more freedom [than a liar does]. His focus is panoramic rather than particular. . . . He is prepared, so far as required, to fake the context as well. What bullshit essentially misrepresents is neither the state of affairs to which it refers nor the beliefs of the speaker concerning the state of affairs. Those are what lies misrepresent, by virtue of being false. Since bullshit need not be false, it differs from lies in its misrepresentational intent. The bullshitter may not deceive us either about the facts or about what he takes the fact to be. His only indispensably distinctive characteristic is that in a certain way he misrepresents what he is up to.
>
> (Frankfurt 2005, 52–54)

> It is impossible for someone to lie unless he thinks he knows the truth. Producing bullshit requires no such conviction. A person who lies is thereby responding to the truth, and he is to that extent respectful of it. For bullshitter, however, all these bets are off; he is neither on the side of

> the true nor on the side of the false. . . . He does not care whether the things he says describe reality correctly. He just picks them out, or makes them up, to suit his purpose.
>
> (pp. 55–56)

Accordingly, the mainstream theories of perfect and imperfect competition are not false but fake having to do with evident misrepresentational intent. In the section on methodology, we implied that it would be legitimate to *undress* the subject under investigation in order to *dress* it up again in thought. However, we cautioned the reader that the process of real abstraction cannot afford to alter the subject in thought by way of speculation or one's fanciful idea toward an axiomatic fabrication.

The category of bullshit employed in this section does not intend to signify an insult in any of its pejorative applications that are prevalent in the public discourse. We use bullshit to categorize perfect and imperfect (or monopolistic) competition, the way in which they were produced, and in a manner that displaced all other theories of competition in the discourse of economics. In order to find that the neoclassical competition is worthy of such description, let us reiterate by way of itemizing the requirements that render bullshit a precise category and a bullshitter distinct from a liar.

First, bullshit is *panoramic*, that is, pertaining to "an open view in all directions"—according to *Webster's New World Dictionary of the American Language*. This is how with bullshit the commitment to particularity is tossed overboard. Second, freedom from particularity and specific scrutiny allows the bullshitter to abandon the context altogether. Third, this gives the bullshitter absolute freedom to ignore and fake the context as he/she wishes. Fourth, having absolute freedom to say anything without any constraint about facts, a bullshitter is not in the business of seeking truth or having any sympathy for it. Fifth, bullshit is not a lie in that it neither intends to subvert the truth about the subject nor about the knowledge of the bullshitter about the subject.

In sum, if fakery, as opposed to falsity, is the prime motivation behind the production of bullshit, then the difference between a liar and a bullshitter is due to the mode of misrepresentation by which the latter conceals one's intent in presenting the facts. What makes the mainstream theory of competition a fakery consist on the fact that (1) that competition is defined panoramically across all historical time—a definition that has no intersection with *specific* truth about capitalist competition; (2) that competition, so defined, is devoid of any content whatsoever; (3) that competition, so defined, is a bundle of perfect harmony, despite intrasectoral and intersectoral contention and mobility of capital; (4) that competition, so defined, has no concern to explore real competition in the presence of concentration and centralization of capital; (5) that competition, so defined, has nothing to do with the truth or the falsity of capitalist competition—it is interested neither in subversion nor affirmation of competition's truth value; (6) that the lack of concern for truth does not render neoclassical competition *false*—it turns it into *fake*; (7) that such fakery then is cloaked in scientific lingo and dispersed for public consumption with intent at misrepresentation across the economic discourse, economic profession, and beyond.

Virtually all "imperfectly competitive" models (including the oligopolistic ones) in and out of mainstream economics, starting with Robinson ([1933] 1969) and Chamberlin (1933) through to Dixit and Stiglitz (1977), Grossman and Stiglitz (1980), Helpman and Krugman (1985), Krugman (1979, 1995), and Brakman and Heijdra (2004) are subsumed under "perfect competition," as melodic variations within the same theme and thus simply by faulty departure from this fanciful forgery. Sadly, the many neo-Marxists of note also descended into this embarrassing quandary by misreading Marx's theory of competition, and by taking refuge in the fashionable concept of orthodox "monopoly," consistent with Lenin's *Imperialism*. In *Monopoly Capital* (1966), Baran and Sweezy acknowledged that the era of "competitive capitalism" was over and that "monopoly capitalism" is now the feature of late capitalism. This conviction may have been reinforced by Sweezy's implicit expansion of Lenin's *Imperialism* to the present and beyond.

The seeds of "monopoly capitalism" were readily planted in Sweezy (1946), where Marx's synthetic competition was thought to be identical to "perfect competition (see for a critique Clifton 1977)." This evidently prepared the ground for *Monopoly Capital* (1966), a complete break with Marx's value theory and Marx's theory of competition. It appears that working with Joseph Schumpeter also did not convince Sweezy to reexamine the origin of competition in capitalism.[39] By acquiescing to the fabrication of mainstream competition, Paul Sweezy, his associates, and numerous others did not appreciate Marx's real competition and mistakenly identified it with the fantasy of "perfect competition" in mainstream economics. Today, this idealization—and its mirror image: monopoly—is visibly dominant in the writings of both left-wing and right-wing economists, not the least of which can be found in the oil literature. And this is despite the remarkable application of Marx's theory of competition and his theory of rent, particularly in this highly integrated sector of the economy (see Bina 1985, 2006).

Concluding Remarks

We have demonstrated that competition in capitalism is neither perfect nor imperfect. Neoclassical competition is an empty axiom in search of a concrete counterpart in the reality of concentration and centralization of capital. It is unlike a utopian vision to be approximated in "imperfect competition," given the turbulent process of "creative destruction" and "destructive creation," a real process with a synthetic implication demands an authentic theory of competition.[40]

We have shown how fittingly one of the most powerful industries of our time, namely oil, was transformed from monopoly (cartel) to competition in the distinct stages of development. This transformation was the consequence of (1) the structural changes at the macro and regional levels toward the development of capitalism, and dismantling of colonial oil concessions, and (2) the overpowering entry of the "independent" oil companies which had long been deprived of exploration, development, and production of oil in nearly all geographical regions of the world (including the US oil region), given the domination of International Petroleum Cartel (1928–1972). Competition from these new entrants (and new oil concessions with the freshly discovered oilfields in Africa and the Middle East), together with the undoing of the whole administered prices under the IPC's sway, had overcome the cartelization of oil and led to rationalization and subsequent globalization of oil through the 1973–1974 oil crisis.

This crisis put an end to the oil monopoly and inaugurated the beginning of a new epoch identified with the globalization of oil and the competitive spot and futures oil markets which thrived along competitively formed differential oil rents across the globe. The intersectoral mobility of capital that prompted the competitive formation of the oil rents also warrants the tendential equalization of the rate of profit across the industries. And, despite the lumpiness of oil reserves in certain geographical clusters (for instance, in OPEC), the magnitude of these differential oil rents is formed independently of any bargaining between the oil rentier—being a state or an individual owner—and the capitalist investor. This is a critical point for competition in the oil sector and contrary to the mainstream *bargaining* theory of rent and oil prices, which may have an implication for reverting to monopoly. As has been demonstrated in this chapter and elsewhere, the oil rents do not arise from the action of the rentier but from the valorization of oil deposits through competition across the globe (Bina 1985, 2012a). This shows that there is little room for the "games theory"—in lieu of the orthodox theory of "market structure"—to be played between the capitalist investor and the owner of the deposits in this industry.

Notes

1 Marx's distinction between land as the landed property (i.e., distinct from capital), and land as capital is *categorical*. We read:

> The representative of land as capital is not the landlord, but the farmer. The proceeds yielded by land as capital are interest and industrial profit, not rent. There are lands that yield such interest and profit but still yield no rent. Briefly, land in so far as it yields interest, is the land capital, and as land capital it yields no rent, it is not landed property. Rent results from the social relations in which the exploitation of the land takes place.
>
> ([1847] 1973, 143–144)

Such distinction is not only consistent but necessary also for a coherent theory of rent in Marx's value theory. Since the modern landed property is precisely the creation of capital and given that the process of valorization is pre-conditioned on their mutuality as well as their distinction, Marx's caveat should not go unheeded. This also creates a problem for rent and its distinction vis-à-vis the interest-bearing and fictitious capital. David Harvey does not seem to appreciate this. Here is what he wrote:

> When trade in [the] land is reduced to a special branch of the circulation of interest-bearing capital, then I shall argue, [that] landownership has achieved its true capitalistic form. Marx does not reach this conclusion directly, although there are various hints scattered in the text [*Capital*, Vol. 3, [1894] 1981, 805–813] to suggest that land-trading could indeed be a form of fictitious capital.
>
> ([1982] 1999, 347)

Then, in the next page, he concludes: "But ought also to specify the historical process whereby *landed property is reduced* to such a condition" (p. 348, emphasis is mine). Harvey, on the one hand, abolishes (by reduction) the category of modern landed property by relegating it to interest-bearing/fictitious capital and, on the other hand, hangs on to its *effect*—the rent. And through this capricious transmutation, *rent* as a category turns to fictitious *capital*. Marx ([1847] 1973) was an admonishing criticism against Proudhon; it could have been just as relevant to be freshly against our contemporary Harvey.

2 This segment is drawn from Bina 2012a, Ch. 4.

3 Marx 1981, 956.

4 An example of the self-propelling tautological system is Piero Sraffa (1960). In this system, anything that matters, including rent, must be defined externally. That is why there is no sign of competition in Sraffa's system.

5 Marx ([1894] 1981, 956).

6 A remarkable illustration of tautology, that is, circular reasoning, can be found in Nitzan and Bichler (2009) where the whole argument about capital begins with power so the authors justify that capital is power.

7 This passage is selected from *A Contribution to the Critique of Political Economy* rather than *Grundrisse*: 105–107, after the comparison of these sections for further fluency in translation.

8 Marx [1859] 1970, 208.

9 Scarcity is behind the construction of many orthodox and seemingly heterodox theories with respect to rent theory. For instance, Sraffa writes: "Natural resources which are used in production, such as land and mineral deposits, and which being in short supply enable their owners to obtain a rent" (Sraffa 1960, Ch. 11, 74). Here, Sraffa's axiomatic system has no room for the specificity of rent in capitalism and thus relies on the generality of "scarcity" that is common to all historical periods, from cave-dwelling folk to the occupant of No. 10 Downing Street in contemporary London. So, the price paid for axiomatic uniformity is absolute hollowness and emptiness as to the specific structure, dynamics, and particularity of capitalism. Rent in the Sraffian system is but an attribute of nature. And thus, the reason for scarcity in nature cannot be found independent of the scarcity in nature. Hence, from the theoretical standpoint, scarcity rent is no other than tautology by other means.

10 The Oil Crisis of 1973–1974 was precisely the crisis of transformation and globalization of the oil industry. The so-called "OPEC offensive" was indeed a catalyst for decartelization and globalization of oil. Globalization of oil, in turn, changed the nature of OPEC from some sort of countervailing power vis-à-vis the "Seven Sisters," to a rent-collecting entity within the competitive (i.e., spot and futures markets) structure of global oil pricing. See Bina 1985, Ch. 6, "Theories of Pure Competition and Competition in Capitalism," pp. 55–65.

11 An excellent source on the Achnacarry Agreement of 1928 and the history of this period is Blair (1976); for further analysis see Bina (2012a, Ch. 4).

12 The wellhead price of oil in the Gulf of Mexico was an administered price based on the highest cost of oil in the world. This price was not a price in a commonplace meaning

of the market, but a "price" based on accounting (market demand) calculations by the cartel. This price then functioned as the basis—thus the connotation, basing-point—for oil from the various geographical locations in the world, plus the transportation cost from the Gulf of Mexico to any delivery points on the planet. It is interesting to note that even if the delivery point were adjacent to, say, oil from the Persian Gulf, the cost of transportation from the Gulf of Mexico was used in the calculations of such delivery. This manner of calculation with respect to the cost of transportation is known as phantom price in the literature of this period.

13 Hobson 1961 was published originally in 1902; Lenin 1963, 667–766. It is disappointing to see that after nearly a century, Lenin's celebrated pamphlet is kept circulating year after year with a subtitle that is more indicting than vindicating. It is my contention that this subtitle should have meant The Higher, not The Highest, for methodological as well as empirical implications, the least of which turn the materialist conception of history on its head. But, alas, the context of Lenin's Imperialism speaks of the latter.

14 An oil concession is essentially a colonial contract like the arrangements by the East India Company.

15 The "posted price" was the price according to which the transfer of crude oil within the worldwide network of the "Seven Sisters" was accounted for.

16 The Organization of Petroleum Exporting Countries (OPEC) was formed in 1960. The original founders were Iran, Iraq, Kuwait, Saudi Arabia, and Venezuela. See Bina 1990, 2012c.

17 See Engler 1977.

18 See Blair 1976.

19 From the standpoint of historical evolution and emergence of oil prices based on a value-theoretic foundation, "cheap oil," both actually and figuratively, is a metaphor for the oil prior to the valorization of landed property by capital in the oil sector. And this irony should not be lost on the issues surrounding the US foreign policy and the colonial-minded authors, such as Daniel Yergin, author of the Pulitzer-Prize-winning, *The Prize* (New York: Simon and Schuster, 1991) and *The Quest* (New York: Penguin, 2011).

20 The so-called posted price was an artificial method by which the IPC disbursed (transferred, swapped, etc.) oil from the basing-point at the Persian Gulf within its international network. Posting of the so-called price was also used to determine the percentage of royalties due to be paid to the oil-exporting countries. The same scheme was utilized for Venezuela and, much later, North Africa.

21 See Bina 1990; Bina and Vo 2007.

22 Sometimes reference to the IPC is made by identifying the cartel as the Transnational Oil Companies (TNCs); this is also interchangeably labeled, in popular jargon, as "Seven Sisters."

23 Bina 1985.

24 Differential oil rent is not the same as "monopoly" rent. It is, rather, a measure of comparative productivity of the various oilfields in competition. As for the Marxian concept of "absolute rent" and its presumable relevance to the oil industry, I wish to make two points. First, from the standpoint of the dynamics of accumulation, absolute rent belongs to a rent-collecting sector (i.e., an industry entangled in "landed property") whose "organic composition of capital" is below the "average." Therefore, the effect of "landed property" upon the investment of capital, via the appropriation of a portion of surplus value, potentially leads to keeping the "composition of capital" below average. Here, "landed property" creates the category of "absolute rent," regardless of the existing qualities of land. In this connection and in Marxian terms, cost price remains below the magnitude of value (or *production price* is below the *value*). Yet, according to Marx, the development of capitalism and the historical limitation of landed property

may lead to the increasing "composition of capital" in agriculture beyond the "average," thus removing the material basis of "absolute rent" (see Engels Marx 1989, 464–477). Second, when the "individual production price" of the least productive land (or oilfield) is the governing "price of production" of the entire industry, then production from such land (or oilfield) may not be possible without payment of rent to the owner. In this case, "absolute rent" (AR) will be a part of the surplus value on all lands, the limit to which is set by the extent of Differential Rent II (DR II). Why? DR II corresponds with the application of varying capital to a specific quality of land already under cultivation, thus bypassing the imposition of additional leasing costs associated with a new lease (see Fine 1979, 1982; Bina 1989a). Yet, AR is not the same as "monopoly rent," an ad hoc category and a point of departure from the fictional notion of competition in neoclassical economics. At any rate, if there will be any AR in the oil industry, it would be in the least productive oilfields of the United States, not OPEC. Moreover, OPEC oil reserves are *not* under the ownership of private sub-surface land. In the context of capital accumulation, these reserves are jointly owned by the capitalist state itself, which also represents the public ownership of the sub-surface land, with no obstruction of the private landed property (see Engels Marx 1989, 519–520, when the landowner and capitalist are one). Consequently, it would be incorrect to attribute the formation of AR to OPEC as, for instance, Chibuzo Nwoke implies. He explicitly reveals his error by stating that "The 'monopoly ownership' of Third World landlord governments would be stronger, and the magnitude of absolute rent exacted by them would be greater, as the demand for minerals expands and the supply of rich mineral deposits becomes more limited" (1987, 30). Perplexed by the Ricardian decreasing margin, Nwoke does claim, mistakenly, that the least productive global oilfields are in the North Sea and Alaska, rather than the lower-48 states of the United States. Nevertheless, the major argument on this issue hinges on the existence of higher-than-average "composition of capital" in the oil sector, and thus AR too is irrelevant to this highly capital- intensive - both in material and value - industry. For further examination of the theoretical points raised in this section, the reader is referred to Bina (1985, 1988, 1989a, 1989b, 1990).

25 This point is drawn from the very meaning of *modern* landed property, i.e., landed property valorized by capital. It is only in this context that is possible to speak of rent in its *modern* connotation. This elementary point is lost on many scholars who ventured to write about this subject. Aside from David Harvey (2003, 2010), Dick Bryan (1990, 176–181) also is guilty of such oversight. Bryan faults Marx for an alleged mishap, namely, that "Marx's theory of rent is limited to pre-capitalist conception of land into a theory of capitalist calculation (i.e., the law of value)." This misreading of rent theory is clear since Bryan has no appreciation of Marx's concept of modern landed property in relation to the valorization of capital. I am afraid that bringing in the mix of Marx's dislike of landlords or separating out the question of "natural" fertility as opposed to fertility caused by capital investment does not cut it. As Mark Twain once said: "you cannot depend on your eyes when your imagination is out of focus." In this context, the problem with Bryan's (and Harvey's) is that they treat the landed property in a stand-alone context, external but engaged with capital.

26 In his PhD. dissertation—which was brought to my attention by someone familiar with the Economics Program at the New School, Fabian Balardini tried to explain the price determination in the international oil market allegedly based on Marx's theory of competition. As I looked over this thesis, I was astonished at how shallow Marx's value theory, theory of rent, and the question of oil prices were treated. Moreover, Balardini does not exhibit any competence in the distinction of intra- and inter-industry competition as it relates to the oil sector. For instance, he misrepresented my position on the formation of *regulating capital* in the oil industry and my theory of differential oil rent (Balardini 2006, 93–101). Some of the key issues that would make Balardini's thesis a non-starter are as follows.

First, the oscillations caused by the conditions of demand (and supply) and the changes that might occur in the magnitude of value and regulating capital were carelessly conflated. This begs the question of the crisis and non-crisis periods in which the former is an indication of a change in value. Balardini's argument blurs this fundamental issue. Second, Balardini trivialized the question of the organic composition of capital in relation to differential rent (DR) and by doing so does not appreciate the mobility of capital in the case of DR. Third, Balardini is innocent of recognizing that the concept of rent in Marx is not a general theory that binds agriculture and all the natural resources together. He fails to notice that rent in capitalism is caused by the landed property, and therefore specificity of rent in oil requires intimate knowledge of the oil industry beyond merely reciting figures. Finally, Balardini relied on what he calls the "hypothetical oil price cycle," an axiomatic construct that relegates the question to a convoluted plane and muddies his conclusions. For instance, Balardini refers to the "lifting cost" of oil and pretends that the cost of production in the oil industry can be limited to this fraction in the long run or for the estimation of value.

It is quite remarkable that these fragmented, inconclusive, and misleading statements were allowed to be made into a dissertation. While my name is also acknowledged in this dissertation, I was not even given the opportunity by Balardini to comment on it before he plans to defend it. See Balardini (2006).

27 These deductions are made explicit in this chapter, so that the reader appreciates the political and ideological implications of the globalization of oil and the enormous impact it had, particularly on US foreign policy.

28 This has a far-reaching implication for liberals and radical leftists who expressly associated the cause of war, for instance, the US invasion of Iraq, with the control of oil in a variety of ways. As I have already demonstrated, such arguments do not have a leg to stand on. One of the reasons is that the ground from beneath such arguments can be easily taken by invoking the globalization of oil and valorization of oil deposits by global capital across the board. But alas, in this confused and confusing world, the spread of disinformation and ambiguity condoned by the US government, and a good deal of nostalgia and ignorance are terrible combinations for anyone to endure. See Bina (2006).

29 These regulating US oilfields are the ones that the *regulating capital* for the entire global oil industry is invested in. The regulating capital governs the production price of US oil and, by implication, the production of all oil across the globe.

30 It should be realized that the extent of this conceptual contamination is not limited to mainstream economics alone. The contagion has not only made a good part of heterodoxy captive but also afflicted many on the radical left in various molds, generation after generation. Aside from the Monthly Review School and well-known rejection of capitalist competition and thus ejection of Marx's value theory, there are scholars whose grasp of capitalist competition (and its pivotal role) does not appear to have been on firm ground but did not reject the theory of value outright. A remarkable example is David Harvey who writes:

> The abandonment of "competitive model" in Marx certainly does entail abandoning the law of value—which, to their credit, Baran and Sweezy are fully prepared to do. The trouble is that we cannot withdraw this, the linchpin of Marx's analysis, without seriously questioning or compromising all the other Marxian categories.
>
> (Harvey [1982] 1999, 141)

Some three decades later Harvey jumps into the ambit of oil, and first revamps the muddled phrase "founder's rent," originally voiced by Robin Murray (1977), in slight variation, namely, the "reserve price" to be paid to the property owner prior to releasing the resource for extraction (Harvey 2010, 81). He then substitutes this for Marx's absolute rent, "because, [as he says] frankly, I do not think it works" (ibid.). As Marx would have said, according to Harvey's method this amounts to the proof of "monopoly rent" in oil (ibid.). Yet, to be safe he tends to play on both sides of the aisle. On p. 82 we read: "In competitive situations this reserve price is typically rather low because if there is abundant land available, producers have choices as to where they go." Mommer (2002) repeats the same shenanigan but calls it "customary ground rent." As can be seen, Harvey moves from branch to branch (i.e., from "monopoly rent" to rent caused by "scarcity") and does notice that his whole argument of his is no more than a tautology and that this view of rent is a sophomoric version of what originally Marshall (1893) put forward. Finally, if the above blunders are not enough, Harvey hammers his last nail in the coffin of capitalist competition, the modern concept of rent, and the foundation of Marx's theory of value. We read:

> In the case of oil wells, however, we are here [sic] dealing with a non-renewable resource, the reserve price on which is given by conditions of relative scarcity. Differential rent on oil well . . . here shades into monopoly rent, as has so obviously been the case with OPEC's control over the release of oil into the world market . . . OPEC's range of action is limited, of course, by the fact that not all states belong to the cartel.
>
> (Harvey 2010, ibid., 82–83)

Save for Marxian analysis. This kind of scholarship—which is now turned into a mouthpiece of radical politics for real change in late capitalism (including the questions of oil, war, etc.)—is an awkward example of percolating orthodoxy beneath the venerated Marxian veneer. I hope the reader is as dumbfounded as I am while probing this case.

31 The phrase "imperfect competition" was initially coined by Joan Robinson under the identical title in 1933. A nearly identical version of this conception, "monopolistic competition," was independently developed by Edward H. Chamberlin as a PhD. thesis at Harvard (defended in 1927) and published at the same time as Robinson's. See Robinson 1969; Chamberlin 1933. It would be also instructive to revisit Joseph Schumpeter's monumental volume, *History of Economic Analysis* (1954), for a glimpse at the backdrop and ambiance of the time in which these two scholars produced these volumes.

32 The fact that many orthodox as well as heterodox economists abandoned the "standard theory" and changed their focus on the "theory of games," attests to the futility of this framework. Such a shift, however, has not been without problems of its own, not the least of which is the axiomatic behavior of interacting agents in isolation from the real structure. See Sen (1977). However, the principal indictment of the "theory of games" can be obtained from rent theory and its competitive formation within Marx's value theory. As I have demonstrated earlier, the magnitude of differential oil rents across the globe is not arbitrary but price-determined; these rents are permanent, not transitory, and their magnitudes are neither subject to a game-theoretic through bargaining by OPEC nor produced by monopoly pricing. These magnitudes are established prior to any bargaining mechanism that might be artificially at work. And OPEC, as I demonstrated time and time again, is not a cartel or a monopolist but an association composed of rent-collecting members (see Bina 1985: Ch. 5–6, 2012a, Ch. 2 and Ch. 4, Note 11).

33 In the context of oil, the reader is alerted to the fact that Marx's theory of competition in mature capitalism is also valid in the presence of rent. For the application of competition, in the presence of a specific theory of oil rent, in the oil and energy industry see Bina (1985, 2012a).

34 The division of the world among monopolies, and the upsurge of finance capital in conjunction with it, in Lenin's *Imperialism*, is illustrative of an early phase of capitalism in which nearly four-fifths of humanity had neither known what capitalism (i.e., a historical-specific social relation) means nor lived under it. In other words, in the epoch of imperialism, described rather specifically by Lenin, capitalism was not on its own. To be sure, while the circuits of capital in its commodity and finance forms were internationalized, the complete social circuit of capital (including the circuit of productive capital) has yet to be developed for, what Marx called, a complete "conquest of the

mode of production" via global competition. On the other hand, allusions, such as "decaying capitalism," must be attributed to the sentiments and anxieties at the time. Many revolutionaries at this juncture believed that the world revolution was at the door. For instance, one can be reminded of Rosa Luxemburg's "theory of breakdown" in capitalism. Therefore, this needs to be taken with a pinch of salt, and this period should be treated as a phase in the development of world capitalism. By the same token, it is also imperative to suspect the reincarnation and currency of similar sentiments, for instance, as "new imperialism" (see Harvey 2003, 2010). Harvey's '*New' Imperialism* is contrary to Marx's theory of competition; and, unlike Sweezy's, it is an oblique thesis on monopoly capital—a masterful smokescreen for the further mystification of the present social change (see Bina 2012a, 2013b).

35 Harvey's ad hoc view of monopoly and monopolization does not allow for appreciation of the above-average "organic composition of capital" in the oil sector, which is the effect of the mobility of capital associated with the inter-sectoral competition of capital beyond the geographical limits. He stubbornly clings to a duality of "territory" (i.e., geography) and "capital" (i.e., social relation), particularly when it comes to oil and oilfields, and then runs with it a circle of tautology to prove that the alleged OPEC monopoly and recent US interventions are connected, and the world has now entered an age of "The New Imperialism" (Harvey 2003). See Fine (2006, 142) and Bina (2012a, Prologue and 110) for a critique of this topsy-turvy observation.

36 The points in this section are in part adapted from Bina (2012a, Ch. 14).

37 See Frankfurt (2005), for further exposition and definition of this phrase.

38 Successive approximation refers to a method in which the intention is to bring the subject closer to the concept (or theory) for the purpose of getting closer to the identification of theory and subject. Methodologically, such mimicking is no other than reducing the theory to an ideal type. *Successive deviation* (a phrase associated with the conceptual distinction of "perfect" and "imperfect" in the neoclassical market structure spectrum) is to theorize by deviating from fiction (see Bina 2012a, Ch. 14).

39 We raise this issue for the obvious reason that Schumpeter and Sweezy had dissimilar views to capitalist competition. Schumpeter (1928) viewed capitalism as turbulent and unstable, whereas Sweezy viewed it as stagnating and monopoly (see Baran and Sweezy 1966). The roots of Sweezy's view, however, were already embedded in *The Theory of Capitalist Development* published much earlier in 1942 (see Sweezy 1946). One wonders why there is no sign of even mild criticism (i.e., critical evaluation) toward Sweezy in Schumpeter (1954).

40 I have long been working on what it means if Schumpeter's "creative destruction" would be placed along with the two aspects of commodities, namely, use-value and exchange value. I thought that the depreciation of capital in recent years had qualitatively changed even beyond what Marx called "moral depreciation." I observed also that the there is a strong mechanism in the fast-paced technology of today that it not only leads to progressively faster rate of obsolescence but also speedily preempts all the commodities (including the labor skills) that were just off the assembly line (or, in the case of skill, obtained recently) that had barely been in use. This has a profound implication for the wholesale evaporation of value (i.e., exchange value) and thus strong motivation that reverses the order of the causality in Schumpeter's and restores the destruction as the cause of the creation from the standpoint of exchange value of the commodities. Thus, the synthesis of "creative destruction" (*à la* Schumpeter)—in line with *use value*—and "destructive creation" (*à la* Bina) —befitting *exchange value*, neatly falling back on Marx's theory of value (see Bina and Davis 2008; Bina 2012d, 2012e, 2021b). Here, in this synthesis, capitalist competition attains the highest intensity.

5 The Origin and Fabric of Globalization

You cannot step into the same river twice.

—Heraclitus of Ephesus

Introduction

Globalization much like beauty is in the eyes of the beholder. It is a popular topic among the left and the right; even the notorious right-wing Ronald Reagan conversed about globalization. There were also economists on the right who jumped on bandwagon of globalization, which in their eyes defined as free trade and exchange supported by the Reagan administration and its right-wing supporters in the 1980s.[1] This of course created an impression as if "globalization" is the new economic policy on the US agenda, and that "neoliberalism"—a fashionable buzzword that depicts policy in place of epoch—is the same as globalization,[2] thus a mistaken belief that the United States is in charge of "globalization" and that the US government is using this "neoliberal" strategy deliberately against the rest of the world.[3] The orthodoxy perceived this as a global triumph and the American influence in international affairs.[4]

This misleading observation is also prevailing in mainstream economics and international relations when it comes to the appraisal of global leadership and the standing of the United States.[5] This captures the balance sheet of the right on this particular issue. As for the liberal and radical left, while *neoliberalism* is to be rescinded, given the damaging impacts and polarizing effects on the society, economy, and hardship and destitution of untold numbers of working population across the world, it is made into an epoch and misidentified as *globalization*.[6] This methodologically displays a state of conceptual dead-end and "poverty of philosophy" on critical issues of our time in which the radical left finds itself. As is implicit in this chapter, the question of globalization is a make-or-break topic in critical political economy and departure from Marx's method or deviation from the universality of capital as a social relation is quite costly.

The critique of the two popular fallacies, namely, the impression conveyed by "deglobalization" and the misconception of beholding multiple globalizations,[7] also remains implicit by placing the singularity of globalization at the

DOI: 10.4324/9781351136785-5

center of our investigation, thus advancing a unique theory of periodization in capitalism. There is a streak of nationalism, in the vintage of "Third-Worldism," behind deglobalization—a tragic vehicle for misplacement of the *cause* and perfunctory struggle against palpable effects.[8] The lack of theoretical perspective and sufficient empirical strength in the proposal of "deglobalization" is the unwillingness to see the universal picture of class polarization and the crises that proceed relentlessly to intense worldwide unevenness, both intranationally and transnationally.[9] The pattern of assuming "globalization" in multiple incidences by allusion to trade and finance in certain periods of history is also a sign of methodological ineptitude on this very subject. These improvised and impressionistic historical subdivisions often turn to unintended consequences.

In addition, it is not the intention in this chapter to contend that one should disregard the notion of a modern nation-state in capitalism. More specifically, the argument here is not of the abolishment of the nation-state in the advent of globalization.[10] The contention is squarely on the historical fact that the institution of the nation-state, like any other establishment in capitalism, is a subject of transformation accordingly. Similarly, the foundation of what is identified as "geopolitics" would also vary markedly with the qualitative transformation of capitalism toward globalization, a measure of all measures, so to speak. Contrary to the allegation of "purity" and the denial of the theoretical foundation for geopolitics, the latter diminishes to scattered narratives on the nation-state, development state, and international conflict.[11] Put differently, geopolitics is neither an ad hoc discipline nor a standalone field nor devoid of dialectical context in capitalist social relations.

Thus, despite the traditional left whose theoretical yardstick for periodization consists of imperialism, monopoly capital, financialization,[12] the golden age of capitalism,[13] neoliberalism,[14] geopolitics,[15] "global north/global south,"[16] and state or nation-state, this chapter relies on *capital* as a social relation for periodization of capitalism.[17] In passing, the "golden age of capitalism" is a phrase coined to describe the period of the postwar boom. This age of course is none other than a period that coincided with the ascent of the *Pax Americana*, a theme elucidated in this volume. As for others, these measures are either transitory, tautological, simplistic, or artlessly anachronistic. Just as an example, the measure of "global north/global south" corrupts Marx's theory of value by transporting "dependency theory" through the backdoor, evoking circularity along with the center/periphery partition, once more.[18] Finally, against all these distractions, appreciation of Marx's methodology and a careful reading of volume I of Marx's *Capital* would deliver much more articulate insights, including a key to the secret of periodization.[19]

Capital: The Secret of Periodization

The focal point of this chapter is the evolution of the capitalist mode of production through historically specific stages in which capital transforms from a *potential* embryo within borders of the nation-state to an *actual* transnational reality beyond it. This historical transformation embodies concentration and centralization as a basic characteristic of capital accumulation in *competition*.[20] Therefore, the accumulation of capital is ultimately accumulation on a global scale. Capital as such is a potential social relation rather than a "thing"—for example, a standalone object.[21] In a capitalist society, capital includes the articles of use (and services) produced for exchange through the market for profit. Profit is an observable phenomenon in both the distribution of national income and individual enterprises across the board. Thus, cost-cutting in all enterprises and production units is the primary motivation for the ongoing business in a capitalist society.[22]

However, the real lever of this cost-cutting, to be persistent and as incessant, is none other than technology and technological change, without which accumulation, via concentration/centralization, of capital has little meaning. In turn, capitalism without concentration and centralization of capital is just a caricature, a cartoon, a parody seen largely in standard theory (and methodology) cast in the neoclassical economics orthodoxy.[23] That is why standard models in neoclassical and mainstream economics are but an ideological fabrication.[24] The impression of a boundary for capital accumulation confines *actual* specificities whose identity is structured by historical and socioeconomic criteria and qualifications. The quality of these criteria sets the stage for epochal change, a propensity that divides capitalism into interludes and epochs.

These epochs are set at an innermost constitution of capital, as a social relation. Here, the "logic" of capital is not *axiomatic*, idealistic, imagined, or fabricated in the lingo of mainstream (neoclassical) economics[25] displayed in popular textbooks, but a real force that organically traverses the trajectories of *territory* and *history*. Social relations are omnipresent in the context of our collective lives. They are the identity of our everyday life as our second nature in the *world* of commodities and capital. Here, in a profit system, production, exchange, and distribution are definite and inseparable parts of an organic whole in the dynamics of accumulation. In other words, we neither have a world with separate "logic" of history and "logic" of territory (or geography) nor capitalism with separate principles for spheres of production, circulation, exchange, and distribution.[26] All these apparent "separations" are the phenomenal forms and tendencies of *capital* as a universal social relation.

An important aspect of Classical Political Economy, particularly Adam Smith and David Ricardo, is in its macro vision as far as it can see the phenomenal forms of capital and the boundaries of the nation-state. The classical school was cognizant of the centrality of production and thus distribution among the classes. Smith and Ricardo spoke of *class* as an omnipresent category. They saw the skeleton of capitalism in its infancy. They looked at the whole first, so far as their *natural law* creed (and its limitation) could allow them to see, and then located the individual parts. Contrary to the neoclassical economic paradigm, the classics did not put the microeconomics *cart* before the proverbial *horse* of macroeconomics. The classical school, despite its other methodological and ideological problems, did not fall into the trap of methodological *individualism*, a dominant, reductionist trend in mainstream economics and political science, particularly via the irony and indeed Orwellian lingo of the "public choice" theory—the narrowest, and perhaps most explicit anti-public (and anti-state) and extreme mindset within the orthodoxy. Here, the forest, so to speak, is dutifully defined by imitation of the single tree and entire macroeconomics diminished to the swelling centrality of microeconomics by the narrowest possible means.[27] The disappearance of *class* in the so-called Marginalist Revolution (of the 1870s, by a trio of Jevons, Menger, and Walras) is no accident; it was the beginning of a protracted and perturbing methodology that in due time placed both the *fallacy* of composition and methodological *individualism*, along with blatant positivism, under one proverbial roof.[28]

This was a deliberate paradigm shift that in due time reduced the political economy utterly and ultimately to a trickle (except for those inspired by Menger), that is, to a timeless *modus operandi* composed of a set of axioms, standardized *individual* behavior, and a collection of a set of individuals identified as a *society*.[29] An ideology that intensely reacted against John Maynard Keynes and the postwar economic policies was also against social democracy and socialism in the heat of the Cold War. Finally, against the backdrop of the crisis of Keynesianism, on the one hand, and the advancement of transnationalization of capital, on the other hand, the state itself—and public institutions—transformed into the appendage of market and market ideology through a full-fledged methodological individualism, which since the 1970s replaced the standard postwar Keynesian policies, as *neoliberalism*.[30]

To observe a contrast, one must go back to the so-called Golden Age of Capitalism, a period beginning with the conclusion of World War II, in 1945, and ending with the breakdown of the Bretton Woods monetary system, in 1971.[31] This of course refers to capitalism seen from the vantage point of the *Pax Americana* (1945–1979), a historic age that nearly overlapped with the "golden age" and essentially ended in the final year of Jimmy Carter's presidency. This means that the Carter administration was the last US government with global hegemony in charge of the postwar Pax Americana, a historical epoch that had just come to a close.[32]

In the aftermath of the detachment of the US dollar from gold by Richard Nixon on August 15, 1971,[33] in addition to a sustained deficit in the balance of payments, the US outsourcing of the manufacturing sector reached its peak by the mid-1980s. This historic marker is known as *plants closing*, a colossal event that triggered a widespread shutdown in the workplace across the United States and eventually led to widespread relocation of manufacturing plants in major domestic industries and primary sectors toward other regions of the world.[34] This would illustrate an instance of global economic shift that was instigated a decade earlier and that now began to mark the displacement of the United States from the center of global production for good. Thus, the Golden Age of Capitalism was not about the *inner* dynamics of capitalism *per se* but about the successful application of *outer* Keynesian (and developmental) economic policies and their eventual failure; it was precisely about a period of relative prosperity and stability in the United States, which was unsurprisingly also coincided with the transitory US global hegemony.

As hinted earlier, capital in embryo stands for a potential that had not yet turned into an actual, full-blown social relation. In this Marxian insight, capital qua capital is conceivable only thru *trans*formation, thus what is known as *commodity* capital, *money* capital, and *productive* capital are but the forms of capital awaiting transformation. In the absence of such a transformation, there is neither ontologically nor epistemically possible to comprehend the true meaning of capital or the change itself; it would be impossible to apprehend the process of accumulation, the reality of technological change, or the frequency of economic crises in capitalist economies. In other words, there is unquestionably no way of grasping the inner dynamics of capital without the necessary motion within the intricate, tripartite circuits of capital in accumulation.

Likewise, it would be impossible to grapple with concentration and centralization of capital as an innermost attribute of capital as a mode of production. It would be also next to impossible to decipher the origin of *competition* in Marxian significance of the term, as opposed to Hobson's *monopoly*,[35] when it comes to the concentration and centralization of capital, a stark reality that reveals itself upside down.[36] Capital in motionless rendition—an epiphenomenon popularized by the neoclassical/mainstream economics orthodoxy—has likewise no resemblance to *capital* at all; it at best is an idealized mass of objects (or services) discretely produced and swapped with money, the latter being speculative, circular, and arbitrary sum. This of course is a familiar portrayal of capitalism in conventional mainstream economics textbooks that see the economy through the pseudo-scientific prism of pure ideology.[37]

Contrary to this parody, a capitalist system in Marx's approach is a *living system* that at the beginning was a potential materialization that gradually turned into a palpable actuality and universal corporeality of today. This historical transformation was brought to bear by means of socio-economic developments that had pervaded and overcome a series of both internal and extremal barriers toward the universalization of capital as a social relation. For instance, the overwhelming borders of the nation-states, eliminating the boundaries of regions and territories, abolishing the traditional walls of social space, and finally bringing the realm of world geography under the universal umbrella of capital are now perceptible by the specialists and non-specialists alike.

Capital: Motion, Barrier, and Epochal Identity

The problem of epochal identity, and indeed periodization of capitalism, is one of the thorniest issues in the critique of political economy that still perplexes the heterodox and radical scholars on the subject. The complexity and burden of historical transformation, combined with sufficient theoretical analysis based on Marx's law of value, have led to a set of controversies that must be cleared up and straightened out on this issue. To be sure, one set of obscurity is comprised of Hobson's imperialism and the perception of monopoly, an enduring influence of which, initially via Hilferding and Lenin, and in due time, Sweezy, Baran, Magdoff, Braverman, and Amin, to name a few, have long been palpable in an alarming manner across the Marxist camp.[38]

To name a few, the undue influence of monopoly is manifest in the works and visions of Rudolph Hilferding, Karl Kautsky, Vladimir Ilyich Lenin, and Rosa Luxemburg early in the twentieth century. As we shall see more in this chapter, this influence (that is., Hobson's) is clearly a departure from Marx's theory of value (and Marx's synthetic competition[39])—a measure of all measures with respect to the capitalist mode of production. The typical argument of course is that capitalism had changed in the "era" of *imperialism* and that the spread of cartels and monopolies then turned out to be the order of the day.[40]

The periodization of the capitalist mode of production is not a simple task.[41] First and foremost, there is the question of finding a framework according to which a proper distinction between the likely periods can be made. Oftentimes, a palpable yardstick, such as emphasis on historical milestones, may accomplish the task of periodization. This approach is familiar in Lenin's *Imperialism*, a celebrated pamphlet that identified the epoch of imperialism as the highest stage of capitalism.[42] This stage, according to Lenin, inaugurated the era of cartels and monopolies, and from the perspective of political economy, any concentration/centralization (of capital) is equivalent to monopoly and the lack of competition, the latter being Hobson's analog of the monopoly.

One should note that according to Lenin or Hobson this period is about the wholesale alteration of capitalism toward monopoly, not as a transitory period but a perpetual one. To unpack the implication of monopoly, of course one needs to be concerned about the accompanying conditions and features, such as economic stagnation, sluggishness of innovation and technological change, and, more importantly, the identification of cartels and trusts with *capital*, dismissing Marx's vision of capitalism as an evolving social relation. This of course was done in Marx's name, with a proviso that capitalism had now altered. This alleged alteration, as we shall see later, is quite justified if one could shift one's attention to the financial form of capital vis-à-vis the nation-state.

This *cleavage* (that is, Lenin's "monkey wrench," so to speak) would simply boil down to the notion of concentration/centralization of capital via Marx's competition as opposed to monopoly, via Lenin. Originated in Lenin's *Imperialism*, this cleavage back then spoke of the highest stage of capitalism in an age where nearly four-fifths of the world population had neither inhabited capitalism nor perceived what the capitalist mode of production would look like. Yet, this *impression*, given the political circumstances after the founding of the Soviet Union, had obtained a mass of supporters on the left and in due time ended up with "monopoly capitalism," via neo-Marxist Paul Sweezy,[43] and survived for a century until today.

It is unfortunate that in this version, capitalism turns into a "monopoly," particularly based on its genesis advanced by Rudolph Hilferding in *Finance Capital*, thus relying on the *form* of financial capital—the lifeblood and an origin of monopoly thesis—and its purported *control* over the industrial capital.[44] Moreover, the ploy of the elimination of competition and the perfunctory reversal of the relationship of "bank" capital and "industrial" capital, which is allegedly due to the "minimization of risks," by the former, in Hilferding's *Finance Capital*, particularly mesmerized Lenin as revealed in his *Imperialism*.[45] These are of course phenomenal forms of deeper changes that materialized at the beginning of the twentieth century. The timing of the so-called *export* of capital is the era in which capital in its *money* (or financial) form negates the borders of nation-states. This is the second negation of capital, the first being negation of capital in its *commodity* form. We must remember that these forms are the two, out of three possible forms, of capital vis-à-vis the accumulation of capital, which would indicate that at this time circuits of capital (in all its three forms) had not yet been broadened beyond the limits of the nation-state. In other words, capital in its productive moment (and its circuits for production and reproduction) is still within the confinement of the nation-state.

That is why at this period, imperialism stands for a historical era with its wide-ranging characteristics, that is, economic, political, and tangible impressions and influences, is in the driver seat. Expressed differently, Hilferding, Lenin, and Luxemburg, among others, essentially had fallen into the trap of deducing tangible impressions of this era by the same tangible impressions as more or less the highest stage of capitalism. This explicit orientation concerning *decaying* and *stagnating* capitalism, voiced by Hilferding and Lenin, had followed Hobson's original instigation of capitalism, verbatim.[46] This of course, besides being, in essence, a liberal view of capitalism, is also a well-known deception in methodologic terms. On the other hand, from the perspective of *capital*—as a social relation—the capitalist mode of production in much of the world had not yet seen the light of the day, let alone the old and decaying days. Hence, a myopic and, as it becomes more evident in this chapter, a fetishistic display of this period that was about to begin with the inauguration of mass production, mass consumption, and mass purchasing power in an intricate interweave of banking and credit systems, in just a fraction of the globe, identified as imperialism and decaying capitalism.

To probe the dilemma of universalization of capitalism in the presence of non-capitalist regions, proposed by Luxemburg in her alleged critique of Marx, the following passage from *The Accumulation of Capital* can be of interest:

> Historically, the accumulation of capital is a kind of metabolism between capitalist economy and those of pre-capitalist methods of production without which it cannot go on and which, in this light, it corrodes and assimilates. Thus, capital cannot accumulate without the aid of non-capitalist organizations, nor, on the other hand, can it tolerate their continued existence side by side with itself. Only the continuous and progressive disintegration of non-capitalist organizations makes accumulation of capital possible. The premises, which are postulated in Marx's diagram of

> accumulation, accordingly represent no more than the historical tendency. . . . Its ultimate aim . . . is to establish the exclusive and universal domination of capitalist production in all countries and for all branches of industry.
> (pp. 416–417)[47]

This much is clear from the aforementioned passage that Luxemburg cannot imagine that capitalism can stand on its own feet, let alone turn into a universal mode of production. She hastily refers to volume II of *Capital* and quickly insists that Marx's analysis on the potential universalization of capitalism "does not lead anywhere," since "The realization and capitalization of surplus value become impossible to accomplish" (p. 417). To see Luxemburg's reasoning, the following passage is pertinent:

> Just as soon as reality begins to correspond to Marx's diagram of enlarged reproduction, the end of accumulation is in sight, it has reached its limits, and capitalist production is in *extremis*. For capital, the standstill of accumulation means that the development of the productive forces is arrested, and the collapse of capitalism follows inevitably, as an objective historical necessity. This is the reason for the contradictory behavior of capitalism in the final stage of its historical career: imperialism.
> (p. 417, emphasis in original)[48]

The reader should realize that *The Accumulation of Capital*, the magnum opus of this revolutionary writer, is accompanied by Joan Robinson's critical preface in her recognition and honor. However, Luxemburg in this book appears to have little clue about Marx's method of investigation, particularly the requisite of reading Vol. I of *Capital* prior to volume II and the self-expanding nature of capital as a social relation, or an inkling of the anticipated periodization of capitalism.[49] Moreover, Luxemburg had little clue about Marx's method of *internalizing* capital as a universal social order. The circular clutch of the *present* time in the early twentieth century seems to have gripped Luxemburg's faculty and thus seemingly compelled her toward a half-baked critique of Marx by brandishing the corollary of *imperialism* and the *breakdown* of capitalism.[50] It is also startling that such an exceptional revolutionary, who had faith in human action and class struggle, would succumb to a perfunctory view of breakdown in capitalism in such an unripe and reflexive fashion.

Here additionally, to quote John Robinson, "[H]er affinity seems to be with Hobson rather than Keynes," denoting Luxemburg's predisposition to *stagnation* and confidence in an illusion of insufficient technological change in capitalism, which also persisted, albeit in a different fashion, in Lenin's (Luxemburg, pp. 20–21).[51] Yet, Luxemburg's peculiar view of capitalism and capital accumulation and its alleged dependability on the "natural" (that is, non-capitalist) economy defines *imperialism* in a new light. Imperialism, a *twin sister* of capitalism and a necessity (in both epistemic and ontological sense) for the accumulation of capital, in her fantastic imagination, was dependent on it. Thus, it is not just due to the underconsumption of the masses (the prevalent delineation of underconsumption) that capital accumulation is doomed to failure but that, as Michael Bleaney articulates, "a general expansion of production in all departments [that is both Department I and II in Marx's *Capital*, vol. II] is not fundamentally justified by any demand."[52] Thus, the phenomenon of imperialism for Luxemburg does not consist of an era, invoked by Lenin in its formalized framework in *Imperialism*, but something quite unlike Lenin's or Hobson's; Luxemburg's imperialism is a quintessential *denial that accumulation of capital can ever be on its own.*[53] Strange as it may seem, it appears that Luxemburg had little clue as to both ontology and epistemology of capital as self-expanding value and a potential social relation toward universality, as Marx had.[54]

Capital: Moments and the Tripartite Negations

As indicated earlier, the focus of this chapter is on periodization and grappling with a measure appropriate to its methodological validation in Marx's vision and in the corporeality of capitalism. The primary complication as hinted earlier, however, is the distinction between historical time and the periods correlated with the span of the tripartite negation of the nation-state by the three *moments* of capital, namely, commodity, money, and productive, leading to the globalization of capital as a *social relation.*[55] To underscore, a sound theory of periodization unfettered by the random pulse of time, affected by concrete organizational transformation within nation-states, and displayed beyond their boundaries could be in accord with self-expanding capital as a social relation.

Following the internationalization of the *moment* of commodity capital, the stipulation for accumulation of capital and thus further concentration and centralization of capital has led to the wholesale reorganization of capitalist enterprises from top to bottom, known as Stock Corporations. This was initiated by separation of the *ownership* from control, thus setting off the entree of fragmented individual properties into the amalgamated and shared property of numerous owners in one pot under an incorporated management *control*[56]; this was a grand invention in capitalism that brought both passive and active investors together, on the one hand, and enhanced the scale and scope of the enterprises, on the other, known as the Managerial Revolution.[57] A corporation is a representation of three notable things: (1) the transformation of private property into the de facto *collective* property of capital, (2) the division of the capitalist class into managers and faceless capitalists, and (3) consequently, capitalism is not a mode of production based on simple *private* appropriation but a system in which private appropriation mediates through *class* appropriation. Here, sociality of the private appropriation is the key to the development of modern capitalism.[58] All this arose in an ultimate sense owing to and preconditioned upon, carrying away several distinctive barriers by capital previously, including overcoming the barriers of the *working day*[59] (via technology and technological change), limitation of individual ownership (by the deployment of a corporation), limitation of a single plant in manufacturing and services (through multi-plant operations), and limitation of single geographical location, to name a few. Here, the phenomenon of the corporation has a deep root in the *sociality* of capital and profundity of the *capitalist state* in both economic and political dimensions in its founding.[60]

Let us be reminded again that in this period in the development of capitalism, there was a process of rethinking and transforming the concept of *time* (and its natural limits) from the finitude of the individual ownership via proprietorship (or partnership) to collective ownership of capital and the perpetuity of *corporation*.[61] The rise of investment banking and further centralization of capital in tandem with mass production in manufacturing and concentration within and across enterprises were the essential features of the period in which capital as money (or finance) negated the boundary of the nation-state, a phenomenon known as the "export of capital" at this time.[62] Thus, from the standpoint of social capital[63] overcoming the boundary of the nation-state by *finance capital* (that is, the *moment* of money capital) is the *key* to the periodization of this period. At this time, simultaneously, several concrete historical establishments and practices, such as colonies, cartels, and trusts, were also in existence, yet the factual truth of these entities should not be an excuse for turning a blind eye to the developments that slowly but surely led to the eradication of colonialism and the implosion of many of such cartels and trusts.

These facts truly existed in concurrence with the aforementioned changes at this historical crossroads and this period, known commonly as the era of *Imperialism*. Yet, as has been fully demonstrated in the example of the International Petroleum Cartel (1928–1972), these monopolies and cartels would implode, collapse, and transform as capital will be universalized and turn to a global mode of production.[64] In the case of oil, decartelization emerged through the crisis of restructuring which then led up to full-fledged globalization of the industry in the 1970s.[65] The completeness of capital as a social relation depends upon the negation of so many barriers, starting with the limitation of working day in the late nineteenth century and extending all the way to the late twentieth century via the negation of the nation-state by the tripartite moments of capital in global accumulation. In this manner, the transnational circuits of social capital finally transcend the barriers of the nation and nation-state. The overcoming of capital as a potential social relation toward actuality has a deeper and deepening side in transcending the walls of the factory and that of the workplace in general, leaping onto the social and political space and by taking the ownership, so to speak, of the entire social fabric of the economy, polity, and society. Put differently, capital advances through the removal of manifold barriers of all categories and kinds, in scale and scope, thus leading to both strengthening and extending social relations across all societies within and beyond the nation-states toward globalization.[66] That is why Marx, in volume III of *Capital*, quite clearly and unequivocally foretold: "The *true barrier* to capitalist production is *capital itself*" (p. 358, emphasis in original).[67]

Thus, from the perspective of globalized capital (as a social relation), the era of imperialism is neither permanent nor deep enough that can stand on itself or that one can hang on one's hat to it methodologically and be able to identify it sufficiently as an epoch for periodization of capital or capitalist mode of production. Overall, the foundation for the proliferation of capital, as a potential social relation, was turning to an actuality a step further, with the negation of the nation-state by capital in financial form. Notwithstanding the presence of cartels and trusts, and the "divisions of the world"—a veritable symbols of imperialism—concentration and centralization of capital and the incessant technological change, via synthetic competition à la Marx (as opposed to Lenin's rivalry, stagnation, and decay), are not only beginning to take hold on its own but also solidly prepared and fortified the development of capitalism much further beyond a handful of capitalist countries early in the twentieth century.

That is why Hobson's vision of monopoly capitalism and the borrowed varied versions by Hilferding, Lenin, Kautsky, Luxemburg, and by the next generations of the radical left, including Paul Sweezy, Paul Baran, and Harry Braverman, Harry Magdoff, Samir Amin, are not only non-Marxian but also anti-Marx in their methodological content. There are also radical scholars like David Harvey who are wavering and vacillating between "imperfect competition" and imperialism (along with two discrete (illusory) "logic"—of *history* and *territory*[68]), thus sadly undoing a modicum of understanding they may have obtained from the reading and rereading of Das Kapital since the 1970s and 1980s.[69] This omnipresent worldview also distorts the corporeality of capitalist production, deludes the dynamics of accumulation, and irreversibly misrepresents the criterion for periodization of capitalism. It is noteworthy that in volume III of *Capital*, Marx concludes, "*In competition . . . everything appears upside down*" (311, italics in original).[70] Marx appears to have anticipated this impulsive measure of competition along the axiomatic spectrum of perfect competition/perfect monopoly in orthodox economics textbooks. Depiction of monopoly—a transposed vision of capitalist competition—theorized and prompted by Hobson and popularized through Lenin's *Imperialism* in radical circles, not to mention revolutionary movements, is an agreed-upon fact by the majority of the left today.[71] Ironically, the same *liberal* (Hobsonian) view of monopoly (and competition), apart from the leftist lexicon and a bit of rewording over the intervening years by orthodoxy, is also a regular staple for the majority of right-wing mainstream economists.[72]

As elucidated earlier, capital manifests itself in three discernible moments, namely, commodity, money, and productive forms. So far, we spoke of the overcoming, thus negation of the barrier of the nation-state by the first two forms (and circuits) of capital. The balance of this chapter is to emphasize the overcoming of the nation-state by the third moment of capital, the productive form. The timing of this negation is crucial since it overlapped with coming to the fruition of the cumulative struggles of enormous masses of humanity, known as the "Third World," for independence, and thus *decolonization* of a significant part of the world in the mid-twentieth century. This was followed in tandem by sweeping changes that gradually but surely transformed the foundations of many of these societies and economies across the then blossoming Pax Americana.

A series of land reform programs aimed at the eradication of the pre-capitalist vestiges in the vast regions known as "Third World" and thus generated the untold number of wage labor en masse[73]; import-substitution industrialization (ISI) accommodated and allocated the seemingly unlimited reservoir of the now available labor to the ISI industries, and planned to boost the incipient domestic market and to connect the newly emerged and enhanced national economies to the world market.[74] Here, the supplemental export-platform industries also reinforced the grip of capital across the economic landscape in many of these countries. From the standpoint of capital as a social relation, this one-two punch socioeconomic strategy, so to speak, is the initial kernel of the newly class-divided and stratified societies coupled with the world economy in flux.[75] As all this is elaborated in detail in this book and elsewhere, this much should be enough for both the dynamics of the Pax Americana and the tip of transnationalization of capital, the purpose in this chapter. These preconditions are a material basis for the moment of capital in the *productive* form to begin to proliferate and overcome the barrier of the nation-states en masse at this time.[76]

The nation-state once created by the nascent capitalism and fundamental to the origins of this mode of production to take hold turned into a contradictory geographical barrier and thus negated by the tripartite moments of capital in an orgasmic social whole in historic strides. These steps are but the development of capital on the road to universality, that is, the fulfillment of conquest of the mode of production and tendency to a worldwide social relation. All this had been possible where social capital in a tripartite negation, moment by moment, virtually seizing and overcoming each barrier to accumulation within the boundaries of the nation-state and beyond their seeming sovereignty, capacity to control, and geography. This is simply a trajectory of historical evolution and dialectical expedition of capital, from the potentiality of much earlier period of "batter[ing] down all Chinese Walls"—to invoke Marx's striking dictum (in *Manifesto*)—to the present day in the twenty-first century. Speaking of the world market in the mid-nineteenth century is a tendency that was potentially propagated and transformed, and eventually turned into a universal manifestation of an actualized mode of production, beyond the border of the nation-state, in the twenty-first century. This is what is meant by (capitalist) globalization in this volume, and it was this very universal tendency that led to the collapse of the interstate Pax Americana (1945–1979) and the irrevocable fall of the American Hegemony.

Periodization of capitalism is a unique theoretical task that must avoid the real appearances, including the imposing institutional imperatives, ideological and doctrinal constraints, economic and political policy reversals, functionality of states themselves, or plain old stochastic processes. A genuine attempt at periodization of the capitalist mode of production must go beyond all the institutional trimmings and trappings of capitalism by starting off with *capital* itself as a self-expanding value that potentially actualizes toward universalization across the limits of geography, that is, a tendency to globalization. In other words, the periodization of capitalism is embedded in the capital itself. This embodies the identification of the tripartite moments of capital in both the deepening and widening of the social relations within, between, and beyond the border of the nation-state toward accumulation on a global scale. This method of periodization is crucial in that we would avoid falling into the trap of the by-products, so to speak, of apparent historical institutions, functional affairs, or historical time (that is, history without theory), while also circumventing the residues or ruins attributed to the old interstate order or diverse strategies, economic testaments, transitory policies, and conceivable doctrines, namely, Keynesianism or neoliberalism, that would appear as genuine and fit for such delicate task. That is why, in both Harvey's *A Brief History of Neoliberalism*[77] and "Thirteen Things You Need to Know About Neoliberalism," by Fine and Saad-Filho[78]—purported intent at periodizing capitalism—nearly all the deployed and displayed signs (in the name of neoliberalism) are but palpable appearances, indeed the *symptoms* of much deeper and much more sweeping changes that have taken place toward globalization since the 1970s. To be sure, neoliberalism is little more than an ideological veneer of transnationalization of capital, an inner and deeper lever of globalization. Let us ask ourselves, is there a coincidence that the underpinning of the manifold neoliberal strategies and policies had lain in the early 1970s? Did Keynesianism and postwar Keynesian policies lead to failure by happenstance, or worse, by peculiarities of "individual capitalisms" in individual countries? Does the end of Keynesianism not demand a coherent and unified theoretical explication far from all these limited and partial accounts we have heard so far? Finally, is it not a periodization (in the Marxian sense of the term) based on neoliberalism versus Keynesianism a scandalous tautology in itself? As we can see clearly, the process of globalization of capital would provide a grand calibration for all possible magnitudes and measures of history, policy, socioeconomic change, geopolitical change, technological change, and any other milestone in the corporeality of capitalism today. It calibrates in periodization and precisely reveals a mode of production that has now turned into a universal social relation across the entire planet.

Capital: The Fabric of History and Geography

The moment of *productive capital* is the last in the chain of tripartite negations, thus the precondition for transnationalization of all circuits of capital toward the stage of globalization. The negation of this moment of capital overlapped with the passing of colonialism-cum-imperialism era in the interwar period, and the beginning of decolonization, following the disintegration of old European empires and the emergence of newly established countries and territories in the mid-twentieth century. Our historical marker, therefore, is the end of World War II and the inauguration of the postwar Pax Americana (1945–1979). The inauguration of the Pax Americana was simultaneous with the official conclusion of the *Pax Britannica*, an archaic colonial system that kept on life support and lived frantically on borrowed time since the beginning of the twentieth century. We call this the end of colonialism-cum-imperialism, the *first* phase of imperialism as a historical period.[79]

The *second* phase of imperialism (as a historical period) is the decolonized period of imperialism in which certain cartels and trusts could operate with impunity at the outset had eventually collapsed under their own weight to an internal change in competition. This conclusion is supported by the decartelization of the most notorious cartel in the twentieth century, namely, the International Petroleum Cartel, in the early 1970s.[80] Therefore, the postwar Pax Americana as a historical period, while thriving on certain cartels and trusts, it nevertheless played a significant role in the transformation and development of capitalism. Yet, this system, just like the vestige of trusts and cartels inside it, had the inadequate capacity and institutional relevance to carry the task of the transnationalization of capital, beyond the defunct Pax Americana into the global landscape. The postwar Pax Americana comprised of the hierarchical arrangement of nation-states that was also complicated by a sizable client states sub-system and fractured in the late 1970s, the tip of which was Iran and Nicaragua.[81]

The transnational capital has been a force much greater than the Pax Americana has; this force could not be confined within this outmoded and unsuitable vehicle, just as the Pax Britannica could not keep the burgeoning capitalism and the system of colonial administration long under one roof and thus was broken down by the hand of time. That is also the story of the disintegration of the Pax Americana, only that the global capitalism had overgrown a world order that led to its maturity toward the conquest of the mode of production in universality. As demonstrated amply in this volume, the Pax Americana exhausted the capacity of the postwar institutions and depleted their relevance by the end of the 1970s, as the tripartite moments of social capital turned into a universal social relation within, between, and beyond nation-states and across the global landscape. Accumulation on a global scale thus obtained its genuine historical connotation with the globalization of capital at large.[82]

Capital without motion, without circuits for transformation, is an aimless object—a "thing"; capital without accumulation is not *capital*; correspondingly, capital without the ability to change into unlimited objects in metamorphosis is no more than a heap of isolated objects of utility. Motionless capital is an artifice. Marx pointedly enunciated, "Capital is not a simple relation, but a *process*, in whose various moments it is always capital" (*Grundrisse*, p. 258, emphasis in original).[83] Similarly, the vision that perceives the moments (or forms) of capital merely in discrete expression, that is, free of transformation, is but in pursuit of the caricature of capitalism. By mere analogy, in the world of physics, say in quantum theory, one would not come across a motionless matter since without motion there is hardly any matter or material at the atomic or even subatomic level to speak of.

In a capitalist system, capital is but a social relation—an inseparable totality. To grasp the nature of this social relation requires a distinction between the form and the substance, the moment in the display from an indivisible whole itself, without an inkling of reduction. In other words, in the analysis of capital, it is not necessary to be an agent of added *fetishistic* mindset in a society in which the mode of production is already born in fetish. The accumulation of capital hinges upon (1) capital as a self-expanding value that perpetually subsists (and expands) on wage labor and (2) capital as a social relation, in motion and constant transformation. These conditions chart the trajectory of capital in the overcoming of all barriers, particularly overcoming of limits of the nation-states across the space and geography of production. The trouncing of these limits is the transmogrifying story of being and becoming capital as a historically unique social relation. These limits are milestones surmounted by trajectories of the advancement of capital, which finally peaked in globalization.

Globalization, therefore, is an epoch of the fulfillment of *capital* an epoch that, in methodological terms, embodies the fabric of history and geography of capitalism in an organic and contradictory unity, an immense force much, much greater than the sum of its parts in geopolitics or any other subscales or subjects today.[84] Transnational, as opposed to "multinational" or *inter*national, capital not only transcends boundaries of nation-states but also boundaries of disciples and sub-disciplines today when it comes to interdisciplinary and transdisciplinary investigation. In this connection, it is critical not to fall for studies that commence with the real appearance of state and power and conclude with the reality of state and power in themselves, and worse, to add an insult to injury, convey with pride that the state was brought back in.[85] Certain sociopolitical schools of thought, namely, World-Systems perspective, are also assembled in their inner core on the panorama of administrative power, thus overlooking the in-built disposition of social relations in capitalism proper. In this light, nation and the nation-state, among other phenomena, are entities in mutability and state of flux, the fluidity of which entails recurrent changes from being to becoming. The seemingly same nation in the 1970s—assuming it remains intact—is not necessarily the same "nation" in the 2020s. These boundaries are sacrosanct only to the myopic vision of nationalism and untutored eyes of tourists who visit them often in causal encounters. Despite all this, the mystery of *globalization* is that it ironically flourishes on such negated, yet intuited and observed barriers, as un undivided social relation universally. Such universality of course accompanies worldwide with uneven development intranationally and internationally, a law that now uniquely operates across the worldwide geography of production.

Notwithstanding all this, it is imperative to note that speaking of transnationalization of capital does not amount to the end or abolition of nation-states as some anti-global, nation-centered, or closeted nationalist scholars led us to believe. Making of the modern nation-state and the issues surrounding the state's politico-economic disposition has been the primary task of capitalism itself from the outset. Yet, as capitalism advanced, the state's disposition and "materiality" had also changed markedly. And, in this very context, brandishing imperialism as a weapon of choice, in as-if-an-era in perpetuity, is nothing short of bashful nationalism and bourgeois obfuscation in a clumsy cloak of contending "radicalism." The epoch of globalization transformed the materiality of the nation-state from top to bottom via cumulative overcoming of nearly all barriers—including the juridical and geography of the nation-state—by capital, toward sweeping shifts in the corporeality of the world capitalism. In the same vein, transnationalization is the negation of *inter*nationalization and thus the earlier centrality of the nation-state, given the tripartite negation of state by global social capital. Thus, globalization is none other than the *study* of the fabric of capitalist social relations (in worldwide accumulation, periodic crises, and intranational and international class polarization) dialectically and universally across the entire planet.[86]

Globalization: A Critique of Uneven and Combined Development

This section offers a brief critical note on "uneven and combined development" (UCD), a popular phrase that is frequently utilized in the traditional left literature, particularly in economic development, international relations and geopolitics. At first blush, an allusion to UCD, particularly concerning its overuse in economic development and international relations literature, appears like a straightforward Marxian concept. Yet, given the context of the self-expansion of capital and the arguments made earlier, in this case, neither the popularity nor the appearance should be a source of confidence and endorsement of this overused epiphenomenon. The expression of "combined" and "uneven development," not unlike a rider tied to an insurance policy, is dutifully cobbled together in nearly all Trotskyist literature on the left. However, an allusion to "combined" is a clear indication that Marx's law of value and self-expansion of capital, as value (and social and material manifestation), was understood poorly and uncritically by the original instigator of uneven and combined development (UCD), Leon Trotsky, and the many followers and promoters of this phrase.

The context and the potentiality-turned-to-actuality of self-expansion of capital beyond national boundaries in intranational and international unevenness is a universal tendency beyond most nation-centered theories that aspire to explicate the expansion of capital to the international arena, via UCD. Yet, in methodological terms, the piggyback of "combined" is neither authentic nor necessary.[87] Embedded in Marx's value theory, self-expansion of capital is uneven both within and between nations. The law of uneven development operates in both an *intensive* and *extensive* fashion. It operates in both deepening and widening modes, in and out of national boundaries. It is a tendency of the self-expansion of capital toward globalization. This also defines the universality of uneven development and capital's self-expansion in the mirror of globalization. Methodologically, UCD is but a mental construct that obscures the embeddedness of capital's self-expansion as a social relation and the organic nature of uneven development à la Marx. Let us hear from Leon Trotsky himself in the passage that follows:

> Unevenness, *the most general law of historic process*, reveals itself most sharply and complexly in the destiny of the backward countries. Under the whip of external necessities, their backward culture is compelled to make leaps. From the universal law of unevenness thus derives another law which, for the lack of a better name, we may call *the law of combined development*—by which we mean a drawing together of the different stages of journey, a combing of the separate steps, an amalgam of archaic with more contemporary forms. Without this law, to be taken of course in its whole material content, it is impossible to understand the history of Russia, and indeed of *any country of the second, third, or tenth cultural class*.
>
> (*History of the Russian Revolution*, p. 5, emphases added)[88]

The previous passage, aside from being a generalized recipe for the caricature of development, confirms the origins of this secondary "law"—the law of "combined" development—a frivolous appendage that ever since unjustly tied to Marx's law of uneven development; uneven development is a fully sufficient effect of Marx's law of value that manifests the trajectory and cumulative footprints of the expansion of capital within and between the nation-states. It is instructive that on this issue Trotsky does not merely speak for Russia: he broadly speaks for an entire mass of humanity in the world that at the time neither lived in capitalism proper nor had a clue on what capitalism would look like, in no uncertain terms. The subsequent points intend to show Trotsky's peculiar methodology in the absence of mediation in theorization, (false) impression of "uneven development" as a *footing* rather than a *manifestation*, and the lack of appreciation of Marx's theory of value, self-expansion of capital, and Marx's method of investigation.

1. Unevenness is the "general law of history," not a specific law in the context of a capitalist society according to the theory of value. This unevenness could be about the deep divide under the reign of Cleopatra VII, Queen of the Ptolemaic Kingdom of Egypt, or the class division in the twenty-first-century United States. Here, the transhistorical view of Trotsky is unmistakable.
2. The "universal law" of unevenness derives "another law," namely, "the law of combined development" (LCD). Here, the status of this secondary "law" is also up in the air, with no speck of a *context* in the specificity of capitalism. Indeed, by invoking the so-called law of combined development, Trotsky (1) camouflages the self-expansion of capital beneath the appendage of "combined," (2) misidentifies "unevenness" as a universal law and by doing so reduces the diverse modes of production in history to their sheer appearances, (3) trivializes capitalism proper and the organic

self-expansion of capital in colonial terms and in context of the "primitive accumulation," and (4) generates an illusion of illumination that extends beyond his own time and pointlessly obfuscate the transnationalization of capital and specificity of the law of value.

3. Given the *panoramic* context of purported "second law"—that is, LCD—the amalgam of "archaic" and "contemporary" quickly turns into a tautological construct that by necessity must revert to the transhistorical law of unevenness itself. In consequence, aside from the political embellishment of Trotsky's supporters, the so-called law of combined development (LCD) itself is but by fiat.
4. The picture alluded to by the "amalgam of archaic with more contemporary forms" is merely a state of affairs that not only relates to revolutionary Russia but also purports to cover the entire world. Trotsky is explicit as to how to deal with this state of affairs; Trotsky points out: "[u]nder the whip of external necessities . . . culture is compelled to make leaps." Those who have studied enough of the pertinent documents and are cognizant of the debates over the New Economic Policy in the immediate period after the 1917 Russian Revolution should have no illusion about the urgency of capitalist development under the guise of the centralized soviet state. In this context, it is imperative to note that the reference to *unevenness* (with or without the piggyback of "combined") invoked by Trotsky was not the same as the uneven development effected by Marx's law of value. These two are different kettles of fish within two different oceans. The point here is a hint at the *difference* of observable phenomenon of uneven development and the theoretical foundation of uneven deployment in the capitalist mode of production. There is little to nothing in Trotsky's own writings on this issue that could convincingly prove otherwise.
5. Those familiar with the literature on the debate between Marxists, on the one hand, and neo-Ricardians (and Sraffians), on the other, must remember the primary point of contention, namely, the focus on the sphere of *production* as opposed to the sphere of *distribution* in the analysis of capitalism. The primacy of production (and articulation with other spheres) over distribution was on the grounds of the distinction between the mode of appearance and the inner dynamics that necessarily lead to such appearances. Thus, a genuine study of capitalism cannot rely on distribution alone. This lesson is also relevant to our critique of Trotsky as to the notion of unevenness. It is then apparent that even if Trotsky were cognizant of his oversight on the panoramic view of history and had revised his notion of unevenness to the specificity of capitalism, he would and could not have been off the hook, so to speak, owing to the insufficiency of unevenness (alone) on the plane of appearance. The same criticism is also relevant to his so-called law of combined development.
6. Without exception, the previous contentions point toward the analysis of real appearances alone, on the part of Trotsky, which then turned to be

delivered as a conclusion. In other words, there is no *theory* here, aside from a detailed account of raw history.

7. Thus, the studies, particularly in global development, geopolitics, and international relations, that would either rely fully on or somehow intersect with the panoramic edict of "uneven and combined development" could not be immune from egregious methodological blunder embedded in this epiphenomenon. A parallel comparison in this case could be the neo-Ricardian approach to theorization in political economy in which the attempt at validation would linger rather tautologically on the surface of the subject under investigation. Trotsky's "uneven and combined development" is not unlike a variation on the same theme and shares a similar predicament. Moreover, the conquest of the mode of production invoked by Marx is a separate proposition that methodologically necessitates the *theory of value*, without which it would turn into an empty shell. On the other hand, as has been shown in this chapter and elsewhere, the allusion to "uneven and combined development" (or "uneven development" without the piggyback) is merely invoking a state of affairs—a descriptive status empty of standing as a *category*—which also lacks a standing (intermediate or otherwise) within Marx's or Marxian theoretical structure.

In this context, the failure of certain revolutionaries, particularly in the 1920s transition, who also badly stumbled on Marx's value theory and methodology is quite understandable.[89] But it is beyond comprehension to witness time and again persistent attempts at resuscitation of certain misleading notions of this period by the traditional leftists, generation after generation, time after time, occasion after occasion in the name of Marxism. Yet, for the sake of completeness, it would be justified to identify the strongest of the arguments in defense of Trotsky's UCD, a further attempt at amelioration of its transhistorical character, before offering a critical retort. Here, Sam Ashman's tenor of argument and delineation of the subject stand out. To uphold the continuity of the materials in this chapter, the points of contention and the critical comments are kept in the endnotes.[90] The so-called law of uneven development-cum-combined development is not unlike the tale of a dead horse whose beating does not produce a sign of getting up; this should be an eye-opener for both the partisan and the reflexive users of the term among radical left, in the view of abundantly available literature on the dynamics of intranational, international, and transnational expansion of capital within a Marxian value-theoretic framework. To be sure, UCD is neither a valid theory, an authentically abstracted concept, nor a fitting *concrete* to be utilized as a proper point of departure; UCD is a mere *mental construct* that tends to avoid detection by camouflaging as an impression of a theory (or a law) and thus infect the analysis through deceit. Here is where Marx's method of theorization turns out to be handy for the detection of both falsity and fakery, beyond the preconceived ideology and doctrinaire politics.

Concluding Remarks

By placing the so-called golden age of capitalism within the context discussed earlier, one could view the ascending phase of the Pax Americana together with the onset of the negation of the nation-state by the *productive* moment of capital.[91] This initiates capital in its tripartite negation (of the nation-state), given that the postwar Pax Americans functioned as an interstate system composed of a hierarchy of nation-states under American hegemony. It is no coincidence that the ascending phase of the Pax Americana should overlap the nascent phase of the tripartite negation, the time in which all three moments (and respective circuits) of capital were tending toward transnationalization. In other words, the ascending (or hegemonic) phase of the Pax Americana would coincide with the early period in which transnationalization of capital was still in its nascent phase before turning into a universal social relation by proliferating across the world. This period is the "golden age" of the United States, an age that the postwar interstate institutions were on the ascent and the order itself was up to the task of international hegemony.

The international monetary system under Bretton Woods (1944–1971) was the cornerstone of this ascendancy, and Marshall Plan and the cartelized oil under the International Petroleum Cartel (channeling cheap oil from the Middle East and elsewhere) dutifully bankrolled the economic reconstruction of Europe and Japan. At the same time, the worldwide land reform programs, designed in Washington, stood as the bedrock of development in the so-called Third World and the client subsystem of the Pax Americana. In this period of ascent, decolonization and nominal independence of the former colonies were the backdrops of the postwar order. Hence, the "golden age" was the composite of far-reaching socioeconomic transformation, including a growing tendency toward transnationalization of capital, that correspondingly punctuated with diehard imperialistic features manifested through foreign policy and Cold War ideology, in the mix.

The eclipse of the "golden age" lies not in the policy—the failure of postwar Keynesianism as the manifestation of the same apparatus was an effect—but in the collapse of socioeconomic and geopolitical institutions of the postwar Pax Americana which in turn led to the loss of the American hegemony. The tendency to breakdown was beginning to take shape in the late 1960s, with the Bretton Woods international monetary system in disintegration and the crisis of decartelization and globalization of oil around the corner. The collapse of Bretton Woods manifested the visible tip of the immense decline that in due time would reverberate across the foundation of the postwar system, leaving behind the façade, the skeleton, and the ideological huff-and-puff, to linger awhile in a decade or two or longer. This speaks loud and clear on the fallacious challenges by those who bestow upon "geopolitics" a defining primacy, a *primum mobile* of epochal change that underpins both politics and international affairs. Considering the arguments presented earlier, seeking out to explicate global change by geopolitics is but a tautological undertaking, the circularity of which should not be hard to decipher by serious scholars in political economy and global affairs. After all, to follow Marx's method, economy and polity are but the two inseparable, interwoven aspects of capitalism as a social relation. Likewise, the reader should have learned by now that the argument here is not about either the "purity" of capitalism or the denial of "materiality" of the nation-state.

The essential point in this chapter is the recognition of the modern nation-state, on the one hand, and the steady loss of its *centrality* (as opposed to its *materiality* or existence), on the other hand, by the historical evolution of forceful tendencies of social relations in global capitalism. One should be both politically and methodologically indifferent to have seen the hierarchical (nation-state) structure of the Pax Americana go by the wayside and would obstinately deny that an implosion of this political magnitude could not have provoked both the transforming and transmogrifying consequences on the disposition of the nation-state. Thus, sanctioning the materiality of state, while need not be the same as the essentialist verdict of perpetual centrality of state, is indubitably compatible with the globalization thesis. Besides, one-sided insistence on the so-called materiality of state in this fashion needs a reminder that Marx's commodity fetishism is also the tip of larger *fetishism* embedded in all state institutions and the nation-state itself since the capitalist state is an institutional *form* of *essential* relations in a capitalist society. Thus, the materiality of the state is one thing, and the fetish-like deployment of such materiality is quite another.[92] The tripartite negation of social capital is the outcome of dialectical unity and contradiction with the modern capitalist state which eventually turned the latter into a transmogrified body beyond a domain of traditional and domestic capital/labor relations, the tendency toward debordering, and global accumulation. This inner permeability of state is but an organic effect of globalization of capital, notwithstanding the outlook of the state in the realm of appearance.[93] Thus, the capitalist state, like any other institution in capitalism, tends to metamorphose from potentiality to actuality along the evolutionary frontiers of materialist history. Finally, there is no denying that the development of capitalism in different countries and regions of the world has been diverse and different from each other; indeed, at the first blush, there are as many capitalisms in many countries around. Yet, from the standpoint of capital (as a social relation), all these countries and regions were in one way or another subject to the universal overcoming and thus organic transnationalization of capital. Yet to declare that these countries have different "capitalisms" is an argument on the *form* and not the *substance* of social relations.[94] Here, the uniqueness of the present period of world history is also a quintessential argument that elucidated in this chapter.

The question of *multipolarity* is also deeply rooted within capital as a potential universal social relation that now turned into a manifold actuality. Such universalization is likewise a reminder that capital can simply exist in multiplicity in national, international, and transnational circumstances, that is, from embryonic form to global manifestation. Thus, the present tendency for multipolarity in the emerging global polity is not merely political but also *structural*, a unique historical transformation that distinctively mirrors the *multiplicity* of capital as a social relation. This was through a series of barrier-breaking, transmogrifying, historically specific journeys beyond the limitations of any nation-state across the planet. It is worth reiterating that the current red-hot issues on multipolarity stand squarely on the innate multiplicity of capital, as a social relation. Such multiplicity stems from the inner nature of capital which has no resemblance to a common taxonomy based on arbitrary struggles among nations, transitory changes of political power, or national capacities and limits, all of which tend to emerge randomly or by contingency as a classification, devoid of theoretical suitability for periodization of the capitalist mode of production. This point once again is not only *methodological*—a safeguard against sliding into historicity, speculative deduction, or exigency—but also *political*, consistent with the corporeality of globalization entwined with the new balance of power suitable for worldwide multipolar polity.

At the very end of the declining chapter of the Pax Americana, the transnationalization of capital underpinned the tectonic plates that moved the ground from beneath the postwar Pax Americana, and by implication overthrown the United States from the throne of international hegemony for good. As noted earlier, the interstate economic and political institutions that once carried the American hegemony had gone by the wayside, starting with the Bretton Woods monetary system, even though virtually all of them remain to this day in the name alone and a façade of that which once stood. This inner dynamic epochal change also changed the balance of political power and contour and quality of the polity in the making forever and thus triggered the deceiving immense nostalgia that bulged and long accumulated within the American leadership and political class. The fall of the Soviet Union emboldened the United States and unsurprisingly intensified a false sense of nostalgia for global supremacy as an alleged rising power by the defunct hegemon. This context is unequivocally critical for appreciation of (1) the irreversible fall of the American-centered world, (2) the irreversible decline of the United States, with or without foreign offensives,[95] (3) the naiveté of the many on the radical left by equating the United States with globalization (via neoliberalism), and worse, upholding the neoliberalism as a pseudo-epoch of capitalism and unwisely swinging at globalization by mocking the counterfeits, and (4) the hyper-Orwellian and pugnacious quality of the US foreign policy, particularly after the loss of hegemony.[96] This is a short clip from the longer story of the "engine of the world economy" whose fortune was revered ironically with the onset globalization of capital in the span of less than four decades (1944–1979).[97]

Thus, the breakdown (and indeed redundancy) of postwar institutions one by one, following the globalization of capital turned in full swing as the hierarchical interstate structure of the postwar order disintegrated from within. This was done without any recourse, without any preventive measures, without any policy antidotes, without any deliberate actions by the "executive committee of the bourgeoisie," or for that matter without volition of the state that for decades held the mantle of hegemony. Here, the larger-than-life image of inner contradictions grander and more potent than any *state* is now standing before us. And those hesitant to see the grand topography of *capital* as a universal social relation are condemned to the limits of fragmented reality, disintegrated theoretical intuition, and patchy methodology.[98] The *order* that held, babysat, and nurtured the transnationalization of capital had finally acceded to a set of transformative dynamics with unintended consequences. The genie's escape from the proverbial bottle was not only the final act, so to speak, but also a milestone that ended American exceptionalism. Again, as William Shakespeare once reminded us, "What is done cannot be undone."[99] The next global order, however, awaits to be built afresh. This should include proper disposal of the ruins and remnants of the postwar institutions and seats of defunct hegemony in order not to contaminate the future.[100] Nevertheless, apart from present disorderly power projection and frequent mischief-making uproars in response to displacement of global power,[101] the world had already disembarked on a new post-American polity in the making.

Notes

1 For instance, see Gupte, Pranay 2004. "Ronald Reagan, Father of Globalization": www.pranaygupte.com/article.php?index=85, retrieved: December 31, 2021. Such a parody, albeit in its lesser scandalous tone, abounds in the think tanks and right-wing media. Of course, such propaganda has two manipulative and misleading aims: (1) that the market ideologies embedded in what is known as neoliberalism are globalization and (2) that the parody of "globalization," so defined, is what is out there and there is no such thing presently as genuine globalization in terms of the conquest of the mode of production globally. Unfortunately, many on the radical left (including Marxists) appear to have fallen for this rather uncomplicated hoax.

2 See Bhagwati, Jagdish 2007. *In Defense of Globalization*. New York: Oxford University Press. This is a view of a more sober scholar that speaks for neoliberalism and the neoclassical economic paradigm—a paradigm that in economic and non-economic terms long dominated, particularly, the disciplines of sociology, international relations, and media studies. However, within the neoclassical economics paradigm, there is another variation on the theme by Stiglitz who despite being steeped in the same methodological caricature, nevertheless appeals to "imperfect information," to depart a little without ever leaving this farcical Alice-in-Wonderland worldview behind. Thus, Stiglitz's "globalization" is a caricature of the caricature itself. See Stiglitz, Joseph E. 2002. *Globalization and Its Discontents*. New York: W.W. Norton & Company. For a detailed critique of Stiglitz's view of economics and policy application, see Fine, Ben and Elsa Van Waeyenberge 2005. "Correcting Stiglitz: From Information to Power in the World of Development," in *Socialist Register 2006: Telling the Truth*. Leo Panitch and Colin Leys (eds.). London: The Merlin Press: 146–168.

3 See Buckman, Greg 2004. *Globalization: Tame It or Scrap It?* New York: Zed Books; Singh, Kavaljit 2005. *Questioning Globalization*. New York: Zed Books; Bello, Walden 2004 [2002]. *Deglobalization: Ideas for a New World Economy*. Update Edition. New York: Zed Press. These three books are a sample of numerous volumes written by the left of the center scholars whose eclectic methodology does not allow them to distinguish between the ontological character of capital (and capitalism) and that of policy, strategy, or doctrine, thus succumbing to petty-bourgeois cynicism and the confusion over the

periodization of capitalism and its global stage. Unfortunately, these progressive souls function in a mode of appearance, a worldview adjacent to the theoretical territory of orthodoxy, and play ironically by the same playbook, albeit in a transposed mode, in bourgeois epistemology.

4 For a critical assessment of the US neoliberal policies labeled Washington Consensus and post-Washington Consensus, see Fine, Ben, Costas Lapavitsas, and Jonathan Pincus 2001. *Beyond the Post-Washington Consensus*. London: Routledge; Fine, Ben and Alfredo Saad-Filho 2014. "Politics of Neoliberal Development: Washington Consensus and the post-Washington Consensus," in *The Politics of Development: A Survey*. Heloise Weber (ed.), London: Routledge: 154–166.

5 See Krauthammer, Charles 1990. "The Unipolar Moment," *Foreign Affairs* 70 (1): 23–33, www.jstor.org/stable/20044692?origin=crossref, retrieved: December 31, 2021; Ikenberry, G. John, Michael Mastanduno, and William C. Wohlforth 2009. "Introduction: Unipolarity, State Behavior, and Systematic Consequences," *World Politics* 81 (1), January: 1–27; Ryan, Maria 2018. "The Rise and Demise of American Unipolarism: Neoconservatives and Foreign Policy," *American Studies Journal* 65 (8), www.asjournal.org/65-2018/the-rise-and-demise-of-american-unipolarism-neoconservatism-and-us-foreign-policy-1989-2009/, retrieved: December 31, 2021. These are a sample of neocon, anti-neocon, and the middle-of-the-road protagonists on the geopolitics of unipolarity by orthodoxy. As can be seen from each of these articles, the context of American power was treated in axiomatic and skin-deep fashion without a fundamental socioeconomic change that was brought to bear by the epoch of globalization.

6 See Wikan, Vilde Skorpen 2015. "What is 'Neoliberalism', and How Does It Relate to Globalization," *E-International Relations*? May 21, www.e-ir.info/2015/03/21/what-is-neoliberalism-and-how-does-it-relate-to-globalization/, retrieved: December 31, 2021. This article is a typical echo of the liberal and leftist view in which globalization is misidentified as a "product" of neoliberalism. Reinsberg, Bernhard, Alexander Kentikelenis, and Thomas Stubbs 2021. "Creating Crony Capitalism: Neoliberal Globalization and the Fueling of Corruption," *Socio-Economic Review* 19 (2), April: 607–634. Given the amalgamation of globalization and neoliberalism, this article is also stranded in the cul-de-sac of IMF.

7 For trivialization of "globalization," see Sachs, Jeffrey D. 2020. *The Ages of Globalization*. New York: Columbia University Press; Michie, Jonathan 2017. *Advanced Introduction to Globalization*. Cheltenham, UK: Edward Elgar.

8 For the typical source, see Bello, Walden 2004 [2002]. *Deglobalization: Ideas for a New World Economy*. Update Edition. New York: Zed Press.

9 It should be reminded of concern over the deepening of poverty due to the transnationalization of capital, on the one hand, and imposition of neoliberal policies across the world, on the other, recounted in Bello's *Deglobalization* and the like, is not only truly justified but must also be critically appreciated by anyone with a modicum of compassion and humanity. Nevertheless, the point here is to penetrate the root cause (that is, materialist inconsistencies and underpinning contradictory interests) of all these widespread calamities, rather than belaboring the effects, and then cursing the mode of appearance of such policies. A significant ideological instance in the mis-presentation of truth about world poverty—a deepening effect of globalization—can be seen in Reddy, Sanjay G. 2005. "Counting the Poor: The Truth About World Poverty Statistics," in *Socialist Register 2006: Telling the Truth*. Leo Panitch and Colin Leys (eds.). London: The Merlin Press: 169–178.

10 There is a near mythological view that divides the world into "globalism" and "localism," fetish-like and in a false dichotomy. This view is motivated by the repercussion of the post-structurist tendencies in social sciences, revealed in postmodernism, exemplified in Hardt and Negri's *Empire*—a parody of globalization. See Hardt, Michael and Antonio Negri 2000. *Empire*. Cambridge, MA: Harvard University Press. Equally

farcical is the view that still habitually divides the world into three parts, namely, First, Second, and Third World, thus misrepresenting the formidable transformation of the world as a whole since once upon a time such characterizations had a social or material reality.

11 See Desai, Radhika 2010. "The Absent Geopolitics of Pure Capitalism," *World Review of Political Economy* 1 (3), Fall: 463–484. Without an agreement in support of either side of this article, it is remarkable that Desai here mocks the grounding of "geopolitics" presented by opponents as "pure" and promotes eclectic narratives exemplified in Desai, Radhika 2013. *Geopolitical Economy: After US Hegemony, Globalization and Empire*. London: Pluto Press.

12 In Marx, Karl 1981 [1894]. *Capital*, Vol. III. New York: Vintage Edition, Ch. 24, Marx speaks of interest-bearing capital as "the superficial form of the capital relation," a fetish that produces "more money, self-valorizing value, without the process that mediates the two extremes[,]" that is, M-M' (p. 515). On p. 516, Marx is explicit that "In the form of interest-bearing capital, capital *appears* immediately in this form, unmediated by the production and circulation process. Capital *appears* as a mysterious and self-creating source of interest, of its own increase" (emphases added). Our emphasis here is to show that so far as the so-called *financialization* relates to this epiphenomenon, it constitutes within *mode of appearance* and thus its universal manifestation must reveal a larger and deeper all-encompassing transformation of capitalism at the global scale and at the limits of the geography of production. Another pertinent point of intertwined significance concerning "financialization" is the development of the complex transnational network of the credit system, including the whole sub-system of financial derivatives that since the 1980s were proliferated without any regulation, toward the creation of *fictitious capital*, anticipated and initially (if potentially and in embryonic form) theorized by Marx (see *Capital*, Vol. III, Ch. 25).

13 "Golden Age of capitalism" is a euphemism limited to the rise of the postwar Pax Americana just before the latter's fall in the late 1970s. It basically capitalizes on the centrality of the US economy in the postwar period.

14 Neoliberalism comprises a set of economic policies and political strategies that first was revealed in the early 1970s as the "Keynesian Counterrevolution." Keynesian Revolution refers to the set of policies and strategies deployed against the Great Depression of 1929–1939, and since the postwar period guided the inter-state system of Pax Americana through its rising phase. Although Keynesianism and neoliberalism hold a distinct period of the history of their own, it would be an egregious mistake to periodize capitalism on that basis. A guanine periodization for capitalism should be beyond the "raw" history of policies, strategies, doctrines, etc., or their manifestation as such, since focusing on the latter is little more than a tautological expression.

15 It is next to impossible to produce a genuine theory of periodization for capitalism out of *geopolitics* alone. In other words, geopolitics, without a firm grounding in capitalism and thus in the inner dynamics of capital (as a social relation), remain a skin-deep subject, which is often absorbed in tautological narratives.

16 The "global north/global south" is a peculiar expression that brings the specter of "dependency" and the center/periphery out in the open with a posturing qualification, "global." It is indeed a whimsical expression of globalization, despite globalization. Why whimsical? Because it is ingenuine to explicate the same division by expressing the same division itself. And yet, sadly, very many traditional leftists subscribe to this circular reasoning.

17 A genuine theory of the periodization of the capitalist mode of production, although mediated by overcoming the manifold barriers through the self-expansion of capital within the nation-state, essentially should constitute the negation of the geographical boundaries of the nation-state in commodity (in trade), money (in finance), and production, that is, sequential negation by all three moments of capital. In other words,

an authentic theory must be internal to capital and its potential-turned-to-actual universalization of capital as a social relation across the globe. Other delineations, such as historical transformation, qualitative change in state apparatus, inter-state system, namely, the colonial Pax Britannica, the era of imperialism, postwar Pax Americana, or policies, doctrines, and strategies thereof that may have overlapped the moments of capital in self-expansion earlier mentioned, are but contingent. All these may be necessary but not sufficient for a genuine theory of periodization reflective of an inner dynamic of capital in its universal conquest of the mode of production. To be sure, in the context of historical materialism, "raw" history cannot be explicated by itself, in a mode of appearance; it would remain at most, a *manifestation*—short of its pertinent essence.

18 One may refer to the writings by those scholars on the "dependency theory" and "center/periphery" view of capitalism who now offer the same contents by turning to global north/global south euphemism. See Amin, Samir 1992. *Empire of Chaos*. New York: Monthly Review Press; Amin, Samir 2013. *The Implosion of Contemporary Capitalism*. New York: Monthly Review Press.

19 Marx, Karl 1977 [1867]. *Capital*, Vol. I. New York: Vintage Edition. Implicit in this volume is both essentially intended at the macroscopic and transnational view of capitalism, despite a few occasional instances to the contrary, that is, capital in *potential* universality.

20 Competition in the context of Marx's value theory is an outcome of a synthesis that increases in turbulence with concentration and centralization of capital. See Marx, Karl 1955 [1847]. *The Poverty of Philosophy*. Moscow: Progress Publishers, Ch. 2, sec. 3: 126–134. This view of competition is implicit in all three volumes of *Capital* and the traces of which can be seen particularly in *Grundrisse*.

21 Marx, Karl 1977 [1867]. *Capital*, Vol. I. New York: Vintage Edition, Ch. 1 (The Commodity), sec. 4 (The Fetishism of Commodity and Its Secret): 163–177.

22 The mother of all cost-cuttings in capitalism is but the cheapening of *labor power*, particularly via centralization of capital and the incessant technological change.

23 The fiction of neoclassical economic competition, that is, "perfect competition," and its analog, "perfect monopoly," designate an idealized spectrum that defines competition without a smidgen of intersection with the truth in capitalism—a mode of production that is embedded and thriving on concentration and centralization of capital. This spectrum, however, operates just like the proverbial *procrustean bed*, cutting up and down and slicing the corporeal of capitalist competition to preordained size—in this case, into shades of *imperfect* (monopolistic) competition and those of the *oligopoly*. This view of competition, embarrassingly as it seems even by elementary school kids, is an official theory in neoclassical orthodoxy and the larger mainstream economics today. This absolute fakery, just like the pandemic coronavirus of 2020–2022, is also spread through heterodox economists, a great number of which is neither immune from this fraud nor vaccinated against a variant of the same virus, namely, monopoly capitalism. For an example of heterodox in name, see a short piece that is intended for review of recent my book by Payam Sharifi, a doctoral student at UMKC (a proud heterodox economics program): Bina, Cyrus 2013. *A Prelude to the Foundation of Political Economy: Oil, War, and Global Polity*. Basingstoke and New York: Palgrave Macmillan, p. 260; Sharifi, Payam 2016. "Book Review," *Review of Keynesian Economics* 4 (3), July: 360–362. Here, the author acts as an inquisitor of the neoclassical basilica to question Karl Marx (and yours truly) for not following the official orthodoxy on the competition. Of course, it takes two to tango, so to speak; the reader also should not be unconcerned about substandard quality of the review process in this newfound journal.

24 Market ideology has a manifold underpinning in mainstream economics; the most popular versions of it are deployed in perfect and imperfect markets. The irony is why other social sciences should be susceptible to such outlandish fabrications, with or without sugarcoating. For a noteworthy analysis on this issue, see Fine, Ben and Dimitris

Milonakis 2009. *From Economics Imperialism to Freakonomics: The Shifting Boundaries between Economics and Other Social Sciences*. London: Routledge.

25 For a vigorous critique of neoclassical economics orthodoxy, see Weeks, John 2012. *The Irreconcilable Inconsistencies of Neoclassical Macroeconomics: A False Paradigm*. New York: Routledge.

26 See Bina, Cyrus 2013b. *A Prelude to the Foundation of Political Economy: Oil, War, and Global Polity*. New York: Palgrave Macmillan, Ch. 5. This chapter, among others, is a critique of David Harvey's dichotomy of the geographical space, that is, the territory, from value theory.

27 A conspicuous example is Barro, Robert J. 1998. *Macroeconomics*. Fifth Edition. Cambridge, MA: The MIT Press. Here in this text, Daniel Defoe's *Robinson Crusoe* is very much alive and well.

28 See Jevons, William Stanley 1957 [1871]. *The Theory of Political Economy*. New York: Kelley and Macmillan; Menger, Carl 1950 [1871]. *Principles of Economics*. Glencoe, IL: Free Press; Walras, Léon 1954 [1874]. *Elements of Pure Economics*. Homewood, IL: Richard D. Irwin.

29 It is noteworthy that Margaret Thatcher and Ronal Reagans of this world do not grow on trees and by happenstance; at the end of his magnum opus, *General Theory*, John Maynard Keynes rather aptly stated: "Practical men [and women], who believe themselves to be quite exempt from any intellectual influence, are usually the slaves of some defunct economist. Madmen [madwomen] in authority, who hear voices in the air, are distilling their frenzy from some academic of a few years back" (p. 383). Keynes, John M. 1964 [1936]. *The General Theory of Employment, Interest, and Money*. New York: Harcourt, Brace & World Inc.

30 In the eyes of many on the radical left, neoliberalism was categorized as a cornerstone for periodization of capitalism, as opposed to Keynesianism, and by doing so created a fictitious background to obfuscate the globalization of capital and to hang on to the fetish of the nation-state as an immutable entity. The fact remains, however, that no periodization theory worthy of the name can be based on a mere sequence of history in capitalism, no matter how interesting or intriguing they may seem. Thus, one must search for a theoretical grounding that would disclose the inner dynamics of this history and not the other way around. Yet, the extent of intoxication of the radical left with the "epoch of neoliberalism" appears to have no conclusion. There is no shortage of examples on this issue; see Harvey, David 2005. *A Brief History of Neoliberalism*. New York: Oxford University Press; Fine, Ben and Alfredo Saad-Filho 2016. "Thirteen Things You Need to Know About Neoliberalism," *Critical Sociology* 43 (4–5): 685–706. This theoretical oversight often gives undue credence to such asinine arguments by the traditional left as if IMF or World Bank (the defunct and hollow institutions of the postwar Bretton Woods system) would be running the usual *hegemonic* show across the globe, at the behest of the United States, long after the collapse of the Pax Americana (1945–1979). Thus, a misplaced fixation on neoliberalism is not only an impairment in judgment but also a cause for numerous conceptual obfuscations.

31 See Marglin, Stephen A. and Juliet B. Schor 1992. *The Golden Age of Capitalism: Reinterpreting Postwar Experience*. New York: Oxford University Press. This edited volume is limited to the analyses of the Keynesian policies of the postwar period and their success and their eventual failure.

32 At this juncture and throughout the 1980s, neither the right nor the left quite understood between the foundation and the facade of the postwar system or how the throne of hegemony (that is, US hegemony) squares with the unraveling of such foundation. The right triumphantly was busy celebrating Reagan's back-to-back presidency and the overwhelming majority on the left, particularly radical left, was treating the United States as if it were a permanent fixture of life as they knew it.

33 See Ghizoni, Sandra K. 1971. "Nixon Ends Convertibility of U.S. Dollars to Gold and Announces Wage/Price Controls," *Federal Reserve History*. www.federalreservehistory.org/essays/gold-convertibility-ends, retrieved: January 7, 2022.

34 See Bina, Cyrus, Laurie M. Clements, and Chuck Davis 2015 [1996]. *Beyond Survival: Wage Labor in the Late Twentieth Century*. New York: Routledge; Bina, Cyrus, and Chuck Davis 2015 [1996]. "Wage Labor and Global Capital: Global Competition and Universalization of the Labor Movement," in *Beyond Survival: Wage Labor in the Late Twentieth Century*. Cyrus Bina, Laurie Clements, and Chuck Davis (eds.), New York: Routledge: 19–47.

35 See Hobson, John A. 1902. *Imperialism: A Study*. London: James Nisbet & Co. Ltd. (electronic reprint: Google Books).

36 For a vigorous and detailed analysis of real competition in modern capitalism, see Shaikh, Anwar 2016. *Capitalism: Competition, Conflict, Crises*. New York: Oxford University Press, Part II, chapters: 7–11.

37 A sample can be found in Frank, Robert, Ben Bernanke, Kat Antonovics, and Ori Heffetz 2022. *Principles of Microeconomics*. Eighth Edition. New York: McGraw-Hill. For a radical critique of mainstream economics theory, see Weeks, John 2014. *Economics of the 1%: How Mainstream Economics Serves the Rich, Obscures Reality, and Distorts Policy*. London: Anthem.

38 Beyond the neoclassical school and outside of the Marxist camp, the influence of monopoly—and degree of monopoly with reference implicit to "perfect competition"—can be seen in the works of Kalecki and Steindl. See Kalecki, Michael 1939. *Essays in the Theory of Economic Fluctuations*. London: George Allen & Unwin; Kalecki, Michael 1943. *Studies in Economic Dynamics*. London: George Allen & Unwin; Steindl, Josef 1952. *Maturity and Stagnation in American Capitalism*. Oxford: Basil Blackwell.

39 Marx, Karl 1973 [1847]. *Poverty of Philosophy*. Moscow: Progress Publishers.

40 It is beyond dispute that Lenin's painstaking quarrel with Kautsky over the nature of imperialism (that is, epoch vs. policy) is a defining moment in the history of the radical left. Yet both Lenin and Kautsky overall were on the same page, so to speak, on the issue of Hobson's monopoly vs. Marx's (real) competition. The reason was that capitalism itself had changed, which of course opened Pandora's box on Marx's value-theoretic analysis of capitalism as opposed to the invention of emasculated, undialectical, and undeniably anti-Marx *monopoly capitalism*. That is why so many self-styled Marxists, such as Ernest Mandel, have been insistently hanging on the epiphenomenon of "development of underdevelopment" for too long while also clutching onto their perceived value theory by Marx. Today, the whole bunch of traditional leftists is doing the same thing with their tattered perpetuity of *imperialism* and tautology of the center/periphery turned global north/global south, in disguise.

41 Laurence Harris, the co-author of *Rereading 'Capital'* (with Ben Fine, Columbia University Press, 1979) presents a summary of periodization in capitalism in *A Dictionary of Marxist Thought* without mentioning Christian Palloix (1975, 1977). This omission was not accidental due to the peculiar atmosphere of Marxism despite Marx, which dutifully compelled many Marxist scholars to pay lip service (if not wholeheartedly) to monopoly. Harris, in *Rereading Capital*, also tends to periodize capitalism into "competitive, monopoly, and state monopoly" without realizing that such a division generates more heat than light, so to speak. Why? Because such a view does stay at the surface of the capitalist society, known as merely *manifestation*, and thus advertently or inadvertently instigates a tautological explanation. See Harris, Laurence 1983. "Periodization of Capitalism," in *A Dictionary of Marxist Thought*. Tom Bottomore (ed.), Cambridge, MA: Harvard University Press: 365–368. See also Palloix, Christian 1975. "The Internationalization of Capital and the Circuit of Social Capital," in *International Firms and Modern Imperialism*. Hugo Radice (ed.), London: Penguin: 63–88; Palloix, Christian 1977. "The Self-Expansion of Capital on a World Scale," *Review of Radical Political Economics*

9 (2): 1–28. In our opinion, these two sources are significant ingredients toward a genuine theory of periodization.

42 Lenin, Vladimir I. 1970 [1916]. *Imperialism: The Highest Stage of Capitalism*. Peking: Foreign Language Press.

43 Sweezy, Paul M. 1970 [1942]. *The Theory of Capitalist Development*. New York: Monthly Review Press; Baran, Paul A. and Paul M. Sweezy 1966. *Monopoly Capital*. New York: Monthly Review Press; Sweezy, Paul M. 1981. "Competition and Monopoly," *Monthly Review* 33 (1): 1–16.

44 See Hilferding, Rudolph 1981. *Finance Capital. A Study of the Latest Phase of Capitalist Development*. London: Routledge & Kegan Paul.

45 For a remarkable study of Hilferding's *Finance Capital* and its influence on the later "neo-Marxists" absorbed in monopoly capitalism, see Zoninsein, Jonas 1990. *Monopoly Capital Theory: Hilferding and Twentieth-Century Capitalism*. New York: Greenwood Press.

46 Without naming names, no amount of sugarcoating of Lenin's view of capitalism by the radical left, including some very known Marxists, would be judicious or wash with the reality today.

47 Luxemburg, Rosa 1968 [1913]. *The Accumulation of Capital*. New York: Monthly Review Press.

48 Luxemburg, Rosa 1968 [1913]. *The Accumulation of Capital*. New York: Monthly Review Press, p. 417.

49 Marx, Karl 1977 [1867]. *Capital*, Vol. I. New York: Vintage Edition; Marx, Karl 1981 [1885]. *Capital*, Vol. II. New York: Vintage Edition.

50 The so-called breakdown of capitalism suffers from two significant symptoms: (1) an epistemic blunder as to the perception of the capitalist mode of production and (2) a lapse in the possibility of its overthrow, without the precondition of collapse, and through praxis. The latter is an irony in the case of Luxemburg, who was among the greatest revolutionaries of the twentieth century.

51 Luxemburg, Rosa 1968 [1913]. *The Accumulation of Capital*. New York: Monthly Review Press, pp. 20–21.

52 See Bleaney, Michael 1976. *Underconsumption Theories: A History and Critical Analysis*. New York: International Publishers, Ch. 9: 193.

53 See Bellofiore, Riccardo 2009. *Rosa Luxemburg and the Critique of Political Economy*. London: Routledge. For a wonderful assessment of Luxemburg's view of capitalism, see a review of this book: Fine, Ben 2012. "Review Article: Revisiting Rosa Luxemburg's Political Economy," *Critique* 40 (3): 449–456.

54 This peculiar point has long been glossed over by the many supporters of Luxemburg, particularly those whose analyses would not exceed adequacy beyond impressions, appearances, and manifestation of capitalism.

55 The reference to globalization should not be mistaken for the rhetoric of "globalization" perpetrated by mainstream economic ideology and proliferated like mushrooms throughout the social sciences. To be sure, the core of capitalism in its globalized state is the transnationalization of capital and thus the application of Marx's value theory universally.

56 See Berle, Adolf A. and Gardner C. Means 1933. *The Modern Corporation and Private Property*. New York: Macmillan.

57 See Chandler, Alfred D., Jr. 1977. *The Visible Hand: The Managerial Revolution in American Business*. Cambridge, MA: Harvard University Press. This book is an emphatic *manifestation* of what is known as managerial capitalism by the orthodoxy itself. It is a manifestation because it deals with the real (that is, palpable) appearance of capitalism as it meets the eye, so to speak. In other words, it is the appearance that must be unstitched so that the inner dynamics of capital in concentration and centralization could be exposed according to Marx's method of analysis. We must remember that if the appearance of subjects under investigation coincided with their essences (that is,

their inner dynamics) we had not had any *science*—had we? This book, which among others, justifies the existence of cartels, is at best a wonderful *raw material* to sift through before a genuine analysis of the foundation of modern capitalism for two reasons: (1) to know what and how the orthodoxy itself thinks about and justifies capitalism and (2) to get hold of the mode of manifestation first before attempting at abstraction and disclosing the innermost dynamics. It is within such a Marxian framework that Duménil and Lévy's recent *Managerial Capitalism*—similarly a *manifestation*—should also be read and criticized. See Duménil, Gérard and Dominique Lévy 2018. *Managerial Capitalism: Ownership, Management & The Coming New Mode of Production*. London: Pluto Press.

58 For a remarkable outline of American capitalism, nearly at its peak, see Galbraith, John K. 1967. *The New Industrial State*. Boston, MA: Houghton Mifflin. Here, one can see the difference between an industrial economy as opposed to the caricature of shopkeepers' nation-state in clear view.

59 See Chapter 10, Marx, Karl 1976 [1867]. *Capital*, Vol. I. New York: Vintage Edition, pp. 340–416.

60 Theoretically and empirically, the *moment* of capital in money hand in hand with capital in productive form was fortified by such enriched *sociality* which of course could not have been accomplished without the active and purposeful ideological and political apparatuses of the capitalist state. The upshot of all this is (1) to make the accumulation of capital independent of the *wealth* that presupposed it and (2) to transform the stand-alone, discreet pockets of potential capital into a perpetual flow of de facto capital ready to be plowed back to the sphere of production toward the continuous production of surplus value.

61 As in the case of Working Day, here capitalism similarly overcomes the limit and discreteness of individual proprietors' lifetime by the perpetuity of corporate form.

62 Export of capital is a concrete act, itself a phenomenal form, a mode of manifestation that must be disclosed for further investigation of its innermost dynamics in money *moment* of capital, which cannot be fully explained by *imperialism*, a yet another concrete phenomenon in need of abstraction, particularly at this stage, that is, at the height of colonialism.

63 The phrase *social capital* here is originated with Marx's notion of social relation and the sociality of capital as a self-expanded value in capitalism. This should not be mistaken with quite unrelated parody, the off-the-cuff euphuism of "social capital" concocted by an offshoot of neoclassical economics via Putnam variety. See Putnam, Robert D. 2000. *Bowling Alone: The Collapse and Revival of American Community*. New York: Simon & Schuster.

64 See Bina, Cyrus 1985. *The Economics of the Oil Crisis*. New York: St. Martin's. Here, the historic collapse of the International Petroleum Cartel, and decartelization, and competitive globalization of the petroleum industry are for the first time theorized. As to globalization of the entire energy industry and the status of OPEC, see Bina, Cyrus 1989. "Competition, Control and Price Formation in the International Energy Industry," *Energy Economics* 11 (3): 162–168; Bina, Cyrus 1990. "Limits to OPEC Pricing: OPEC Profits and the Nature of Global Oil Accumulation," *OPEC Review* 14 (1): 55–73; Bina, Cyrus and Minh Vo 2007. "OPEC in the Epoch of Globalization: An Event Study of Global Oil Prices," *Global Economy Journal* 7 (1): 1–49.

65 See Bina, Cyrus 2006. "The Globalization of Oil: A Prelude to a Critical Political Economy," *International Journal of Political Economy* 35 (2): 4–34.

66 The conventional wisdom for many of the left, particularly leftist of the traditional stripe with an unbounded obsession with the primacy of the nation-state, endlessly squabbling against globalization as if the latter is alien to the former. Many in this group are hesitant as to the use of "transnationalization," instead of internationalization, even if the context, not the relation of the two or more nations, is the subject of investigation. While these tendencies are not the same in emphasis or ideological motivation, the vast

majority is unable to see that the very context of globalization of capital is preconditioned by overcoming the geography of the nation-state, and that such overcoming need not produce a dichotomy between globalization and the nation-state by fiat.

67 Marx, Karl 1981 [1894]. *Capital,* Vol. III. New York: Vintage Edition.

68 See Harvey, David 2003. *The 'New' Imperialism.* Oxford: Oxford University Press; Harvey, David 2011. "The Urban Roots of Financial Crises: Reclaiming the City for Anti-Capitalist Struggle," in *Socialist Register 2012.* Leo Panitch, Gregory Albo, and Vivek Chibber (eds.), London: Merlin Press: 1–35.

69 For a critique of Harvey's view on competition and his superficial partition of "history" and "territory," see Bina, Cyrus 2013b. *A Prelude to the Foundation of Political Economy: Oil, War, and Global Polity.* New York: Palgrave Macmillan, Ch. 5, sec. (Orthodoxy and the Euthanasia of Capitalist Competition): 144–147.

70 Marx, Karl 1981 [1894]. *Capital,* Vol. III. New York: Vintage Edition.

71 Today, many on the *traditional* left across nearly all political and ideological stripes tend to exhibit the influence of Hobson's view of competition and monopoly in bifurcation and as a display of a state of affairs, rather than as the inner dynamics of capital accumulation toward concentration and centralization. This legacy is not different from the neoclassical theory of market structure, a construct linked to a spectrum of perfect competition/perfect monopoly.

72 Aside from its Austrian faction, the Marginalist Revolution played a firm backdrop for modern neoclassical economics to idealize competition as "perfect" to be contrasted with equally idealized "perfect" monopoly in a mental construct of a theory of market structure. The sad part of this farcical ploy is that the same idealized spectrum sets a standard for the variants in duopoly (remember Sweezy's "Kinked Demand Curve"!) and oligopoly, a tragic parallel for leftists predisposed to *monopoly capitalism.*

73 See Lewis, Arthur 1954. "Economic Development with Unlimited Supplies of Labor," *The Manchester School* 22 (2): 139–191. Despite the criticism by the antagonists mostly confined to the neoclassical economics paradigm, this article anticipated the policies that were in the pipeline, so to speak, in the mid-twentieth century concerning the eradication and rationalization of pre-capitalist agriculture resulting in a reservoir of new migrant labor moving to the emerging urban industries across the developing world.

74 See Bina, Cyrus and Behzad Yaghmaian 1988. "Import Substitution and Export Promotion within the Context of the Internationalization of Capital," *Review of Radical Political Economics* 20 (2–3): 234–240.

75 Concerning such developments, it should be reminded that invoking the catchphrase, "uneven and combined development," habitually, or perhaps dutifully as certain political creed within the radical left does, is not only superfluous but also little more than a tautology.

76 See Bina, Cyrus and Behzad Yaghmaian 1991. "Postwar Global Accumulation and the Transnationalization of Capital," *Capital & Class* 43: 107–130.

77 Harvey, David 2005. *A Brief History of Neoliberalism.* New York: Oxford University Press. Harvey even invented the word, "neoliberalization" and obsessively added more confusion to the readily existing muddled view of *neoliberalism* among the traditional left as a stand-in for "globalization" (see p. 117).

78 Fine, Ben and Alfredo Saad-Filho 2016. "Thirteen Things You Need to Know About Neoliberalism," *Critical Sociology* 43 (4–5): 685–706. This article sums up a view from two serious Marxist economists who despite what one of them, namely, Ben Fine, had preached on the necessary distinction between the appearance and the essences in Marxian methodology, for instance against neo-Ricardian and Sraffian methodological blunder, now succumbing to a parallel slipup in the periodization of capitalism by invoking *neoliberalism.*

79 It is imperative not to fall into Hobson's vision of imperialism, that is, *monopoly capitalism* rubbed off on Lenin's *Imperialism: The Highest Stage of Capitalism* which turned into a

perpetual political vernacular on the traditional left till this date. This chapter is not only trying to avoid that but also to show why it is irrevocable harm (1) to obfuscate Marx's value theory and his theory of capitalist competition and (2) to depict a caricature of the capitalist mode of production, particularly at its global stage. Marx is utterly unambiguous on this very issue:

> As long as capital is weak, it still itself relies on the crutches of past modes of production, or of those which will pass with its rise. As soon as it feels strong, it throws away the crutches, and moves in accordance with its own laws (p. 651). See Marx, Karl 1973 [1939]. *Grundrisse: Foundation of the Critique of the Political Economy*. New York: Vintage Edition.

80 For the collapse of the International Petroleum Cartel and the transformation of the entire petroleum industry worldwide in the 1970s, see Bina, Cyrus 1985. *The Economics of the Oil Crisis*. New York: St. Martin's Press. This was the beginning of the competitive markets in spot and futures prices, on the one hand, and the formation of differential oil rents in competition, on the other, across this globalized industry. See *inter alia* Bina, Cyrus 1989. "Competition, Control and Price Formation in the International Energy Industry," *Energy Economics* 11 (3): 162–168.

81 In the late 1970s, there emerged a major political tremor that in two separate places disrupted the postwar order of the Pax Americana, namely, Iranian and Nicaraguan Revolutions, neither of which proved rectifiable despite the US obstinate intrusion and taking sides against the popular uprising, and ultimately instigating counterrevolution in both countries. In the case of Iran, see Bina (2021b). This was more than a symbolic gash in the underbelly of American order; it was the beginning of the dismantlement of the client-state portion of the Pax Americana. The economic underpinnings of the order, along with the postwar economic institutions, were already in a state of breakdown since the early 1970s; the underpinning of American hegemony eventually manifested in what is identified in the United States as the wholesale plants closing. The trimmer of disorder was also running through the inter-state polity concurrently, at least a decade before the collapse of the Soviet Union in 1989–1991. This unraveling and disorder materialized in the final year of Jimmy Carter's presidency, in which recently the People's Republic of China was officially recognized as the sole representative (i.e., one China) in the United Nations, and Taiwan's flag was accordingly removed from the display.

82 From the standpoint of Marx's theory of value, appealing to transnationalization of capital is but the acknowledgment that the tripartite circuits of capital had essentially overcome the border of the nation-state and that such an advance was via the inner dynamics of capital via *real* competition as opposed the neoclassical *fib* of "perfect" or "imperfect" competition. This means that the workers worldwide, across the industries and the various sectors, are now competing with one another, and thus the establishment of the socially necessary labor time (SNLT- measure of *abstract* labor) is beyond the border of the nation-state. The worldwide competition of workers, on the one hand, and the diffusion of technology (and technological change) beyond the nation-states, on the other hand, imply that the concrete labor of any kind and quality across all industries and sectors tendentially find a *common denominator* as abstract labor. The tendency of differential wage of course has been an impetus in this becoming at the early stages; yet the *effect* of "cheap labor" would become limited due to the intensity of capital accumulation relative to its original accessibility, as an "external" source. Deep down, however, the globalization of capital is organically interwoven with the "cheapening" of the labor power—as opposed to cheap labor—through the power of competition and incessant technological change. Finally, the complex particularities of social, moral, and historical elements in the formation of the value of labor power in each country would not remain unaffected by global competition and the transnationalization of the means subsistence across the board. Accordingly, the corollary of all this is threefold: (1) that alluding to

"multinationals" and insinuating "national" capitalism is but a mirage, (2) that attributing (capitalist) competition to the contending nation-states (under the rubric of rivalry) is an utter reduction which would echo the real appearance for deeper social and political relations, and (3) that relying on geopolitics alone and viewing of the surface of the struggles for power (based on haphazard circumstances) is little more than a tautology. The latter point can be exemplified by superficial debates induced, particularly by the United States and the Western corporate media, on US–China relations.

83 Marx, Karl 1973 [1939]. *Grundrisse: Foundation of the Critique of the Political Economy*. New York: Vintage Edition.

84 This immense transformation in terms of its ontological origins and its direct epistemological effects should be sensibly set apart from (1) the secondary influences of the mainstream economics orthodoxy across nearly all social sciences, which reasonably, assiduously, and uniquely pointed out by Professor Ben Fine and (2) the prevalent trends in several social sciences and across the social media manifested in pseudo-globalization, postmodernism, etc., from the philosophy of sciences point of view, are also the product of the methodological weakness and epistemic fragility of their own. For instance, since branching out of the political economy in the late 1800s, the discipline of sociology is still struggling to fill the gap in the centrality of its mission and the similarity of context and differentiation of focus from, say, anthropology, economics, geography, social psychology, urban studies, race relations, international relations, development studies, gender and women studies, criminology, etc. Today, this discipline degenerated into a mere name. Therefore, there should be no surprise that sociology has been a prime target of mainstream economics orthodoxy and the very first experimental ground, to use Fine's lexicon, in *imperialist* expansion. For more details, see Fine, Ben and Dimitris Milonakis 2009. *From Economic Imperialism to Freakonomics: The Shifting Boundaries Between Economics and Other Social Sciences*. London: Routledge.

85 For a superb review of conventional literature on the debate on transnationalization, including the false dichotomy of state and globalization, see Radice, Hugo 1999. "Taking Globalization Seriously," in *Socialist Register 1999,* Vol. 35. Leo Panitch and Colin Leys (eds.), London: The Merlin Press: 1–28. It is worth mentioning though that "globalization" is frequently identified as neoliberalism; also see Radice, Hugo 2015. *Global Capitalism: Selected Essays*. London: Routledge.

86 It must be pointed out that the characterization of periodic crisis as "accumulation by dispossession" misrepresents the dynamics of crisis in capitalism proper; here the side effect of the crisis, exemplified in Harvey's, is mistaken for its cause. See Harvey, David 2004. "The 'New' Imperialism: Accumulation by Dispossession," in *Socialist Register 2004: The New Imperial Challenge*, Vol. 40. Leo Panitch and Colin Leys (eds.), London: The Merlin Press: 63–87.

87 On the application of "combined" with reference to economic development, the reader may go to Lenin's *The Development of Capitalism in Russia*, a luminous book detailing the transformation of both manufacturing industry and agriculture in the post-agrarian-reforms in Imperial Russia. In Chapter V, sec. 8, Lenin speaks of the "combination of the industry with agriculture," describing their *mutual* development (pp. 335–388). Lenin here clearly follows the contour of development according to Marx's notion of capital's self-expansion and its tendential change across the sectors of the economy. In other words, "combination" here in Lenin's is not the same as the piggyback of "combined" in Trotsky's. The latter is a fictitious impression of a transformation (and transition) that is not quite informed by the self-expansion of capital. See Lenin, Vladimir I. 1974 [1899]. *The Development of Capitalism in Russia*. Moscow: Progress Publishers.

88 Trotsky, Leon 2008 [1917]. *History of the Russian Revolution*. Chicago, IL: Haymarket Books.

89 It is important to note that there is also occasional brilliant scholarship of a 100% unadulterated Marxian vintage produced in pre-revolutionary Russia. For a quintessential

example of this, see Lenin, Vladimir I. 1974 [1899]. *The Development of Capitalism in Russia*. Moscow, Progress Publishers. This book, not *Imperialism*, should be considered a *magnum opus* for Lenin.

90 See Ashman, Sam 2009. "Capitalism, Uneven Development and Combined Development and the Transhistoric," *Cambridge Review of International Affairs* 22 (1): 29–46. The intent of this article is to delineate the boundary of UCD (U&CD) to the capitalist mode of production and by doing so apparently resurrect it once more as a useful "concept" for the analysis of what is known as the transnational system within the subject of international relations. While Ashman succeeded in such delineation by correctly arguing against both Callinicos's and Rosenberg's points of view on UCD (U&CD), she is absolutely mistaken in resurrecting Trotsky's superfluous impression. Here is why. First, Ashman points to "the limitations in Trotsky's analysis" by turning to Marx's analysis of capitalism and transformation to "the real subsumption of labor to capital" and "international division of labor," among others (p. 32). Second, Ashman points out that "Trotsky is limited in the extent to which he spells out the mechanisms and relations involved, but prescient in his recognition of the importance of finance for 'late' development and of the importance of the state for facilitating rapid accumulation" (p. 32). Third, after some discussions then Ashman concludes: "once capitalism is established in one part of the world it affects and changes *the form of transition to capitalist development elsewhere*. The relatively advanced exert pressure on the relatively backward through both the international division of labour and the international system of states" (p. 37, emphasis is mine). Fourth, by invoking the "international division of labor," Ashman asserts: "Those on the 'periphery' of the system become tied or forced into an international division of labour where they specialize in the production of primary products" (p. 38). Fifth, Ashman leaps further, so to speak, by maintaining: "For those parts of the world that are forced into capital's orbit via colonialism, *the colonial state* needs to be seen as a *variant of the capitalist state*" (p. 38, emphasis is mine). Sixth, to elevate Trotsky's imaginary achievement, Ashman further speculates that "whilst Trotsky clearly assumes Marx's analysis of competitive accumulation to be the driving force behind the creation of world economy—and therefore the basis for U&CD as a phenomenon—it is not something he ever articulates fully" (p. 38). Finally, "U&CD [operates] at two levels. First, as a *mediating* level of analysis [between] the abstract concept of the capitalist mode of production [and] a concrete social formation or society . . . . Second, as a *tool* for looking at particular societies at particular points in time and how the '*amalgam of the archaic and the contemporary*'" (p. 43, emphasis is mine). The disagreement as to the sevenfold points of contusion above should be obvious to the reader in the view of this volume and elsewhere. What is significant here is to see that UCD (U&CD)—a combination of "uneven development" and "combined development," either singly or in combination is but an effect of the capitalist mode of production. Such *effects*, if treated as *concrete*, that is palpable concrete, would be little more than an *impression* about capitalism or transition to capital. On the other hand, if such *effects* are treated as an abstract (or the alleged mediating *semi-abstract*), thus needing a particular concrete to be abstracted from, so to speak, we need to identify such a concrete, other than impressions of Trotsky's off-the-cuff generalization of what he appears to have made from his work, *History of the Russian Revolution*. One cannot explicate the "international" system by invoking either "uneven development" or uneven development with the piggyback of "combined." Nor can anyone produce a genuine theory of inter-state system in an axiomatic, like the undo generalizations of the so-called *Realists* in the orthodox international relations paradigm. In other words, there is no general theory of international relations just as there is no general theory of political economy *per se*. The concrete to go by genuinely for the twentieth century and beyond is the collapse of the old empires, primarily the Pax Britannica, the rise and fall of the Pax Americana, and the emerging pot-American polity. These concrete historical systems have their counterparts in capitalism in periodization

toward globalization. The transnationalization of capital organically encompasses uneven development both intranationally and internationally. Here, the self-expiation of capital (as a social relation) and the role of the state are implicit. The redundancy of UCD (U&CD) is crystal clear as shown directly and indirectly in this volume.

91 Those familiar with Marx's method and the dialectic of capital should know that negation (and the tripartite negation of the nation-state by capital, as a social relation, in this chapter) is *not* the same as a (false) dichotomy of the nation-state and globalization, prevalent and propagated in both orthodox and heterodox literature.

92 See Desai, Radhika 2015. "Introduction: The Materiality of Nations in Geopolitical Economy," *World Review of Political Economy* 6 (4), Winter: 449–458. In light of our ponderings in this chapter, this article is an emblematic rearview image of profound changes that had taken place, since the Bolshevik Revolution, for more than a century across the world. The tone and tenor of stocking up on Trotsky's transhistorical (and trans-modal) "uneven and combined development," on the one hand, and uncritical dependence on everlasting notion of imperialism and thus fetish-like fixity of the nation-state, on the other hand, is the hallmark of this old wine in a new bottle, branded as Geopolitical Economy. This article is an introduction to a symposium titled: the Materiality of Nations in Geopolitical Economy, co-edited by Radhika Desai, as a special issue in the aforementioned journal. There are five remaining papers in this issue, starting with Jonathan Pratschke, "Clearing the Minefields: State Theory and Geopolitical Economy," 459–481. Pratschke reviewed four recent books, including Desai's (*Geopolitical Economy* 2013), and concluded that Desai did not produce a state theory relevant to the "materiality" of state. The remaining contributors are O. Moussaly, G. Montalbano, P. Kurecic and E. Sebag de Magalháes, H. Farias, and Z. Viera. None of the participants in this last group produced something new, something significant or relevant that would explicate the transformation of the nation-state or formidable global sea change over the last 50 years. For instance, Kurecic (pp. 522–543) put on the song-and-dance of the control of non-renewable resources (oil?) by the state and made an imaginary scenario of state's "materiality." As for the question of "Clearing the Minefields," as has been demonstrated in the present chapter and throughout this volume, the identification of minefields requires first and foremost a thorough knowledge of the field itself and then the circumstances and period in which such proverbial mines were being laid. For starters, the holdover of *imperialism* is the first landmine in front of our nose to be defused.

93 Here is not a place to engage in the assessment of "regulation school"; yet the reader should be reminded that there are left academics, drawn to such a vintage, who are fixated on the fetish of *state* (as a predetermined entity), particularly vis-à-vis the globalization of capital. A typical example is Barrow, Clyde W. 2021. "Globalization and the Emergence of the Fortress State," *Science & Society* 85 (2): 170–177. Barrow stunningly states: "I argue that globalization, in its current form, is actually the new form of American global hegemony and empire" (pp. 173–174); he continues: "the United States is acting as the superintendent of global capitalism" (175).

94 This issue is raised by both liberals and radicals (even certain Marxists) on the left for various reasons. One of the reasons that compel certain radicals is their legitimate concern about the pseudo-globalization tendencies that since the mid-1990s are floating around across the social sciences in a variety of expressions, e.g., quintessentially in postmodernism, neoliberalism, etc. However, what is not legitimate is the identification of such bizarre sentiments as *globalization* in combative terms; obsession with the counterfeit seemingly forced the radical critics to overlook the pertinent issues surrounding the *inevitability* of the transnationalization of capital, a driver of (real) globalization. In addition, the implausible periodization of the capitalist mode of production purportedly in "competition, monopoly, and state-monopoly capitalism" appears to be the culprit and tell-tale sign behind caricaturing the real process of *globalization*, the effect of a genuine theory of periodization based on geographical self-expansion of capital itself. Here, the

inverted image of competition in the (real) appearance of "monopoly," together with an undue fixation on *state*, had led to this misguided original sin. Speaking of the original sin, see Fine, Ben and Laurence Harris 1979. *Rereading Capital*. New York: Columbia University Press, chapters 7 and 8. Samir Amin is another scholar that suffers theoretically from similar symptoms in "periodization," and thus succumbs to misidentification of the United States (and the defunct Pax Americana) with the epoch of globalization of capital, and consequently scrambles the political issues and badly fumbles on pertinent contradictions of our age. See Amin, Samir 1992. *Empire of Chaos*. New York: Monthly Review Press; Amin, Samir 2013. *The Implosion of Contemporary Capitalism*. New York: Monthly Review.

95 See Bina, Cyrus 2007. "America's Bleeding 'Cakewalk'," *EPS Quarterly* 19 (4): 1–4.

96 See Bina, Cyrus 1992. "Global Oil and Unviability of 'Pax Americana'," *Economic and Political Weekly* 27 (28): 1467–1469; Bina, Cyrus 1993. "The Rhetoric of Oil and the Dilemma of War and American Hegemony," *Arab Studies Quarterly* 15 (3): 1–20; Bina, Cyrus 2004. "The American Tragedy: The Quagmire of War, Rhetoric of Oil, and the Conundrum of Hegemony," *Journal of Iranian Research and Analysis* 20 (2): 7–22.

97 See Bina, Cyrus and Chuck Davis 2015 [1996]. "Wage Labor and Global Capital: Global Competition and Universalization of the Labor Movement," in *Beyond Survival: Wage Labor in the Late Twentieth Century*. (eds.) Cyrus Bina, Laurie Clements, Chuck Davis New York: Routledge: 19–47; Bina, Cyrus 2013b. *A Prelude to the Foundation of Political Economy: Oil, War, and Global Polity*. New York: Palgrave Macmillan.

98 Those familiar with the analysis of concrete and real differentiation (and fragmentation) in the capitalist mode of production in Marx's sense of the term should be careful not to misidentify it as if a fragmented theorization of capitalism would apply, and thus tendency (and countertendency) toward overcoming the barrier of geography at large should not be in the cards, so to speak.

99 The crudeness of America's power projection and the simplistic view of the world, particularly after the fall of the Soviet Union, is a symptom of the loss of American hegemony and American delusion over its recovery by any means necessary; this is the predicament of the United States.

100 This of course a lot depends on so many contingent factors, which first and foremost includes class struggle, universal solidarity, and purposeful praxis beyond narrow and prejudicial national or regional boundaries.

101 At the time of the final editing of this chapter, the American China policy (particularly, China-bashing) and the festering wounds of the United States, and the latter's conduct and deliberate duplicity during the fall of the Soviet Union led, among others, to a new political crisis on Ukraine again, the root cause of it is an expansion of NATO. As the tenor of this volume anticipates, NATO (or not NATO) is but an irony of the American decline that also speaks of the strategic weakness and pitiful political position of the European partners of the now-defunct Pax Americana. The reliance on the expansion of NATO is as whimsical as Macbeth's confidence in the impossibility of the appearance of Birnam Woods at Dunsinane, in Shakespeare's celebrated tragedy.

6 Globalization: Identity, Fallacy, and Spurious Temptations

There are three classes of people: those who see, those who see when they are shown, those who do not see.

—Leonardo da Vinci

Introduction

This chapter does not intend to investigate the literature on the international relations, value theory, or the critique of political economy; we are not seeking a detailed assessment of any of these subjects or the combination thereof. This chapter is committed to the identity of our epoch and its critics, spanning the post-Marx radicals of the 1910s and 1920s, a precursor to monopoly capitalism via Monthly Review School,[1] and the perpetuity (and indeed plasticity) of imperialism, as an epoch of all epochs, perceived by the majority of the traditional left.[2] This issue will be pursued further with a critique of World-Systems,[3] Geopolitical Economy,[4] and Empire[5] perspectives, in succession, in order to demonstrate the methodological inconsistencies, fallacies, and underlying flaws of each in light of Marx's methodology, Marx's theory of value, periodization theory, and the corporeality of today's global capitalism. In a way, this chapter is a mirror of irreconcilable differences between Marx and the traditional left, while at the same time investigating the failure of the latter to appreciate the epoch of globalization.

The task here is to add a slender but necessary piece to a larger puzzle in this book, namely, (1) an emphasis that the present (and concrete) corporeality of global capitalism is a two-way street for the journey of *abstraction* and concretization of the consequent abstract in return, with an eye on the materialist history and emergence of today's globalization; and (2) a specific touch on the conceptual *origins* and tendencies of certain post-Marx radical scholars whose Marxism would neither square with Marx's methodology (and his optimist worldview) nor with today's corporeality of capitalism. The reason for both aims is far from dwelling on conceptual points that mattered to Marx for one's intellectual curiosity or satisfaction. But for the fact that approaching the old puzzle of *how to change* the world, besought some 180 years ago in "Thesis

DOI: 10.4324/9781351136785-6

Eleven"[6] by Marx, also necessities a strong footing in the recognition of an *epoch* that distinctively identifies with our world, here and now; a universal guidepost that would envelop our collective struggle and our collective survival.

Don Quixote[7] of social activism who would rather toy with off-the-rack wooden swords of dilapidated political ideas and eternal trial and error are a contrast to Thesis Eleven as originally intended in praxis. The stubborn facts on the ground are craving for genuine analysis. These facts cry out loud in this crowded, cruel, and deeply unequal world whose identity, its GPS, so to speak, remains fuzzy or questionable in the mind of scholars from the right to the left, including radical left, Marxists, and non-Marxists alike. Therefore, the points discussed in this chapter (and this volume) should not be treated as an academic theme and subject of curiosity. The whole issue here wraps around the urgency of the identity of our epoch, which also reflects the identity of ourselves and the conditions of our own commitment to an organic, global, and social transformation.

For sake of clarity, this chapter is divided into two parts. Part I centers on methodological issues and fallacies that take center stage in the critiques in Part II. This section is decidedly composed of the identity of several falsities that are usually encountered by both orthodox and heterodox scholars in economic, political, and social issues, particularly in political economy and international relations. The delineation of fakery, as opposed to falsity, is also accomplished in Part I, thus extending the demarcation that exceeds the limits of dominant true-false binary in assessment and verification of economic, political, and social issues at hand. In Part II, the attention is placed on the origins of methodological cleavage between Marx's view of capitalism and those of the post-Marx Marxists whose perception of capitalism unambiguously pointed to Hobson,[8] not Marx. Among this group, the works of Hilferding,[9] Lenin,[10] and Luxemburg[11] are particularly of interest in this paradigm shift, primarily pertaining to the perceived nature of capitalism as monopoly and its consequence on circumventing Marx's law of value.[12]

In Part II, the spotlight is also on the neo-Hobsonites,[13] exemplified by Monthly Review School and its intellectual guru, Paul Sweezy,[14] and the multitude of proliferating scholars in the 1950s, 1960s, and 1970s who began to publish in support of *monopoly* thesis and the purported last stage of capitalism in imperialism across the world. This follows by a critique of the World-Systems perspective and those of the geopolitical economy and Hardt and Negri's Empire, showing their incapacity, their irrelevance, and their lack of specificity toward the perception of capitalism and the identification of the present epoch. It is demonstrated that the World-Systems view essentially thrives on the confusion of the pre-capitalist and capitalist accumulation in a collage of "systems" in the panorama of history, itself a cardinal lapse in methodology. The geopolitical economy is a different kettle of *new* fish that, among others, survives on the perpetuity of imperialism, evasion of transnational footprints of capital as a social relation, and the denial of globalization by mistaken identity. It is shown that it also consists of a compendium of eclectic materials with little originality or theoretical consequence. This view is uncritically set off by the tautology of "uneven and combined development" (UCD), enchanted by an essentialist identity of the nation-state and its transmodality (be it capitalist or "socialist"), before capitalizing on the state's policymaking properties.

Finally, it is shown that Hardt and Negri's Empire and the invention of "multitude" is quite an aberration in the post-Marx tradition of nearly all radical left worthy of the name. It is elucidated in Part II that Empire, aside from injustice to Marx and Marxism, tosses away the very *context* of capitalism before cutting it off from the body of history in a putative style of postmodernism. It is argued that the critique of all these perspectives also has a profound implication for a genuine account of the rise and fall of the postwar Pax Americana (1945–1979)—having to do with the rise and fall of American hegemony; a significant interstate system that prospered till its peak by the sustenance and support of transnational accumulation of capital, yet in due time its hierarchical interstate institutions (and the related idiosyncratic paraphernalia) turned superfluous and incompatible with maturity and universality of capitalism, and eventually superseded by global capitalism and full-blown globalization of social relations of capital.[15] Moreover, in our critique it will be shown why social relations should take precedence over international relations.

Some Preliminary Reflections

The fall of the Soviet Union saddened the longtime scholars and activists who learn their Marxism from the Soviet experience. Others on the left were not far behind. Hobson's monopoly, Hilferding's finance capital, Lenin's *Imperialism*, Luxemburg's underconsumption, supplemented by the Monthly Review School and an eclectic set of tendencies with little variation across much of the radical left, advertently or inadvertently drew an insurmountable line against Marx and his method of investigation, until the 1970s when Marx was finally back. Yet, it has been an uphill battle for some of us who were suspicious of the residue of the so-called Soviet Marxism with a peculiar vision of capitalism, presetting and mechanization of dialectics, and a double-sided concept of imperialism/monopoly capitalism in the mix, thus leading to unnecessary ambiguity or worse, outright abrogation of the theory of value.[16]

Thus, the delineation for comparing these two incongruent methodologies and worldviews, namely, Marx's and what is known as today's Marxism, are (1) the corporeality of capitalism at the stage of globalization on the ground and (2) Marx's vision and the predictive power of his value theory and his insightful method of investigation as to the development of capital as a universal social relation in contemporary capitalism. While these two intertwined find narrow expression in the breakdown of the Pax Americana in this book, this chapter provides a tiny part. It is important to note that in so doing, we always take the *concrete* reality—that is, a multilayered contradictory amalgam of immediate and unmediated facts that ordinarily meet the eye—as a point of departure for our investigation. Thus, the *theory* is necessarily the result of mediation and has nothing to do with evacuating those facts of their content, on the one hand, which by the intercession of mind emerges as an abstract double, so to speak, of the same original concrete phenomena, on the other.[17] Therefore, one must make a distinction between *real* abstraction and *axiomatic* abstraction, a demarcation that distinguishes true, false, and axiomatic fake.

Here, the well-known encounter between Anwar Shaikh and Robert Solow, in the early 1970s over the validity of Neoclassical Aggregate Production Function comes to mind, where a seemingly "scientific" construct by Solow, the winner of the 1987 Sveriges Riksbank (Bank of Sweden) Noble Memorial Prize in Economic Sciences, shown by Shaikh to be but a masqueraded "humbug."[18] The word "humbug" was an approximation at the time for impressions of fake and fakery (as opposed to false and falsity), namely, "bullshit," theorized brilliantly in a gem of a petite book, in 2005, by Harry G. Frankfurt. Therefore, returning to Marx (and Marx's methodology) is indispensable; for instance, on this issue, invoking "purity" or "impurity" by fiat along with an accusatory tone is but self-indictment.[19]

There are certain pitfalls in theorization, one of which is the trap of idealism and idealization of the external world. Another is the trap of fascination with the face value of the external world, known as empiricism. Examples of the latter are plentiful on popular issues surrounding the periodization of capitalism into "competitive capitalism" and "monopoly capitalism," exemplified by Paul Sweezy, eminent neo-Marxist economist, and Harry Braverman, popular labor historian, who apparently took the concentration and centralization of capital on face value, as a monopoly.[20] There is another example that relates to the traditional left and what it considered as "monopoly oil," even after the worldwide crisis of *decartelization* and globalization of oil in the early 1970s, and the subsequent worldwide competitive spot and futures markets in crude oil.[21]

In recent literature, one may come across views that speak of earlier periods of "globalization" as if it reincarnates multiple times. *The Ages of Globalization* by Jeffrey Sachs is a recent attempt at *trivialization* of history (and indeed pre-history) through the *artifice* of globalization literally in an extended panorama of some seventy millennia back to the pre-historic Paleolithic Age. "Humanity has always been globalized," the book pontificates, "since the dispersals of modern humans from Africa some seventy thousand years ago" (p. 1). This magnitude of overgeneralization and lack of vision or interest in the distinctiveness of various historical periods, let alone capitalism, is a rarity even for the orthodoxy in mainstream economics. Projecting the present into a distant past, Sachs proposes: "Globalization . . . involves the intricate interplay of physical geography, human institutions, and technical know-how" (p. xiii).[22]

No wonder that hardly anyone in mainstream economics and with a mainstream mindset and methodology could ever make out the consequence of globalization as an epoch. Aside from this "beam-me-up, Scotty" moment, Jonathan Michie too declares multiple globalizations in his *Advanced Introduction to Globalization* and blunders on a similar test of *specificity*, against the ploy of plasticity, on the exclusivity of globalization as a definite stage of capitalism.[23]

Such perspectives, aside from whether expressed in the heterodox or orthodox tradition, have little grasp of the uniqueness of today's globalization in which capital has turned into a worldwide social relation across the globe.[24] In the same vein, invoking the "world market" in a blanket and timeless fashion, as frequently appears in much of the leftist literature, which often advertently or inadvertently takes away the world-shattering and groundbreaking changes that had been materialized since the nineteenth and the twentieth centuries toward the universalization of capital as a social relation. To be sure, the world markets in capitalism (and the sphere of exchange, in general) are no more than a vessel, so to speak, that carries and conveys the omnipresent content of social relations.

Finally, empiricism, the twin sister of idealism, is also commonly on display in the aforementioned cases, and regardless of familiar divisions between heterodoxy and orthodoxy in economics and politics, among others. The catchall lexis of "imperialism" is another mishmash of panoramic magnitude which also without limit carries monopoly and monopoly capitalism on its façade.[25] Another empiricist trap is the seemingly popular "global north/global south" division, a clever camouflage for the outmoded "dependency theory" and the tautology of the center/periphery promoted by proponents of the World-Systems perspective and certain self-styled Marxists.[26] Likewise, eclecticism is but an appeal to empiricism by other means, often dressed in belittling theorization and depreciating commitment to abstraction.[27] Eclecticism is none other than collage of several different facts arranged in a cherry-pick order, employed by the left and the right in pursuit of an end without a coherent and irrefutable theoretical framework. This approach thrives on dodging the main question by concocting a mental gap between the root cause and effects of the argument at hand.

Part I: A Note on Methodology—True, False, Fake

Overview of Some Pertinent Issues

Just as commodity fetishism in Marx's *Capital*, social relations, in general, is the driver of forms of their expression.[28] These expressions manifested in sum total of economic and political relations through the state, as an arbiter and a complex and convoluted reflection and representation. Thus, a state (that is, a capitalist state) is but a mediating institution that commonly expresses these social relations in a concrete and fetishized manner. Therefore, the idea that somehow a capitalist state everlastingly determines the social relations of capital—that is, capital as a social relation—is a nonsensical tautology. In other words, while there is enough fetish to go around in capitalism, one need not add fuel to the fetish-making machinery of *state*. Here, economy and polity are also different expressions of the same social relations. Hence, the dichotomy of economics and politics, a habitual reflection among many on the radical left, has no originality in Marx or Marx's method: the so-called superstructure is but an outward expression of the same structure, not two different things, in a capitalist mode of production.

Similarly, the negation of all three forms of capital along with their intertwined transnational circuits is a strong indication for recognition of the corporeality—that is, the sum total of economic and political institutions and the constitution of state itself—toward its wholesale transformation. Therefore, holding to a generic and persistent view of state or nation-state (as a foremost unit of analysis), in terms of geopolitics, geoeconomics, and the like, and at the same time beating one's chest for, say, "socialism" is pitifully silly. To be sure, the state is not an intrinsic entity grounded upon itself. Therefore, one cannot erect a coherent theory of periodization for capitalism centered on the *state* just as in modern astronomy one cannot develop a cogent theory for the origin of the universe, by deliberate observation of the gigantic gravitating and floating masses of matter and gas, as an intrinsic or innate given known as constellations. In both cases, it would be whimsical to claim authenticity and materialism by advocating idealism in the guise of essentialism.[29]

It is imperative to note also that any commitment to historical materialism must eschew analyses that are bordering on idealistic outlook and ideal types as to the future of capitalism. In this vein, the "purity/impurity" of capitalism is a classification that fits well with the bourgeois method of axiomatic abstraction. Marx's abstraction is beyond the purity/impurity dichotomy. The example of *abstract* and *concrete* labor in Marx should illuminate this remarkable distinction. In capitalism, the mutuality of production, exchange, and distribution generates the commensurability of all labor in *value* and *value form*. This commensurability is warranted by inner competition of *concrete* labor (that is, incommensurable labor of all kinds and qualities) spent in production and exchange of numerous and diverse commodities that all share a common denominator in value, namely, *abstract labor*. The latter, contrary to *axiomatic abstraction*, constitutes a *real* means of commensurability, the magnitude of which originated and thus measured by the socially necessary labor time through competition in the sphere of production.[30]

Thus, *real abstraction* is an abstraction beyond the usual mental constructs of purity-impurity variety; it is beyond axiomatic abstraction, that is, mental abstraction prevalent in mainstream economics and dominant orthodoxies in nearly all social sciences. Incidentally, in methodological terms, this speaks clearly on the priority (and ineluctability) of *value*—and the price of production—over observable market prices in all capitalist economies. Here, neither the idealization of "aggregate demand"—based on "interpersonal utility"—nor the tautology of "aggregate production function"—circularity of viewing production and distribution, in aggregate (and equilibrium)—has a wiggle room to upset the proverbial applecart, as the dichotomy of abstract and concrete is justifiably relegated to con-artists, neoclassical economists, and vulgar political scientists and international relations specialists.

It is not possible, except by tautology, to analyze commonly experienced concrete facets of capitalism without the *mediation* of a theory. Capitalism aside, there is nothing tangible or intangible, animate or inanimate under the sun that can be measured, so to speak, or elucidated without a theory. Why? Because no subject can be examined by itself or replication of self. Thus, a theory is not meant to be a replica of the subject of investigation, yet what's more, it should not be alien to it so that it could illuminate the subject thoroughly in abstraction. This clearly separates an abstraction, that is, genuine abstraction, from other varieties of mental constructs, natural or unnatural that include pipedreams. In the philosophy of sciences, there is extensive literature on this issue. The task here, however, is to briefly distinguish two types of abstractions—axiomatic versus real abstraction. These abstractions embrace two different outlooks on the purpose of theorization and the nature of knowledge, like day and night. The axiomatic approach relegates the task of abstraction directly to individual mind and preconceived axioms (or assumptions) that are immune from scrutiny in advance. The axiomatic method relies on the reduction of the external world to an idea via a set of axioms that enables the mind to *speculatively* express it and thus generate an idealized identity for it. In other words, all axiomatic systems are both *ahistorical* and *asocial*. To be sure, vulgar neoclassical economists alone do not have a methodological monopoly on this idealized view. To illustrate, a quintessential example of this tendency can be found in the Japanese Kõzõ's Uno tradition on the mistaken connotation of *commodity*, in Marx's *Capital* (vol. I, Ch. 1), as a transhistorical rather than a specific entity belonging to a system of generalized commodity production, namely, capitalism, and thus divorcing equivalent form of *money* from its substance, *abstract labor*—a cardinal sin in Marx's method—in an axiomatic and idealized fashion.[31] Kõzõ Uno is also guilty of invoking "pure theory" in contradistinction to "historical stages of capitalism" and "the actual phenomena"—a three-stage separation.[32] To know the profundity of Uno's methodological quandary, one should appreciate that (1) invoking "pure theory" is *a priori* and thus an axiomatic construct and (2) claiming a "historical" stage-theory without an embedded theorization is but a *tautological* construct. As demonstrated here in this volume, the theory is neither a separate reality nor independent of the "historical stages" in the evolution of capitalism, but a real abstraction expressing the embeddedness of capital in self-expansion in these historical stages. In other words, "stage theory" is not fancifully separated from capital (as a social relation) as a "level of analysis," a setting prevailing in much of the Uno-inspired literature without embedded theorization. Another example is the theory of numbers in mathematics that constitutes an axiomatic system and thus cannot hold within the theory of numbers itself. This principle has a larger implication for all deductive systems, proved by Kurt Gödel in his pathbreaking "incompleteness theorem."[33]

Today, many mainstream economics textbooks are replete with examples of this brand of theorization in which axiomatic individuals do the task of the maximization of both utility and profit in a timeless, society-less, classless, genderless, powerless, and realistically senseless void in a robotic fashion.[34] These *procrustean* models and idealized constructions are held onto in crude emulation by fiat against the external world and then leveled indiscriminately against the unsuspecting freshmen and sophomores in economics as the first dose of ideological indoctrination toward adulthood.[35] This is the story of how the so-called mainstream economics has taken to center stage in the name of "science," simply by methodological deception and with carte blanche of ideology.[36] Real abstraction, on the other hand, is preconditioned upon what is specifically being perceived, thus overcoming the infractions of perceiving mind in idealism; here "existence precedes the essence [of perceiving mind]," so to speak. Real abstraction is an abstraction from the complexities of concrete reality for the purpose of laying bare its basic core. In a sense, it is the undressing of the concrete reality layer by layer.

Popular Fallacies and Occasional Fakes

The fallacy of *incongruent equivalence* is a syndrome that is frequently, but not exclusively, exhibited in the political economy and international relations literature. This pitfall debases the subject by robbing it of its *specificity* and then turns the query into a panoramic babble. This fallacy is the nemesis of precision and methodic analysis in the periodization of capitalism, notably the particularities of epochal change. A prime example of this fallacy is the equivalent comparison of the nineteenth-century *Pax Britannica* (the British Empire) and the twentieth-century *Pax Americana*. The intention is to plant an aura of fusion in minds of uncritical viewers in advance so that in due time the barrage of panoramic verbose would eventually accomplish the task of persuasion.

Aside from the orthodox international relations literature, which is replete with this fallacy from top to bottom, the radical left too by clinging to "finance capital" in the twenty-first century and drawing an equivalent-in-perpetuity on *imperialism*, that is, "export of capital," Lenin's "highest stage," and "monopoly capitalism," credulously perpetuates this fallacy. As noted in the application of the dialectical method, any dialectical concept worthy of the name should know its own limits, when it comes to fitting imperialism into the capitalist mode of production in its maturity, in perpetuity, pretending that there is no time limit to this effusive epoch that founded by Hobson and popularized by Lenin. Hanging onto specifics and specificities in analyzing stage-by-stage capitalist transformations demands creative imagination and careful work. Clutching onto vestiges of early capitalism with certain contemporary embellishment is apparently much more comfortable to pass.

To be sure, the phrase "classical Marxist theory of imperialism,"[37] à la Lenin, Bukharin, Hilferding, Luxemburg, etc., is an inflated phrase, if not totally an oxymoron, in the view of the fact that it has neither to do with Marx and Marx's methodology nor with capitalism in its maturity.[38] This phrase at best could fit in a particular period where cartels and trusts were roaming the landscape, a time that capital had not yet been on its own as a social relation; and at worst consistent with a lauded Hobsonite proposition camouflaged conveniently as Marxism. It must be remembered that two things are evoked by *imperialism*, particularly in Lenin's case: (1) that it is the last stage of capitalism and (2) that capitalism at this stage is perpetually stagnant with limited and little technological change, both of which were not only flatly false but hold as evidence also of how little did he—and his aforementioned contemporaries—know of inner dynamics of the capitalist mode of production, capitalism's genuine periodization, and of Marx's law of value.

Notwithstanding well-known transhistorical parables, there is also the transidentification fallacy that cuts across the entire political spectrum, from left to right, particularly in the political economy and international relations literature. On the left, the frequency of this fallacy infected the economic and political analysis by injecting unnecessary ambiguity and opacity into the distinction between *capitalism* and *socialism*. This fallacy has a long history that is rooted in Pierre-Joseph Proudhon's view of socialism in the nineteenth century and flowered in seeming socialism in "electrification and central planning" in the early days of the Russian Revolution in the twentieth century.[39] The refreshed version of this fallacy has now found frequent usage in some leftist circles concerning twenty-first-century China.[40] Traces of this fallacy are also implicitly laid behind the nation-centered perspective known as the geopolitical economy, a halfway between geopolitics and an eclectic mix of orthodox and heterodox economics. From the standpoint of methodology, the transidentification fallacy does more damage to the discovery of truth than simple misidentification due to its potent strategic quality in vacating the genuine identity and uniqueness of the subject of its core constitution.

In recent decades, another popular fallacy among the traditional left is the blending of "primitive accumulation" and "capitalist accumulation" in one pot, as if old-fashioned beef stew boils in multiple ingredients. Such amalgamation bears three deluding repercussions: (1) it instigates grave miscategorization of the pre-capital accumulation and capital accumulation proper, (2) it provides ammunition to those that hitherto behold to raw "plunder" and the limitless era of "imperialism" as contemporary capitalism rather than relying on Marx' value theory, and (3) it unwisely replaces the cause of periodic crisis with an outward effect of "dispossession."[41] Here, *category* and categorization would appear as something exotic or unnecessary in the arsenal of knowledge; the amalgamation of distinct periods and epochs and blending of categories, sprinkled with Marxian parlance, are more palatable to populist radicals. Yet this fallacy is a litmus test for the separation of genuine analysis from the mock. In other words, this fallacy stands between capitalism that essentially accumulates based on its own internal dynamics in Marx's verdict, on the one hand, and the one that depends on or implies outright plunder, reminiscent of pre-capitalist era, monopoly, imperialism, "systems of protection," and systematic manipulation of an imperial state, on the other. Let us be blunt on this make-or-break issue. We need not fudge the categories in the style of the many on the radical left frozen dutifully in ideological debates and theoretical "inventions" of the 1910s and 1920s. The issue is to identify the core—the social relation of capital and tendency toward self-expansion within a relevant periodization of capitalism—aside from the incidental embellishments that may surround capitalism in terms of convoluted appearances and of everyday life experiences. By analogy, the study of inner dynamics of the Solar System proper is not the same as observation of the passage of the itsy-bitsy meteors that intermittently cross over, say, from the outer reaches of the Kuiper Belt to the inner space of our Solar System.

There is a fallacy associated with orthodoxy in international relations literature, such as "Hegemonic Stability," which expresses the phenomenon of the Cold War in panoramic and circular reasoning. The transhistoricity attributed to hegemonic stability theory (HST) is apparent upon rudimentary inspection of its manifold versions that similarly warrant its application to dominant powers in the modern, medieval, and ancient world, which also comprises both the Pax Britannica and postwar Pax Americana. Here, the centrality of this fallacy is the domination of leading powers aside from a particular history, epochal manifestation, social composition, and socioeconomic relations. To be sure, specific analysis and thus the epochal distinction between the Roman Empire, the British Empire, and the Mongol Empire led by Genghis Khan or the Achaemenid Empire under Cyrus the Great would be of little consequence. For HST sustained domination by *any means necessary* is what really matters. In other words, all it takes for HST to stick is an imaginary pattern of power and a panorama of improvised application. HST is a one-size-fits-all scheme at the disposal of power. Simply put, *stability* of domination is at the core of this fallacy, which is expressly exemplified by the practice of colonial conquest and administration. In other words, HST is a panoramic discourse camouflaged as stability, without specificity.

The circularity of HST is embedded in its axiomatic structure. It reduces all historical periods to fictional archetypes and employs the concept of hegemony commonly and uncritically for almost any kind of power-grab, such as domination. The notion of hegemony displayed here in the present volume is *not* domination; it is a specific power relation that comes across through the mediation of hegemonic institutions, the properties of which are specific and bundled up with a distinctive period in capitalism; it is not transhistorical or is it a mental yardstick. From the writings of the Italian Marxist Antonio Gramsci, hegemony infers a historical circumstance and political setting in which *consent* and *force* find synthetic unity that materializes into political power.[42] Based on close readings of Gramsci, we maintain that hegemony (that is, the structure of hegemonic power) represents the organic fusion of *consent* and *force*, just as Albert Einstein's fabric of the Universe rests upon the synthesis of time–space. The nature of hegemonic power (and the litmus test for its lack thereof) also depends on historically specific and distinctive mediation of specific institutions.[43] In this manner, consent and force are not two separate, standalone entities that tend to switch between the two poles in the middle of the game. Instead, despite the popular but inaccurate perspectives, consent and force do not operate like digital binaries but represent the constituent parts of a synthesis that defines hegemony as an organic whole.

By comparison, HST is a whimsy little ideological trick for maintaining the status quo. That is why *gunboat diplomacy* by the defunct British Empire or the twenty-first-century invasion and occupation of Afghanistan or Iraq by the post-hegemonic United States (that is, by a defunct and expired hegemon) is not a sign of hegemony.[44] These subtleties point to not only the vulgarity of HST by right-wing orthodoxy in international relations literature but also in the crudity of the many on the left who also equate hegemony with domination and unmediated force.[45] As theorized in this book, hegemony is not about the intrinsic power of the hegemon but the indispensability of the hegemonic system and hegemonic institutions. Once the hegemonic system disintegrates, the hegemon is out of business. This principle has a profound implication for the historic breakdown of the postwar Pax Americana explicated throughout this volume.

A quintessential illustration of parting with specificity and thus precise analysis is the application of "uneven and combined development" (UCD)—a postulate (a combination of two separate "laws") in connection with the post-revolutionary Russia by Leon Trotsky.[46] This preposition invoked the state's role in capitalist and non-capitalist development. However, the panoramic nature and departure from specificity render UCD a methodological liability in several different ways. First, blanket deployment of "uneven development"—an effect of capitalist accumulation—is but relying on a corollary rather than a cause; in Marx's methodology, "uneven development" is a superficial appearance of the deeper dynamics of capital, in need of a return to the underpinning of such a development in unevenness and indeed social relations according to the law of value. Second, aside from the centrality of value theory in uneven development, as a precondition, the role of capitalist states differs in different conditions, which would lead us to a necessity for the specific analysis of the context of nation-states' actions and strategic and policy issues involved. Here, uneven development is not the be-all and end-all in itself. Third, any encroachment on the part of capital necessarily embodies the overcoming of barriers, which coincides with *capital*'s self-expansion as a social relation toward universalization. This of course brings us to the purported necessity of the piggyback of "combined" on the "uneven development," given the embedded potentiality of capital toward universalization beyond the borders of the nation-state. Put differently, in methodological terms, without the theory of value, UCD is little more than a mental construct; and with it, it turns into a pointless encumbrance. The panoramic application of UCD utilized for capitalist and pre-capitalist (and, as some argue, for "socialist") development is an exercise in confusing the traditional left literature on monopoly capitalism theory and underdevelopment, among others, on the one hand, and Marx's anticipated conquest of the mode of production and the eventual universalization of social relation of capital across the globe.[47]

The fallacy of "economic specialization" is one more parable told by caretakers of colonial Pax Britannica, which was circulated in the academy through the Ricardian theory of "comparative cost."[48] This fallacy is then paired with the tautology of "opportunity cost" and turned into a standard axiom as the "theory of comparative advantage" in neoclassical/mainstream economics of today.[49] Capitalized on the colonial version of "free trade" and an eye on the plunder of natural resources of nearly four-fifths of the world that was neither lived under capitalism nor aware of what capitalism would feel or could be imagined.

Thus, free trade dogma—a colonial and coercive policy known in universal terms as "primitive accumulation"—was thrown into the hopper, so to speak, of imperialism whose palpable consequence in the early capitalism at home revealed contradictory effects in Hobson's writings of monopolies and cartels, and subsequently of Lenin's *Imperialism*. The ghost of "free trade"—a catchall political ploy with larger latitude—has since been behind the fallacy of economic specialization as it still thrives as a colorful justification in the established order and through conformist ideologues in think tanks and the academy, including orthodox economics and international relations textbooks.[50]

Let us conclude this subsection with a brief introduction of yet another view, an amalgam of several fallacies enumerated earlier, that identifies itself under the rubric of Geopolitical Economy.[51] This view rests on a methodology that singularly sticks to *state* in generic form at the exclusion of the remaining approaches across the political economy and international relations that may hold up to the international (or transnational) transformations of the globe and global polity—the latter belittled and polemicized as "metropolitan."[52] This fallacy is triggered by "uneven and combined development" (UCD), a transhistorical construct captivated by nation and fixated rather generically on the transmodality of state (be it capitalist or "socialist"), and the skin-deep doctrines, strategies, and implements of policymaking by state.[53]

In a nutshell, this transhistorical paradigm views nearly all transformations and commotions in the world economy and polity, from the nineteenth century through to the twenty-first century, instigated by the purported logic of "contender state/contender development." This of course—given UCD's futility—remains an unwarranted tautological proposition without a footing on methodological ground.[54] Thus, any potential multipolarity in contemporary polity, based on the "geopolitical economy" paradigm, is not only on a shaky foundation based on attitude alone but also due to inaccurate conceptions and egregious methodological errors. Conversely, as demonstrated throughout this book, specific periodization of capitalism, critique of imperialism as the highest stage of capitalism, capital as a social relation, and finally the rise and fall of the Pax Americana provide a theoretically rigorous, historically consistent, and politically credible framework for the identity of our epoch in today's watershed toward a multipolar polity.

Thus far, the distinction of *true* from *false* was the focal point of our attention, where all scientific inquiry across all disciplines, including social sciences in general, are normally treated. The fallacies enumerated earlier are a small subset of larger series of falsity across the board. These falsities are an instrument of distortion or inversion of truth, either partially or totally. True and false are thus parts of a mutually exclusive binary that is traditionally utilized in research. Since the publication of *On Bullshit* by Harry G. Frankfurt, however, we have one more category, besides true and false, for evaluating the genuine quality of research, particularly in social sciences where among others, controlled experiment in a laboratory setting is nonexistent.[55]

In this context, categories are *true*, *false*, and *fake*. Here, the effect and intention of "bullshit" are to spread fakery, not falsity. As Frankfurt elucidates:

> [T]he essence of bullshit is not that it is *false* but that it is phony. In order to appreciate this distinction, one must recognize that a fake or a phony need not be in any respect (apart from authenticity itself) inferior to the real thing. What is not genuine need not also be defective in some other way. It may be, after all, an exact copy. What is wrong with counterfeit is not what it is like, but how it was made. . .. What bullshit essentially misrepresents is neither the state of affairs to which it refers nor the beliefs of the speaker concerning that state of affairs. . .. The Bullshitter may not deceive us, or even intend to do so, either about the facts or about what he takes the facts to be. What he [she] does necessarily attempt to deceive us about is his [her] enterprise. His [her] only indispensably distinctive characteristic is that in a certain way he misrepresents what he [she] is up to.
>
> (pp. 47, 53–54)[56]

The previous passage draws a clear distinction between false (and falsity) and fake (and fakery) the difference of which lies in concealing truth through falsity as opposed to concealing one's intent through fakery. The latter is synonymous with bullshit: an act or production equated with emitting excrement, or "matter from which everything nutritive has been removed."[57]

Part II: Post-Marx Marxism and Misidentity of Our Epoch

In this section, an attempt will be made to shed light on the corporeality of capitalism. The framework of our analysis, as noted in the first part of this chapter, is inspired by Marx's methodology. As the basic feature and innermost tendencies of capital come to further light, the stark difference between Marx and what is known as Marxism from the standpoint of the method of analysis, worldview, and the palpability of today's capitalism would become intelligible. This dissimilarity neither is inconsequential for the identity of our present epoch nor hinges on youthful nineteenth-century capitalism in Marx's time. This latter point invoked at the outset is to clarify that there is no doubt that the world (under capitalism) has evolved so much that it would be impossible to find any resemblance between now and its nineteenth-century image of some 150 years ago. But the intention here is to demonstrate that it is the same potential social organism with nearly the same DNA, so to speak, that guided its maturation and development accordingly. To be sure, this parallel speaks on the inner core and basic constitution of capitalism, far from the undialectical and deterministic views of structure/superstructure variety. The DNA analogy agrees with Marx's account at the opening of *The Eighteenth Brumaire of Louis Bonaparte* that "Men [and women] make their own history, but do not make it as they please; they do not make it under self-selected circumstances, but under circumstances existing already given and transmitted from the past" (p. 15).[58] At the same time, one must be reminded of the dialectical conception of turning from potential to actual manifested in Marx's methodology, particularly in his theory of value, as to the transformation of the capitalist mode of production.

Moreover, the basic tenet of capital (and capital accumulation) is attributable to its embedded dynamics from a *potential* that over time turns to an *actual* as capitalism transforms. This transformation also embodied the potentiality of capital as a social relation in its early development. The same attribute, not unlike an imprint of DNA, pertains to capital's manifold *overcoming* of the multifaceted *barriers* to its eventual universality. Some of these barriers were the working day, size of individual capital, isolated production units, discrete method of production, rudimentary organizational structure, scattered and undisciplined working-class, rarity of middle class, insufficient scale and scope of production, limitation of geographical space, limited size of capital, and inadequate concentration and centralization of capital which in Marx's perspective translates to the inadequacy of capitalist competition.[59]

Overcoming all this was what established the capitalist mode-of-production proper based on the production of *relative surplus value* in scale and scope. The sustained accomplishment of the latter includes the establishment of what Marx identified as joint-stock companies which are drawn on the separation of ownership from control for the purpose of generating a joint mass of unlimited capital in perpetuity and unconstrained by each individual property owner. This is known as the "corporate revolution," in the parlance of modern management. Here, the task of centralization of capital is to unleash capital in money form through the credit system, across the spheres of production, exchange, and distribution. The credit system hand in hand with the corporate revolution led to overcoming the natural limits of the *present* time by its intertemporal extension into the future, thus projecting the presence of capital in perpetuity and without interruption, which also opened the door for rampant speculation. Marx identified this early on in dialectical terms as follows:

> This is the abolition of the capitalist mode of production within the capitalist mode of production itself, and hence a self-abolishing contradiction, which presents itself *prima facie* as a mere point of transition to a new form of production.
>
> (*Capital*, Vol III, p. 569, emphasis in original)[60]

Marx's expression of the critical change *within* the capitalist mode of production concerning the "self-abolishing contradiction" is a significant demonstration of overcoming the insularity of private property as an instrument of the trade by an up-and-coming mode of production that in essence craves *capital*, an entity that had shed its *individuality* and transmuted into a *sociality* in a *genuine* capitalist mode of production worthy of the name. Marx was also careful in the previous citation to qualify his observation by the watchword of *prima facie* to indicate that he is not speaking of the "new" mode of production other than capitalism, notwithstanding the new managerial sub-class. Indeed, it would be quite fantastically out of ordinary to presume that the capitalist mode of production in its tender age, where nearly four-fifths of the world's population lived under various pre-capitalist modes, would lead to a new mode of production.[61]

A corporate form and *corporation*, an entity arising from the separation of ownership and control, is an indispensable *vehicle* for the systematic persistence and *regularity* of concentration and centralization of capital in capitalism proper. In Marx's lexicon, this "self-abolishing contradiction" is an organic part of accumulation and thus identifies the mode of production in which the capitalist class includes a sub-class of managers. This also ties in with the development of the credit system (including investment banks and elaborate financial structures) and systematization of both concentration and centralization of capital, the latter a definitive source for persistent technological change. All this of course reveals a *new form* of production and not a *new mode* of production, unless one appeals to a caricature of embryonic and immature capitalism of the early nineteenth century, built on the *idealization* of "free competition" and mode-of-production-in-the-making of pre-corporate age, as Hobson, Hilferding, Lenin, and Luxemburg, among others, appears to have been making. Marx did not have any illusion whatsoever about that kind of capitalism, a lampoon of capitalism, as his theory of value today is more relevant than ever.

It is also incredible to idealize capitalism, as orthodoxy does, in scattered production units and workshops in equally idealized "free competition," without concentration and centralization of capital.[62] If Marx's value theory were about capital minus concentration and centralization (that is, without accumulation), it would not be worth the plain paper it was written on. After all, the transformation of property relation that led to the sociality of capital is the first step toward the inner capacity of capital as a social relation, far from the rudimentary corpus of scattered objects of utility. To be sure, there should be a sharp distinction between private property and capitalist property in *private form*, as a negation of the former. The sociality of capitalist property in corporate form is also a *negation of negation* within capitalism. This is similarly true for capitalist competition, which is a negation of the negation of feudal monopoly. Let us be blunt in the face of those in the habit of tossing around the phrase "free competition," as capitalist competition. A casual display of elementary, small, stand-alone, and scattered units of production under the proprietor ownership is not yet competition; this was known to Marx, and it is known to any perceptive individual who appreciates the ins and outs of today's capitalism in practice. Just as matter without motion has no consequence in particle physics, capital without accumulation is not capital.

Timewise, this transformation was virtually synchronized with a series of pivotal changes in the labor process and restructuring of the workplace under the rubric of Taylorism (that is, "scientific management" by the reorganization of workstations thru control of time and motion à la A. P. J. Taylor) that displayed the *inner competition* of capital as the competition among workers, toward rationalization of production, standardization of the socially necessary labor time, and the control and regimentation of the working class vis-à-vis the emerging changes in technology; this, in turn, paved the way for further reduction in the socially necessary labor time, via the assembly line, on the way to further *competition* in mass production, alongside mass consumption and mass purchasing power fostered by the newly emerged credit system. This is a remarkable pattern of further competition, a corollary of further concentration and centralization of capital before the naked eye, and the very telltale of an innermost tendency of capital activated toward maturity. This of course has colossal methodological ramification against Hobson's "monopoly capitalism" and—aside from combative language—against Lenin's "highest stage of capitalism" and the alleged perpetuity of imperialism prevalent across the traditional left lexicon and literature.

Imperialism: Specificity, Plasticity, and Panorama

As indicated earlier, specificity is a necessary feature of a concept or theory that is worth the name, by distinguishing *true* from either *false* or *fake*. Therefore, the litmus test for a valid concept or theory is limited to the subject of investigation, and not the other way around. In other words, contrary to the axiomatic, idealized, or unconstrained constructs, genuine theorization is constrained by the limitation of the subject, that is, by the very constitution of its specificity. As a result, we are confronted with two different levels of specificity: specificity of the subject and the specificity of the theory that intends to elucidate it, that is, the level of ontology side by side with the level of epistemology. An example of this violation at the ontological level is the promotion of the capitalist economy for all human history and civilizations promoted by ideological precepts of neoclassical economic theory, a mockery of scientific analysis, and a monumental scandal the trace of which can be evidenced through the mainstream economics discipline.

An example of the violation at the epistemological level is an outright abolition of classes, first by the trio of the Marginalists in the 1870s, and through various incarnations in the twenty and twenty-first centuries, festooned mainstream economics textbooks with a timeless, classless, nationless, genderless, robotic individual that automatically shifts between production, exchange, and consumption, and a profit maximizer and utility maximizer in one that fills the entire universe with the glitter of capitalism for eternity.[63] As Frankfurt reminds us, in *On Bullshit*, the consequence of impingement on specify need not be false in a true-false binary but worse: the corollary of the aforementioned examples in a pseudo-scientific garb is but *fake* and *fakery*. The lack of specificity and concern for truth is the telltale sign of fakery as opposed to falsity in this case. Again, Frankfurt is keen on this subtlety:

> The liar is inescapably concerned with truth-values. In order to invent a lie at all, he[she] must think he[she] knows what is true. And in order to invent an effective lie, he[she] must design his[her] falsehood under the guidance of that truth. On the other hand, a person who undertakes to bullshit his[her] way through has much more freedom. *His[her] focus is panoramic rather than particular. He[she] does not limit himself[herself] to inserting a certain falsehood at a specific point*, and thus he[she] is not constrained by the truths surrounding that point or intersecting it. *He[she] is prepared, so far as required, to fake the context as well.*
>
> (pp. 51–52, emphases added)[64]

The question of specificity is also a litmus test for the concept of imperialism, its structural and institutional underpinnings, and any other demarcation that intersects with it, from the standpoint of historical change and epochal identity. The first error in Lenin's *Imperialism* is the identity of concentration and centralization of capital in the capitalist-mode-of-production proper and the palpable presence of cartels and monopolies that manifested in this critical and convoluted period of transformation and struggles against colonialism in this period of the history of the world. That identity compels Lenin to exceedingly be concerned about the role of "finance capital"—a stand-in for monopoly borrowed from Rudolph Hilferding—in the colonies. Lenin, like many of his revolutionary comrades and contemporaries in this period, had little foresight as to the imagination of capitalism in a wider spectrum from *potential* to *actual* that would eventually carry forward once the self-expanding system of capital, as a social relation, takes roots, as Marx had. And contrary to frequent citations and references to Marx, his readings of Marx's value theory and method appears skin-deep and artificial. For instance, Lenin in his own mind, in a casual illustration of *Imperialism*, "corrected" Marx's portrayal of a tendency to the universalization of the financial codes of "book-keeping" in the colonies, as "monopoly."

Lenin also hastily reads the period of the pre-1870s "free competition" in the same way as Hobson reads it, and as Hilferding and Luxemburg both would emulate it and misread and misunderstand Marx's notion of capitalist competition, a synthetic and dialectical theory without which his value theory would fall by the wayside. In the heat of the moment, Lenin, and his contemporaries, advertently or inadvertently, *replaced* the context of inner dynamics of *capitalism* with Hobson's outlook of the world, namely, *monopoly capitalism*. This clever *switch*, however, marked the origin of grand fakery—as opposed to falsity—that obfuscated century-old post-Marx political debates among the radical left of all stripes. This misstep was the corollary of three interlinked factors: (1) overwhelming influence of Hobson upon the intellectual left in this period; (2) colonial trade, ongoing anti-colonial struggles, and the existence of prohibitive cost of the administration; and (3) tautological view of monopoly and scant awareness of Marx's anatomy of capitalism, particularly his theory of *competition*.[65]

Hence, Marxism was turned to empiricism via Hobson's monopoly and underconsumption, and then predictably settled as "the highest stage of capitalism" till this day as we speak. To be sure, the category of *imperialism* belongs to a period in which the inner dynamics of capitalism and capital as a universal social relation had yet to emerge. It is the period that primitive accumulation of capital, that is, pre-capital accumulation, is at its height and capitalism is in its burgeoning, not highest, stage. Therefore, in this period, panoramic references to monopoly and cartel should not be miscategorized as an outcome of the inner dynamics of capitalism, namely, concentration and centralization. This is an egregious error of monumental proportion that breaks the underpinning of *imperialism*, at the highest stage, and duly indicts all those who pulled off this fakery in perpetuity. What Hobson, Hilferding, Lenin, and Luxemburg did in this unconstrained, panoramic scenario is not short of mental construction, that is, idealization through the fallacy of *incongruent equivalence*. To be sure, we do not deny the presence of cartels in the capitalist mode of production, particularly in the postwar Pax Americana (1945–1979); their configuration, their functioning, their interval, and their eventual collapse in conjunction with the inner dynamics of capital accumulation should be an ultimate arbiter. A remarkable example of this is the eventual collapse of the International Petroleum Cartel (1928–1972) on its own weight due to decartelization and globalization of capital across the petroleum industry early in the 1970s.[66]

Lenin's *Imperialism* succinctly summarizes the underpinning of imperialism as a "special" stage of capitalism, before he assigns the highest stage to it,[67] as follows:

1. Concentration of Production and Monopolies,[68]
2. Finance Capital[69] and the Financial Oligarchy,
3. Export of Capital,[70]
4. Division of the World Among Capitalist Associations,
5. Division of the World Among Great Powers.

These conditions are *prima facie* perceptible during the period between the late 1870s and 1916 when this pamphlet was written. So, the question is not on their prima facie perception but on the structural unity and logical consistency as to the specificity of this period of transition. In other words, we need to decipher a cogent theory from this laundry list, so to speak.

The first point amalgamates the concentration of capital with monopoly as the bourgeois economics texts treat the accumulation of capital in today's academic arena. This is the first litmus test of the *text* of monopoly by the *pretext* of monopoly. The second point is on "finance capital" and the role of the nascent banking system. It is a mishmash of *apparent* oligarchy, on the one hand, and the actual development of the circuit of capital in money form, on the other. Here, both Lenin and Hilferding (the original instigator) miss the forest, so to speak, by counting the trees in the immediate vicinity and unmediated observation. The export of capital, as opposed to commodity export, is the third on the list. Yet its significance as a *moment* of capital in money form and a step in the organic transformation of capital, that is, a potential social entity in the systemic overcoming of the existing barriers, including the borders of the nation-state—other than as an instrument of plunder in the colonies—was completely and cluelessly forsaken.[71]

Finally, the two remaining facets of imperialism relate to the division of the world among "capitalist association," that is, among trusts, syndicates, and cartels, on the one hand, and among the great powers, on the other hand. These two interwoven divisions would certainly qualify imperialism as an international relations theory as well. The capitalist economy and polity viewed in this fashion are the perpetuity of a handful of monopolies operating across the world, in cahoots with the great powers that divide the world, and, in tandem with these (national) monopolies, is reminiscent of the empires of the yesteryears. This simply depicts that Lenin's *Imperialism*, which is precisely a caricature of the capitalist system, without an inner dynamic of its own and devoid of mediating institutions, is much worse than the vision of vulgar economists who perceive the economy as a heap of physical objects to be divided in whatever fashion among a handful (or plentiful) of muscle-flexing bidders. It is phony even in the bourgeois sense of the term. It betrays that notion of potentiality turning to actuality in Marx's sense of evolution toward actuality. Lenin's outward *rivalry* against monopolies is not the same as Marx's theory of competition.[72] Lenin's *Imperialism*, overall, is a fundamental letdown of Marx's method and Marx's value theory.[73] *Imperialism* (perpetuating as the highest stage of capitalism) is a caricature of an international relations theory in the twenty-first century, an artifice that appeals to both *power* and *conflict* without mediation (and adequate methodological grounding) at the surface of the international polity. And no amount of manipulation, modification, patching up, and jiggling toward generalization of this charade does not change its basic tenet. Notwithstanding Marx's theory of value in *Capital*, Vol. I (and his *synthetic* competition in *The Poverty of Philosophy*), one could imagine that Karl Marx's bones would turn in his grave repeatedly as many of his self-identified followers submissively fiddle with imperialism and endorse it in perpetuity.[74]

Monthly Review School and Mismeasure of Capitalism

As pointed out earlier, the seed of the panoramic view of imperialism was sown across the political landscape of the left by Vladimir I. Lenin. This vision, although in certain variations, was also shared by Rudolf Hilferding, Rosa Luxemburg, and even Karl Kautsky. However, John A. Hobson, a well-known underconsumption theorist, since Malthus and Sismondi, and the author of *Imperialism: A Study* (1902), was an undeniable source of emulation for the many on the left. Aside from the USSR Marxist education, the majority of the neo-Marxists in the West quickly accepted the panorama of imperialism, jointly with the axiom of "monopoly capitalism," as an unreachable fact. In the United States, the most influential scholars on the left had clustered at the Monthly Review (MR), a newly formed journal that inaugurated its first issue displaying Albert Einstein's lead article "Why Socialism" in May 1949.

The backlash of McCarthyism in the United States, among others, led to the flourishing of MR in subscription and at the newsstands, and an avalanche of translations and publications of Marxist orientated materials hit the public and private libraries across the world, including what was then identified as the "Third World." The burning issues were varied and fittingly relevant to economic development, and politics of the 1950s and 1960s and, among others, tangent to the Cold War and imperialism. While Marx was in the background, the entwined question of monopoly and monopoly capitalism was expressly kept to the front, in MR. The Lenin-Hilferding-Kautsky-Luxemburg ponderings of the 1910s (and 1920s) on imperialism and the political aura surrounding the aftermath of the Russian Revolution, among others, once again were subject of publishing, republishing, and interest as an order of the day.

To make a long story short, in 1966, *Monopoly Capital: An Essay on the American Economic and Social Order* by Paul Baran and Paul Sweezy took center stage. The authors in no uncertain terms wrote:

> We must recognize that competition, which was the predominant form of market relations in nineteenth-century Britain, has ceased to occupy that position, not only in Britain but everywhere else in the capitalist world. Today the typical economic unit in the capitalist world is not the small firm producing a negligible fraction of a homogenous output for an anonymous market but a large-scale enterprise producing a significant share of the output of an industry, or even several industries, and able to control its prices, the volume of its production, and the types and amounts of its investments. . .. In an attempt to understand capitalism in its *monopoly stage,* we cannot abstract from monopoly or introduce it as a mere modifying factor; *we must put it at the very center of the analytical effort.*
>
> (p. 6, emphasis added)[75]

At the very outset and in one stroke, upon its publication, the previous passage sets the tone of the entire book by implanting the mindset and method of the *Monthly Review School,* a refurbished version of Hobson/Hilferding/Luxemburg/Lenin's vintage of "new" capitalism, as an alternative source of emulation for the radical left worldwide, particularly for the Third World intellectuals, even the revolutionaries. To be sure, Sweezy alone had tried through *The Theory of Capitalist Development,* in 1942 (reprinted in 1956), to undo Marx's vision of capitalism in *Capital* in earnest and with some qualification, yet in this book (coauthored with Baran), he had gone for the jugular, so to speak, to not to just a temporary separation but to a complete divorce from Marx, Marx's theory of value, and Marx's concentration and centralization of capital via *real competition*, by a deliberate U-turn toward monopoly capitalism and the parody of *market structure*, borrowed from neoclassical economics. In a nutshell, this simply speaks for the intransigent position of the Monthly Review School from the 1960s till the present as we speak. *Monopoly Capital*, as shall be elucidated later, contextually hinges on monopoly (as opposed to its counterparts pure competition), borrowed from Hobson, and stage-managed in several iterations, including "Demand Under the Conditions of Oligopoly" (the famed "kinked demand curve") by Sweezy himself, another sign of theoretical commitment to up and coming mainstream economics all the way through.[76]

As for the status of topics in the balance of *Monopoly Capital*, aside from their perceptible truth or falsity under capitalism, they are there *not* for their truth value, *given the context*, but merely as an inventive disguise of the authors' original intent, namely, an intent to *misrepresent* capitalism. For instance, one need not be capitulated to the parody of monopoly capitalism to appreciate the nature of "The Giant Corporation" (Chapter 2), "Militarism and Imperialism" (Chapter 7), "Race Relations" (Chapter 9), and "Quality of Capitalist Society" (Chapter 10), or for that matter notice that the irrationality of capitalist system is bad for one's health and well-being (Chapter 11). Methodologically, the truth values of all these important subjects covered in this book are quite incidental to and independent of the context of monopoly capitalism, just as the truth value of the Holy Ghost in the eyes of those indifferent to Catholicism. The promotion of monopoly capitalism alone in this book is an intent that is carefully camouflaged by these subjects.[77] In other words, all such subjects could be elucidated with more cohesion without even a remote reference to monopoly capitalism. To be sure, placing monopoly "at the very center of analytical effort," to explicate monopoly in this book is a circular methodology that had persisted since the era of Hobson and Lenin's Imperialism.

Monopoly capitalism is a consequence of a tautology that externalizes competition as monopoly and individualizes the impersonal inner dynamics of social capital in the perceived collusion of oligopoly in the worst possible manner. This view tends to stay on the surface of appearance, on the one hand, and trivializes the investigation by mismeasuring empiricism, on the other. Some of the significant side effects of this malady are as follows:

1. Abrogation of Marx's law of value and the changeover of voluntary control by means of the handful of individual capitalists (in the person of the corporation) at the helm.
2. Annulment of Marx's theory of surplus value and the changeover to *unmediated* surplus and super profit.
3. The reliance on the outward *symptom* of *underconsumption* and *realization* (and likewise the tautology of *disproportionality*[78]) rather than confidence in the *inner* cause of periodic crises in capitalism.[79]

4. The alleged monopoly control and its corollary the fallacy of declining technological change in capitalism.
5. Endorsing the stagnationist thesis and persistence on the long period of stagnation in the economy, and the use and abuse of the theory of long waves.
6. The panoramic view of imperialism and its unconstrained perpetuity.
7. The speculative mindset and monopolistic view of the global economy.
8. The undefined and uncertain attitude toward global polity and international relations.
9. Subscribing to the "method of successive approximation," a prevalent bourgeois method of investigation that successively sways the *concrete* (that is, the object of investigation) to approximate the *ideal* (the theory). Here, the theory is but a perceived axiom and a point of departure in Sweezy's investigation, just like the idealized analysis by the mainstream orthodoxy and despite his radical rhetoric. Sweezy's own testimony is crystal clear: "[T]he decisive units of the economy are unmistakably moving toward a definite, recognizable pattern, and this pattern itself is much more important than any of the concrete approximation to it" (p. 15, paragraph 3).[80]
10. Finally, contrary to the fact that imperialism was grounded on cartels, trusts, and controlling institutions in a specific historical period, monopoly capitalism (as a school of thought) submissively would count any act of conflict across the world as imperialism.[81]

The reincarnation of irreconcilable cleavage between Marx's unique methodology and evolutionary view of capital and capitalism, on the one hand, and the Hobson–Hilferding–Lenin–Kautsky–Luxemburg deviation (that is, the original cluster of post-Marx scholars), on the other hand, took to new heights in Sweezy' thesis, its resolute supporters and numerous scholars that in one way or the other for years surrounded the Monthly Review School (MRS). Hobson, a liberal non-Marxist, was included in the earlier group because of his originality in the first place, and for being a source of emulation in this methodological irreconciliation. At the same time, debates, such as the "breakdown controversy," the so-called transformation problem, or the "value controversy," also emerged in reprints and came to surface further reading and reconsideration. There were many eclectic tendencies and influences that emerged in the 1950s and beyond, particularly on the issues surrounding economic development, namely, the "dependency theory," development of underdevelopment, center–periphery divide, etc., that their full assessment is outside of the purview of this volume. In all these issues, the Monthly Review School, for obvious reasons, kept Marx's value theory in the background and monopoly and imperialism, front and center.

The upshot of the previous critique is to perceive capital (1) as a social relation and (2) in the process of overcoming the social, political, legal, physical, and ultimately geographical barriers that stood to its expansion. And it is the footprints of such overcoming that provided us with a measure for periodization of capitalism in the context of globalization. In this context, Marx's competition has no inconsistency with the process of concentration and centralization of capital.[82] If anything, both intrasectoral and intersectoral competitions are dialectically part and parcel of it. In other words, contrary to the *external* view of competition in neoclassical economics, replicated by mainstream social scientists and the traditional left, competition is *internal* to the dynamics of capital accumulation. And as social capital frows and proliferates beyond the borders of the nation-state in a complete (tripartite) negation, competition hand in hand with concentration and centralization of capital increases. Hence, the radical left's lip service to "rivalry" and sticking to "monopoly" is not other than fainthearted capitulation to bourgeois economic orthodoxy and *parody* of competition.

Here is where the insurmountable fault line was laid from day one, between Marx, on the one hand, and the Hobsonites and neo-Hobsonites, on the other. In historical terms, imperialism had its own specific historical period which was overlapped with the negation of the nation-state by capital, in *commodity* and *money*, short of universalization, thus lingering awhile through the postwar Pax Americana (1945–1979), before the transnationalization and universalization of capital as a social relation. Therefore, *imperialism*, like everything else in life, must have a specific lifespan, in historical time. This specification, both ontologically and epistemologically, is indispensable for the tenor of politics and rhetoric of imperialism in today's political deliberations. But, alas, *imperial fetishism* (and another side of the same coin: stealthy nationalism), together with the ghosts of cartels, trusts, and monopolies of the yesteryears, are seemingly hunting the imagination of the many on the traditional left, a tradition that has little to do with Marx's.

World-Systems and the Transhistorical Dilemma

As hinted earlier, the political and methodological influence of the MRS among a wide spectrum of the radical left is unmistakably hefty. Yet, such appeals are punctuated in the various degrees of overlap with other schools of thought, thus generating an eclectic collage across the political left today. This is despite the revival of Marx, Marx's value theory, and his methodology concerning the identity of capitalism in its various stages since the 1970s. For instance, the advent of World-Systems (WS) perspective in sociology and its sway in political economy and international relations began to appeal to those who were already steeped in the panoramic view of social phenomena, and the long and convoluted history of the last five centuries, along the line of historian Fernand Braudel. The advantage of WS was seen in its umbrella-like capacity that brought all the seemingly standalone subjects, such as "dependency theory," center-periphery divide, unequal exchange, etc., under one broad, amalgamated heading. Its disadvantage is of course the consolidation of incongruent historical periods and developments, literally from soup to nuts, in one hell of a panorama that had decidedly done away with *specificity* for good.

Here, again, from the standpoint of methodology, the misrepresentational persistence of *panoramic context* underlying the theoretical constitution of WS makes the subject, any subject, under consideration, neither true nor false, but fake. In other words, at first blush, WS appears a unified theory but in essence, it represents a giant quilt that is stitched together by fiat and a flurry of divergent narratives. For instance, references to "systemic cycles of accumulation" intended to smooth out the incongruent and incompatible parts of capitalist accumulation and those of the hodgepodge of untimely pre-capitalist entities. A quintessential sample of WS is Giovanni Arrighi's *The Long Twentieth Century* in which the author does not redo, so to speak, the whole nine yards of the past 500 years, though he tends to cover enough to remain faithful to the panoramic purpose of this perspective. Arrighi maintains:

> All four states—Venice, the United Provinces, the United Kingdom, and the United States—have been great powers of the successive epochs during which their ruling groups simultaneously played the role of the leader in processes of *state formation* and of *capital accumulation*. . .. [The] networks of *power* and *accumulation* . . . enabled the states in question to reorganize and control the world system[.] . . . It can thus be seen that the expansion of capitalist power over the last five hundred years has been associated not just with interstate competition for mobile capital, as underscored by Weber, but also with the formation of political structures endowed with ever-more extensive and complex organizational capabilities to control the social and political environment of capital accumulation on a world-scale. Over the last five hundred years[,] *these two underlying conditions of capitalist expansion* have been continually recreated in parallel with one another.
>
> (pp. 14–15, emphases added)[83]

Our intention, among others, is to show a handful of red flags in this brief passage:

1. As can be seen, the very context of a historically specific social relation under capitalism has been cleverly switched with a sleight of hand in the panorama of the *World-Systems*. The latter of course is *a priori* construction that has no autonomous authenticity except thru tautology. And no amount of historical narrative or political pleading would be able to restore that.
2. The persistent deployment of *accumulation* in the previous panorama is an affront to specificity, particularly to capitalist accumulation. For instance, under the guise of "power" and "accumulation," the author knowingly blends and intermingles the two separate and distinct categories of "primitive accumulation" and accumulation in capitalist-mode-of-production proper, in the mix. Thus, the catchall expression of "systemic cycles of accumulation" is but an incongruent equivalence.

3. The panorama of *power* is a significant aspect of WS, yet it cannot be identified independently and detached from the corpus of the administrative state, except by tautology. Power is also a corollary of the administrative state as an undifferentiated category.
4. As an epistemology, the entire façade of WS holds up on governance and the projection of state power in a transhistorical framework and the object of thought. Yet, state and governance as real appearances are cut on the horn of dilemma in circularity, that is, as a point of departure and a point of return. The allusions to trade, money, finance, capital, and capital accumulation in this tautological framework are also a part and parcel of a larger reality in a manifold mode of appearance.
5. The British Empire, a colonial system with few embryonic *mediating* institutions, and the postwar Pax Americana, among others, are the quintessential example of comparing apples and oranges in this book.
6. The notion of hegemony in Arrighi's, although not defined as "domination," and on the face of it conforms to Gramsci's *embryonic* consent and force, is faulty in two ways: (1) it is deployed panoramically without any binding restriction and (2) it is intrinsic to the state's generic role and character, as opposed to specific mediating institutions of hegemony. This misapplication in Arrighi's is also the tip of a common blunder in much of WS literature on hegemony.
7. The references to competition in Arrighi's book appear casual and generic portending rivalry, not unlike rivalries among Hobson's monopoly blocks. Whereas Marx's capitalist competition is internal to capital and its inner dynamics as a social relation. Arrighi also cites Marx's circuits of commodity and money with little clue as to the meaning of *money* in the capitalist mode of production (as a manifestation of abstract labor), a category incommensurate with the finance associated with the Genoese' or the Dutch merchant capitalism.
8. The panoramic view of history, on the one hand, and of capitalism, on the other, by WS is one thing. The lack of adequate abstraction and abstract categories underlying the multiple layers of concrete reality related to today's world economy and polity toward globalization is evidently another; this much is clear from the syllogism of "systemic cycles of accumulation" deployed by WS.
9. A glance at the "Epilogue: Can Capitalism Survives Success" should point to the *fault line* in the misidentification of the postwar Pax Americana (1945–1979) and the contemporary global capitalism. This blunder is not unique but similarly the Achilles' heel of the vast majority in the political economy and international relations, particularly on the traditional left. Here, Arrighi's "networks of power" and "accumulation" are but the mode of appearance of economy and polity, the circularity of which turns the entire analysis into a ramshackle of theoretical disarray and speculative guesswork.[84]

This section is not complete without the mention of Emmanuel Wallerstein, the de facto founder of this school in sociology and history whose extensive work includes multiple volumes on the modern world-systems.[85] Wallerstein follows the same central tenet that distinguishes and demarcates WS from other heterodox groupings. It goes without saying that the collage of the pre-capitalist and capitalist modes of production and thus transhistorical methodology also runs through the fabric of scholarship within his work.[86] The previous critique is methodologically applicable to the corpus of Wallerstein's work as well.

Traditional Left: The Predicament of the Rest

There are other left-leaning tendencies that intend to explicate the contemporary transformation of the world and contemporaneous conditions of global polity and economy.[87] These inclinations are overall the variegated echo and offshoots of the original cleavage that started by post-Marx, radical Hobsonites of the early twentieth century and that which renewed to its full capacity by the Monthly Review School and its political and ideological supporters to this day. Samir Amin is a typical example among the scholars that spent nearly all their life in the alleged reconciliation of Marx's value theory and monopoly capitalism, before appealing to the mode of appearance and raw empiricism and eventually joining sides with the latter. Amin's final verdict in *The Implosion of Contemporary Capitalism* is "[T]he capitalism of generalized, financialized, and globalized monopolies" (p. 7). He then underscores his long-established stance that "Capitalism and imperialism, in their historic reality, are the two faces of a single coin" (p. 8).[88] As indicated earlier, the irreconcilable differences between vision of capitalism à la Marx, on the one hand, and that of Lenin's and his contemporaries, on the other, have relegated the 1950s, 1960s, and 1970s, to a new generation of neo-Hobsonites (dubbed neo-Marxists) around Sweezy's thesis.[89] Given the incommensurability of the context of these writings, no amount of persistence at reconciliation over Marx's value theory, for instance, in Amin's prior work, namely, *The Law of Value and Historical Materialism*, was conceivably possible.[90] Holding to historical materialism and keeping up with the mode of appearance is not a methodology worthy of a Marxist. The tenuous partition between "global north and global south," contra to value theory, in Amin's later work is the legacy of this misconception. And one may wonder to call all this the revenge of Marx or the curse of Hobson.

An arbitrary dichotomy of the "logic" of territory and "logic" of history à la David Harvey, together with his mistaken identity of "neoliberalism" as a stand-in for a "new epoch," is another dimension of the traditional left's uneasy attitude toward globalization.[91] Here, any periodization theory, worthy of the name, of capitalism must challenge these two seemingly unrelated subjects. We hold that the resolution to Harvey's hang-up on such a dichotomy is due to the lack of appreciation of the fact that "neoliberalism" cannot be a genuine measure for the periodization of capitalism and that what happened to capitalism in the structural sense of the term cannot be papered over by references to a set of public policies, official strategies, or posited doctrines, and accepted as an authentic yardstick for capitalism's change over. In other words, the common usage of neoliberalism, particularly by the traditional left, since the 1970s, need not make it essentially a new era except by fiat.

Harvey's vacillation on "new" imperialism, imperfect competition, and evidently patchy knowledge of Marx's method and vision of capitalism, appears to have proven an impediment to the discovery of this rather elementary point. The *dichotomy* of territory and history of capitalism is but one of those peculiar appeals to appearance. Capital is a self-expanding social relation with a unique history and potential territory in the process of overcoming all possible barriers, except the barrier of its own, that is, being capital itself. The barrier of territory and geography unquestionably includes all these manifold overcomings. After all, the tripartite negation of the nation-state by self-expanding capital is the very *context* of the deepening and widening of social relations toward universalization across all geography.[92] This also shows that globalization is not only a matter of *epistemology* but also of *ontology*, which in due course stamped out and done away with the vestiges of the pre-capitalist social formations as well.

It must be noted that these tendencies, which are either absorbed in the panorama of the monopoly-cum-imperialism or, like World-Systems perspective, occupied by some kind of *a priori* syllogism, elicit their own geopolitical view of a polity under investigation. In other words, the geopolitics of any stripe, including the paradigms discussed earlier, drive their strategic substance and initiatives from the directions set by the paradigms themselves. The dominion of geopolitics is not an independent jurisdiction. This is illustrated by a new geopolitical vintage, bidding to fortify the given arguments and disputations as *Geopolitical Economy*, a project that is seemingly planned to sidestep and suspend any transformation that may look like the negation of the nation-state toward transnationalization and by slighting as "cosmopolitan."[93] The *state* is treated as an innate and intrinsic entity (beneath the edict of "materiality,"[94] an alleged "novel interpretation of Marx and Engels"[95]); imperialism, a panorama that mimics Lenin's "highest stage of capitalism" in perpetuity[96]; and the decline of the United States and the rise of China not unlike the display of seesaw in a mechanistic brush, via the catchphrase of "state contender development,"[97] demanding a multipolar world. The author Radhika Desai writes:

> The multipolar moment of the twenty-first century closes the long chapter in the history of imperialism in which single powers could dominate . . . the capitalist world order. . . . Imperialism has not come to an end: the more powerful states, the poles of the multipolar capitalist world, will still attempt to stall further diminution of the unevenness that favors them by new bouts of contender development. However, their very multiplicity works against them, and accelerates instead an evolution towards ever more numerous and less powerful poles, and a world order in which unevenness becomes progressively less consequential.
>
> (Desai 2013, 262)[98]

The previous passage is an instance of some methodologic errors in this "new" approach. First, in the context of Marx's value theory, uneven development is an *effect* of the self-expansion of capital as a social relation. Therefore, *unevenness*, an object of investigation and a real appearance, as it stands, necessarily precludes the underlying sources of its manifestation, as it stands here in this passage and indeed throughout this book. Hence, with or without the *piggyback* of the "combined,"[99] it cannot be a point of departure and a point of return at the same time.

Second, any discernable and consequential hint of unevenness in a capitalist economy is a product of the inner dynamics of capital itself; to put it plainly, in Marx's parlance, an individual capitalist or a group of capitalists or capitalist state in toto is but an *impersonator* of social relations of capital. In this light, a phenomenon of unevenness is no more and no less than an outward consequence of the contradictions that permeate, transfuse, and manifest through the state. Hence, frequent appealing to *unevenness*, in this volume, is not short of building a house of cards on apparent tautology.

Third, the tip of a mental construct, exemplified in the previous passage on *imperialism*, defined by the dominance and power of "the more powerful states," in circularity, supplemented by the tautology of "unevenness," is the height of a self-indicting methodology in this volume. The corollary of the circularity of power, on the one hand, and the idealization of the multiplicity of states of smaller size, capable of "new bouts of counter development," on the other, are the ingredients of diminishing polarity and "unevenness" in this proposed "world order." Hence, the "unevenness" and "imperialism" can be sponged on the road to a multipolar world in this bizarre mental construction. Here, "counter development" and "unevenness"—the epiphenomena that find centrality in the argument—are the constituents of the circular edifice that thru the caricature of geopolitics substituted the inner competition of capital, à la Marx, with Hobsonite rivalry and uneven development of capital, intrinsic to Marx's law of value, with apparent action of the state, by fiat. Here, a whiff of untimely nationalism, stashed in the *fetish* of imperialism, is in the air.[100]

Fourth, misidentifying the fallacy of "Hegemonic Stability Theory" (HST) with hegemony à la Gramsci and belittling the role of hegemonic institutions in the postwar Pax Americana is yet another methodological mishap in this volume. The lack of necessary theorization of the US role in the early part of transnationalization of capital, insufficient analysis of the circumstances surrounding the rise and fall of the US hegemony, and the lack of insight as to the organic connection between US decline and the collapse of hegemonic institutions of the Pax Americana could be among the factors that contributed to this mishap. The denial of US hegemony, however, has neither validity nor a bearing on the hegemonic reality of the postwar system as demonstrated in this volume.[101]

Fifth, the panorama of imperialism, a centerpiece of the neo-Hobsonite worldview, on the one hand, and the unyielding transhistorical tendency, for instance, the incongruent comparison of the Pax Britannica and postwar Pax

Americana, on the other hand, is also the Achilles' heel of this contending view in geopolitics and international relation. Here, the perpetuity of imperialism and plasticity of its untimely application provide a smokescreen for obfuscation of the periodization of capitalism and speculative attitude toward the significance of the now-defunct Pax Americana and the irreversible decline of the United States. Here, the tip of contradiction, namely, the negation of the US power by the emerging epoch of globalization, except by anecdotal rumor, is not only overlooked but also left entirely *untheorized* genuine geopolitics, as opposed to the speculative variety, devoid of a theoretical footing consistent with a periodization of capitalism compliant with the materiality of the epoch-making globalization.

Sixth, relying on fictitious rhetoric of "globalization," à la Washington, and depreciating the genuine tendencies of the globalization of capital is a context for this globalization-denial author in *Geopolitical Economy*. Speculating on the sustained power of the United States and counting on the minutia of Robert Reich's proposal in the Clinton administration purportedly toward the US revival (Chapter 7), the author eagerly mocks the globalization of capital under the pretext of "Reichian Globalization" turned "Stiglitzian Globalization" (p. 198), as if globalization was an American prerogative or if it is a choice. Enchanted by real appearances and beset by the mistaken identity not once but twice of the subjects under investigation, this book is a true portrayal of a sizable segment of the traditional left, in so many ways and so many iterations, in both methodology and ideology, today. The incongruent equivalence of the United States, a part of the whole, with the globalization of the world, the whole, is the tip of parody in this volume.[102] In a condescending strategy, the author also attempted to preempt other traditional leftists (among them self-styled Marxists) by accusing them of a "pure" approach and the failure to deal with the palpable reality.[103] Desai then takes to offense, as a defense, to boost the geopolitical economy as a new approach to contemporary world economy and polity under the guise of multipolarity.

Finally, as denoted in Part I and elsewhere in this book, crude reliance on the "uneven and combined development" (UCD) inescapably leads to distorted arguments and confusing conclusions, particularly on sensitive issues involving geopolitics and international relations. UCD appears to have obtained its magical place in *Geopolitical Economy*, as its functionality twisted toward "contending" and "counter development," against panoramic "unevenness," and ultimately to a stand-in for socialism in either the vintage of the former Soviet Union or contemporary China.[104] This, of course, opens the pandora's box of numbers of old and contentious issues that divide the radical left since the inception of the Bolshevik Revolution in Russia, an area beyond the aim of our subject. At any rate, in *Geopolitical Economy*, UCD and refurbished imperialism in the vintage of Hobsonite tradition explicit in the centrality of nation and nationalism play a defining part in the panoramic methodology and speculative understanding of multipolarity in the present post-American world.

Finally, the treatment of "uneven development" is a critical part of any study that deals with capitalist development. It is the issue that intimately relates to the law of value and thus class polarization intranationally, on the one hand, and international polarization, on the other, the sum total effects of which ultimately lead to transnationalization of capital (as a social relation) and eventual class polarization universally on a global scale. In a historical-materialist framework, this transformation represents a depiction of organic and enduring change across the seemingly inevitable and unchanging *center-periphery* division. This "division" then circularly taken up in the erection of *dependency* theory, a somewhat glorified version of it find survives in World-Systems theory, and the whimsy jumble of its latest incarnation, the embodiment of "global north/global south" partition, now appeals for the explanation of the same global phenomenon. This also shows the poverty of approaches that not only revolve around the limits of the nation-state or national boundary but also utterly are devoid of an embodiment of class and the value-theoretic Marxian analysis. It is unmistakable that methodologically, the concept of *uneven development* should cut across the national boundaries as a mode of appearance of the encroaching capital as a *potential* universal social relation, and more important as a precondition for (1) the identity and disposition of such state and (2) the state's policy and its very action. In other words, nation-states do not grow on trees just by happenstance.

Empire: Owl of Minerva and the Nightfall of Amnesia

This is a glance at a particular post-Marx Marxist tendency on the road to Marx-Beyond-Marx that in the end turned away from Marx's method, Marx's notion of exploitation, and Marx's vision of capitalism, and decidedly toward postmodernism, Empire, and a dystopia of a "non-place" where history, not unlike the light from a black hole, may not reveal a glimpse. Here, Empire is devoid of the past collective memory (known as history), the sense of reminiscences in time, the identity of time as history, the dawn, and the dusk at which time Owl of Minerva could spread its wings. Hence, fragmented subjectivity, disaffected by history—any history—turns up as a *text* detached from historical *context*; and this by itself is a grand irony vis-à-vis social activism and serious political struggle in this fantastic world of postmodernist imagination.[105]

Empire embodies an incomparable intoxication with the mode of appearance, a project that removes the context of capitalism by fiat, drains humanity of their history, and opens the door to endless collective amnesia and suspended animation of the new polity in the making.[106] This book was written in the aftermath of the collapse of postwar Pax Americana (1945–1979), the breakdown of the Soviet Union (1989–1991), and the illusion of American "unipolarity," in the 1990s, a unique and complex period that appeared to the naked eye as hotchpotch and undetermined.[107] As will be explicated later, the caliber of deception in Empire is not quite the same as the traditional left along the line of those examined earlier; Empire is a class by itself for obliterating, refashioning, and manifestly manufacturing the context and constitution of time, place, mode of production, social relations, etc.—that is, everywhere and everything we had so far learned and understood for sake of our survival under the sun.

Empire (i.e., the concept) is in effect science fiction motivated by postmodernity, a vision mesmerized by an arbitrary distinction of history as modern and post-modern, and accordingly, a capitalism that is morphed into distinction. Like neoclassical and neo-Ricardian economics, the study of reality according to this latter segment, that is, the postmodernist version of capitalism, ends up with real appearances alone.[108] *Empire*, by Hardt and Negri, conceived and choreographed explicitly as a world order without history, would speak for itself as follows:

> The concept of Empire is characterized fundamentally by a *lack of boundaries*: Empire's rule has *no limits*.[109] . . . Second, the concept of Empire presents itself not as a historical regime . . ., but rather as an order that effectively *suspends history*.[110] . . . From the perspective of Empire, this is the way things *will always be* and the way they were always meant to be. In other words, Empire presents its rule *not as transitory moment in the movement of history*, but as a regime . . . *outside of history* or at the end of history.[111] Third, . . . Empire presents the paradigmatic form of *biopower*.[112] Finally, although the practice of Empire is continually bathed in blood, the concept of Empire is always dedicated to peace—a perpetual and universal peace outside of history.
>
> (*Empire*, Preface, pp. xiv-xv, emphases added)

This is a description of history-less individuals and societies that despite the universality of life in both physical complexity and social dimensions, "always be" without a scintilla of becoming, a bizarre hyper-idealization not only of reality on Earth but also from the standpoint of a conscious observer of the Universe out there, so far as we experienced. And yet in this universal drama, known as *life*, any imaginable becoming of any kind, be it natural, social, intellectual, or political, cannot willfully avoid the dimension of *history*, old or new, that is, the willful avoidance of the sum of all cumulative subjectivities measured across in time. In other words, *being* and *becoming* are always the two faces of the same coin. Thus, the previous passage in its deepest logical core remains a crude mental construction despite its oracular tone, if not a hallucinatory aura, reminiscent of the ancient scripture.

The detailed critique of *Empire* or *Multitude* (also by Hardt and Negri) is neither our intent nor a parameter within our purpose in this volume and much less in this chapter. The aim here is merely a *hint* that our thesis of globalization has little to do either with Negri's earlier book, *Marx Beyond Marx*,[113] or his subsequent volume co-authored with Hardt—*Empire*. It should be noted that in *Empire*, Hardt and Negri do not present a critique of monopoly or imperialism; they have no qualms with Hilferding's, Lenin's, or Luxemburg's; Negri particularly does not seem to care about Marx's method or Marx's theory of value or, for that matter, methodic transnationalization of capital as a social relation. Moreover, he and his co-author Michael Hardt, at this historic moment in universalization of the capital's social relations decided to do away with class, history, and anything that smacks capitalism, as we know it, by the fiat of "virtuality" in *Empire*.[114] Hardt and Negri's allusion to globalization is merely rhetorical which has neither a grounding in Marx's value theory nor a footing in the capital as a social relation.[115]

The globalization of capital presented in this volume, however, is a different genre in both method and the vision of capitalism, its inner dynamics, and its aftermath. Our globalization has a long history that begins with the study of decartelization and globalization of oil (sector) in the 1970s. Globalization is a theory embodied in the periodization of capitalism, on the one hand, and manifested through the manifold overcoming by the capital of barriers and remaking of economic, cultural, legal, political, and social institutions across the board, on the other hand. This includes overcoming the limits of workplaces—industrial and otherwise—and appropriation and reordering of social structures and political space and arenas subject to footprints of capitalism. To simply use Marx's expression, this is nothing short of the conquest of "mode of production in all respects" worldwide.[116] The allusion to "non-place" symbolized in Hardt and Negri's *Empire* is but the very symptom of deepening division in class, gender, race, and widespread inequity inherent in the dynamics that necessarily accompany the globalization of capital.

The substitution of the class by "multitude," a grave methodological blunder, coupled with the perceived liberation of "virtual" work and imaginary autonomy of "digital" capitalism[117]—a crude and skin-deep view of social reality under capitalism—rips to pieces the very context and identity of capitalism, namely, *exploitation*. The multitude itself is also a double-edged weapon of choice for capital; indeed, a high point of fetishism that dutifully obfuscates the foundation of class struggle. It should be reminded that Marx's method of analysis should be an arbiter of elusive depiction and garbled envision of pseudo-globalization in Hardt and Negri's *Empire*. The allegory of "inside" and "outside" vis-à-vis the "multitude" in *Empire* also should be contrasted with capital's most distinguishing property in its early, embryonic anatomy, discovered some 160 years ago by Marx, namely, that "[t]he *true barrier* to capitalist production is *capital itself*" (*Capital*, Vol. III, p. 358, emphases in original).[118]

Here, the *inside* is the key to the *outside* for liberation. Contrary to Marx's methodology, Empire's "lack of boundary" and "rule [that] has no limits" both betray the DNA of capital and fly in the face of contemporary capitalism. What is the test—the litmus test, here?—ontologically, the existing boundary of the corporeality of capitalism itself; epistemologically, Marx's method and the trajectory and limit of Marx's theory of value at its core. Yet Hardt and Negri's Empire glides on the surface of reality and the palpable politics submerged in postmodernist ideology. In all seriousness, one should ask: Does this by any stretch of the imagination have any kinship with Marx beyond Marx that would show a faint semblance to Marxism? Finally, the appeal to the globalization of capital in Empire is but an intent at misrepresentation as to what the *text* is up to. It is neither about the reality or the true meaning of globalization nor about the authors' knowledge of the reality or author's knowledge of the true meaning of globalization; the allusion to globalization (indeed, pseudo-globalization) in *Empire* has one single purpose only, namely, to camouflage the intent of the text.[119] In methodological terms, a departure from the anachronism of *imperialism* and arrival in the futuristic regime of *Empire* has a schizophrenic quality and mental mutation that should not be discounted at either end of this transition.[120]

Time is a palpable measure of history as no one can refer to time without invoking history. Thus, evoking time is implicit in the recognition of history and ultimately in a "grand narrative"—as opposed to randomized, isolated, and fragmented narratives, oblivious to their encompassing historical origins, social context, and organic connections, in the name of *relative* subjectivity. *Empire* is infused in the latter vision, namely, the postmodernist view of the world. Here, the amputation of the *present* from the *past* takes center stage in a skin-deep epistemology that is detached from the backdrop of history and immersed in the mental construction of reality by fiat. This points to the lineage of the so-called Marx beyond Marx with Marx's value theory and his method of analysis.[121] By the way of analogy, the "arrow of time" is an artifact of the *observer*, according to modern cosmology, revealing that "time" in the physical world (in the absence of an observer) has no meaning whatsoever. In other words, without a conscious observer or subjective mind, historical time is meaningless, the obverse of which means that the subjective mind is also the creature of history, aside from social interaction. By standing "outside history," the logic of Hardt and Negri's Empire categorically has no room for an observer, to sense the *time* and feel the *history* (in memory of time–space), so to speak, while doing the task of passive observation, let alone active social and political struggle, in this whimsical dystopia where there is no sign of life, let alone society or capitalism. Don Quixote de la Mancha[122] himself could not have felt more at home in this twenty-first chimera than in his own fantasy in the sixteenth century.

Concluding Remarks

In Part I, the attempt was made to develop a framework for identification of certain fallacies that underpin the prevalent orthodox, heterodox, and the so-called radical views of capitalism and perceived transformation of it, particularly by the traditional left. There is a cluster of fallacies in this section that exposes the political and methodological divisions, old and new, and thus provide further lucidity to the critiques and disputations of Part II, and make them more intelligible to the reader. The ideological divide that beset the traditional left—particularly within its radical ranks today—belongs to an earlier bifurcation that set off the radical Hobsonite's newfound tradition of the 1910s and 1920s against Marx's methodological tradition. Thus, the old and insurmountable cleavage of the past, like a festering old wound, together with new cleavages, cannot be set aside in the name of unity or Marxism. The periodization of capitalism toward globalization, on the one hand, and critical assessment of the Hobsonite and neo-Hobsonite departure prompted the themes in this chapter, the corollary of which is critical for the modus operandi of the collapse of the Pax Americana and the rise and fall of the American hegemony.

The fallacies presented in Part I are a shorthand for the preemption of methodologies that in manifold variation broadly follow Hobson/Hilferding/Kautsky/Lenin/Luxemburg's tradition of monopoly capitalism; a tradition immersed in cartels, monopolies, and crises of underconsumption and a worldview incongruent with indigeneity of concentration and centralization of capital, and thus alien to the internal dynamics of capitalism based on synthetic competition embedded in Marx's theory of value. The bifurcation indicated earlier cannot be simply reduced to the alleged change in the outlook of capitalism in historical time, between Marx's and, say, Lenin's lifespan, but squarely grounded in critical contrast between Marx's methodology and worldview, and those of Lenin's, Hilferding's, Bukharin's, or Luxemburg's. In other words, the contrast between Marx's view and Hobsonites' vision of capitalism is methodological and as a matter of inconsistent epistemologies. This contrast is also a matter of ontology concerning the corporeality of capitalism as hinted earlier in this chapter. Similar incompatibility with Marx's also runs through the generations of the neo-Hobsonites who also maintain that monopoly capitalism and imperialism, the two sides of the same coin, constitute the highest stage of capitalism. Whereas Marx's capitalism is organically explicit in (1) distinction of "primitive accumulation" (pre-history of capital) and capitalist accumulation, (2) distinction of perfect/imperfect competition and the real competition as inner dynamics of capital accumulation, (3) expressed manifestation of competition in concentration and centralization of capital, and thus cheapening of labor power universally, and (4) tendency of capital as a self-expanding value toward eventual universality. For Marx, all these attributes are irreducibly organic and intensely on display as capitalism grows into maturity. On the other hand, for Hobsonites and neo-Hobsonites penetrating below the surface of appearance does not play the first fiddle, which also was an epistemic attribute of Hobson himself.

The aforementioned fallacies are, in one way or another, symptomatic of post-Marx Marxism either in its Hobsonites original vintage in the 1910s and 1920s or, as demonstrated earlier, in the neo-Hobsonite vintage of the following decades, prominently in the writings of Paul Sweezy, Paul Baran, Harry Magdoff, Harry Braverman,[123] and Samir Amin, among many more. Given our interest in the globalization of capital à la Marx, Part II attempted to run alongside the neo-Hobsonite tendency, a critique of three additional perspectives that utterly fail the test of specificity and thus relevance as to the identity of capitalism and the epoch of globalization, namely, World-Systems theory, geopolitical economy, and Empire. These approaches also failed to pay sufficient attention to the particularities of hegemonic power and the role of mediating institutions in the rise and fall of postwar Pax Americana and their paradoxical link in the irony of globalization of capital. As pointed out in some details, all these perspectives are either methodologically unfit or historically anachronistic and panoramic or, in the case of Empire, a masquerade of fantastic spectacle leading to a shadowy "non-place." As for the grounding of our critique in alternatives of true, false, and fake—as opposed to the standard true-false binary—the rationale is given in Part I.

Similarly, the identity of the *present* is lost on nearly all these alternative approaches, as each was sidetracked by the minutia of trifling narratives without originality or theoretical consequence. The identity of our epoch is crucial for the identity of our common struggles and by inference the defining measure of our own social and individual identity. As denoted earlier, the fetish of imperialism, overblown by allusion to convoluted appearances and by misidentifying the *present* as the habitual *past* by the traditional left, is but camouflage for misidentification of the American capitalism with the epoch of globalization, inevitably leading to a mangled view of contemporary geopolitics. Given the palpable global realities surrounding the rise of China, certain supporters of this view while muddying the water are now on the defensive. The story of the non-traditional left, exemplified by Hardt and Negri's *Empire*, is even more bizarre. Here, Empire is but a caricature of globalization, embedded in the tautology of power and façade of "biopolitics" à la Foucault, glitteringly giving off a whiff of the avant-garde. Thanks to the mystifying aftermath of the Soviet collapse and fakery of American "unipolarity," perceived by the Marx-beyond-Marx silliness and postmodernist swank. The "suspension of history," in this charade, is also explicit in holding off Owl of Minerva in suspended animation for the balance of life as we know it. The incongruent equivalence of the epoch of globalization and the United States is nevertheless a misrepresentation shared by both the traditional and non-traditional left.

Globalization is the mother of all negations and as such an ultimate overcoming of the barriers, from the barrier of working day in the late nineteenth century to the boundaries of geography across the planet in the twenty-first century. It is the de facto conquest of the mode of production, as Marx remarkably predicted some 160 years ago at the peak of his investigation. And it is the omnipresence of globalization that stands as a measure of all measures and the context of all contexts in an epoch that Marx's law of value finds universally across the globe. As elucidated amply in this book, the postwar Pax Americana (1945–1979) was eventually collapsed by the inner dynamics of globalized capital—that is, capital as a social relation. This also crystalizes Gramsci's insightful observation that international relations "follow" social relations (Gramsci 1971, 176).[124]

Notes

1 See Cypher, James 1979. "Internationalization of Capital and the Transformation of Social Formations: A Critique of the Monthly Review School," *Review of Radical Political Economics* 11 (4): 33–49.

2 The phrase "traditional left" here refers to all those on the radical left who think that Marx's view of capitalism, including his method and the law of value, is reconcilable

with those of the radical Hobsonites, such Hilferding, Lenin, and Luxemburg, to name a few; it is this undue reconciliation that twists the contemporary capitalism into something that is not.

3 Wallerstein, Emmanuel 2004. *World-Systems Analysis: An Introduction.* Durham and London: Duke University Press.

4 Desai, Radhika 2013. *Geopolitical Economy: After US Hegemony, Globalization and Empire.* London: Pluto Press.

5 Hardt, Michael and Antonio Negri 2000. *Empire.* Cambridge, MA: Harvard University Press.

6 Marx, Karl 1983 [1845]. "Theses on Feuerbach," in *The Portable Karl Marx.* Eugene Kamenka (ed.). Harmondsworth, England: Penguin: 155–158.

7 Miguel de Cervantes' prominent character in a book of the same title.

8 Hobson, John A. 1902. *Imperialism: A Study.* London: James Nisbet & Co. Ltd. (electronic reprint: Google Books).

9 Hilferding, Rudolf 2019 [1910]. *Finance Capital: A Study of the Latest Phase of Capitalist Development.* London: Routledge (reprint).

10 Lenin, Vladimir Ilyich 1970 [1916]. *Imperialism: The Highest Stage of Capitalism.* Peking: Foreign Language Press.

11 Luxemburg, Rosa 2003 [1913]. *The Accumulation of Capital.* London: Routledge (reprint).

12 See Marx, Karl 1976 [1867]. *Capital,* Vol. I. New York: Vintage Edition; Marx. Karl 1981 [1885]. *Capital,* Vol. II. New York: Vintage Edition; Marx, Karl 1981 [1894]. *Capital,* Vol. III. New York: Vintage Edition; Marx, Karl 1973 [1939]. *Grundrisse: Foundations of the Critique of Political Economy.* New York: Vintage Edition.

13 After nearly five decades of painstaking study, I have coined the term Hobsonites as to the first serious methodological cleavage between Marx and the prominent followers of Hobson in the 1910s and 1920s, namely, Hilferding, Lenin, and Luxemburg, among others, who in the opinion of the traditional left made an advance over the master himself. As demonstrated throughout this book, Hobsonites' first foot was backward, not forward. The second round of explicit methodological breaks with Marx took place in the 1950s and 1960s, culminating in the 1966 publication of *Monopoly Capital* by Baran and Sweezy. This, in weightlifting parlance, was a "clean and jerk" cessation that made it crystal clear to everyone that the wagons were about to be circled, so to speak, and the neo-Hobsonites, particularly those associated with Monthly Review, meant business from then on. But, as the 1970s realities set in, low and behold, Marx was back on the saddle and with vengeance.

14 See Baran, Paul A. and Paul M. Sweezy 1966. *Monopoly Capital: An Essay on the American Economic and Social Order.* New York: Monthly Review Press.

15 See Bina, Cyrus 1994a. "Farewell to the Pax Americana," in *Islam, Iran, and World Stability.* Hamid Zangeneh (ed.). New York: St. Martin's: 41–74; Bina, Cyrus 2004. "The American Tragedy: The Quagmire of War, Rhetoric of Oil, and the Conundrum of Hegemony," *Journal of Iranian Research and Analysis* 20 (2):7–22.

16 See Chattopadhyay, Paresh 2019 [2018]. *Socialism and Commodity Production: Essays in Marx Revival.* Chicago, IL: Haymarket Books. This book reveals the misperception of those so-called Marxists within the traditional left, who may have little clue about social relations in capitalism defined by Marx's theory of value since the early 1910s.

17 See Bina, Cyrus 2013b. *A Prelude to the Foundation of Political Economy: Oil, War, and Global Polity.* New York: Palgrave Macmillan, Ch. 5, sec. "A Note on Methodology": 130–133.

18 Solow, Robert M. 1957. "Technical Change and the Aggregate Production Function," *The Review of Economics and Statistics* 39 (3), August: 312–320; see also Shaikh, Anwar 1974. "Laws of Production and Laws of Algebra: The Humbug Production Function," The *Review of Economics and Statistics* 56 (1), February: 115–120; Shaikh, Anwar 1980.

"Laws of Production and Laws of Algebra—Humbug II," in *Growth, Profits and Property*. Edward J. Nell (ed.). Cambridge, UK: Cambridge University Press: 80–95.

19 It is important not to get sidetracked by authors who insist on the priority of "geopolitics" without a proper underpinning in theory concerning the stage of development of capitalism. As is demonstrated in this chapter and elsewhere in this book, it is also imperative to not fall for the clichés, such as "imperialism" and "uneven and combined development" (UCD), in order to come up with a proper theory and practice of geopolitics in today's globalized economy and polity. For a contrary example, see Desai, Radhika 2010. "The Absent Geopolitics of Pure Capitalism," *World Review of Global Economy* 1 (3): 463–484. Aside from the context of the dispute, the allusion to "pure" in the title of this article is problematic. This will become perceptible as we proceed in this chapter.

20 Look at Paul Sweezy's earlier book, namely, *The Theory Capitalist Development*, prefaced by Sweezy at Dunster House, Harvard University Campus, on August 1, 1942, and reprinted verbatim by MR Press (New York and London) in a paperback edition in 1968. The inspection of Chapters 14 and 15, particularly, reveals that Sweezy from the get-go believed that concentration and centralization of capital are but a monopoly and that Marx's competition is the same as the neoclassical theory of "pure competition." The further evidence of this is even more revealing: his 1939 article, "Demand Under Conditions of Oligopoly," *The Journal of Political Economy* 47 (4), August 1939: 568–573, known as the kinked demand curve. This shows that Sweezy was not by any stretch of the imagination even remotely close to his mentor, and later his senior colleague, Joseph A. Schumpeter, at Harvard's Economics Department, on capitalist competition, at the time. In other words, Sweezy had ample time to learn and change his mind on the parody of competition in mainstream economics orthodoxy, but he didn't. As for Harry Braverman, the title of his book speaks for itself: Braverman, Harry 1974. *Labor and Monopoly Capital*. New York: Monthly Review Press.

21 See Bina, Cyrus 1985. *The Economics of the Oil Crisis*. New York: St. Martin's Press.

22 Sachs, Jeffrey D. 2020. *The Ages of Globalization*. New York: Columbia University Press.

23 Michie, Jonathan 2017. *Advanced Introduction to Globalization*. Cheltenham, UK: Edward Elgar.

24 This should not be mistaken with the assorted sentiments that appeared in the social and cultural milieu under the rubric of "globalization," particularly with the advent of digital technology, in the late 1990s.

25 A specific example is Amin, Samir 1992. *Empire of Chaos*. New York: Monthly Review Press.

26 See Amin, Samir 2013. *The Implosion of Contemporary Capitalism*. New York: Monthly Review Press.

27 A typical example is Desai, Radhika 2013. *Geopolitical Economy: After US Hegemony, Globalization and Empire*. London: Pluto Press.

28 See Marx, Karl 1976 [1867]. *Capital*, Vol. I, Ch. 1 (The Commodity), sec. 4 (The Fetishism of Commodity and Its Secret): 163–177. Here is also a key to sociability (or sociality) of capital and capitalist relations which in developed forms express themselves not only in exchange relations but necessarily also in the sum total of state's institutions and in the guise of the nation-state itself. Marx's introduction early on to fetishism here in this volume is remarkable evidence of his complete grasp of capitalism in its developed form within its embryonic development in the nineteenth century. Here, I wish to remind the reader that Gérrard Duménil and Dominique Lévy, in their recent book, are victims of fetishism, besides being methodologically inconsistent with Marx's theory of (synthetic) competition, and the originality of his value theory for capitalism's all-embracing mode of production till its contemporary globalization. See Duménil, Gérard and Dominique Lévy 2018. *Managerial Capitalism: Ownership, Management & The Coming New Mode of Production*. London: Pluto Press.

29 As an example of an essentialist approach to viewing the nation-state under the guise of "materiality," see Desai, Radhika 2013. *Geopolitical Economy: After US Hegemony, Globalization and Empire*. London: Pluto Press, Ch. 2.

30 This process emerges in a historical materialist domain with *abstract labor* as its social consequence which in turn is represented by *money* in exchange. This is the essence of value theory in Marx. We must carefully notice three significant points here: (1) that abstract labor is not the consequence of a mental process but the result of real abstraction and real competition; (2) that the formation of value, as the center of gravity of prices of production and observable market prices, is neither an "equilibrium" theory nor a result of equilibrium; and (3) that money is not an arbitrary numéraire (or arbitrary sum) but real and a necessary part of the same process. While on the subject, we wish to alert the reader to the so-called *monetary theory of value*, by Michael Heinrich, which completely disregards Marx's labor theory of value by vacating the abstract labor, value, and the value-form and externalizing "money" as the measure of "value" across the society or economy by fiat. The cause of such fiat appears to be in the fact that Heidrich put himself in Marx's body and soul and decided for him what Marx should have done in the early 1850s with his theory of value. In other words, Heinrich concocts a story that Marx's project remained "incomplete," not due to any probable intervening incidents, but because in Heinrich's "logical" mind, Marx wanted to (or should?) have made the change long before the writings of the *Grundrisse*, and all three volumes of *Capital*. This is a bizarre claim and bizarre attitude by someone who craves to impose his methodology and his own thinking about how capitalism works, or how it would turn up, in the name of Marx. For details, see Liedman, Sven-Eric. 2018. *A World to Win: The Life and Works of Karl Marx*, London: Verso, Ch. 11, section (The Interpreters): 430–434, section (Essence and Appearance; Form and Content; Surface and depth): 434–439; Bina, Cyrus 2013b. *A Prelude to the Foundation of Political Economy*. New York: Palgrave Macmillan, Ch. 5, section (A Note on Methodology): 132–133; Heinrich, Michael 2014. *An Introduction to the Three Volumes of Karl Marx's Capital*. New York: Monthly Review Press. Michael Heinrich appears as a closeted post-Modernist.

31 See a remarkable critique by Samezö Kuruma, a leading Japanese Marxist of lesser-known tradition in the West. Kuruma is correct in his criticism of Uno's on Marx's theory of money and his cult of supporters in the West. Kuruma, Samezõ 2018 [2017]. *Marx's Theory of the Genesis of Money: How Why, and Through What is a Commodity Money?* Chicago, IL: Haymarket Books. For further critique of Uno's value theory, see Lange, Elena Louise 2021. *Value without Fetish: Uno Kõzõ's Theory of 'Pure Capitalism' in Light of Marx's Critique of Political Economy*. Leiden: Brill. While on the subject, there are three significant points that have not sufficiently been appreciated in Marx's value theory: (1) that, in capitalism, spheres of production and circulation are organically intertwined, that is, the latter is the apparent manifestation of value (abstract labor) and *inner* competition in their *first-appearance*; (2) money has no direct relation with market price without the mediation of value in production; and (3) that commodity, commodity exchange, and money in pre-*capital* is not the same as a commodity (including commodity *labor power*), generalized commodity production and exchange, and *money* (general equivalent form) in *capital* proper (and capitalism). This may respond to some of "much ado about nothing" on the alleged priority of money and value form over the *abstract labor* in some fringe quarters.

32 See Uno, Kõzõ 1980 [1964]. *Principles of Political Economy*. Essex, UK: The Harvester Press Ltd. In addition to this three-stage a priori division, which makes a mockery of Marx's value theory and method of abstraction, Uno's view of money as an unmediated phenomenon in exchange opens the pandora's box to a variety of misadventures into the methodological ramification of value theory, including the so-called monetary theory of value, neo-circulationist view of value theory, and return to the idealism of Hegel through the "systematic dialectic." For a sample of the latter incursion, see Arthur,

Christopher J. 2014. "Marx, Hegel and the Value-Form," in *Marx's Capital and Hegel's Logic: A Reexamination*. Fred Moseley and Tony Smith (eds.). Chicago, IL: Haymarket Books: 269–291.

33 This pivotal point in mathematical logic and the larger arena of methodology is known as Gödel's Proof. See Nagel, Ernest and James R. Newman. 1958. *Gödel's Proof.* New York: New York University Press.

34 There is an exception for the Carl Menger side of the Marginalist school, known as Austrian economics, in which there is room for *time* and *process* but subjectivism, "praxeology," and methodological individualism are prevalent. See, for further details, Milonakis, Dimitris and Ben Fine 2009. *From Political Economy to Economics*. New York: Routledge, Ch. 13.

35 The so-called mainstream economics is not a benign paradigm but a subject that is profoundly ideological. For a remarkable critique, see Weeks, John 2014. *Economics of the 1%: How Mainstream Economics Serves the Rich, Obscures Reality and Distorts Policy*. London: Anthem Press.

36 For a glimpse of typical neoclassical economics texts, see Mankiw, N. Gregory 2020. *Principles of Microeconomics*. 9th Edition. Samford, CT: Cengage Learning; Frank, Robert H., Ben S. Bernanke, Kate Antonovics, and Ori Heffetz 2019. *Principles of Microeconomics*. 8th Edition. New York: McGraw-Hill.

37 This phrase is an oxymoron in strict Marx's methodology and worldview of the capitalist mode of production. Given its origins in Hobson, it cannot be Marxian. It is a strange case of guilt by association. An appropriate term with decidedly less ideological yet accurate connotation could be "classical theories of imperialism."

38 For an example of communication between the traditional left scholars beyond economics, see Callinicos, Alex and Justin Rosenberg 2008. "Uneven and Combined Development: The Social-Relational Substratum of 'the International'? An Exchange of Letters," *Cambridge Review of International Affairs* 21 (1), March: 77–112. The interesting about this exchange is that it exposes a pattern of methodological obstacles that many on the left are confronted with. Yet, the setback for Trotskyists is compounded by a dutiful fixation on "uneven and combined development," a notion that is discussed amply in this volume. This exchange reveals (1) that any theorization in the context of "international" must necessarily hold on to the perpetual motion of imperialism, (2) that the "classical theories of imperialism" are necessarily an extension of Marx's theory, (3) that the fallacy of incongruent equivalence is at the heart of the discussion, and (4) that, in footsteps of orthodox theory, there is such thing as a *general theory* of international relations.

39 For a remarkable critique of Lenin's view of socialism, the immediate period after the October Revolution, and of the nature of the so-called socialism in the Soviet Union, see Chattopadhyay, Paresh 2019. *Socialism and Commodity Production*. Chicago, IL: Haymarket Books. This critique, in addition to many revolutionary contemporaries of Lenin following the revolution, is relevant to today's traditional left concerning this trans-identification of socialism and capitalism by real appearances.

40 For an overview of selected traditional leftists' views, see McKelvey, Charles 2021. China and the Left: A Socialist Forum, *Knowledge, Ideology, and Real Socialism in Our Times* September 24, retrieved: December 10, 2021: https://charlesmckelvey.substack.com/p/china-and-the-left. Among several leftists in this interview essay, Radhika Desai reiterates her dutiful stance on the perpetuity of "imperialism"; she also acknowledges that contemporary China is socialist.

41 This should raise a red flag on a profound error by writers, such as Harvey, who stock up on "neoliberalism" and pretend to have explicated the post-1970s economic upheavals as "accumulation by dispossession." David Harvey implicitly and erroneously draws a parallel between Marx's "primitive accumulation" (an accumulation prior to the development of capital accumulation proper) and the fully developed, globalized capitalism of

post-1970s, under the guise of "new" imperialism. Neoliberalism for Harvey consists of state policies that lead to privatization, "financialization," state redistribution, and manipulation of crises by the state since the 1970s. Accumulation by dispossession of course smacks Luxemburg's view of capitalism that—as we explained earlier in this volume—is not capitalism with its inner laws of motion and dynamics at all. Harvey's egregious blunder is methodological on several fronts: (1) he misidentifies neoliberalism, a set of policies, with globalized capitalism and its laws of motion; (2) he unwisely releases the ghost of imperialism from its tattered closet; (3) he muddies the accumulation of capital with its pre-accumulation by displacing of the cause (inner dynamics of capital) and its effect: dispossession; (4) he uses neoliberalism in a tautological manner and expounds the actions of the state in neoliberalism; (5) he turns Marx's theory of competition to "perfect/imperfect" competition in orthodox neoclassical economics; and (6) consequently, he has little (methodological) clue as to the profound structural changes that have taken place since the 1970s toward globalization. See Harvey, David 2004. "The 'New' Imperialism: Accumulation by Dispossession," *Socialist Register* 40: 63–87; Harvey, David 2003. *The 'New' Imperialism*. Oxford, UK: Oxford University Press.

42 See Gramsci, Antonio 1971. *Selected from the Prison Notebooks*. New York: International Publishers.

43 See Bina, Cyrus 2013b. *A Prelude to the Foundation of Political Economy: Oil, War, and Global Polity*. New York: Palgrave Macmillan, Ch. 7: 188–191.

44 Bina, Cyrus 2004. "The American Tragedy: The Quagmire of War, Rhetoric of Oil, and the Conundrum of Hegemony," *Journal of Iranian Research and Analysis* 20 (2):7–22.

45 A typical example of traditional left's misunderstanding of *hegemony* can be seen in Desai, Radhika 2013. *Geopolitical Economy: After US Hegemony, Globalization and Empire*. London: Pluto Press, Ch. 5.

46 Trotsky, Leon 2008 [1917]. *History of the Russian Revolution*. Chicago, IL: Haymarket Books.

47 The reliance upon what comes into view as "uneven" within the nation-state and augmentation via an artifice of "combined" generate a framework that looks like development with an international dimension. This is UCD's significance for certain post-Trotsky scholars. But it appears as a sneaky way of claiming monopoly capitalism without falling into the trap of flat-out abrogation of Marx's theory of value. An expressive example of the unbending deployment of UCD can be found in Ernest Mandel's *Late Capitalism*, where the author takes issue with Christian Palloix on the "international equalization of the rate of profit," a tendency that Marx's law value (and his theory of synthetic competition) had long predicted. Mandel writes:

> The hypothesis of international equalization of the rate of profit cannot be sustained either theoretically or empirically. Theoretically, it presupposes *perfect* international mobility of capital—in effect, the equalization of all economic, social, and political conditions propitious to the development of modern capitalism on a world scale. Such equalization, however, is completely contradicted by the law of uneven and combined development which dominates this development (Mandel 1978, 352, emphasis added).

First, Mandel speaks of the "perfect international mobility of capital"—a reference that smacks the neoclassical theory of "pure competition" as opposed to Marx's synthetic competition. There is no such thing as perfect or imperfect mobility or competition. Second, Mandel speaks of presupposition for such mobility, and cannot envisage that the tendency of mobility for capital in competition (an inner nature of capital itself) had already been working and in full force at the time of his writing. Third, sticking to UCD (an epiphenomenon that appears as international development and expansion of capital) is in complete conformity with his view of *underdevelopment* (albeit on a capitalistic basis, p. 352), an outlook quite reminiscent of *dependency theory* and undeniably contrary to Marx's theory of value. Fourth, neither Mandel nor other traditional leftists captivated by monopoly and perpetuity of imperialism (as an epoch) appear to have no other recourse other than to hold onto the dogma of UCD as a make-believe international development theory. Finally, Mandel's *Late Capitalism* is after all monopoly capitalism with punishing vacillation between Lenin and Marx. See Mandel, Ernest 1978. *Late Capitalism*. London: Verso Press.

48 Ricardo, David 1911 [1817]. *The Principles of Political Economy and Taxation*. Second Edition. New York: J.M. Dent; E.P. Dutton, Ch. 7.

49 Embedded in Say's Law, Ricardo's comparative cost theory is a theory of trade in goods between nations where the balance of trade between the deficit and surplus country is settled by the transfer of gold from deficit nation to surplus nation in order to stabilize prices in both countries. Hence, this theory for classical political economy stands for (1) a theory of domestic prices and (2) a theory of balance of trade and payments. The logical conclusion of Ricardo's theory of comparative cost is complete specialization. In the context of the British colonial empire, such specialization was not without direct ideological implications concerning trade the bulk of which was decided with colonies. The story of the concept of "comparative advantage" à la neoclassical economics is a separate genre in that it is grounded in the tautology of "opportunity cost"—the cost of the next best alternative—in a microeconomic framework, reflecting the individual choice. The comparative advantage also promotes specialization. In this connotation, this reincarnation has no sophistication as to even pretending as an instrument for balance trade or payment. Yet, each of these fallacies has its own specific ideological bent in caricaturing the truth.

50 For a critical assessment of free trade, see Shaikh, Anwar 2007. "Globalization and the Myth of Free Trade," in *Globalization and the Myth of Free Trade: History, Theory, and Empirical Evidence*. Anwar Shaikh (ed.). New York: Routledge, Ch. 3: 51–68.

51 See Desai, Radhika 2013. *Geopolitical Economy: After US Hegemony, Globalization and Empire*. London: Pluto Press.

52 See Desai, Radhika 2010. "The Absent Geopolitics of Pure Capitalism," *World Review of Political Economy* 1 (3), Fall: 463–484.

53 See Desai, Radhika, *Geopolitical Economy* 2013, Ch. 1.

54 See Desai, Radhika, *Geopolitical Economy* 2013, Ch. 9.

55 See Frankfurt, Harry G. 2005. *On Bullshit*. Princeton, NJ: Princeton University Press.

56 Frankfurt 2005. *On Bullshit*: 47, 53–54.

57 Frankfurt 2005. *On Bullshit*: 43. For an application of bullshit to recent debates on US intervention in Iraq and the cause of war, see Bina, Cyrus 2012a. *Oil: A Time Machine*. Second Edition. Ronkonkoma, New York: Linus Publications, Ch. 14.

58 Marx, Karl ([1852] 1963). *The Eighteenth Brumaire of Louis Bonaparte*. New York: International Publishers.

59 For Marx's view of capitalist competition as opposed to prevalent view in both orthodox and heterodox economics, see Marx, Karl 1955 [1847]. *The Poverty of Philosophy*. Moscow: Progress Publishers, Ch. 2, sec. 3: 126–134.

60 Marx, Karl 1981 [1894]. *Capital*, Vol. III. New York: Vintage Edition.

61 The lack of adequate appreciation of the fact that capitalism is a social system from the ground up, on the one hand, and Marx's *synthetic* competition leads to further concentration and centralization of capital and the latter to further competition, compels Lenin to speak in the dawn of capitalism of "transition from the capitalist system to a higher socio-economic order." Lenin, Vladimir I. 1970 [1916]. *Imperialism: The Highest Stage of Capitalism*. Peking: Foreign Language Press: 148. For a critical assessment, see Bina, Cyrus 2013b. *A Prelude to the Foundation of Political Economy*. New York: Palgrave-Macmillan, Ch. 5: 133–144. Concerning Marx's scant remark on the "new" mode of production in *Capital*, Vol. III, in their new book *Managerial Capitalism* (2018), Gérard Duménil and Dominique Lévy make the same mistake about the *sociality* of capitalism as if it is something new and external thus claiming a new mode

of production. It is a matter of primary importance to note that such sociality needs to be understood as a potential turned actual in the dialectic of transformation of capital as a social relation. To be sure, Marx's allusion to the "new" mode is a reference to a mode of appearance alone. Otherwise, Marx would be a fool to publish his first volume of *Capital* with such enthusiasm in 1867, nearly three 3 years hence, and promote it too as it was for the rest of his life. Incidentally, the authors' illusion of Marx's general theory of history also in this book, not unlike Samuel Clenmce's early obituary, is highly exaggerated.

62 For a critique of the orthodox view of competition, see Clifton, James A. 1977. "Competition and Evolution of the Capitalist Mode of Production," *Cambridge Journal of Economics* 1 (2): 137–151; Shaikh, Anwar 1980. "Marxian Competition versus Perfect Competition: Further Comments on the So-Called Choice of Techniques," *Cambridge Journal of Economics* 4 (1): 75–83; Weeks, John 2013. "The Fallacy of 'Competition' Markets and the Movement of Capital," in *Alternative Theories of Competition: Challenges to the Orthodoxy*. J. Moudud, C. Bina, and P. Mason (eds.). New York: Routledge: 13–26; Bina, Cyrus 2013a. "Synthetic Competition, Global Oil, and the Cult of Monopoly," in *Alternative Theories of Competition: Challenges to the Orthodoxy*. J. K. Moudud, C. Bina, and P. Mason (eds.). New York: Routledge: 55–85.

63 This trio is William Stanly Jevons, Carl Menger, and Léon Walras, who separately laid the cornerstone of the individualization of economics as a universal and ahistorical subject in the 1870s. This is an ideological paradigm shift that ironically landed at the time that capitalism was in the process of further sociability symbolized in corporate form.

64 Frankfurt, Harry G. 2005. *On Bullshit*. Princeton, NJ: Princeton University Press.

65 For an elaborate and detailed investigation of competition as an innermost dynamic of the capitalist mode of production, see Shaikh, Anwar 2016. *Capitalism: Competition, Conflict, Crises*. New York: Oxford University Press, Chapters 7–11.

66 See Bina, Cyrus 1985. *The Economics of the Oil Crisis*. New York: St. Martin's Press; Bina, Cyrus 2006. "The globalization of Oil: A Prelude to a Critical Political Economy," *International Journal of Political Economy* 35 (2): 4–34; Bina, Cyrus 2013a. "Synthetic Competition, Global Oil, and the Cult of Monopoly," in *Alternative Theories of Competition: Challenges to the Orthodoxy*. J. K. Moudud, C. Bina, and P. Mason (eds.). New York: Routledge: 55–85.

67 Lenin, Vladimir I. 1970 [1916]. *Imperialism, The Highest Stage of Capitalism*. Peking: Foreign Language Press.

68 We should have realized so far that from the standpoint of Marx's *Capital*, not any and every prima facie concentration and/or centralization is an outright monopoly.

69 The euphemism of "finance capital" is encryption for monopoly borrowed verbatim from Hilferding's *Das Finanzkapital* (1910); for the English version, see Hilferding, Rudolph 1981. *Finance Capital. A Study of the Latest Phase of Capitalist Development*. London: Routledge & Kegan Paul.

70 Export of capital is but the negation of the nation-state's border by self-expanding capital in money form. Money (finance) is one of the three possible forms of capital in a transformative motion.

71 Without naming names, whitewashing Lenin's view of the "export of capital," a sign of the awareness of Marx's circuit of moments of capital as a tendency to international accumulation, is not a proper way of approbation of this great and incomparable figure of the twentieth century. To be sure, Lenin took "export of capital" out of Hilferding's mouth, specifically in a connotation that would reinforce Hobson's monopoly, in the context of "finance capital." For a remarkable source on Hilferding's view, see Zoninsein, Jonas 1990. *Monopoly Capital Theory: Hilferding and Twentieth-Century Capitalism*. New York: Greenwood Press. Similarly, the fiat of "labor aristocracy" is a sign of an artificial view of capitalism and Lenin's unshakable monopoly capitalism.

72 The notion of *rivalry* in Lenin's is not unlike "oligopoly," an offshoot of market structure orthodoxy in neoclassical economics.

73 It is a pity that a brilliant scholar and author of *The Development of Capitalism in Russia*, and an incomparable Marxist revolutionary, such as Vladimir Ilyich Ulyanov (Lenin), should be absorbed by extraordinary circumstances in this fashionable conceptual U-turn at this time. See Lenin, Vladimir I. 1974 [1899]. *The Development of Capitalism in Russia*. Moscow: Progress Publishers.

74 To be sure, we hold that imperialism signifies the characteristics of a specific period only.

75 Baran, Paul A. and Paul M. Sweezy 1966. *Monopoly Capital: An Essay on the American Economic and Social Order*. New York: Monthly Review Press.

76 Sweezy, Paul M. 1939. "Demand Under Conditions of Oligopoly," *The Journal of Political Economy* 47 (4), August: 568–573.

77 With all due respect, the argument here is not whether there is something wrong with these subjects, that is, the question of *falsity*; it is rather the more subtle question of *fakery* (of the context) that is the very focus.

78 On the notion of "disproportionality," it would be instructive to read Marx's passage in *Grundrisse* as follows:

> Finally: *proportionate production* . . . only when it is capital's tendency to distribute itself in correct proportions but equally its necessary tendency . . . to drive beyond the proportion. (In *competition* this inner tendency of capital appears as a compulsion exercised over it by *alien capital*, which drives it forward beyond the correct proportion with a constant *march, march!* . . . . Conceptually, *competition* is nothing than the inner *nature of capital* . . . appearing in and realized as the reciprocal interaction of many capitals . . . the inner tendency as external necessity).
>
> (pp. 413–414, emphases in original)

79 It is no accident that Sweezy tried tooth and nail to demonstrate that Marx was devoted to underconsumption in his theory of crisis. He tried like a first-class criminal lawyer to plant doubts in the mind of the unsuspected jury, so to speak, to distract them from the Tendency of the Rate of Profit to Fall, an all-inclusive key to the inner competition of capital through the crisis in the capitalist mode of production. So, the best defense was an offense by resorting to a dog-and-pony sideshow to put the underconsumption (an epiphenomenon) at the center and dovetail it in mutuality with his monopoly theory, not unlike Hobson. For more details, see Bleaney, Michael 1976. *Underconsumption Theories*. New York: International Publishers, Ch. 6. To be sure, underconsumption underly all class societies in human history, just like scarcity. To fall for the mimic of underconsumption is not unlike being duped by the neoclassical price theory based on *scarcity*.

80 Baran, Paul A. and Paul M. Sweezy 1966. *Monopoly Capital: An Essay on the American Economic and Social Order*. New York: Monthly Review Press.

81 Confirmation of lockstep with Sweezy's thesis is the emulation of the current editor of *Monthly Review*, John Bellamy-Foster. See Bellamy-Foster, John 2015. "The New Imperialism of Globalized Monopoly-Finance Capital," *Monthly Review* 67 (3), July–August: 1–22; Bellamy-Foster, John 2019. "Late Imperialism," *Monthly Review* 71 (3), July–August: 1–19. It appears that Bellamy Foster is so deeply preoccupied with his dutiful task that he had to put an additional qualifier on "finance capital" to make it appears more monopolized, even though Hilferding's phrase, namely, *finance capital*, itself has a fastidious undertone for monopoly.

82 See Shaikh, Anwar 1983. "Centralization and Concentration of Capital," in *A Dictionary of Marxist Thought*. Bottomore, Tom, Lawrence Harris, V. G. Kiernan, and Ralph Miliband (eds.). Cambridge, MA: Harvard University Press: 68–69. Concentration and centralization of capital are an inner engine of capital accumulation in competition in

Marx. As the latter leads to the former, the accumulation of capital increases and leads to further competition. Marx refers to concentration as an increase in scale and *quantity* of capital in size, and to centralization as an enhancement in *quality* of capital, in conjunction with the credit system, interwoven with technological change. The two processes are entwined and hand in hand with (synthetic) competition in Marx. Contrary to Marx, Ernest Mandel changes this very context by invoking "the imperialist monopoly capitalist phase . . . . until entire branches of industry were dominated by a handful of trusts companies and monopolies, and common price agreements" (p. 311). See Mandel, Ernest 1978. *Late Capitalism*. London: Verso Press. Here, how the irreconcilable Hobson's position on monopoly, albeit in Lenin's vernacular, and Marx's competition had blindsided Mandel and eventually surrendered him to the neo-Hobsonite's vision, despite his excruciating efforts to remain loyal to Marx's theoretical point of view. For *synthetic competition* and the disintegration of the greatest monopoly in recent memory, namely, International Petroleum Cartel (1928–1972), see Bina, Cyrus 2013. "Synthetic Competition, Global Oil, and the Cult of Monopoly," in *Alternative Theories of Competition: Challenges to the Orthodoxy*. J. K. Moudud, C. Bina, and P. Mason (eds.). New York: Routledge: 55–85.

83 Arrighi, Geovanni 2010 [1994]. *The Long Twentieth Century*. New & Updated Edition. New York: Verso.

84 Arrighi 2010 [1994]. *The Long Twentieth Century*. Epilogue: 336–370.

85 These are some of Wallerstein's recent books: Wallerstein, Emmanuel I. 2000. *The Essential Wallerstein*. New York: New Press; Wallerstein, Emmanuel I. 2003. *The Decline of American Power: The U.S. in a Chaotic World*. New York: New Press; Wallerstein, Emmanuel I. 2004. *World-Systems Analysis: An Introduction*. Durham, NC: Duke University Press.

86 It is interesting to note that *transhistorical* methodology is not a monopoly of the World-Systems approach alone. There are quite a few scholars on the radical left, even Marxists, whose scholarship suffers from the same theoretical blunder. A prominent example is Dick Bryan who writes:

> International accumulation predates capitalism, and it [*sic*] pre-dates nations. Capitalism and nations were conceived in a world in which capital was mobile. Yet this book (Bryan 1995) has addressed the internationalization of capital as a 'recent' process—not a fundamental transformation of the nature of capitalism, but a change which is of some significance in determining a broad spectrum of contemporary social relations. How can internationalization be a change in a system which is inherently international? (p. 181). Bryan, Dick 1995. *The Chase Across the Globe: International Accumulation and the Contradictions for Nation States*. Boulder, CO: Westview Press.

87 See Amin, Samir 1992. *Empire of Chaos*. New York: Monthly Review Press. This book is the lens through which one could clearly see chaos surrounding the mind of the author—seriously. It is *chaos* within that sees chaos without. This of course is a chaotic scene perceived by an "average Joe" on every street corner. Yet it comes to the observation of a wise scholar; the same chaos underlies a systematic order that cries for discovery. Had it not for Amin's susceptibility to monopoly and unmediated imperialist ghosts of the yesteryears, he could have seen a bit of regularity and order in all this despite the abrupt collapse of the Soviet Union at the time of his writing. He perhaps could have envisaged the collapse of the Pax Americana (1945–1979), a decade prior to the fall of the Soviets; or Amin could have appreciated the notion of competition in conjunction with (not despite?) the concentration and centralization of capital toward globalization. But, alas, neither "could have" nor "should have" is a part and parcel of a real-life story.

88 See Amin, Samir 2013. *The Implosion of Contemporary Capitalism*. New York: Monthly Review Press. As the tenor of the argument in this book reveals, Amin attempts to

one-up Sweezy's "monopoly capitalism" (1920–1970), and by the way of emphasis produces an *Age* for "generalized-monopoly capitalism" as the "last phase" of capitalism since the 1970s. Of course, he also throws in by punctuating "globalization" for the hell of it, so to speak; see Ch. 1: 15–41, and Conclusion: 149–155.

89 To be sure, there were others on the left who did not reconcile with Marx's method or conformed to Sweezy's strict thesis; it is true also that there were many who began to explore Marx's theory of value and his methodology in the dawn of the 1970s when Marx was back.

90 Amin, Samir 1978. *The Law of Value and Historical Materialism*. New York: Monthly Review Press. This book shows clearly where Amin stood (or drifted) on Marx's theory of value and on Marx's method and vision of capitalism in general. Aside from contemplation on monopoly, Amin is completely wrong about Marx's theory of ground rent (Ch. 4) and "Theory and Practice of Mining Rent in the Present-Day Capitalist System" (Ch. 6), where he has no clue about the context (or the subject), yet sticking his nose into all aspects, including technology, by invoking "technological rent." This alone infuriates the present writer who devoted nearly five decades of his adult life to petroleum, energy, Marx's rent theory, oil crises, decartelization of oil, globalization of oil and had developed a value-theoretic theory of rent for oil and energy, among others.

91 See Harvey, David 2003. *The 'New' Imperialism*. Oxford, UK: Oxford University Press; Harvey, David 2005. *A Brief History of Neoliberalism*. New York: Oxford University Press.

92 For a critique of Harvey's dichotomy on the "logic" of history and "logic" of territory, see Bina, Cyrus 2013b. *A Prelude to the Foundation of Political Economy: Oil, War, and Global Polity*. New York: Palgrave Macmillan, Ch. 5.

93 See Desai, Radhika 2010. "The Absent Geopolitics of Pure Capitalism," *World Review of Political Economy* 1 (3), Fall: 463–484. Among a handful of disputed issues here, this article argues for the primacy of the nation-state policies and actions as the *primum mobile* of international relations. Yet it falls back on the nation-state in order to explicate such policies and actions in a circular manner and without showing an interest in changes in the structure, context, and quality of global polity, which itself is also dependent on the socio-economic transformation of the globe as a whole. We also must realize that *global polity* is much more than the sum of all nation-states held in mutuality within it. The disparaging reference to "metropolitan" is not an accident here.

94 See Desai 2013, Ch. 2 (The Materiality of Nations). To know more about this "materiality" and the drift of its caricature, see the special issue of *World Review of Political Economy* on "The Materiality of Nations in Geopolitical Economy," co-edited by Radhika Desai, 6 (4), Winter 2015. This issue and the level of scholarship and the caliber of perception of those participating in it should speak for themselves.

95 See Desai 2013, Ch. 1 (Introduction): 19. The off-the-cuff references such as this would indicate how little the author knows about Marx's views or his methodology or for that matter Engels's and their possible difference.

96 On imperialism and its perpetuity, see Desai 2013, Ch. 2: 43–53. Imperialism is a typical staple of the traditional left not unlike maize for the Aztecs.

97 See Desai 2013, Ch. 9 (Conclusion). The notion of "counter development" is deliberately kept ambiguous to be used as a catchall phrase for "rivalry," in the case of imperialism, for "socialism," in the eyes of the beholder, or for plain capitalist development by the so-called countering states. In methodological terms, it is a pitiful way of dodging a specific and genuine analysis.

98 Desai 2013. In this paragraph, the tenor of the entire book on "imperialism" and its manifold reincarnation since Hobson and Lenin is revealed in black and white, so to speak. Unevenness here stands for the measure of imperialism as it appears to the naked eye; that is, the connotation of "unevenness" is about the economic size of the states, not an inner dynamic of capital, as Marx would have it. Consequently, a solution to get rid

of "unevenness" is also the solution to get rid of "imperialism." It should be reminded once more that this bizarre *mental* construct is not unlike the origins of price theory in neoclassical economics where all assumed numerous firms of the same size live together evenly ever after in "perfect competition." Here, even Lenin's bones would turn over and over again in his eternal resting place.

99 On the piggyback of "combined," an essential part of UCD, and its obsessive use by a certain segment of the traditional left, see Part I of this chapter. Desai 2013 is uncritically replete with this fallacy and indeed makes the bulk of its foundation.

100 Desai 2013, Ch. 9.

101 Desai 2013, Ch. 5.

102 Desai 2013, Ch. 7.

103 See Desai, Radhika 2010. "The Absent Geopolitics of Pure Capitalism," *World Review of Political Economy* 1 (3), Fall: 463–484. This is a remarkable example of skating on thin ice in geopolitics—superficial to the core. The context of the argument is not a matter of concern here, since I take issue with all three of the scholars, namely, Rosenberg, Teschke, and Callinicos, in both substance and methodology concerning both the global economy and polity. The issue here is the accusation of "pure" against these scholars in order to distract the audience from what the author is up to. That is intended at the misrepresentation of pushing something that has no *nutrient* and no significance as something quite fresh, innovative, and just off the oven for body and soul. This is a fundamental methodological issue that was addressed in Part I of this chapter.

104 Desai 2013, Ch. 9. For a remarkable critique of socialism in the USSR, Chattopadhyay, Paresh 2019 [2018]. *Socialism and Commodity Production: Essays in Marx Revival.* Chicago, IL: Haymarket Books. This critique is relevant to contemporary China as well.

105 It should be realized that we are critical of any *essentialism* in explanation without falling into the trap of relativism at the heart of postmodernism. A remarkable example here is *abstract labor,* a quintessential concept for Marx's labor theory of value and a social outcome; here, there is no essentiality involved in an axiomatic sense of the term. Because the concept of abstract labor is not made by an assumption but by the mediation of social reality surrounding the capitalist labor process in production and exchange, here, essentialism (as identified by the critics) has no role to play. Yet, understanding abstract labor is essential (the figure of speech!) for the understanding of the corporeality of capitalism to its core and the notion of exploitation. Antonio Negri and Michael Hardt have long abandoned this very concept before settling on the pastiche of undifferentiated concepts, such as Empire, Multitude, and Commonwealth.

106 Hardt, Michael, and Antonio Negri 2000. *Empire.* Cambridge, MA: Harvard University Press.

107 Amin (1992) speaks of an "empire of chaos"; the confusion in the immediate aftermath of the collapse of the Soviet Union is not particular to post-Autonomist-turned-postmodernist Antonio Negri. The overwhelming majority of the traditional left remained astounded for a considerable period.

108 The mode of appearance is an initial encounter with reality in any investigation. The question is where to go from that point on. Why? Because the acceptance of any real appearance is but a convoluted *concrete,* and thus concrete as such may not reveal an inner dynamic of the subject under investigation. In the case of the neo-Ricardian emphasis on the *distribution* alone, the underlying (*abstract*) production relations are decidedly left out of the investigation. For further details on this issue, see Fine, Ben, and Laurence Harris 1977. "Surveying the Foundations," in *The Socialist Register 1977.* Ralph Miliband and John Saville (eds.). New York: Monthly Review Press: 106–120. The same problem exists with Empire and its two authors. The background that had led to *Empire* runs through the so-called cognitive capitalism and "immaterial Capital,"

both of which are but a mode of appearance devoid of adequate abstraction. In this context, Empire is ineptly erected on a shifty foundation.

109 The subject of "limit" has a long discussion beyond our purpose; suffice it to say that there is nothing either physical or mental in the entire universe, so far as we know, that could live or appear to live without a limit. Here, the *limit* is also a hint of transformation in both a historical and epistemological sense. According to Kurt Gödel, even the number system in mathematics has a limit that is based on external assumptions. See Nagel, Ernest, and James R. Newman. 1958. *Gödel's Proof*. New York: New York University Press.

110 Nothing can "suspend" history either internal or external to itself. Since the "internal" suspension of history amounts to an analogy with the Almighty that can (cannot) create a huge stone which he/she cannot (can) lift, in either case, the Almighty negates being an Almighty. In the case of "external" suspension of history, every schoolchild knows that it is an impossibility—for instance, how could you and I suspend the rotation of Earth around the Sun in broad daylight? Or how could the white man in America ever suspend (or purify?) American history from the annihilation of the natives and the slavery of the African blacks? So, we can see at first blush that such claims do not even have the honor of being false but are drenched from head to toe in clumsy *fakery*.

111 It is one thing to say that the United States (presumably the symbol of Empire) is outside its own time that once played as a hegemon during the Pax Americana and that now descended further toward the level of colonial Pax Britannica, a history that has long gone—as we argue all along in this volume—and quite another to claim that the whole post-American world is outside of history or "at the end of history." Aside from real appearances, neither the contemporary world looks like Hardt and Negri's Empire nor the United States is as powerful as these authors want us to believe nor the postmodern epistemology has the wherewithal to crack the foundation of global capitalism before unleashing a *relative* subjectivity-gone-mad.

112 The "Biopower"—a spectacle of real appearance gone berserk—originated in Michel Foucault's writings. Terry Eagleton has a striking description of Foucault as follows:

> Michel Foucault, a student of Louis Althusser, was a post-Marxist heretic who found Marxism unpersuasive on questions of power, madness, and sexuality, but who continued to move for a while within its general ambiance. Marxism provided Foucault with a silent interlocutor in several of his most renowned works (Eagleton 2003: 35). See Eagleton, Terry 2003. *After Theory*. New York: Basic Books.

The mention of Althusser in the above passage is not an accident; Althusser has done more harm than good to Marx (and Marxism) by axiomatizing Marx and then revising his assessment of capitalism by getting rid of the backdrop of history. In Eagleton's words, "If Louis Althusser rewrote Marxism from the inside, he opened the door in doing so through which many of his disciples would shuffle out of it altogether" (Eagleton 2003: 37).

For a detailed critique of Althusser, see Thompson, Edward P. 1978. *The Poverty of Theory and Other Essays*. New York: Monthly Review.

113 Negri, Antonio 1991. *Marx Beyond Marx: Lessons on the Grundrisse*. London: Autonomedia/Pluto.

114 The fact that the *appearance* of the "virtual" labor, and its unqualified misinterpretation, is a part and parcel of *Empire* and Negri and Hardt's subsequent writings are of little doubt.

115 This point is worth emphasizing for those who do not differentiate the origins of globalization in Marx's theoretical work and those of Hardt and Negri's variety.

116 See Marx, Karl 1973 [1939]. *Grundrisse: Foundations of the Critique of Political Economy*. New York: Vintage Edition: 729–730.

117 See Jeon, Heesang 2010. "Cognitive Capitalism or Cognition in Capitalism? A Critique of Cognitive Capitalism Theory," *Spectrum: Journal of Global Studies* 2 (3), Summer: 90–117.

118 Marx, Karl 1981 [1894]. *Capital,* Vol. III. New York: Vintage Edition.

119 The camouflage of the text particularly amplifies the postmodernist spectacle of relative subjectivity centered on a cursory critique of imperialism and the imagined notion of the multitude. There are two more books by Negri and Hardt that follow *Empire* in a similar fashion and methodology, entertaining the same issues in this entertaining scenario, namely, *Multitude* and *Commonwealth*; the former, the biggest show on earth in tautology, and the latter an incredible playact, like Santa Clause, offering something to everyone in the name of communism. See Hardt, Michael and Antonio Negri 2004. *Multitude: War and Democracy in the Age of Empire*. New York: The Penguin Press; Negri, Antonio and Michael Hardt 2009. *Commonwealth*. Cambridge, MA: Harvard University Press.

120 See Hardt and Negri 2000. *Empire*, Part 3.

121 It is an irony that Antonio Negri could not catch a drift of Marx's method of analysis in *Grundrisse*—a very method that underpins the foundation of Marx's *Capital*. Negri keeps emphasizing the "missing volume," not that whatever is "missing" must be restored accordingly but to dish out a counterfeit in the name of the missing volume of Marx. Negri's (and Hardt's) problem demonstrably limits to hyper-activity and hyper-subjectivity, in the most relative sense of the term, that is, surfing on the surface of capitalism by invoking "multitude" and playing Santa Clause at the expense of Marx and Marxism.

122 A novel by Miguel de Cervantes about Don Quixote and his "squire" who tries to prove that chivalry is not dead and aspiring to be heroes.

123 See Braverman, Harry 1998 [1974]. *Labor and Monopoly Capital*. 25th Anniversary Edition. New York: Monthly Review. This edition includes a new introduction by John Bellamy Foster. For a critique of Braverman's monopoly and one-sided deskilling, see Bina, Cyrus 2020b. "A Note on Technical Change, Skill Formation, and Economic Instability," *International Journal of Political Economy* 49 (1): 89–91. DOI: 10.1080/08911916.2020.1733776.

124 Gramsci, Antonio 1971. *Selected from the Prison Notebooks*. New York: International Publishers: 176.

7 COVID and Negative Price of Oil

Prediction is very difficult, especially if it's about the future.

—Niels Bohr

I

The freefall of contract oil (i.e., the futures market in WTI) in the middle of the pandemic in April 2020 was due to an immediate halt in global demand for the various sectors of the world economy. This includes nearly all modes of transportation (both recreational and commercial), the bulk of worldwide supply chains associated with the production and distribution of goods and services, and the unavoidable conservation of fuel and energy conditioned by shelter-in-place and quarantines across the world. The freefall of the price benchmark for crude (WTI) in the United States, given that crude oil is a globalized industry, had correlated impacts on other benchmarks in the larger crude oil markets globally and directly compressed the average value of stocks in the United States and around the world.

The *uncertainty* caused by the COVID-19 pandemic had instantaneously turned into universal uncertainty within the core of global supply chains and transportation networks worldwide. The same uncertainty plagued the oil industry, from Saudi Arabia to the United States, oil producers in desperate need of cash and flooded with the oversupply of oil, buckled under pressure; in the United States, producers also long encountered the shortage of oil storage facilities and high cost of oil once it was produced. The oil price had no place to go but down, and very fast. As the crisis beleaguered the industry (as demonstrated in my earlier work on oil and theory of value, reflected in this volume), a stable magnitude that normally synchronizes the amplitude of short-run market fluctuations has given way to oblivion.[1]

II

The phenomenon of moving into "negative territory"—the term used by the industry—is indeed unprecedented since the inception of the futures oil

DOI: 10.4324/9781351136785-7

market in 1983. This signaled the fact that, as many oil analysts unanimously acknowledge, there was no space left in the United States to store an already produced crude oil. This included storage facilities on the ground and in tankers anchored near the shore. Consequently, this is an American drawback relative to other oil producers, for the following reasons:

(1) The United States has been producing oil for years by what is known as "fracking"—the injection of liquid at high pressure into subterranean rocks, boreholes, etc.—and by horizontal drilling, freely without any oversight and environmental safeguards.
(2) The US government, in cahoots with a powerful oil lobby, frequently boasts of being "self-sufficient" in oil, and acts as if such a false pretense would increase US domestic security and supposedly bolster the US foreign policy and American power in the world.

Little do these double-speaking bureaucrats (who are by and large the spokespersons for the capitalist system) know that there is no such thing as "self-sufficiency" in capitalism, and someday the idea of the unlimited production of oil will come back to bite them. As demonstrated in this volume, oil has been a global industry since the crisis of decartelization and competitive globalization in the early 1970s, and "national" self-sufficiency and other deceptive arguments, such as an OPEC "cartel," are mere gimmicks.[2]

III

The spot oil price (both WTI and Brent) has already dropped between 35% and 40% in two or three phases since the pandemic became known and duly acknowledged by the UN agency, the World Health Organization (WHO). The spot price is the competitive price of oil traded on daily basis at the designated exchanges across the world. The spot market and futures market are supposed to complement each other by linking the present to the defined future, thus delineating the calculable risk by taming of chance. This entwines the levels and distributes risks for the purpose of professedly informed speculation, having to do with the so-called trade on paper barrels and thus speculative finance. It is therefore important to point out the difference between calculable *risk* and *uncertainty*.

Risk refers to an event that occurs with the knowledge of prior probability distribution concerning chances, and thus it is subject to and appears under the jurisdiction of probability theory. To put it another way, a typical example is the issuance of a life insurance policy for a particular age, gender, or certain medical conditions. Here, the underwriter has access to readily collected information about a particular population and its demographic characteristics. Thus, by referring to the available probability distribution, the risk is clearly calculable. Uncertainty, on the other hand, has no probability distribution in advance of the event itself. An outstanding example of an uncertain event was the global pandemic of COVID-19 that is currently wreaking havoc in and across every nook and cranny of the globe. Even with the availability of vaccines, the occurrence of so many variants and sub-variants associated with this virus, and the possibility of unforeseen mutation, are not within the realm of calculation. There is little prior experience with patients and little information on the pattern of immunity so far.

IV

Contrary to mainstream economics, the mechanism of demand and supply cannot lead to the determination of commodity prices *by itself*, given the fact that in a typical capitalist market with disaggregated consumers and producers of all kinds, the market could not be cleared in the short run and thus the price would remain indeterminable. This should lead us to Léon Walras and his externally produced *auctioneer* (see Walras [1871] 2014).[3] In other words, there is no guarantee that there will not be a freefall (or unlimited rise), so one must look for the hidden reason for the stability of market prices in normal times.

Here is where Marx's theory of value comes in and eloquently explains why and how the stability of prices is guaranteed in normal times.[4] Here "value" plays as a center of gravity around which market prices tend to fluctuate. The amplitude of the fluctuation depends upon the commonplace disparity between demand and supply in a disaggregated capitalist market in the short run. Neither is the price of oil an exception. During the crisis, however, this state of normalcy disappears, and the possibility of freefall is on the cards. This works even with a change in the magnitude of value, an occurrence through the restructuring of capital in accumulation via the persistent periodic economic crisis.

Speaking of crisis, the mainstream has no concept of the economic crisis in a theoretical sense, since there would not be a breakdown in the circuit of capital when one capitalizes on harmony and the ideal axiom of the system of prices. That is why, during the real crisis, like this pandemic, and over the price of oil, orthodox economists (and their counterparts in the media) engage in improvisation by hanging onto Saudi Arabia or Mr. Putin or other drummed-up conspiratorial schemes toward justifying the 2020 freefall in the price of oil. A similar tendency also prevails in certain leftist circles whose monopoly view of oil drives them toward collusion and conspiracy.

Moreover, an off-the-cuff and casual approach, away from the specificity of this crisis and the lack of attention to competitive globalization oil (as opposed to monopoly), provides a breeding ground for the spread of ideologically constructed materials to the public at large. A quintessential example is the treatment of OPEC as a cartel throughout the news media. This very misconception then allows the mass media to take the next step to bring the individual nations into this fraudulent echo chamber either for credit or for the blame, each time the price of oil tumbles or rises.

V

Given the tendency for the slowdown of the global economy prior to this pandemic, I particularly wish to emphasize that a decline in the global demand for oil was inevitable. In this context, the precarious oversupply of oil in the United States had already led to the abandonment of too many oil fields in the United States and Canada; for instance, those in North Dakota's Bakken oilfields and Alberta's Athabasca tar sands. Due to fracking, however, the storage capacity in the United States was already at its peak even several years before the arrival of this ongoing pandemic. In other words, American oil producers should have known that something or someone had to give—but, given the short-term profit, they did not give a hoot. Thus, the day of reckoning, unprecedented in the not-too-long history of global markets, eventually caught up with them.

VI

The COVID-19 pandemic is, in a sense, internal (not external) to the current global economic crisis, in that it reveals the open secret of the "conquest of [the] mode of production," a very powerful prediction made by more than 150 years ago by Karl Marx (see *Grundrisse*, pp. 729–730).[5] As I have established much earlier and also in this volume (see Bina 2019),[6] the periodization of capitalism necessarily involves worldwide encroachment and appropriation through the geography of production in which the mode of production and the social relation of capital attain universality. Yet, such a conquest also comes with (1) the across-the-board devastation of the environment, (2) the hasty acceleration of human-induced climate change, (3) the eradication of species upon species and widespread invasion of the entire natural habitat, and (4) consequently harmful exposure of human life to a myriad of unknown pathogens, both knowingly and unknowingly. It is not necessary to be super-intelligent to realize that a pandemic of such a global proportion and of such an extraordinary speed must be organically the very consequence of the globalization of capital that concurrently binds a dual crisis of health and economy together.

VII

In recent years, much ink has been spilled on the issues surrounding the 2008 global financial crisis and the role finance played in it. However, the role of finance should not be detached from the rest of the moments of capital in circulation and accumulation. After all, finance is an aspect of capital as a whole—a moment of capital in money form. Yet capital influx depends on two other entwined moments, namely, commodity and productive capital. Thus, from the standpoint of Marx's methodology, the so-called financialization cannot be analyzed but within the context of globalization. As has been shown in this volume, this also goes for "neoliberalism," an expression that enjoys utmost popularity within the radical left over the last two decades or so. Some scholars are so in sync with neoliberalism as an all-embracing vision of the world opposed to globalization that intuitively put inverted commas around *globalization*. Saad-Filho (2020) is one of those scholars who did that in his recent paper on the current bio-economic crisis and present pandemic.[7]

Likewise, in his previous work with Ben Fine, Saad-Filho followed the same style by insisting as if neoliberal economic policies were a suitable substitute for the periodization of capitalism (see Fine and Saad-Filho 2016).[8] Others, too, have tautologically reduced globalization to the "American Empire," a phrase that betrays a limited understanding of American wherewithal in light of the observable facts on the ground concerning the collapse of the Pax Americana (1945–1979), and the bankruptcy of nearly all institutions of postwar polity and economy.[9] The great American author, Mark Twain, said something that perfectly fits such ideas. He said, "You cannot depend on your eyes when your imagination is out of focus." Now, the positive aspect (if there is any) of this coronavirus crisis is that it teaches us that globalization is real and that it will remain so with or without neoliberalism.

This crisis is fundamentally different from the previous ones, including the Great Depression of 1929, the 1987 crisis of saving and loan association, and the 2008 global financial crisis. The COVID-19/Economic Crisis of 2020 got swiftly underway by hitting at the heart of production and disrupting the global supply chains and distribution centers, while also instantaneously crippling commercial transportation systems worldwide (Bina 2021a). The brunt of the crisis then led to the rapid disruption of the oil and energy around the world and quickly transmitted the initial decline that emerged from China's outbreak; the massive quarantine of the financial sectors across the world—from Shanghai, Tokyo, London, and eventually Wall Street—was the result of the first wave of this pandemic (Bina 2020a).

Finally, the decline by some 40% early on, and then by a freefall that eventually moved the WTI futures (oil) market—available for delivery in May (2020)—into negative territory, we have witnessed an oil crisis unprecedented in the history of globalized oil across the globe. One must bear in mind that, among others, there are two entwined and critical factors in this crisis: (1) the universality of speed and (2) the universality of scope. This is equally so whether we speak of global oil or the entire global economy. These by themselves should provide a clue to the ubiquity of globalization. See DiSavino and Soreng 2020; Geiger 2020a, 2020b; The Guardian 2020a, 2020b; Heath 2020; Kool 2020; Sergent and Bravo 2020. These references are provided for the reader keen on the specifics of the nosedive in the price of oil and other indicators surrounding the economic crisis and why this bio-economic crisis is unique in the history of all market crashes so far.

Notes

1 See Bina (1985, 2006, 2013a). The value in Marxian theory preconditions the stability of short-term market prices in a disaggregated system, such as capitalism. Contrary to Walras and Marshal's untenable verdicts on short-run equality of demand and supply, and the resultant market-clearing prices, value functions as the long-run center of gravity and thus simply clears the markets, in the absence of such imbalances in normal times. The issue of freefall comes in when the economy is in crisis, and given break in the circuits of capital, value too is subject to restructuring and thus unable to operate as in normal times.

2 See Bina (1990, 2012a, 2012b, 2012c) and Bina and Vo (2007). Contrary to mainstream economics, the 1973–1974 oil crisis was neither about OPEC nor essentially about negotiation between the oil-producing and oil-consuming countries. This was the mother of all crises about decartelization and globalization of oil as modern industry. Globalization has two intertwined effects: (1) it put an end to the colonial and semi-colonial structure of the petroleum sector and (2) it sliced off the umbilical cord of American foreign policy of monopoly oil. The advent of globalization also led to the burgeoning spot markets for oil and soon thereafter (in 1983) to the futures markets. OPEC and non-OPEC producers across the globe take their cue from these competitive markets ever since. In other words, OPEC is neither a cartel nor a monopoly.

3 See Walras ([1871] 2014), Ackerman (2002), and Moffatt (2020). The mechanism of market-clearing prices has since Léon Walras' Elements of Pure Economics (1871) been the issue in neoclassical economics. The crucial question of short-run market clearing prices in the presence of disaggregate economy in which there are many buyers and sellers compelled Walras to pull an "auctioneer" out of his "Marginalist Revolution" hat and then cleverly escort the exchange toward a market-clearing price. Walras was aware that no market in capitalism could internally clear without this external device in the person of auctioneer, not unlike falling back on God of certain evangelists who tend to resolve the earthly problems by pray or fiat. The assumption of "perfect information" and the malleability of time across the past, present, and the future leave not much imagination for a typical neoclassical economist to reveal the secret of real markets and real economy in terms of their genuine process. Similar delusions are common in topics like global oil, oil rent, or OPEC where the signpost of governing orthodoxy is in control.

4 Based on Marx's value theory, value of a commodity is the center of gravity of fluctuating market prices. While demand exceeds the supply, price would be above the value, and when supply exceeds the demand, price would be below the value. Now, if there's no value, as center of gravity, there's no stability for any price to hold, since market fluctuations could send the prices to either free-rise or free-fall. In either case, in normal (non-crisis) times, there is a necessity for a center of gravity in long run. This task is performed either by an entity external to the system, i.e., the auctioneer, or by a mechanism internal to the system, the value. The choice is obvious for those who are well versed in oddity of Walrasian equilibrium. This was for the none-crisis times. For the crisis period, the value itself cannot hold and the center of gravity falls by the wayside.

5 Karl Marx, *Grundrisse*. London: Penguin Edition, 1993: 729–730. Here, Marx reveals the tip of the periodization of capitalism, which obtains theoretical conclusion in the first volume of Capital, a decade later.

6 Bina (2019) takes its cue from Marx's approach to the periodization of capitalism (originated first in Grundrisse and then advanced further in Capital). In this article, I review the prevailing view of the periodization of capitalism by the left scholars informed (mostly) of Lenin's approach to this perplexing subject. In this newly published piece, I beg to differ by following Marx's post signs, which involves the theory of value and the conquest of the mode of production across the geography of production worldwide. Here, while the theory of globalization gives a concrete foundation along with the theory of value,

I interrogate David Harvey's pointless dichotomy concerning the "logic of history" and "logic of territory." See Bina (2013b)), Ch. 5, for further information.

7 See Saad-Filho (2020) for a dramatic reduction of COVID-19 pandemic to neoliberal policies, rather than pinning down the outbreak to the very "conquest of [the] mode of production" across the globe, as Marx would have declared, an objective ground for implementation of such policies. Saad-Filho goes on to the details of these dreadful policies in order to demonstrate that era of "neoliberalism" is over. Reading this article more than once, I wonder (1) what happened to the Saad-Filho whom I once knew and (2) what is the difference between, say, Bernie Sanders and a Marxist economist concerning the critique of these neoliberal policies?

8 In this article, titled "Thirteen Things You Need to Know about Neoliberalism," Fine and Saad-Filho attempt to persuade their readers that neoliberalism and neoliberal policies since the 1970s consist of an era—and not the corollary of the transformation of the world toward the era of globalization. Yet nearly all the "things" the authors itemized and authorized as an era are but the very distinguishing insignia of globalization. Being intimately familiar with Fine's work and much appreciative of his pioneering contributions to Marxian theory and critique of political economy, I am nevertheless at loss at his blundering way of treating the periodization of capitalism. For further discussion over periodization and critique of Ben Fine, see Bina (2019).

9 For an ample critique of writers on the postwar Pax Americana, American Hegemony, and the shift in the balance of power in the world, see Bina (2019).

References

Ackerman, Frank (2002). "Still Dead After All These Years: Interpreting the Failure of General Equilibrium Theory," *Journal of Economic Methodology* 9 (2), 119–139.

Bina, Cyrus (1985). *The Economics of the Oil Crisis*. New York: St Martin's Press.

Bina, Cyrus (1990). "Limits of OPEC Pricing: OPEC Profits and the Nature of Global Oil Accumulation," *OPEC Review* 14 (1), Spring.

Bina, Cyrus (2006). "The Globalization of Oil: A Prelude to a Critical Political Economy," *International Journal of Political Economy* Special Issue: Oil in Global Economy 35 (2), Summer.

Bina, Cyrus (2012a). *Oil: A Time Machine*. Ronkonkoma, NY: Linus Publications, Second (Revised) Edition: https://linuslearning.com/product/oil-a-time-machine-2nd-edition/

Bina, Cyrus (2013a). "Synthetic Competition, Global Oil, and the Cult of Monopoly," in *Alternative Theories of Competition: Challenges to the Orthodoxy* (eds.) J. Moudud, C. Bina, and P. Mason. London: Routledge.

Bina, Cyrus (2013b). *A Prelude to the Foundation of Political Economy: Oil, War, and Global Polity*. New York: Palgrave/Macmillan.

Bina, Cyrus (2019). "Specter of Globalization: Marx, Gramsci, and Disjointed Time," *World Review of Political Economy* 10 (4), 484–518: www.jstor.org/stable/10.13169/worlrevipoliecon.10.4.0484?seq=1

Bina, Cyrus and Minh Vo (2007). "OPEC in the Epoch of Globalization: An Event Study of Global Oil Prices," *Global Economy Journal* 7 (1) Article 2, March 2007: www.worldscientific.com/doi/10.2202/1524-5861.1236

DiSavino, Scott and Eileen Soreng (2020). "US Oil Rigs See Biggest Decline in a Week since February 2015," Baker Hughes," *Reuters* April 17: www.reuters.com/article/us-usa-rigs-baker-hughes/u-s-oil-rigs-see-biggest-decline-in-a-week-since-february-2015-baker-hughes-idUSKBN21Z2XO

Fine, Ben and Alfredo Saad-Filho (2016). "Thirteen Things You Need to Know About Neoliberalism," *Critical Sociology* 43 (4–5), 685-706, August 19.

Geiger, Julianne (2020a). "Extreme Volatility in Oil Continues as WTI June Contract Tanks 65%," *Oilprice.com* April 21: https://oilprice.com/Energy/Oil-Prices/Extreme-Volatility-In-Oil-Continues-As-WTI-June-Contract-Tanks.html

Geiger, Julianne (2020b) "The Largest Rig Count Collapse in 5 Years," *Oilprice.com* April 3: https://oilprice.com/Energy/Energy-General/The-Largest-Rig-Count-Collapse-In-5-Years.html

The Guardian (2020a). "Oil Prices Deep Below Zero as Producers Forced to Pay to Dispose of Excess," April 20: www.theguardian.com/world/2020/apr/20/oil-prices-sink-to-20-year-low-as-un-sounds-alarm-on-to-covid-19-relief-fund

The Guardian (2020b). "Complacency to Chaos: How Covid-19 Sent the World's Markets into Freefall," March 28: www.theguardian.com/business/2020/mar/28/how-coronavirus-sent-global-markets-into-freefall

Heath, Thomas (2020). "Oil Prices Extend Slide One Day after US Crude Drops below Zero; Dow Plunges more than 600 Points," *The Washington Post* April 21: www.washingtonpost.com/business/2020/04/21/oil-crash-stocks-today-coronavirus/

Kool, Tom (2020). "A Massive Wave of Shut-Ins Fails to Halt Oil Price Crash," *Oilprice.com* April 21: https://oilprice.com/Energy/Energy-General/A-Massive-Wave-Of-Shut-Ins-Fails-To-Halt-Oil-Price-Crash.html

Moffatt, Mike (2020). "The Definition and Significance of the Walrasian Auctioneer," *ThoughtCo* February 11: www.thoughtco.com/overview-of-walrasian-auctioneers-1147333

Saad-Filho, Alfredo (2020). "Coronavirus, Crisis, and the End of Neoliberalism," *The Bullet* April 17: https://socialistproject.ca/2020/04/coronavirus-crisis-and-the-end-of-neoliberalism/#more.

Sergent, Jim and Veronica Bravo. (2020). "6 Charts Offer Lessons from Past Bear Markets," *USA Today* March 17: www.usatoday.com/in-depth/money/2020/03/17/coronavirus-how-stocks-moved- previous-bear-markets/5011397002/

Walras, Léon ([1871] 2014). *Elements of Theoretical Economics*. Cambridge: Cambridge University Press.

8 COVID's Bio-Economic Crisis and Post-Pandemic World

To be or not to be, that is the question.[1]

—**William Shakespeare**

Preface

Pandemics are pervasive but it is for the first time that the capitalist mode of production reached the outer limits of biology, biosphere, ecology, economy, geography, and international relations in unison resulting in a multifaceted crisis that universally devastated the entire planet. The upshot of this pandemic has overwhelmed the infrastructure of public health across the globe with stunning speed and with infections in tens of millions in just a few months and the velocity of economic damage and devastation much worse than the Great Depression in the last century. It is also the "proof of the pudding" for "conquest of the mode of production"—à la Marx, against the ideological view of the majority on the left that misleadingly classify globalization as neoliberalism—thus holding a doctrine as a justification for an epoch that pretends to measure the periodization of capitalism. It is implicit that this crisis must alarm those assembling within and across both the orthodox and heterodox international relations theory that either hold unto a mirage of "neoliberal international order" or revert to imperialism, ad hoc power politics, fatalistic power structure, and, worse, the supposed hegemony of the United States, respectively. This chapter underscores the authenticity of the value-theoretic periodization of capital toward the identity of the present epoch.

Introduction

To imagine a world beyond the twin COVID-19 Pandemic/Economic Crisis that emerged in 2020, it would be necessary to appreciate the essential features of the pre-pandemic world and the contextual trigger and timing of this bio-economic crisis. It is not the first time that capitalism has been on the brink of collapse. The Great Depression of the 1930s is an outstanding example. However, it is the first time that capital, as a global social relation, reached the outer

DOI: 10.4324/9781351136785-8

limits of biology, ecology, economy, geography, and international relations in unison, wreaking havoc in the animate, immeasurable, inclusive, and certainly catastrophic crisis across the planet. As Karl Marx cogently elucidated:

> No social order is ever destroyed before all the productive forces for which it is sufficiently have been destroyed, and new superior relations of production never replace older ones before the material conditions for their existence have matured within the framework of the old society.
>
> (Marx [1859] 1970, 21)

This crisis attests yet to a deeper issue surrounding the notion of globalization, a theory that originated deep from an inner dynamic of capital toward the periodization of capitalism and spells out the universal identity of our epoch as opposed to courses of actions, proposals, projects, and the application of certain strategic goals embodying "neoliberalism." The capitalist mode of production represents a social relation that is for all intents and purposes irreducible to concrete and convoluted categories, such as the state policy or an administrative strategy. Neoliberalism, aside from its apparent timing, is neither a valid category suitable for the periodization of capitalism nor a fitting contender for the identification of our epoch. It is critical therefore not to fall into the temptation of timing and practice of such neoliberal policies and by doing so justify their epochal import as a marker of periodization. Commitment to reduction is one of the cardinal sins in methodology, particularly Marxian methodology. Globalization is not the same as neoliberalism, as COVID-19 may very likely obliterate the latter; the former although shaken and shocked, as demonstrated in this volume, is to stay as a norm in the post-pandemic world universally.

The following sections provide a universal context for the pre-Corona world that may depict an implied view of the world to come. The post-pandemic world is visible through the wobbly foundation of capitalism, and the sum of the terrified, trembling, and dilapidated public health institutions encountered with super-calamities that are much larger than their deliberately restricted capacity. The telltale of this crisis is infallible. The universal failure of the capitalist mode of production is registered and widely chronicled through this crisis and throughout the world. The millions upon millions of observers in the nook and crannies of this planet bore witness to this inability and were affected simultaneously by the overall incapacity of capitalism when it comes to the nitty-gritty of everyday life. The inhabitants of the globe realized in this instance that another world is not only possible but also necessary.

The Tautology of Neoliberalism and the Left

The pandemic of COVID-19, while instigated by a specific strand of tiny pathogen linked to an assembly of viruses, known as the coronavirus family, is not by itself a cause for the present crisis that had engulfed all four corners of the globe so quickly. Indeed, the speed of contagion and the overwhelming bearing it had upon the prevalent socioeconomic structure, and functional fabric of capitalism across the world, should be a point of departure as to the exclusivity of this crisis. Yet the word "exclusivity" here is a misnomer if the focal point of attention shifts quickly and head-on to *globalization*. Since the 1970s, globalization perceived as either identical or analogous to "neoliberalism" by an array of traditional leftists, from social democrats to radical Marxists. This pandemic, however, is but a corollary that thrives universally on the material foundation of "conquest of the mode of production" across the globe. This "conquest" entails the trajectory of a potential tendency, carefully anticipated by Marx more than 150 years ago, that has since heralded the de facto transformation and dissemination of social relations (of capital) en mass across the geography of world production.

Indeed, in the first place, this pandemic mirrors the universality of globalization and the social relation of capital. The impact of this bio-economic crisis is both intranational and international, following the pattern of intrasectoral and intersectoral competition across the worldwide geography of production. It is not unlike the metaphor of the ill-fated ocean liner Titanic that suddenly struck an iceberg in the North Atlantic Ocean in 1912; COVID-19 is a manifestation of the simple fact that globalization may have different compartments (intranationally and internationally) but does not allow for two different sets of validation or in this case value theory, one for "rich nations" and another for "poor nations"—indorsed by "monopoly capitalism," which unambiguously display the mental division of "global north/global south."[2] The celebrated value theory by Marx and the specificity of his theories of uneven development and synthetic competition are contrary to such post-Marx reconstructions. COVID-19 is not only a specter of doom but also a harbinger of lucidity and light, reflecting the depth of class polarization both intranationally and internationally and gesticulates the overarching of the two embroiling transnationalization of capital and thus globalization across the worldwide geography. Besides, the climate change itself, and its universal impact on the planet, is yet another proof of this universality. Indivisibility and universality are the two intertwined qualities that underly the economic, political, social, and natural aspects of our planet at this stage of capitalism.

The pandemic of COVID-19 (and now its manifold variants), although compelled us to wear masks, ironically led to the unmasking of the circularity of the arguments employed by the majority of traditional leftists, including Marxists, in the false *identity* of state policy (and strategy) and the inner dynamics and intrinsic structure of capital in a period in which capital has secured organic unity in its tripartite circuits of accumulation across the globe. In other words, the present structural/epochal manifestation, known as globalization, is a formidable category belonging to a much deeper level of analysis than the perceptible epiphenomenon of neoliberalism, since the Reagan/Thatcher ideological coup d'état on the two sides of the Atlantic in the late 1970s and early 1980s. While the multiplicity of signs assigned to neoliberalism is in concord with globalization, there is hardly any of them (or their collection as a whole) could stand on its own alone without their structural underpinning and epochal identity, namely, globalization. Indeed, the transnationalization of the three moments of capital underpins the global circuits of social capital since the 1970s. This provides a contextual background for neoliberal *ideology* and policies, in contradistinction with Keynesian policies in the prior period that also deployed a series of developmental policies, such as Import-Substitution Industrialization in the formerly "Third World" counties under the postwar Pax Americana (1945–1979).[3]

Thus, the epoch of globalization, from the methodological standpoint takes precedent over a set of neoliberal policies that could not have been plausible in the first place let alone implemented independently. In other words, one has to avoid placing the cart before the proverbial horse in this sardonic parody. Ironically, the arrival of this tiny virus that causes COVID-19 presents us with a mixed blessing that *inter alia* subdues the claim of the two known Marxist scholars who precipitously persist in the promotion of "neoliberalism into a theoretical (epochal) category in order to explain the contemporary phase of the capitalist mode of production" (see Fine and Saad-Filho 2016; Saad-Filho 2020). They appear to be turning a period of raw and unmediated history into a theory. The universal impact of COVID-19 cannot be truly understood by the casual observation of its effects on neoliberal policies via neoliberalism. It is true that the crisis surrounding COVID-19 and the requirements for recovery stand in sharp contrast to the ideology of market and market-worshiping economists, such as Friedrich von Hayek and Milton Friedman. Yet, focusing on these policies and their negation by way of celebration has little bearing on the understanding of globalization as an epoch. This virus reveals just how intensely and organically connected, yet deeply uneven, the world has become since the 1970s and what that means when we speak of the transnationalization of capital and universalization of capital's social relation. Thus, contrary to Saad-Filho (2020), and others who take comfort in the failure of "neoliberalism," the supposed diminishing of such policies would have little effect on globalization itself.[4]

Thus, COVID-19 unveils an all-too-common methodological blunder by many who hang onto neoliberalism—a set of outward expressions—as a tool for periodization, through misjudging the appearance as the essence and by circular reasoning. As Marx once declared, "all science would be superfluous if the form of appearance of things directly coincides with their essence" (Marx [1894] 1981, 956). Sadly, positing neoliberalism without mediation may not also be immune from encountering the concurrence of the point of departure and the point of return. Saad-Filho (2020) is an example of such a view when the author places *globalization* within the inverted commas, before quickly zooming against neoliberal policies that in his judgment are the culprit in this pandemic. Our point is not that the neoliberal policymakers were not caught off guard by this pandemic and they need to adjust their policies. But to stress precisely on a deeper transformation that was brought to bear by globalization, a widespread situation that is now manifested through this pandemic. Many radical authors, including Harvey (2005), on "neoliberalism" do not appear to appreciate the difference between the "trigger" and the "firing mechanism"—in this case, the apparent state policy and the deeper dynamics of capitalism. Oddly enough, this tiny virus is now casting a speck of light on all this.

Globalization and Universalization of Social Relation

To appreciate the theoretical footings of the present epoch, one needs to go back to the outline of Karl Marx toward a critique of the political economy in *Grundrisse*. Here, Marx attempts to address a plethora of issues about the corporeality of capitalism and comprehensible and consistent theory that elucidates its regulating mechanism, and the capacities and incapacities through periodic crises. *Grundrisse* is a compendium of telegraphic notes from Marx to himself, which according to their evident significance and theoretical implication were selectively polished and utilized in *Capital*. One of these refined notes is the "necessary tendency to conquer the mode of production in all aspects, to bring them under the rule of capital"—that is, geographical gesticulation of capital in all its critical forms or moments as an organic and universal social relation (Marx [1939] 1973, 729–730).[5] In *Capital*, vol. 1, Marx begins his cogent theory with a perceptible appearance in order to grasp the fetishized and imperceptible form of value embedded in the concept of capital and "the victory of its mode of production" beyond not only of a unit of capital or an entire sector (known as Microeconomics) but also through overcoming the geographical borders of the nation-states. In other words, capital could not become a universal value unless it transforms (i.e., "to become" as opposed to "to be") from potential to an actual thus it would be able to propagate its mode of production universally. This universality, therefore, is a precise context for the law of value across the geography of production, distribution, and exchange displayed unambiguously by globalization today.

The "victory of [the] mode of production" and its cumulative impact on the ecosystem (and climate change), on the one hand, and its critical consequence for the numerous species that are already extinct or currently on the verge of extinction, on the other hand, is the very identity of globalization. The capitalist mode of production has historically been uneven intranationally, internationally, and transnationally. Yet, among a myriad of barriers, the previous two very distinct barriers (ecological system and life-support/specie preservation system) are conspicuously overcome and overwhelmed by capital in recent decades. The brunt of this overexpansion and conquest unsurprisingly coincides with globalization when the worldwide geography of production is overwhelmed by the interwoven circuits of social capital via transnational production, transnational finance, and the transnational commodity exchange since the 1970s. A further manifestation of these is a disastrous expansion into the natural habitat of multitudes of species and pathogens, known and unknown, due to impulsive urbanization, wholesale deforestation, and mindless conquest for the short-term profit. In other words, as Marx fittingly and ironically put it: "The *true barrier* to capitalist production is *capital itself*" (Marx [1894] 1981, 358; emphasis in original).

As this pandemic is in its multiple surges and its recurrence in several more variants and sub-variants remain on the horizon, the question is why the advanced capitalist countries, including the United States, had not anticipated this pandemic, given the outbreak of SARS-CoV-1 in the 2010s, and hence why not ready to keep sufficient hospital beds, ventilators, ICU facilities, medical staff, and assorted technical resources to handle such probable emergencies. Had these advanced countries anticipated all this, one may surmise, they may have been able to handle the brunt of the consequence. The same question, either implicitly or explicitly, raised by the majority of radical leftists with exclusive attention to "neoliberalism" and draconian economic policies of the "neoliberal era" since the 1970s. While the neglectful impact of these neoliberal strategies is a catalyst for exacerbation of the worldwide pandemic/economic twin crisis, the answer is much deeper than such apparent and skin-deep frameworks. The façade of "neoliberalism" (like the veneer of Keynesianism earlier) itself conceals the very inner dynamics of accumulation on a global scale and the very underpinning of capital in its periodization toward the present stage of globalization. As Marx put it more than 150 years ago:

> Capitalist production . . . should never be depicted as something that it is not, i.e., as production whose immediate purpose is consumption, or the production of means of enjoyment for the capitalist. This would be to ignore completely its specific character, as this is expressed in its basic inner pattern.
>
> (Marx [1894] 1981, 352)

Thus, relying upon the traditional rationale and being surmised for the lack of facility and provision for arrangements that sustain life itself is little more than grasping strews on manifestations and away from fundamental reasoning and critical assessment of deeper forces that have led a worldwide calamity and this twin crisis, in the first place. Similarly, a deeper critique beyond "neoliberalism" is necessary to show in a more radical and decisive manner why market ideologues, such as von Mises, von Hayek, or the infamous "Chicago boys," had not yet learned their lesson on the corporeality of capitalism, away from the ideal types. And why indeed "public choice" is the code word for private plunder. In fact, this twin crisis should tell us volumes about the epoch of globalization of social capital and the shaky foundation of capitalism itself. Yet, the end of neoliberalism, if ever, is not the end of globalization or the end of capitalism.[6]

COVID-19, Globalization, and Worldwide Crisis

The pandemic that started with a contagion of a tiny virus as SARS-CoV-2, officially COVID-19, had spread across the world with more than 500 million cases and upward of 6.3 million deaths—and counting—according to official statistics as of late April 2022 (see Virus-Documentary Film 2020 on PBS, World Statistics 2022; WHO 2020, 2022). Official tallying on this, however, is far from accurate due to the lack of adequate testing and pertinent information about the number of cases and fatalities across the world. The numbers of cases and death toll, in nearly all countries, including Brazil, India, Iran, Mexico, Russia, and the United States, among others, are often many times greater than the official statistics. In countries in the war zone, such as Yemen, Syria, Afghanistan, Iraq, and several in Africa, with devastated infrastructure, slight medical care, chronic malnutrition, and persistent starvation due to the lack of access to basic food is the killing ground of biblical proportion due to COVID-19. The question of the availability or lack thereof of vaccines to the countries in West Asia, Africa, and Latin America also opens Pandora's box of deep social inequality both intranationally and internationally again and again manifested by this worldwide pandemic.

The COVID-19 pandemic uncovered many faults and tectonic plates in the lithosphere of economy, ecology, and geography across this globalized world. First, it has shown that we are much closer to each other than we thought and all of us are vulnerable. Second, it confirmed that the notion of the "national economy" is a long passé despite the nearly total disruption of production chains and the chain of supply and transportation networks across the globe. The virus does not need a passport to cross the borders. Third, it highlighted the profound divide between the haves and have-nots and clearly illustrated that class (and the class division) is consistently the supreme and unqualified underpinning of capitalism. Fourth, it established that capitalist markets are all concealment of the deeper relations in the labor/production process, and apt references to *essential workers* in this pandemic are the very first pedagogical lesson in economics. Fifth, it revealed that neoliberalism—old and new—consists of a set of policies that would cut one's nose despite one's face, and that Thatcherite/Reaganite ideologues of yesteryears and Austrian market-mongers of today should both wear a mask and zip their mouth. Finally, the COVID-19 pandemic has shown us that we are all now living in a globalized world evidenced by the instant spread and exceptional speed of this deadly disease. This pandemic also exposed the bare bone of the bygone American power and the feeble skeleton of the US hegemonic past that is still persistently marching across the world in search of renewal in desperation. Here, the pandemic touched the realm of geopolitics and international relations as the mummified carcass of the Pax Americana and the empty declaration and claims by the American political class on foreign policy could not find an iota of reconciliation. As demonstrated here and throughout this volume, and contrary to the many on the right and the left, including the radical left, globalization is incompatible with the political posturing of the American state and American foreign policy.[7]

The COVID-19 is a stage upon which the wherewithal of the United States, as a defunct hegemon and the present contender in the world economy and polity, is manifestly on display. COVID-19 does not determine but reveals rather vividly a post-American global economy along with a multipolar polity flexible enough for possible collective governance in the not-so-distant future. Yet, in the aftermath of the post-pandemic world, in all likelihood, the class polarization (along with a profound racial tension) would likely be deepened further both within the national borders and between nations across the globe. COVID-19 also reminds us that the Pax Americana is clearly a distant memory, calibrating a true impression of the United States amid a pile of disintegrated and decayed postwar international institutions, on the one hand, and the deeply divided and unequal domestic society, in both race and class, on the other. The COVID-19 cases and fatalities, respectively, as of late April 2022 in the United States alone are 83 million and over one million, with the number of new cases and new variants and sub-variants still rising since January 2020. The United States, with 4.25% of the world population, has over 16% of COVID-19 for both the number of cases and fatalities relative to those of the world according to official statistics, initially via *World Statistics* 2020, and then as of late April 2022 (*World Statistics*, April 21, 2022). This shows that the United States so far impacted nearly four times as much relative to the world's average in both the number of cases and fatalities during this pandemic.

The convergence of COVID-19 and the chronic police brutality is the combined symptom and outward manifestation of fractured America, despite the repeated denial by the leadership in Washington and the political posturing at the international level (Bina 2019). To be sure, the COVID-19 worsened the class division and aggravated race relations in the United States, which generated some 50 million unemployed (just between mid-March and early August 2020) and nearly a hundred million on the verge of eviction from their dwellings thereafter, and millions more underemployed as we speak. Back to the earlier Trump administration—given this prototype "confederate" presidency and the infantile mantra of "Make America Great Again"—an unambiguous manifestation of internal political decline and the specter of pervasive societal interruption is hovering everywhere in the United States. This internal disorder was long expected to disembark but the onset of the Trump administration precipitated its arrival. The external and internal decline is now visible to the naked eye as both the presidency of Donald Trump and the entrance of the Biden administration and provocation toward the terrible war in Ukraine are the latest symptoms (see Bina 2013b, Ch. 7; Bina 2017).

COVID-19 interrupted the entire global supply chains and their interconnected sequence of global production in one sweeping swipe. What COVID-19 has done in this worldwide economic crisis is to deliver a *direct* blow at the heart of production and the major arteries of global supply chains and transport channels, thus effectively interrupting the global production process for a substantial bulk of traded goods and services across the world economy. Normally, the symptom of capitalist crises would first appear in the finance, credit system, and financial markets and then permeate through the industrial circuits of capital into the heart of production. This time around, production was hit head-on across the global supply chains and transpiration networks, before sending signals to intertwined circuits of commodity and financial capital. Therefore, this bio-economics crisis sets a new normal. However, the financial markets quickly registered and transmitted the brunt of this colossal calamity across the world. The blue chips on Wall Street *inter alia* plunged more than 1300 points on March 18, 2020, thus "erasing nearly all of its Trump-era gains" (Telford and Heath 2020). The transportation networks across the world came to a trickle if not to a screeching halt. This propelled the energy markets into a steep nosedive. In April 2020, NYMEX WTI crude oil futures registered -$37.63 (negative)—unparalleled in the history of global oil since the establishment of this index in 1983 (see NYMEX 2020). The oil markets around the world, both spot, and futures, also registered a tremendous fall accordingly. The lack of demand, on the one hand, and the universal uncertainty created across the world by COVID-19, on the other, hung the world economy in the balance.[6] Events surrounding the freefall in the price of oil quickly transmitted to the stock markets across the world and triggered further plunge (see Bina 2020a). As I articulated elsewhere:

> [T]his crisis though is fundamentally different from previous ones, including the Great Depression of 1929, the 1987 saving and loan association crash, and the 2008 global financial crisis. The COVID-19/Economic Crisis of 2020 got swiftly underway by hitting at the heart of the production, as well as disrupting global supply chains and distribution centers, while simultaneously crippling commercial transportation systems worldwide.
>
> (Bina 2020a)

One of the peculiar features of the COVID-19/Economic Crisis of 2020 is the speed of its transmission matched by the speed of transmission of COVID-19 itself. By comparing the S&P data for all recessions and depressions since the Great Depression of the 1930s, the two crises of 1929 and 1987 are the only ones that virtually come close to the COVID-19 crisis of 2020 in terms of the speed of transmission. Here, in the case of the 1929 crisis, it took 35 "trading days" to move from a bull market to a bear market. The measure for the 1987 Saving and Loan crisis was 38 days, while for the COVID-19/Economic Crisis of 2020 the same measure was[8] merely 16 trading days—greater than 2.2 times the speed of these two historic economic crises (see Sergent and Bravo 2020). These are only a subset of the multidimensional effects associated with the outbreak of this epidemic, which provide us with the larger picture of the systemic fragility of the economic system that had already been fraught with profound instability, deep class division, and the staggering inequality across the board. The post-pandemic world is an opportunity for tending the wounds and striving collectively to heal and to cleanup.

Notes

1 Hamlet, Act 3, scene 1.
2 Monthly Review is the primary source for the dissemination of monopoly capital. For a further critique of monopoly theory, see Bina (2013a); Moudud et al. (2013). For the notion of "global north/global south," see Amin (2013). For a critique of Monthly Review School and Samir Amin, see Bina (2019).
3 The postwar Pax Americana is the period in which Keynesianism was the hallmark of economic policy, and development policy essentially revolved around Import-Substitution Industrialization (ISI). Here, Pax Americana is a structure and Keynesianism is a policy. On ISI and its part vis-à-vis transnationalization of capital, see Bina and Yaghmaian (1988, 1991).
4 An extensive spectrum of opinions among the radical left tends to identify neoliberalism with globalization or sometimes utilizes them in succession as a phrase, i.e., "neoliberal globalization." Here are a few samples that casually speak in this fashion as related to COVID-19: Jan Orbie and Ferdi De Ville (2020), Paul Rosenberg (2020). Fine and Saad-Filho (2016) and Saad-Filho (2020) identify "neoliberalism" not only as a period of policymaking by the state but as a new epoch also of the capitalist mode of production.
5 This point is critically important for the appreciation of a dialectical unity between historical and geographical dimensions of value theory in conjunction with the periodization of capitalism. The notion of globalization owes a great deal to this misunderstanding. Davis Harvey's dichotomy of "logic of history" and "logic of Territory" allows neither a relevant theory of periodization nor a cogent notion of globalization, based on Marx's value theory (see Harvey 2003). But the most misleading piece by Harvey is his A Brief History of Neoliberalism, a cursory assemblage made to camouflage as an "epoch." Harvey even invented the term "neo-liberalization," an expression that wittingly sounds like an objective process. For a critique of Harvey, see Bina (2013b, Ch. 5; 2019).
6 The points raised in Rosenberg (2020) do not appear to appreciate the depth of capital as a social relation in its epoch of universalization, that is, globalization. Globalization is not policy or program or something that would go by the wayside by this pandemic or worse. The only hope here is a massive, vigorous, and continuous worldwide struggle at every level of life as we know it that could be a match with this behemoth.
7 One may retrace this very issue, for instance, in Panitch and Gindin (2012).
8 It is a habit of orthodoxy to lump categories of risk and uncertainty together and carelessly submit them to the law of probability. This habit persuaded Alan Greenspan (former chairman of the Federal Reserve) to boast before the US Congress (that was probing the roots of the 2008 financial crisis) that he was not a total failure but "seventy percent" successful on the issues surrounding the financial market and the role of derivatives. Little did he know while the risk is calculable, based on the available probability distribution, uncertainty has no probability distribution in advance of the event and thus cannot be calculated (see Knight 1921; Hacking 1990; Bina 2020a).

References

Amin, S. 2013. *The Implosion of Contemporary Capitalism*. New York: Monthly Review Press.

Bina, C. 2013b. *A Prelude to the Foundation of Political Economy: Oil, War, and Global Polity*. New York: Palgrave Macmillan. https://link.springer.com/book/10.1057/9781137106971

Bina, C. 2013a. "Synthetic Competition, Global Oil, and the Cult of Monopoly." In *Alternative Theories of Competition: Challenges to the Orthodoxy*, edited by J. Moudud, C. Bina, and P. Mason. New York: Routledge.

Bina, C. 2017. "Homecoming to Nostalgia: The Inauguration of Donald J. Trump." *The Bullet*, January 25. https://socialistproject.ca/2017/01/b1361/

Bina, C. 2019. "Specter of Globalization: Marx, Gramsci and Disjointed Time." *World Review of Political Economy* 10 (4): 484–518. www.jstor.org/stable/10.13169/worlrevipoliecon.10.4.0484?seq=1

Bina, C. 2020a. "Oil, COVID-19, and the Global Economy." *New Cold War*, April 28. www.newcoldwar.org/oil-covid-19-and-the-global-economy/

Bina, C., and B. Yaghmaian. 1988. "Import Substitution and Export Promotion within the Context of Internationalization of Capital." *Review of Radical Political Economics* 20 (2–3): 234–240.

Bina, C., and B. Yaghmaian. 1991. "Postwar Global Accumulation and the Transnationalization of Capital." *Capital & Class* 43: 107–130.

Fine, B., and A. Saad-Filho. 2016. "Thirteen Things You Need to Know About Neoliberalism." *Critical Sociology* 43 (4–5): 685–706.

Hacking, I. 1990. *The Taming of Chance*. Cambridge: Cambridge University Press.

Harvey, D. 2003. *The "New" Imperialism*. Oxford: Oxford University Press.

Harvey, D. 2005. *A Brief History of Neoliberalism*. Oxford University Press.

Knight, F. H. (1921). *Risk, Uncertainty and Profit*. Boston: Houghton Mifflin Company.

Marx, K. (1859) 1970. *A Contribution to the Critique of Political Economy*. Moscow: Progress.

Marx, K. (1894) 1981. *Capital*, vol. 3. London: Penguin.

Marx, K. (1939) 1973. *Grundrisse*. London: Penguin.

Moudud, J., C. Bina, and P. Mason. 2013. *Alternative Theories of Competition: Chanllenges to the Orthodoxy*. (eds.). New York: Routledge.

NYMEX. 2020. "Crude Oil WTI May." *NYMEX*, April 21. www.barchart.com/futures/quotes/CLK20

Orbie, J., and F. De Ville. 2020. "Will the COVID-19 Crisis Herald the End of Neoliberal Globalization . . ." *United Nations University* (UNU-CRIS), April 30. http://cris.unu.edu/covid-19-end-of-neoliberal-globalisation

Panitch, L., and S. Gindin. 2012. *The Making of Global Capitalism: The Political Economy of American Empire*. New York: Verso.

Rosenberg, P. 2020. "Does the Coronavirus Pandemic Mean the End of Globalization? Good!" *Salon*, May 7. www.salon.com/2020/05/07/does-the-coronavirus-pandemic-mean-the-end-of-globalization-as-we-know-it/

Saad-Filho, A. 2020. "Coronavirus, Crisis, and the End of Neoliberalism." *The Bullet*, April 17. https://socialistproject.ca/2020/04/coronavirus-crisis-and-the-end-of-neoliberalism/

Sergent, J., and V. Bravo. 2020. "6 Charts Offer Lessons from Past Bear Markets." *USA Today*, March 17. www.usatoday.com/in-depth/money/2020/03/17/coronavirus-how-stocks-moved-previous-bear-markets/5011397002/

Telford, T., and T. Heath. 2020. "Wall Street Seizes up as Pandemic-Fueled Volatility Sends Dow into a Deep Dive." *The Washington Post*, March 18. www.washingtonpost.com/business/2020/03/18/markets-economy-live-updates-coronavirus/

Virus-Documentary Film. 2020. "The Virus: What Went Wrong?" *Frontline* (PBS), June 16. www.pbs.org/wgbh/frontline/film/the-virus/

World Health Organization (WHO). 2020. "Coronavirus Disease (COVID-2019) Situation Reports." April 19. www.who.int/emergencies/diseases/novel-coronavirus-2019/situation-reports

World Health Organization (WHO). 2022. "Coronavirus Disease (COVID-2019) Situation Reports." April 19. www.who.int/emergencies/diseases/novel-coronavirus-2019/situation-reports

World Statistics. 2020. "Coronavirus Cases." April 19. www.worldometers.info/coronavirus/

World Statistics 2022. "Coronavirus Cases." April 19. www.worldometers.info/coronavirus/

9 Conclusion

The Rise and the Fall of American Power

What goes up, must come down.

The Postwar Economy and Polity

The corpus of all foregoing chapters is the blend, balance, and display of three fundamental manifestations (1) that the postwar Pax Americana was an interstate system that upon its rise both historically and institutionally mediated the transformation of social capital intranationally and internationally for the balance of the twentieth century; (2) that a genuine periodization of capitalism should be grounded in three *moments* of capital, namely, commodity, money, and productive forms had overcome, *inter alia*, the boundaries of the nation-states toward globalization; and (3) that the transnationalization of capital, that is, the core of globalization, led to the collapse of the hierarchical structure of Pax Americana (1945–1979), and with it the fall of the American hegemony. The implosion of the postwar Pax Americana must be understood not only in the context of historic and irreversible change in the balance of power across the globe but also in the wholesale disintegration of the institutions of postwar economy and polity.

Therefore, holding up to hollow skeletons and façade of IMF, World Bank, and the like—as commonly, for instance, a good deal of writings on the traditional left does—is not short of an affront to an intelligent and serious view of today's post-American economy and polity.[1] The rise, decline, and fall of the Pax Americana, however, cannot be satisfactorily defined based on the functionality of institutions or the changing trajectory of postwar history. Thus, any references to these dynamics have no sufficiency in themselves; they necessarily must be theorized in a larger context of the periodization of capitalism identified by moments of capital overcoming the boundaries of nation-states. On the obverse side, it would be through the mediating rise and fall of postwar Pax Americana that the periodization of capitalism in transnationalization of capital in all its three moments, namely, commodity, money, and productive forms, find real expression beyond the boundaries of the nation-states.

DOI: 10.4324/9781351136785-9

The postwar Pax Americana was a contradictory system in which outright colonialism, in the vintage of the Pax Britannica, had steadily contracted, yet there was a tendency for newly liberated countries to be shunted into the sphere of influence political and economic in modern imperialism. This was intermixed with Cold War, a deliberate hegemonic phenomenon initiated by the United States and continued as multifaceted ideological weaponry, as a countertendency to the assorted national liberation and anti-imperialist (national) movements around the world. To be able to perceive the caliber of such contradictions, the reader is reminded of the series of Central Intelligence Agency (CIA) coups inflicted upon the budding, fragile, and independent democracies, starting "officially" with Iran (1953), by the United States.[2] As a matter of course, the boogeyman in these covert interventions was always the Cold War (and prevention of the so-called communism), although the ulterior motive in nearly all cases was none other than economic. For instance, the objective of the 1953 coup in Iran was safeguarding the tentacles of the International Petroleum Cartel (1928–1972)[3] over Iranian oil, itself being the tip of cheap Middle East oil, a vital mainstay of the Marshall Plan for the postwar reconstructions of Europe and Japan.

It is important to understand the complexities of economic development under the Pax Americana, which the rising part of it dabbed the "golden age of capitalism," manifested in the commencement of reconstruction and continued implementation of assorted Keynesian policies and strategies across the board. In addition to the so-called welfare state in the United States, there emerged a proliferation of strategies, known as import substitution industrialization (ISI), prompted by the nearly universal land-reform programs across the Pax Americana having to do with the eradication of self-sustaining production in the countryside and switching to the production of commercial crops for the world market. The ISI strategy relied on the vast surplus of labor freed from the countryside, on the one hand, and the emerging internal market that banked on import-substituting industries that laid the cornerstone of industrialization through the imports of inputs and technology, and manufacturing of imported goods domestically, on the other. Here, the target of ISI[4] was (1) preconditioned by agrarian reform programs, eradicate the remains of self-sufficiency and petty commodity production from the countryside, while generating an abundant supply of fresh labor on the way to urban industries; (2) to link up the countryside based on the type of products demanded buy to the world market; and (3) to organically hook up the rest of the individual economies via both inputs and technology, on the one hand, and the final products, be it, consumer or producer, on the other, to the world market.[5]

These steps of course were either accompanied or supplemented by export-platform strategies that, both directly and indirectly, laid the foundation of transnationalization (and eventual tripartite negation of the nation-state by all three *moments*) of capital, *inter alia*, from the angle of the "Third World," the client-state fragment of the Pax Americana. In the postwar period, within the capitalistically developed core of the Pax Americana, known as the industrialized nations, capital (a potentially universal entity since inception) turned to actuality and tendential manifestation in terms of transnationalization of capital. This was contrary to the euphemism of "national capital" (an accepted oxymoron) and assorted nationalistic and semi-nationalistic accounts either in *multi*national corporate context or within the "imperialist globalization" mold, *inter alia*, by the radical left and liberal right, and in contradistinction of the innermost nature and dynamics of capital itself. We must be reminded that the incessant removal of legal, moral, social, physical, technical, and geographical boundaries has long been (potentially) the quintessence of accumulation of capital from day one, perhaps since the historic overcoming of the limits of the working day. And all such overcoming in the cumulative sense of the term consists of tendencies and countertendencies appropriate to the mother of all tendencies, an eventual accumulation of capital on a global scale. This is what Marx called, the conquest of the mode of production, overcoming all possible barriers, except the barrier of *capital* itself, which is in a nutshell and in Hegelian (methodological) lingo establishes both a "positive" and a "negative" critique of capitalism in its organic unity and contradiction. Here, the *world market*, in its early embryonic capitalist form, say, in Marx's time, too, steadily but surely had acquired its innermost substantive core in fully developed capital as a social relation, thus transformed from potential to an actual conduit at the service of proliferation, reproduction, and amplification of scale and scope of the conquest of the mode of production across the globe. Therefore, speaking of the world market or money and finance or cartels and trusts is not only not the same as what was once perceived (by the likes of John A. Hobson) in the late nineteenth and early twentieth centuries, in which colonialism and cartels were running the roughshod over a world whose nearly four-fifths of the population had neither lived nor knew what *capitalism* would look like, but also an unmitigated caricature of what capital, as a social relation, and the innermost dynamics of concentration and centralization, a lever of capitalist competition, is all about.

Pax Americana and the Dialectic of Global Reach

As explicated directly and indirectly in this volume, no period of history, significant or otherwise, can ever be defined or examined by itself, that is, as a point of *departure* and a point of *return*, at the same time, without tautology. In other words, any historical period worthy of the name must be necessarily mediated through a process of theorization for the purpose of delineation and identity. These periods could arise in sub-periods, say, from certain set of socioeconomic policies, strategic and political shifts, or, for that matter, an entire interstate system across the international arena, like the postwar Pax Americana, that would encompass and be a context for any of economic, political, and social policies and their possible shifts in the sub-periods. What is significant here is to note that (1) no historical period, in and of itself, could necessarily be a ground for a genuine theory of periodization for the capitalist mode of production, and (2) no set of state economic policies, strategies, doctrines, policy shifts, and policy reversals of sorts in any relevant sub-periods or in the whole period under investigation could be an appropriate ground for the periodization of capitalism. Why? Because the (methodological) reliance upon such historical periods themselves is necessary but not sufficient without the *mediation* of a germane theory of periodization; a theory that while detached yet arises from the inner dynamics of capitalism in those periods and thus, within an unencumbered context of abstraction, clearly disclose both the contradictory character and limits of such specific periods. Here, following Marx, the methodological requirements of circumventing the occurrence of a tautology is a guide for theorization and the primacy of a fully-fledged theory of periodization grounded in the social relations of *capital* itself. In other words, the rise and the fall of postwar Pax Americana cannot be theoretically explained without an adequate theory of periodization for capitalism, stage by stage.

In this context, by adopting the theoretical approach unique to Marx's study of capitalism, this book advances a pivotal foundation for several burning questions of our time, namely, that (1) the postwar Pax Americana was a hierarchical interstate/international system in which outright colonialism took a backseat to client-state sub-system, displayed in imperialism; (2) the Pax Americana was a *passage* for the spread of capitalist social relations across the world, yet it relied on cartel and strict administered pricing in certain "strategic" sectors; (3) the Pax Americana was hegemonic by the virtue of its mediating hegemonic economic and political institutions, *inter alia*, the Bretton Woods international monetary system (1944–1971); (4) the American hegemony was absolutely dependent upon the sum total of hegemonic institutions of the Pax Americana; (5) the rise and the fall of the Pax Americana are both intertwined and contradictory effects of the development of capitalism in the successive stages of internationalization and transnationalization of capital; (6) the systematic rise and the fall of the Pax Americana cannot be explicated by resort to speculation as to the singling of internal constituents or, for that matter, to external elements; (7) the loss of American hegemony is adamantly and indisputably the consequence of the fall of the Pax Americana; (8) the rise of China as an explanation for the fall of America is as absurd as a belief that your cat is losing weight since your neighbor's dog is getting fat; (9) the promotion of neoliberalism as a yardstick for periodization of capitalism is not unlike a "dog and pony sideshow" that wittingly or not (a) obscures the reality of American decline, (b) obfuscates the connotation of a genuine periodization, and (c) diverts attention from the dialectic of American decline and the rise of globalization; and finally (10) the corollary of all these is inevitably an irrevocable and critical change in the global balance of power in the world today.

The postwar Pax Americana thrived on three legs of the stool, three interwoven dimensions: economy, polity, and cultural/ideological/public relations,[6] the latter gigantic and dynamic machinery for ideological reproduction in both the inside United States through the educational, religious, and cultural institutions, and outside, across the world, by means of immense, imaginative, and intoxicating precision, and true Orwellian vintage.[7] The economy in the Pax Americana essentially consisted of the institutions surrounding the Bretton Woods arrangements, notably, IMF and World Bank, that propelled and enveloped the transformative tendency and countertendencies of development and capital accumulation across the world. As indicated earlier, all this should be conjoined early on with Marshall Plan and in due time dovetail in the 1950s and 1960s with worldwide agrarian land reforms programs, the former intended to reconstruct Europe and Japan while the latter aimed at the eradication of precapitalist production and self-sufficiency, and uniting "Third World" economies to the world market. As demonstrated earlier in this volume, this is just a glimpse of a long, diverged, yet irreversible passage toward the metamorphosis of capital in eventual transnationalization, which promptly disrupted the very foundation of the Pax Americana. The postwar order thrived on the sum total of its institutions, whose strength was ultimately dependent upon the vibrancy of the economic institutions and the power of transforming technology. On the political front, these translated to the de facto political power that ironically reinforced the US three-pronged containment strategy, a hallmark of polity (and geopolitics) in the Pax Americana. To be sure, all the so-called security arrangements (including all treaties) in the Pax Americana unequivocally revolved around the three-partite of containments of (1) the Soviet bloc, (2) the nationalist and budding democracies (and movements) in the "Third Word," and (3) the radical organizations and progressive movements in the United States and other advanced countries in the West. Concerning the containment of the latter category, the era of McCarthyism in the United States is only the tip of the iceberg. This is how the rhetoric of the "free world," the craftiest stunt of the Cold War, was born.[8]

Overall, the interwoven quality and character of the economy, polity, and public relations in the practice of foreign policy were remarkably profound. As for public relations, successful diplomatic conduct normally involves a healthy dose of public relations, yet in the Pax Americana, and under the US auspices, foreign policy had turned into a dangerous dialectic of covert (and overt) actions and public relations.[9] The unswerving course of various CIA coup d'états is a telltale of contradictory nature of US foreign policy and a sign of punctuated hegemony due to both built-in instabilities of the order and stupidity of those who oversaw the foreign policy (and the conduct of the international relations) on behalf of the hegemon, the United States.[10] The consequential overthrow of Mossadegh, over the nationalization of cartelized oil in Iran, is a quintessential illustration of both *imperialist* manifestation and proclivity of inner dynamics of the Pax Americana, and imperial quality and essential feature of the US foreign policy so far as the conduct of its hegemon is concerned.[11] Those who attribute this, and similar conducts by the United States, to Cold War are either not aware of the circularity of this explanation or, given an awareness, are possibly in the business of counterfeit-making.

To be sure and more specifically, the 1953 nationalization of oil in Iran and the subsequent Anglo-American coup reveal the tip of contradictory dynamics that not only had to do with geopolitics at the time but also a hint of what defined the heart and soul of the Pax Americana. Here, notwithstanding some 70-year examination by various historians and international relations specialists, putting the overthrow of an elected government, particularly the popular government of PM Mossadegh in Iran, in a larger context of the Pax Americana, not for absolution but for the excavation of its disposition, would shed some light on the intricacy of an interstate system that consistently presented itself as the beacon of freedom and democracy to the outside world as well as inside. It is noteworthy that our critique here is not ethical but immanent, having to do with the inner capacity (or incapacity) of the postwar system, which had served as a credible threshold for both the economic and political conduct of the hegemon. To understand the cause for cartelized oil how tenuously could relate to Cold War and by implication to the boogeyman of "communism," one must remember that cartelized cheap Middle Eastern oil, under the aegis of the International Petroleum Cartel (1928–1972), had been an integral part of Marshall Plan, an economic vehicle for reconstructions of war-torn Europe and Japan—itself a vital interest to the Pax Americana. This would clearly demonstrate that the antidemocratic (i.e., antiliberation and autocratic) tendency was a built-in characteristic of the Pax Americana from the get-go, despite its anticolonial predisposition, particularly against the British Empire. However, the subtlety of this point is lost on liberal historians in the repeated CIA coup d'états, particularly in the well-known case of the nationalization of oil in Iran in which judiciously amicable compensation and orderly arrangement by the government of Mossadegh (1951–1953) were planned, yet fictitious rationale of the Cold War and other ancillary and misleading justifications muddied the *pimum mobile* of the Pax Americana and twisted the postwar history, largely toward the rubric of international *stability* (and worse, international *security*) and thus center stage of "anti-communism." Yet straight, sober, and *inward* look at the Pax Americana could not be more disagreeable.

In addition, Pax Americana's polity had grounded in the arrangements surrounding the United Nations. In addition to the containment of the Soviet Union, the United States drove the runaway Chiang Kai-shek, and the island of Taiwan, to the UN seat, following the 1949 Chinese Revolution. In other words, in 1950, less than 8 million Taiwanese (headed by right-wing reactionary renegades) were to represent some 550 million people in the People's Republic of China (PRC).[12] This simply would display a glimpse of the lopsided structure of the United Nations, which was commonly the subject of American use and abuse to the detriment of targeted states, especially developing and revolutionary nations, by the United States. Therefore, notwithstanding the precepts of the UN Charter, the caretakers of Pax Americana (particularly, its hegemon) had dutifully behaved as if the United Nations was the *de facto* (and exclusive) part of their "political jurisdiction" and polity and thus attached to the postwar American hegemony. Those who may not quite agree with our assessment here should stick to their homework and comb through the pile of available documents in the UN General Assembly, UN Security Council, and elsewhere, for these years to observe a consistent pattern of use and abuses of the "rule of law" by the United States.[13]

Nevertheless, despite all these political intrusions and intermittent covert actions, the real power had rested upon the mediation of the Pax Americana's institutions, without which the entire system would have turned into an arbitrarily ambiguous and indeterminate *military* force in circularity.[14] Furthermore, the nature of power under the Pax Americana was *hegemonic*, that is, having necessarily to do with the mediation of specific institutions at a specific historical time in modern capitalism.[15] The economy in post-war Pax Americana was the core of capital accumulation and transformative engine of capitalist development, which decidedly led to the eradication of self-sufficient production, development of the internal market, and production, consumption, and exchange according to the world market, albeit contradictory tendency and countertendencies in much of the "Third World." This was simultaneous with the generation of a limitless supply of wage labor that departed from the countryside and frequented at the margins of the urban interiors and metropolitan districts of the developing countries where light and heavy manufacturing, and service sectors had clustered. The effect of all this was, *inter alia*, intensifying, and deepening class polarization in all these societies and of course critical tendency to political discord and possible revolutionary upheaval. The rising Pax Americana also witnessed the internationalization of all three *moments* of capital, in commodity, money, and predictive forms, with one's own tendencies and countertendencies, across the board.

Globalization and the Collapse of Postwar Order

Globalization is neither external to the Pax Americana nor external to the capitalist mode of production; it is a consequence of *historical* transformation through the passage of the Pax Americana[16] and the (*theoretical*) corollary of negating capital in all its three moments vis-à-vis the nation-state. In the theoretical context, globalization rest upon the intertwined dynamics of intranationalization and internationalization and transnationalization of capital as a social relation, while from the perspective of history, it goes beyond the emergent and eclectic era of imperialism, and traces through the rise and demise of the Pax Americana, displayed in every nook and cranny of the world in the conquest of the mode of production.[17] In a larger transdisciplinary context, therefore, this particular view of globalization uniquely articulates a theoretically-endowed and historically-informed (critical)[18] theory for both political economy and international relations in one. As demonstrated in this volume, any neglect either on the theoretical side or on the historical side of globalization simply obfuscates and misrepresents the corporeality of capitalism in the present epoch. And none of such misrepresentations is more unwarranted than the *periodization* of capitalism based on Keynesianism and neoliberalism.[19] Hence, the collapse of the Pax Americana (and the fall of American hegemony) appeals to a common historical cause that has properly rooted in the globalization of capital as explicated earlier.[20]

The decline of the Pax Americana began in the late 1960s when the postwar international monetary system, the Bretton Woods, was overwhelmed by overprinting of US dollars (known as Eurodollars) backed up by a fixed exchange rate in gold. This was a crack in the foundation of the Bretton Woods and the attendant economic institutions of the postwar system, which compelled the Nixon administration to dismantle the system on August 15, 1971. On the political side, the war in Vietnam, culminating in the 1968 Tet Offensive, topped the standoff in the confrontation back in 1953, in the Korean war,[21] and led to an indubitable defeat by the United States.[22] The late 1960s was a preamble to Pax Americana's eventual eclipse, as the tectonic plates of earth-shattering change also set in motion against the American hegemony,[23] by the end of the 1970s. The crisis of the Bretton Woods was not over a simple switch between fixed to the flexible exchange-rate regimes, as neoclassical economic orthodoxy led us to believe, it was a gamechanger of epochal quality that set the beginning of the end. This poor judgment also carried into certain heterodox economic analyses whose *a priori* methodology and perfunctory political perspective did not allow for deeper insights.

The transnationalization of capital was nowhere so clearly revealed than in the oil sector in which the crisis of decartelization led to the collapse of the International Petroleum Cartel (1928–1972), known as the 1973–1974 oil crisis. This was a worldwide crisis that swept across OPEC and non-OPEC regions leading up to the competitive globalization of the (crude) oil industry. This was the end of cartelized oil—a significant economic component of the Pax Americana (via Marshall Plan) and a potent political and ideological weapon in the arsenal of US foreign policy in the postwar period. In a value-theoretic context, other sources within the fossil-fuel energy category, such as coal and natural gas, are also governed by the value of oil since globalization.[24] In the aftermath of the oil crisis, contrary to the whimsical public outcry in the news media and fictitious claims by both the Ford and the Carter administrations neither the bellicosity of American exceptionalism nor silly calls for "energy independence"[25] nor deliberate badmouthing of OPEC did change larger and persistent picture of decartelized and globalized oil.[26] Incidentally, this should be a lesson to so many crowd-pleasing, yet clueless, traditional leftists who deluded the public by misplacing the cause of the 2003 US invasion of Iraq as *oil*, or the 2001 US invasion of Afghanistan as *pipeline*, given the very fact that the United States, despite the so-called self-sufficiency in oil and gas well over the last decade or so, is still in the business of invading or interfering, either directly or by proxy, in nearly every part of the world, particularly in the Middle East. On this issue, the traditional left does not commit to untruth but to counterfeit, the essence of which is not simply negating truth but disguising one's indifference to it.[27] It is a shame that so many progressive, antiwar radical leftists are so theoretically naïve and methodologically impressionistic.[28]

In the 1970s, both the *polity* and *economy* of the Pax Americana, to put succinctly in Gramsci's terms, the "war of position" was on the losing side, and "manufacturing consent" was on the offing. The third leg of the stool of the Pax Americana, that is, the machination of *ideology*, was also run over itself. And there was a crude but cumulative political awakening in the client-state subdivision of the Pax Americana. The tip of all this can be seen in the Iranian and Nicaraguan Revolutions, both of which came to a head in 1979, and both of which were subverted by the United States, first, covertly by aiding and abetting the counterrevolutionary Islamic forces (under the leadership of anti-communist/anti-nationalist Khomeini), and thus nipping the Iranian revolution in the bud and covering southern borders of the USSR with "green belt" of Islam and, second, overtly, by financing, hiring, and equipping mercenaries, known as Contras, against the burgeoning people's revolution in Nicaragua. In due time, the "war of maneuver," which was started in these two separate countries across the globe, was spread and engulfed the entire subdivision of the Pax Americana. The European Union, apart from Britain, potentially had an ambivalent relationship with the United States, and given the anti-Soviet sentiments of the Western European bourgeoisie and convenient cover of the "nuclear umbrella," their de facto deviation appeared a bit intensely right after the fall of the Soviet Union. The transnationalization of capital, however, was an underlying power of change in the interest of the grand bourgeoisie in both manufacturing and trade, which led to separate unity and the eventual formation of a new global currency, the euro. In the meantime, toward the end of the presidency of Jimmy Carter, both the pace of outsourcing in manufacturing and deregulation of the US banking system and unification of the entire financial system were the manifestation of much deeper forces of globalization. This was the preamble to a much larger upheaval, known as wholesale *plants closing* across the United States in the mid-1980s, displayed as a colossal mop-up operation across the United States, which promptly unseated the United States from the throne of hegemony[29] and removed it categorically from the center of global production for good. In political terms, the overturning of such material centrality, together with the implosion of the Soviet Union, generated an immense disorder in the transition to a somewhat ordered multipolar world till now. Therefore, the question of global security is either broached rather falsely in demand for the status quo ante or leapfrogging by the United States, a declining power fascinated by the *appearance* of the power vacuum.[30]

Finally, contrary to public opinion, it would be meaningless to measure the decline of the United States with, say, the rise of China. Such a comparison overlooks the very point about the transformation of the world as a whole; it also neglects the fact that the post-Pax Americana world cannot be hegemonic in the way that the Pax Americana once was, that is, an intermediate period on the way to transnationalization of capital and eventual tendency toward a *universal* social relation across the globe.[31] And it is within such universality that there would not be any room for a state—no matter how powerful—or a system of states to be exceptionally hegemonic. Unlike domination, hegemony is neither dependent on military power nor subject to political volition. Hegemony is the *whole*, and the concept of the whole in the context of globalization is defined by the social relations of capital across the economic and political landscape.

Globalization and the Babble of "New" American World Order

It is not a coincidence that Karl Marx amended Hegel's vexing remark that "all great world-historic facts and personages appear, so to speak, twice." Marx elucidates: "He forgot to add: the first time as tragedy, the second time as farce."[32] The fall of the Berlin Wall (November 9, 1989)[33] and eventual (and official) collapse of the Soviet Union (December 26, 1991)[34] were godsends for George H. W. Bush and the rest of the American leadership who unilaterally declared a "new world order" (April 13, 1991)[35] and force-fed the world that the United States is a "unipolar" power. Yet, it must also be remembered that this upbeat announcement had come after a massive permanent militarization of the Persian Gulf by the US forces, in apparent response to Saddam Hussein's invasion of Kuwait (on August 2, 1990), which decidedly targeted the indiscriminate destruction of Iraq (January 17, 1991—February 28, 1991). Those keen on subtleties should not be too hard to gaze at these dates and opportunistic actions and not be persuaded that all this points to an ominous portrayal of the United States as a power-grabbing loose cannon from the outset. Yet, sadly, the very superficial appearance—in conjunction with the rhetoric of the moment and the parade of military might and to be sure quick and cowardly slaughter (not a war, with reasonable rules of engagement defined by Geneva Conventions) of Iraqi forces under George H.W. Bush[36]—that had concealed the inner transformation of this period captured the imagination of copious mélange of onlookers, from the right of the right to the left of the left in the political spectrum. Adjunct to this topsy-turvy and false narrative is the labeling of *states* (and new countries), which resulted from the breakdown of the Soviet bloc, as *emerging markets*,[37] thus accentuating an illusory rise of the United States. As a result, this ploy, through media frenzy and hand in glove with US foreign policy, purposely played down and disguised the rise of globalization and the fall of American power. In the meantime, with the collapse of the Soviet bloc—the number one adversary—the crawling neoconservatives and cold worriers, advancing to the center of the American foreign policy, were at work on finding a substitute and thus suitable "enemy" to justify both the theoretical (and ideological) and operational and empirical cause of the US strategic expansion and aggressive move. Samuel Huntington's piece in *Foreign Affairs* is one of the early attempts toward this collective posture.[38] The fall of the Soviets was palpable even by savvy schoolchildren, but the collapse of the Pax Americana earlier needed considerably more insight and less hubris. There were those among more philosophically refined ideologues who doubled down on the mirage of American rise. Francis Fukuyama was the one who dared to go for the jugular, so to speak, and invoked "the end of history."[39] As we have demonstrated in this book and elsewhere, the shoe has all the while since the 1980s been on the other foot, and what had finally ended is ironically the very *history* of the Pax Americana.[40]

In this context, in the aftermath of the Soviet collapse, the dog-and-pony sideshow of "we won the Cold War without firing a shot," by Washington, must be scrutinized within the larger choreography toward not only the mere restoration of the Pax Americana but also exceed it by (wishful) turning off the clock way back by sheer military means in the direction of the empires of the yesteryears. It is within this grand scenario that, first, the perpetuation of NATO and, second, NATO's takeover of former Soviet states and its deliberate expansion inch by inch toward the borders of the Russian Federation,[41] concurrently with the so-called pivot to Asia (read China), would make a perfect sense. Skating on the thin ice of nostalgia both at home and abroad and endowed with a thick presence of firepower and trigger-happy military machine scattered in nearly 800 bases around the world, it is how and why the United States would not let go of NATO.[42] Yet, no military might (or application of external force) would be able to change or to sustain a world order that is not truly amicable to the inner dynamics of the global economy and polity of today, not to mention, the sheer resolve of several billion of masses of humanity, as the American (and NATO) defeat after defeat in not-so-distant past in Afghanistan, Iraq, and Syria[43] (to name a few) had already shown.

Since the 1980s, deep down beneath the tendency of unsettling and destabilizing US behavior is the globalization of capital, the new ground that—following the manifested finale of plant closings explicated earlier—had cracked the foundation and bashed the entire superstructure of the postwar Pax Americana from within. As pointed on in detail in this book, globalization is a concept that has intimately to do with the structural and organic change in the material, social, political, geographical, and at last environmental aspects of life under capitalism toward the conquest of the mode of production. This conquest, which is palpable in nearly all quarters of the world and touching billions of people as we speak, is explicable by the development of capitalism in a value-theoretic manner expounded and anticipated in Marx's *Capital*—not to be confused with Piketty's *Capital*.[44] This view, in abstract, encapsulates why the growth of the embryo of capital as a social relation is dependent upon, *inter alia*, the overcoming of natural, social, organizational, political, economic, and geographical barriers, which also embrace negation of the boundaries of the nation-state and the threshold of environmental capacity. And how this negation, particularly of the nation-state, led to the transnationalization of capital and transmogrification of the state beyond imperialism, late colonial and hybrid-colonial (in both the prewar and postwar Pax Americana) era that posed as an antecedent to globalization.

In a nutshell, the primary aim of this book has been to show (1) that *periodization* of capitalism is a key to spotting the kernel of inner dynamics of change, particularly in the postwar and post-postwar period since the 1970s; (2) that the theorization of a genuine periodization of capitalism, as opposed to popular but counterfeit genre, must be founded within capital itself; (3) that the globalization of capital is subject to the "conquest of the mode of production" manifested through negations of nearly all material, social, political, and geographical boundaries, including the borders of the nation-states; (4) that, for purpose of theorization, any intended division between different parts of history for the purpose of theorization in capitalism proper, must be mediated through the three *moments* of capital, namely, commodity, money, and productive forms; (5) that both conceptually and materially, unlike the past, the present-day world market is intimately interwoven with global production; (6) that the fall back on "monopoly capitalism" is but the poverty of philosophy of our time, a pandemic version of it palpable in various degrees among the clueless (and theory-less) left fascinated by the echo of emulating days of Hilferding and Lenin; (7) that, aside from its specific historical identity, speaking of imperialism is little more than a juxtaposition of separate levels of analysis fused and confused, the least of which is the likening of cartels (and trusts) to concentration/centralization of capital and crudity of *direct* political power in perpetuity[45]; (8) that the rise and the fall of Pax Americana (1945–1979) are cogently explicable by trace, and more importantly, mediation of the transnationalizing capital; and finally (9) that the fall of the Pax Americana sealed the fate of the US hegemonic power and put an end to American political order for good.

It is necessary to note that there is no shortage of alternative views on capitalism, the postwar economy, and the characteristics of the global economy since the 1970s. As has been shown in this book, by critically looking at a somewhat persistent and popular spectrum of the traditional (and non-traditional) leftist tendencies, along with an inventory of *blind spots* common to all, the views that by and large cluster around the notion of imperialism in perpetuity (and monopoly capitalism), either relegated Marx to a mere appendage of Lenin (more correctly, Hobson) for explication of contemporary capitalism or rather paid lip service to Marx's theory of value, his theory of synthetic competition, and their ramification for the conquest of the mode of production across the globe. Amid this methodological and ideological disarray, Monthly Review School had taken the mantle of anti-value theory and has been playing a crucial role in the cult of monopoly since the 1950s. In the meantime, the perplexing issues surrounding the post-1970s unparalleled shifts in the global economy and global polity, and the turbulent crises of restructuring and readjustment, should be a litmus test for those who huffed and puffed as Marxists for years and yet played a variation or two, day in and day out, on the same old theme, and dutifully revived the tautology of "imperialist rivalry," circularity of "center-periphery," or "the duality of global north/global south." The clink of once historically specific *imperialism* rings much like a timeless nursery rhyme in the ears of the infantile left, while in whose eye every perturbing political event or conflict under the sun turns rather submissively into a game of table tennis, now ping, then pong, without end. And almost any and every economic or political event in the world is religiously phrased in a blanket display of "imperialism." In a parallel context, another radical scholar appealed to the duality of the two so-called *logics*: of history and of territory, while curiously joggling between "monopolistic competition" and "monopoly" at the margins of the theory of value and contemporary capitalism.[46] Such a cat-and-mouse drama, aside from its theoretical inaptness, advertently or inadvertently corrupts the substance of periodization of capitalism and distorts the meaning of globalization of capital in both the value-theoretic and realistic terms. The nature of these blind spots and theoretical mishaps are also varied according to both methodological and ideological tendencies of each view, including issues tangled with transhistorical fixation and the degree to which certain critics did not abide by the criterion of specificity and *differentia specifica* of capitalism.[47]

There are also distinct yet methodologically flawed approaches concerning worldwide transformation and the global sea change other than the application of World-Systems perspective (exampled by Arrighi's *The Long Twentieth Century*) whose critique is available in this volume.[48] We are as a rule critical of the garden variety of pseudo-globalization theories, those whose foundation either lacks the social relation of capital and thus rather superficially speaking of global technology, and global markets and the *neoliberal* world or else has turned the table on their presumed Marxian pedigree and thus freeing themselves from both theoretical, institutional, and political imperatives of *class* in modern capitalism.[49] At the pinnacle of critique here is *Empire* (by Hardt and Negri), an approach that at the first blush jettisoned the class and embraced the *multitude*, thus abrogating Marx's theory of value from the foundation of the emerging worldwide transformations.[50] This reversal of course is not accidental but the direct effect of capitulation to, not the falsity, but absolute *fakery*[51] of postmodernism and voluntary amnesia toward history, particularly the history of capitalism. In this context, any reference that the era of imperialism is passé, and thus globalization, is but a mere clever maneuvering for dishing out the phantasm of "empire" to the unsuspecting reader.

In sum, the periodization of capitalism proper is internal to capital itself as a social relation toward universality. Such universality must also be substantiated by the theory of value and theory of synthetic completion to be genuine. As indicated in this book, synthetic competition in Marx is the opposite of the vulgar division of capitalism into competitive and monopoly, and thus any periodization that bears a resemblance to "competitive, monopoly, state-monopoly capitalism" must be dubious. Likewise, any such division based on pure historical interludes, that is, without the mediation of capital (that is, without the mediation of its tripartite *moments*) itself or, for that matter, identified according to a particular doctrine, state economic policy, or political strategy, such as Keynesianism versus neoliberalism, is equally misleading.[52] The irony is that among those on the left who committed this methodological blunder there is a peculiar overlap between these two approaches. Of course, the saturation of social and political space with the assorted pseudo-globalization theories, in both right-wing and left-wing vintage, cannot be discounted as a factor for a downright anti-globalization obsession among the left, particularly those Marxist scholars who desperately struggle to explain away the present epoch in such inept and inaccurate terms. To conclude this chapter, we wish to hint in passing that the approach taken in this book is far from Kõzõ Uno's "three-level analysis," and its manifold variants, in the study of capitalism. We contend that such a "stage theory" unnecessarily axiomatizes the notion of capital as "pure" and thus mechanically segregates the development of capital from potentiality to actuality. In other words, Uno's method of analysis dichotomies the inner dynamics of capital from their manifestation in these rather mechanical stages.[53]

Finally, the globalization of capital is but an organic context for the globalization of contradictions, the pinnacle of which is the globalization of class struggle. Along this indispensable trajectory, any movement worthy of the name, in what is discerned as the "butterfly effect,"[54] would spread across the world. Within the same context, the critical question of climate change is readily palpable in every nook and cranny of the globe. This and the speed of the spread and universal effects of COVID-19 are *inter alia* the two concrete manifestations of globalization both because and beyond the globalization of capital. In other words, stage by stage, outer limits of the geography of capital accumulation have now been achieved, in a cumulatively deepening and widening organic unity (and contradiction and turbulent competition[55]) in globalization; and history and geography conjoined in the universality of capital as a social relation, overcoming all but itself—*capital*.[56] At the heart of issues displayed and discussed in this book is the critique of political economy entwined with the theory of international relations (and geopolitics) from the perspective of both orthodoxy and heterodoxy, including the supposed militant variety regurgitated and consumed across the radical left today.[57] Here is where the rubber hits the road, so to speak, and the collapse of the postwar Pax Americana (1945–1979) and fall of the American power can be understood theoretically, historically, scientifically, and without prejudice.

Notes

1 Habitual references that carelessly put the IMF, World Bank, and other paraphernalia—institutions belonging to the now-defunct Pax Americana—at the center of the contemporary world, are simply misleading and pitiful, particularly by disparaging pseudo-leftist writers.

2 See Elwell-Sutton, Laurence P. 1955. *Persian Oil: A Study of Power Politics*. London: Lawrence and Wishart; Elm, Mustafa 1992. *Oil, Power, and Principle: Iran's Oil Nationalization and Its Aftermath*. New York: Syracuse University Press.

3 Blair, John M. 1976. *The Control of Oil*. New York: Pantheon Books; Engler, Robert 1977. *The Brotherhood of Oil*. Chicago, IL: University of Chicago Press.

4 Bina, Cyrus and Behzad Yaghmaian 1988. "Import Substitution and Export Promotion within the Context of the Internationalization of Capital," *Review of Radical Political Economics* 20 (2 & 3), Summer: 234–241.

5 Contra Karl Polanyi's approach and views, the nineteenth century is neither a "market society" nor a "market economy." These seemingly innocent and fitting characterizations are simply *fictitious* if not entirely misleadingly dangerous. These two phrases are *perceived* appearances of something deeper that must be identified through theoretical mediation (that is, adequate abstraction) and then demonstrated why they *appear* as they do in such pattern or exactitude. We must note carefully that the contention here is not over the

narrative of the prevalent ideology of capitalism, in this period, but precisely the method of analysis (and theorization) in the advancement of capitalism. See Polanyi, Karl 1967 [1944]. *The Great Transformation: The Political and Economic Origins of Our Time.* Boston, MA: Beacon Press. In this book, despite wonderful expositions and detailed narratives, Polanyi fails a theory of either market economy or market society. Why? Because he failed to *mediate* his history (that is, raw history) with precise theoretical construction. He failed because he used the narrative to explicate the narrative, a costly tautological undertaking that is also consciously, or unconsciously, lost on so many of his admirers among the liberal and radical left. To be sure, my objection to Polanyi (and the Polanyi-brandishing supporters) is not toward his magnificent storytelling and the collage of so many useful slices of historical accounts and developments, but to his claim at conceptualization (and theorization) which is empty of mediation of a theory to accompany the history without falling into the trap of *tautology*. In other words, Polanyi's "market society" and "market economy" are both mental constructs, indeed a fickle device to claim rather fictitiously to (1) "society as a whole" over class-based capitalism, (2) society over class, (3) sociality over individualism, (4) "rationality" over irrationality, (5) peace and harmony over conflict, and (6) "politism" over "economism"—all on the same level and within a transhistorical context (see Ch. 13 for most parts). Such claims of course are a tall order that could not be critically understood within Polanyi's nonexistent methodological framework, yet they somehow turned into loud ballyhoo in a cheeky cottage industry of branching Polanyi against Marx, for instance, on the purported economism of the latter, and presumably justified political (and social) framework of the former, by a miscellany of liberals and left-leaning radicals in the mix. Specifically, Polanyi fooled his audience by the shallow examples of "economic protectionism" vis-à-vis *laissez-faire*—and thus an impression of infringement for "social whole"—and by neglecting a much deeper transmogrification of capital's (class) Interest, as *public interest*, by the fetish of capital itself (see Ch. 12 and Ch. 13). In addition, Polanyi's observation in Chapter 6 ("The Self-Regulating Markets: Labor, Land, and Money") comes very close to the reality of capitalist mode of production but, alas, without a firm theoretical basis other than tautological narration and superficial intimation; these issues effectively addressed and coherently theorized some 80 years before Karl Polanyi's by Karl Marx. Being a progressive scholar, Polanyi must have been acquainted with such concepts, yet certainly without sufficient theoretical understanding of their organic roots, not so much in the market, per se, but in the capital. We must say this in no uncertain terms to those who accuse Karl Marx of "economism," with a straight face, that (1) speaking of polity (and politics) without a mediating analysis and genuine theorization as to the inner dynamics is but an empty talk, and (2) throwing around phrases like market society, the market economy, geopolitical economy, imperialist globalization, neoliberal capitalism, Empire, *inter alia*, is not far from sticking with the real appearance, or skin-deep reality, and thus rudimentary imagery not deep enough to be able to capture inner dynamics and essential core of social and political aspects of capitalism as has been known.

6 Antonio Gramsci's magnificent point on the cultural institutions aiming at reproduction of ideology by "war of position" is unequivocally pertinent here. The role of the church, both Catholic and Protestant churches, in anti-communism, on the one hand, and Xenophobia and hostility to anti-imperialist movements in the developing countries, on the other; the role of educational institutions, particularly schools of foreign policy, history, political science, economics, and sociology in the United States, and by extension across the geography of Pax Americana; and the role of the establishment media and the propaganda machine of all, movie industry in Hollywood, *inter alia*, are the delicate and distinguishing characteristics of the Pax Americana, besides economy and polity.

7 The culture of the so-called *American exceptionalism* has remained as a cherry on top of other ideological distractions, potently wreaking havoc with the American psyche not only in the highly schooled population, such as Barack Obama himself, but also across

the barely schooled, isolated, downtrodden, and simple rural population in the United States. To my astonishment, I also observed a whiff of this in liberal European writings, even after the fall of the Pax Americana, in the political science and international relations literature.

8 It is deplorable that after the collapse of Pax Americana and the implosion of the Soviet bloc one should witness the resurgence of this empty rhetoric (i.e., "free world") in the media and public discourse, particularly at the present that the United States has very little to show for either on the foreign-policy front or domestic front, concerning human rights, civil rights, or freedom.

9 Essentially, marketing-on-steroids comprised a lion's share of American diplomatic comportment during the height of the Cold War, the core of which was the weaponization of everything, from soup to nuts, not only against the Soviet Union but also, besides deliberate covert interventions, against nationalist movements, budding democracies in the "Third World," and the nationalist figures across the three continents, such as Mossadegh (1953), Arbenz (1954), Lumumba (1960), Villeda Morales (1963), Goulart (1964), Bosch (1965), Sukarno (1965–1966), Umberto Illia (1966), Nkrumah (1966), Torres (1971), Allende (1973), and Isabel Perón (1976), to name a handful.

10 For a glimpse of the US covert interventions and CIA coup d'états, see Blum, William 2003 [1986]. *The CIA: A Forgotten History*. Revised Edition. Monroe, ME: Common Courage Press.

11 It should be recognized that imperialism is a specific (historical) period in the development of capitalism where cartels and trusts are at center stage. This period consists of a lower stage in which colonialism is still in the mix and the moment of capital in money form is just beginning to overcome the border of the nation-states known as the "export of capital." In the upper stage of imperialism, a period that coincides with the Pax Americana, however, colonialism was rescinded, the development of capitalism is much more advanced, the *moment* of capital in *productive* form had begun to overcome the border of the nation-state, and by and large, the accumulation of capital had thrown the crutches of cartel and trusts by the wayside. As the fate of the Pax Americana (1945–1979) was sealed by the epochal forces of globalization, the closure of imperialism, a specific period in the history of capitalism, was inevitable. That is why appealing to "imperialist globalization" is but an oxymoron.

12 The respective comparison of the population of Taiwan and PRC is less than 15 million and some 818 million in 1970, while Taiwan had a secured seat at the UN General Assembly and PRC had none. It was not until 1971 that PRC was officially recognized as a member; Taiwan's flag, however, was removed from the display at the UN Headquarters in New York in 1979, the final year of the presidency of Jimmy Carter.

13 The UN documents would tell us that, among other nations, the United States (and not to mention, Israel since its inception) has the highest record of violation of international law since the signing of the UN Charter. And the frequent reference to the "rule of law" by the US leadership is a cruel irony.

14 To comply with hegemony (and hegemonic power) in Gramsci's connotation, "military hegemony"—a common expression among the left and the right—is an oxymoron.

15 For the specific implication and categorization of hegemony (and hegemonic power), see Bina, Cyrus 2013b. *A Prelude to the Foundation of Political Economy: Oil, War, and Global Polity*. New York: Palgrave Macmillan: 188–191.

16 It is noteworthy that the inter-state system of Pax Americana was belonging to a *specific* period of history (as opposed to the transhistorical variety) and so is our theory behind it.

17 That is why, I have long insisted that the present epoch (i.e., globalization) is the epoch of Karl Marx, not of Vladimir I. Lenin and his like-minded contemporaries. Likewise, contrary to pontification by certain protagonists on the radical left, an accurate grasp of capitalism should make a hell of a difference to (accurate) praxis, in contradistinction from simple trial and error.

18 The inference to *critical* here is intended to parallel Marx's critique of political economy and has nothing to do with the "critical theory" espoused by the Frankfort School or any other.

19 Next to this myopic and circular view is an equally inaccurate and deceiving view on periodization based on "monopoly," that is, *competitive, monopoly, and state-monopoly capitalism.*

20 It goes without saying that the transformation of the Soviet Union and of China (particularly under Deng Xiaoping) should be considered as part of the same trend toward capitalist globalization. The contentions insinuating communism or socialism in both countries are hollow and rather thin.

21 Those who wonder about the hostile position of North Korea and the behavior of its leader should return all the way back to the original sin of not signing off on the peace agreement by the United States, right after the armistice in 1953. One should note that both the Soviet Union and the People's Republic of China signed the peace treaty there and then, yet the United States not only did not agree to the peace but doubled down also by keeping some 30,000 US troops on the border for some 70 years till now.

22 The US military defeat in the protracted Vietnam War was the mother of all defeats that stamped its ultimate verdict on every single American military conflict in the world hence. It has been the litmus test of US military power, its functionality, and its strategic value (i.e., lack thereof) when it comes to invading other countries with or without a pretext. That is why the frequent reference by the traditional left to some 800 US military bases around the world is not a sign of American hegemony (an oxymoron) or control. This is an occasion in which many self-styled leftists in the vintage of Hobson, particularly those in a radical version of Leninist-Trotskyist tradition, sadly think with their eyes rather than their head.

23 Hegemony and hegemonic power are defined by the organic unity of the underlying institutions of economy and polity; power defend in this fashion has nothing to do with domination or sheer military prowess. Hence, neither hegemonic power nor hegemony is something of their own but an organic *relation.*

24 It is striking that several years after the globalization of oil and the fall of American hegemony there are those who habitually stick to their rusty guns and speak of the world oil and American hegemony as if nothing had changed in the intervening time. See Bromley, Simon 1991. *American Hegemony and World Oil.* University Park, PA: Pennsylvania State University Press; Bina, Cyrus 1994b. "Review of American Hegemony and World Oil," *Harvard Middle Eastern and Islamic Review* 1 (2): 194–198.

25 Those familiar with the calculus of commodity production in capitalism (and anathema of self-sufficiency) should know that question of oil here is about crude oil available on the competitive global market but a telltale sign of *sour grapes* of losing the cartelized (foreign) oil, following the collapse of International Petroleum Cartel (1928–1972), and globalization of oil in daily (competitive) prices in both spot and future's markets across the world.

26 One must remember the founding of the Rapid Deployment Force by the Carter administration, in 1979, which was allegedly ready to go to the Persian Gulf to "secure" the production of oil. The dubious course of US actions and mentality of the US leadership at this juncture are quintessentially important from the standpoint of both bewilderment in viewing new reality and new reality itself. With the collapse of the International Petroleum Cartel, in 1972, the umbilical cord of the US foreign policy was hanging loose and thus there was a panic attack in the corridors of power in Washington. See Bina, Cyrus 1993. "The Rhetoric of Oil and the Dilemma of War and American Hegemony," *Arab Studies Quarterly* 15 (3): 1–20. In the meantime, badmouthing of OPEC as a "cartel" is a corollary of fictitious competition in orthodox neoclassical economics and its reckless rendering in much of the leftist literature. For a critique, see *inter alia* Bina, Cyrus 1990. "Limits to OPEC Pricing: OPEC Profits and the Nature of Global Oil Accumulation," *OPEC Review* 14 (1): 55–73; Bina, Cyrus 1989a. "Some

Controversies in the Development of Rent Theory: The Nature of Oil Rent," *Capital & Class* 39: 82–112.

27 This is exactly the definition of bullshit (and bullshitting or faking), which is worse than a lie or falsity. See Frankfurt, Harry G. 2005. *On Bullshit*. Princeton, NJ: Princeton University Press.

28 For a quintessential example of this rather dominant tendency on the left, see Klare, Michael 2004. *Blood and Oil: The Dangers and Consequences of America's Growing Tendency on Imported Petroleum*. New York: Metropolitan Books; Klare, Michael 2003. "It's the Oil, Stupid," *The Nation*, May 12. Sadly, in twisting the cause of the recent US invasions, Klare and his like-minded supporters misinformed the public and thus played in the hands of the US government by masking and softening the culpability and criminality of such invasions as if "energy need" or "oil dependency." For a critique of this view, see Bina, Cyrus 2004a. "Is It the Oil, Stupid?" *The URPE Newsletter* 35 (3): 5–8; Bina, Cyrus 2014. "Global Oil and the Fallacy of Middle East Oil Dependency," in *The Sage Handbook of Globalization*, vol. 1, Ch. 19. Manfred B. Steger, Paul Battersby, and Joseph M. Siracusa (eds.), Thousand Oaks, CA: Sage Publishers: 299–319.

29 As demonstrated in this volume and elsewhere, hegemony is a holistic and undivided concept belonging to the entire system, in this case, the Pax Americana. Here, the mutuality of the status of the hegemon and the system is unmistakable.

30 It has been pointed out in this volume that the reasoning behind "power vacuum" is but tautological; it simply overlooks the inner dynamics of change and clings onto the superficial appearance.

31 At this juncture, it must be pointed out that some scholars persistently accused Karl Marx of "Eurocentric" tendencies by brandishing certain cherry-pick citations, for instance, on India under the Brutish (sorry!) British Empire, thus badmouthing the theoretical foundation of capitalism (and its center, value theory) in Marx. As implicitly and explicitly demonstrated in this book, the theory of value has no country or region, for that matter, as *Capital* (starting with vol. 1) does not embed in a country or region, but all about the whole, which was potential and becoming. The references to Britain are also mere illustrations. Finally, the undue amalgamation of the pre-capitalist development, known as "primitive accumulation" and that of capitalism, and the vulgarity of the *reduction* of capitalism to colonialism (exacerbated by Hobson and his counterparts among the follower of Marx) should assume the lion's share of this misunderstanding. To be sure, Marx's theory of value has no country but the world.

32 Marx, Karl 1975 [1852]. *The Eighteenth Brumaire of Louis Bonaparte*. New York: International Publishers: 15.

33 Tomforde, Anna 1989. "The Fall of the Berlin Wall—Archive, November 1989," *The Guardian* November 10. Retrieved: February 20, 2022: www.theguardian.com/world/from-the-archive-blog/2019/oct/30/the-fall-of-the-berlin-wall-archive-november-1989.

34 Contrary to shoddy deceptions, such as Ronald Reagan's infamous phrase: "Mr. Gorbachev! Bring Down this Wall" or Cold War pressure by Americans, the collapse of the Soviet Union was unequivocally an internal phenomenon, a consequence of tangled economic and political crises that long being encountered yet differed without solution before the sudden implosion in the late 1980s. To be sure, the development of capitalism eventually caught up with and outpaced the institutional capacity and political control of the state from within.

35 President George H.W. Bush spoke at the commencement of the Air University in Maxwell Air Force Base in Alabama University on the New World Order. www.c-span.org/video/?17541-1/commencement-address-world-order (April 13, 1991). Retrieved: February 20, 2022.

36 This is a small pictorial lens on this US invasion of Iraq, in 1991, that was delicately televised as a showcase for power projection across the world while the Soviet Union was

falling. Taylor, Alan 2016. "Operation Desert Storm: 25 Years Since the First Gulf War," *The Atlantic* January 14 (38 Photos). Retrieved: February 20, 2022: www.theatlantic.com/photo/2016/01/operation-desert-storm-25-years-since-the-first-gulf-war/424191/.

On US invasion of Iraq, in 1991, *inter alia*, see Hooglund, Eric 1991. "The Other Face of War," *MERIP* July/August. Retrieved: February 20, 2022: https://merip.org/1991/07/the-other-face-of-war/. My intention here is to emphasize the origins of the post-Soviet US foreign policy that began with George H.W. Bush who willfully, in doublespeak, planned and persecuted a war of aggression toward the militarization of the Persian Gulf, in 1991, by any means necessary, the least of which was arms-twisting members of the UN General Assembly. Hence, the criminal roots of much deeper and wider aggressions that emerged during the Bush-Cheney administration, beginning in 2001 (Afghanistan) and 2003 (Iraq), reside in the George H.W. Bush administration. Furthermore, speaking of world order either by reference to postwar Pax Americana (1945–1979) or whimsey "new world order," claimed by the likes of George H.W. Bush or George W. Bush, would not expunge the durability of present realities of both the world disorder and substantial change in the balance of power in the world.

37 Likening states (and nations) to *market* is one of those methodological reductions that not only reveal the *functionalist* attitude of both business and politics in the West but also disclose the extent of fetish-mongering and ideology-peddling institutions in capitalism.

38 See Huntington, Samuel 1993. "The Clash of Civilizations," *Foreign Affairs* 72 (3): 295–302. To know the political atmosphere, at this time Huntington was working at the Center for International Affairs at Harvard, located in the same building that also housed the Center for Middle Eastern Studies at which I worked and, among others, published Bina, Cyrus 1993. "The Rhetoric of Oil and the Dilemma of War and American Hegemony," *Arab Studies Quarterly* 15 (3), Summer: 1–20. This minute juxtaposition is the mere tip of political and ideological debates following the fall of the Berlin Wall at Harvard. The so-called *theorization* of finding a *new enemy* at this historic moment should not be discounted for the very reason that orthodoxy in international relations needed an explanation to feed the minds of the armies of inductees and students, a fertile ground for breeding and propagating ideologues, operatives, and apologist in political science departments and international relations schools across the West.

39 The context of such flimsiness can be seen in Fukuyama, Francis 1989. *The National Interest* 16 (Summer): 3–18; Fukuyama, Francis 1992. *The End of History and the Last Man*. New York: Free Press.

40 See Bina, Cyrus 2013b. *A Prelude to the Foundation of the Political Economy: Oil, War, and Global Polity*. New York: Palgrave Macmillan, Ch. 7.

41 The deliberate strategy for expansion of NATO was realized first in 1999 (The Czech Republic, Poland, Hungary) and then in 2004 (Bulgaria, Estonia, Latvia, Lithuania Romania, Slovakia, Slovenia); and attempted in Georgia and Ukraine in 2008, which led to war in the former and dragged on till February 2014 in a US coup that backfired and led to the Russian annexation of the Crimea (an entity attached by Nikita Khrushchev in 1954 to Ukraine and was leased as a naval base by the Russian Federation since 1991) in the same year. The Russian invasion of Ukraine, on February 24, 2022, is the latest response to the United States concerning the eastward expansion of NATO in the most discernable fashion to date. This is how the falling former hegemon, namely, the United States, is vividly more dangerous to global peace and tranquility than a rising power. And that is how the world disorder since the full-scale militarization of the Persian Gulf by the George H.W. Bush administration, in 1991, deliberately set the stage for a full-fledged global conflict and world disorder (rather brazenly under the rubric of "new" world order) ever since.

42 Embedded in the political instability of the intervening period between the fall of the Soviet Union and the present is the covert and overt expansion of NATO, particularly from 1997 onward, instigated by the United States, which in the case of the Russian invasion of Ukraine is crystal clear.

43 In each of these interventions, the American reason (associated with deeds) and American rhetoric (brewed for public consumption) were decidedly apart, as the double-speak of *freedom*, *democracy*, and *sovereignty* being stuffed into the ears of the public in these countries and across the world through mega airwaves of disinformation and indoctrination.

44 See Piketty, Thomas 2014. *Capital in the Twenty-First Century*. Cambridge, MA: Harvard University Press. Despite its voluminous size, this book offers next to nothing about the inner dynamics of capital (as a social relation) other than the *veneer* of distribution albeit by a mere *empirical* means. In other words, it is not about a *theory* of distribution but an impression of it in a limited scope of the amassing wealth by tracing its impression. Piketty's *Capital* is barely an elementary-school story of capitalism or even the tip of Marx's *Capital.*

45 Imperialism is a theoretical construct within the context of specific history. As a theory, imperialism must be an outcome of the mediation of capital. Such mediation is through the moments of commodity and principally money. Hence, transnationalization of capital in all its moments, namely, commodity, money, and productive forms, is the *theoretical* limit to imperialism. In other words, the globalization of capital is an embodiment of fading away of imperialism as a specific epoch that it really was. Thus, it would be idiotic to consider branding any and every act of war or smidgen of conflict in the world as imperialism; imperial-mindedness, imperial policy, penchant for invasion, and what is appearing as imperialist acts in this time and era are *not* equivalent to the era of imperialism. But, alas, there are too many hardcore leftists of traditional vintage that are dogmatically clutching onto "inter-imperialist rivalry" and other paraphernalia of the imperialist epoch to no avail. As this manuscript was going to the publisher, referring to the current Russian invasion of Ukraine, a known Trotskyist scholar, Davis Yaffe, wrote: "It was a long time in the making and we are witnessing the brutal outcome of inter-imperialist rivalry—both ideologically and materially" [*OPE] Ukraine and the Current World Crisis*, https://mail.google.com/mail/u/0/#inbox/FMfcgzGmvLWSRVHcfGSLLpshwdppQDNq (email: March 9, 2022). On the same theme that is also saturated by the ascendence of the United States and is visibly relying on spurious US "new world order," Alex Callinicos pontificates that "more fundamentally he [Vladimir Putin] wants Russian imperialism to be recognized by the US as a global player, not the 'regional power'." See Callinicos, Alex 2022. "Why the Ukraine Crisis has Dragged On," *Socialist Worker* February 21. Retrieved: March 11, 2022: https://socialistworker.co.uk/alex-callinicos/why-the-ukraine-crisis-has-dragged-on/. These are the latest examples of the comedy-tragedy of the traditional left, including self-styled Marxists, whose umbilical cord has not yet been detached from Hobsonite and neo-Hobsonite views of the world as we speak.

46 It is worth restating that Marx's theory of competition is not the same as neoclassical economics fiction of "perfect competition," the origin of the mainstream economic theory of market structure, namely, imperfect (or monopolistic) competition, oligopoly, and monopoly. Marx's competition is synthetic and *consistent* with concentration and centralization, and turbulent accumulation of capital. Here, I need also to point out that, contrary to many Marxist scholars, Marx's competition is first and foremost an attribute of capital in production manifested in distribution. In other words, competition is the property of capital (as a whole) before the distribution of surplus value into the constituent parts, such as profit, rent, and interest. Finally, it is critical to recognize that there are two distinct levels of competition in Marx's value theory, namely, *intra*-sectoral and *inter*-sectoral competition, the former leads to different profit rates and a uniform market value in a single sector, while the latter to a uniform rate of profit with different prices of production for entire sectors of the economy. This suggests (1) that the formation of value has nothing to do with equilibrium and (2) that the transformation of value into the prices of production is a necessary part of this dynamic.

47 The problem in the literature under investigation, say, in the World-Systems approach, is not only transhistorical proclivity but also (in the "geopolitical economy" approach) the identification of "electrification and central planning," in the Soviet Union, and the current advances in contemporary China, as socialism.

48 Arrighi, Giovanni 1994. *The Long Twentieth Century: Money, Power and the Origins of Our Times*. New York: Verso.

49 The imperative of class in the capitalist society both locally and globally is the principal distinction. Other categories, such as race, gender, etc., although important, cannot be understood, both methodologically and institutionally, without the foundation of class in the capitalist mode of production. The reversion to the *multitude* (in *Empire*) *inter alia* is but a clumsy recategorization and deceptive dismantling of all these categories.

50 I refer the reader to Hardt and Negri's relatively recent article in which the authors restate their customary narrative in terms of a caricature of global transformation (and globalization), combining an ad hoc philosophic pretext, elusive view of geopolitics, and misleading the labor process dynamics, on the twentieth anniversary of *Empire*. See Hardt, Michael and Antonio Negri 2019. "Empire, Twenty Years On," *New Left Review* 120, (November/December): 67–92.

51 For the distinction between falsity and fakery, see Frankfurt 2005. *On Bullshit*.

52 See *inter alia* Fine, Ben and Alfredo Saad-Filho 2016. "Thirteen Things You Need to Know About Neoliberalism," *Critical Sociology* 43 (4–5): 685–706. This piece is among the most explicit articles that identify the contemporary global transformation as neoliberalism. Yet, as has been demonstrated rather extensively in the present volume, nearly all displayed signs of the purported stage of neoliberalism are but globalization symptoms.

53 See Uno, Kōzō 1980 [1964]. *Principles of Political Economy*. Essex, UK: The Harvester Press Ltd. In addition to this flawed stage theory, Uno's value theory is also defective in the placement of the category of *money* before that of capital and thus corrupting the foundation of Marx's value theory. For a pertinent critique, see Kuruma, Samezō 2018 [2017]. *Marx's Theory of the Genesis of Money: How Why, and Through What is a Commodity money?* Chicago, IL: Haymarket Books. For a glimpse of the Uno School among supporters, see "Is the Uno School Approach Relevant to Understanding Present-Day Capitalism?" the special issue, edited by Yokokawa, Nobuharu and Richard Westra, *The Japanese Political Economy* 45 (3–4), December 2019. Again, concerning Uno's stage theory, I wish to emphasize that such a disjointed framework and its supposed resuscitation via "critical realism" would NOT improve this approach to value theory a bit since the latter is but a transhistorical (and not historically specific) scaffold itself. For such an attempt, see Westra, Richard 2021. *Economics, Science and Capitalism*. London: Routledge.

54 The *butterfly effect* is the materialization of chaos theory, a nonlinear pattern of change that enlarges with slight change locally (that is, initial condition) and gives rise to subsequent substantial change at the end of the path. The theory of chaos was discovered by Edward N. Lorenz, an MIT mathematician, and meteorologist as he was running a numerical computer model for the prediction of weather in 1961. Lorenz's fascinating and accidental discovery need not detain us here. What is significant is the absence of randomness and organic context of both the life and social phenomena as we know them. For an introduction to chaos theory, see Gleick, James 1988. *Chaos: Making a New Science*. New York: Penguin.

55 For further study of turbulence and competition, see Shaikh, Anwar 2016. *Capitalism: Competition, Conflict, Crises*. New York: Oxford University Press, Chapters 7–11.

56 This is Marx's central precept that is also persisting throughout this book.

57 For display of political naiveté, lack of theoretical spine, and utter confusion on the global sea change since the eclipse of the Pax Americana and the rise of globalization

by radical leftists (even self-styled Marxists), see their reaction to the Russian invasion of Ukraine on February 24, 2022, in just first 2 weeks into this war. The radical left has been browbeaten by trailing the right in theory and ideology, and worse, following the right-wing propaganda by idiotically echoing the cause of war as "Putin, Putin, Putin" on television and social media. This is aside from scores of liberal ideologues in the West whose bone and flesh are made of obfuscation of the inner dynamics and deep roots of this and other similar conflicts since the 1990s. The basic question to all these concerned leftist activists and scholars is this: Aren't all these half-truths an outcome of your phony theoretical posturing and de facto capitulation to bourgeois directions? Aren't you being played by the very hands that you yourselves were opposed to and have long been struggling to expose, in this war?

Bibliography

Abrams, Floyd (2021). "Daniel Ellsberg's 'Heroic Conduct' in Leaking the Pentagon Papers"—Opinion Letter, *The New York Times* August 14, 2021; retrieved: August 20, 2021: www.nytimes.com/2021/06/14/opinion/letters/pentagon-papers-daniel- ellsberg.html

Ackerman, Frank (2002). "Still Dead After All These Years: Interpreting the Failure of General Equilibrium Theory," *Journal of Economic Methodology* 9 (2), 119–139.

Adelman, Kenneth (2002). "Cakewalk in Iraq," *The Washington Post* February 13, A27.

Amin, Samir (1974). *Accumulation on a World Scale*. New York: Monthly Review Press.

Amin, Samir (1978). *The Law of Value and Historical Materialism*. New York: Monthly Review Press.

Amin, Samir (1992). *Empire of Chaos*. New York: Monthly Review Press.

Amin, Samir (2013a). *Three Essays on Marx's Value Theory*. New York: Monthly Review Press.

Amin, Samir (2013b). *The Implosion of Contemporary Capitalism*. New York: Monthly Review Press.

Anderson, Benedict (1991). *Imagined Communities: Reflections on the Origin and Spread of Nationalism*. New York: Verso.

Anderson, Perry (1976–1977). "The Antinomies of Antonio Gramsci," *New Left Review* 100, Winter: 5–78.

Anderson, Perry (2002). "Force and Consent," (Editorial), *New Left Review* 17, September/October: 5–30.

Anderson, Perry (2013). "American Foreign Policy and Its Thinkers," *New Left Review* (Special Issue) 83, September/October: 113–167.

Anderson, Perry (2017). *The H-Word: The Peripeteia of Hegemony*. New York: Verso.

Arrighi, Giovanni (1990). "The Three Hegemonies of Historical Capitalism," *Review: A Journal of the Fernand Braudel Center* 13 (3): 365–408.

Arrighi, Giovanni (1994). *The Long Twentieth Century: Money, Power and the Origins of Our Times*. New York: Verso.

Arthur, Christopher J. (2014). "Marx, Hegel and the Value-Form," in *Marx's Capital and Hegel's Logic: A Reexamination*. Fred Moseley and Tony Smith (eds.). Chicago, IL: Haymarket Books: 269–291.

Ashman, Sam (2009). "Capitalism, Uneven Development and Combined Development and the Transhistoric," *Cambridge Review of International Affairs* 22 (1): 29–46.

Ayers, Alison J. (2008). *Political Economy and International Relations*. (ed.). London: Palgrave Macmillan.

Balardini, Fabian (2006). "Producer Behavior and Price Determination in the International Oil Market: An Alternative Model of Oil Price Based on Marx's Theory of Com- petition and Market Value," unpublished PhD dissertation, New School for Social Research, UMI Microform 3239926.

Baran, Paul and Paul Sweezy (1966). *Monopoly Capital*. New York: Monthly Review Press.

Barrow, Clyde W. (2021). "Globalization and the Emergence of the Fortress State," *Science & Society* 85 (2): 170–177.

Battle, Joyce (2003). National Security Archive, "Shaking Hands with Saddam Hussein: The US Tilts Toward Iraq, 1980–1984," *National Security Archive Electronic Briefing Book No. 82* February 25: www.gwu.edu/~nsarchiv/NSAEBB/NSAEBB82/index.htm

Belew, Kathleen (2018). *Bring the War Home: The White Power Movement and Paramilitary America*. Cambridge, MA: Harvard University Press.

Bellamy-Foster, John (2015). "The New Imperialism of Globalized Monopoly-Finance Capital," *Monthly Review* 67 (3), July-August: 1–22.

Bellamy-Foster, John (2019). "Late Imperialism," *Monthly Review* 71 (3), July-August: 1–19.

Bellamy-Foster, John and Robert W. McChesney (2012). *The Endless Crisis: How Monopoly-Finance Capital Produces Stagnation and Upheaval from the USA to China*. New York: Monthly Review.

Bello, Walden ([2002] 2004). *Deglobalization: Ideas for a New World Economy*. Update Edition. New York: Zed Press.

Bellofiore, Riccardo (2009). *Rosa Luxemburg and the Critique of Political Economy.* (ed.). London: Routledge.

Berle, Adolf A. and Gardner C. Means (1933). *The Modern Corporation and Private Property*. New York: Macmillan.

Berry, Kim (2003). "The Symbolic Use of Afghan Women in the War on Terror," *Humboldt Journal of Social Relations* 27 (2): 137–160.

Bhagwati, Jagdish (2007). *In Defense of Globalization*. New York: Oxford University Press.

Bina, Cyrus (1985). *The Economics of the Oil Crisis*. London and New York: Merlin and St. Martin's.

Bina, Cyrus (1988). "Internationalization of the Oil Industry: Simple Oil Shocks or Structural Crisis?" *Review: A Journal of the Fernand Braudel Centre* 11 (3): 329–379.

Bina, Cyrus (1989a). "Some Controversies in the Development of Rent Theory: The Nature of Oil Rent," *Capital and Class* 13 (3): 82–112.

Bina, Cyrus (1989b). "Competition, Control and Price Formation in the International Energy Industry," *Energy Economics* 11 (3): 162–168.

Bina, Cyrus (1990). "Limits to OPEC Pricing: OPEC Profits and the Nature of Global Oil Accumulation," *OPEC Review* 14 (1): 55–73.

Bina, Cyrus (1991). "War over Access to Cheap Oil or the Reassertion of U.S. Global Hegemony," in *Mobilizing Democracy: Changing the U.S. Role in the Middle East*. G. Bates (ed.). Monroe, ME: Common Courage Press: 71–81.

Bina, Cyrus (1992). "Global Oil and Unviability of Pax Americana," *Economic and Political Weekly* 27 (28), July 11: 1467–1469.

Bina, Cyrus (1993). "The Rhetoric of Oil and the Dilemma of War and American Hegemony," *Arab Studies Quarterly* 15 (3): 1–20.

Bina, Cyrus (1994a). "Farewell to the *Pax Americana*: Iran, Political Islam, and the Passing of the Old Order," in *Islam, Iran, and World Stability*. H. Zangeneh (ed.). New York: St. Martin's Press: 41–74.

Bina, Cyrus (1994b). "Review of American Hegemony and World Oil," *Harvard Middle Eastern and Islamic Review* 1 (2): 194–198.

Bina, Cyrus (1995). "On Sand castles and Sand-Castle Conjectures: A Rejoinder," *Arab Studies Quarterly* 17 (1 & 2), Winter/Spring: 167–171.

Bina, Cyrus (1997). "Globalization: The Epochal Imperatives and Developmental Tendencies," in *The Political Economy of Globalization.* S. D. Gupta (ed.). Boston, MA: Kluwer: 41–58.

Bina, Cyrus (2004a). "Is It the Oil, Stupid?" *The URPE Newsletter* 35 (3): 5–8: www.academia.edu/33487296/BinaArticlePages_URPENewsletter_Spr2004_pdf

Bina, Cyrus (2004b). "The American Tragedy: The Quagmire of War, Rhetoric of Oil, and the Conundrum of Hegemony," *Journal of Iranian Research and Analysis* 20 (2): 7–22.

Bina, Cyrus (2005). "Industrielle Reservearmee [Industrial Reserve Army]," in *Historisch- Kritisches, Wörterbuch, Des Marxismus.* Band 6/II (IMPERIUM BIS JUSTIZ). Herausgegeben von Wolfgang Fritz Haug (ed.). Berlin: für diese Augabe Argument-Verlag: 1003–1011.

Bina, Cyrus (2006). "The Globalization of Oil: A Prelude to a Critical Political Economy," *International Journal of Political Economy* 35 (2): 4–34.

Bina, Cyrus (2007). "America's Bleeding 'Cakewalk'," *EPS Quarterly* 19 (4): 1–4.

Bina, Cyrus (2009). "Post-Election Iran: Crossroads of History and a Critique of Prevailing Political Perspectives," *Journal of Iranian Research and Analysis* 26 (2), Fall; retrieved: January 15, 2022: http://www.iran-echo.com/echo_pdf/bina-post-election_iran.pdf

Bina, Cyrus (2010). "Economic Crises: Marx's Value Theory and Twenty-First Century Capitalism," *Radical Notes Journal* May 9: https://radicalnotes.org/2010/05/09/economic-crises-marxs- value-theory-and-21st- century-capitalism-an-interview-with-cyrus-bina/

Bina, Cyrus (2011). "Globalization, Value Theory, and Crisis," in *Political Economy, Crisis & Development.* I. Siriner, et al. (eds.). London: IJOPEC Publication: 19–24.

Bina, Cyrus (2012a). *Oil: A Time Machine—Journey Beyond Fanciful Economics and Frightful Politics,* 2nd ed. Ronkonkoma, NY: Linus Publications: https://linuslearning.com/product/oil-a-time-machine-2nd-edition/

Bina, Cyrus (2012b). "Oil," in *Encyclopedia of Global Studies,* vol. 3. M. Juergensmeyer and H. K. Anheier (eds.). Thousand Oaks, CA: Sage Publishers: 1259–1263.

Bina, Cyrus (2012c). "Organization of Petroleum Exporting Countries (OPEC)," in *Encyclopedia of Global Studies,* vol. 3. M. Juergensmeyer and H. K. Anheier (eds.). Thousand Oaks, CA: Sage Publishers: 1276–1278.

Bina, Cyrus (2012d). "Technology Sector," in *Encyclopedia of Global Studies,* vol. 4. M. Juergensmeyer and H. K. Anheier (eds.). Thousand Oaks, CA: Sage Publishers: 1623–1625.

Bina, Cyrus (2012e). "Deskilling," in *Encyclopedia of Global Studies,* vol. 1. M. Juergensmeyer and H. K. Anheier (eds.). Thousand Oaks, CA: Sage Publishers: 396–398.

Bina, Cyrus (2013a). "Synthetic Competition, Global Oil, and the Cult of Monopoly," in *Alternative Theories of Competition: Challenges to the Orthodoxy.* J. Moudud, C. Bina, and P. Mason (eds.). New York: Routledge: 55–85.

Bina, Cyrus (2013b). *A Prelude to the Foundation of Political Economy: Oil, War, and Global Polity.* New York: Palgrave Macmillan.

Bina, Cyrus (2014). "Global Oil and the Fallacy of Middle East Oil Dependency," in *The Sage Handbook of Globalization,* vol. 1, Ch. 19. Manfred B. Steger, Paul Battersby, and Joseph M. Siracusa (eds.). Thousand Oaks, CA: Sage Publishers: 299–319.

Bina, Cyrus (2015). "What's at Stake for Iran in Syria?" *The Real News Network* October 30; retrieved: September 3, 2021: www.youtube.com/watch?v=9g4sV8GXWCc

Bina, Cyrus (2017). "Homecoming to Nostalgia: The Inauguration of Donald J. Trump," *The Bullet* January 25: https://socialistproject.ca/2017/01/b1361/

Bina, Cyrus (2018). "Bicentenary of Marx's Birth, His Legacy, and His Last Laugh (1818-2018)," *People's Daily* (China) May 5.

Bina, Cyrus (2019). "Specter of Globalization: Marx, Gramsci and Disjointed Time," *World Review of Political Economy* 10 (4), Winter: 484–518: www.jstor.org/stable/10.13169/worlrevipoliecon.10.4.0484?seq=1

Bina, Cyrus (2020a). "Oil, COVID-19, and the Global Economy," *New Cold War* April 28: www.newcoldwar.org/oil-covid-19-and-the-global-economy/

Bina, Cyrus (2020b). "A Note on Technical Change, Skill Formation, and Economic Instability," *International Journal of Political Economy* 49 (1), April: 83–91.

Bina, Cyrus (2021a). "Corona's Bio-Economic Crisis and the Post-Corona World," *International Critical Thought* 10 (4), January: 566–574.

Bina, Cyrus (2021b). *The 1979 Revolution and Counterrevolution in Iran* (in Persian). Process Publisher (eBook); retrieved: September 3, 2021: https://newprocess2010.files.wordpress.com/2021/05/cyrus-bina-57-new-1.pdf

Bina, Cyrus, Larry Clements, and Chuck Davis ([1996] 2015). *Beyond Survival: Wage Labor in the Late Twentieth Century.* (eds.). New York: Routledge.

Bina, Cyrus and Chuck Davis ([1996] 2015). "Wage Labor and Global Capital: Global Competition and Universalization of the Labor Movement," in *Beyond Survival: Wage Labor in the Late Twentieth Century*. C. Bina, L. Clements, and C. Davis (eds.). New York: Routledge: 19–47.

Bina, Cyrus and Chuck Davis (2000). "Globalization, Technology, and Skill Formation in Capitalism," in *Political Economy and Contemporary Capitalism*. R. Baiman, H. Boushey, and D. Sunders (eds.). Armonk, NY: Sharpe: 193–202.

Bina, Cyrus and Chuck Davis (2008). "Contingent Labor and Omnipotent Capital: The Open Secret of Political Economy," *Political Economy Quarterly* 4 (15): 166–211: www.socialcapitalgateway.org/content/paper/bina-c-davis-c-2009-contingent-labor-and-omnipotent-capital-open-secret-political-econ

Bina, Cyrus and Minh Vo (2007). "OPEC in the Epoch of Globalization: An Event Study of Global Oil Prices," *Global Economy Journal* 7 (1), Article 2: 1–49.

Bina, Cyrus and Behzad Yaghmaian (1988). "Import Substitution and Export Promotion within the Context of the Internationalization of Capital," *Review of Radical Political Economics* 20 (3): 234–240.

Bina, Cyrus and Behzad Yaghmaian (1991). "Postwar Global Accumulation and the Transnationalization of Capital," *Capital & Class* 43: 107–130.

Blair, John M. (1976). *The Control of Oil*. New York: Pantheon.

Bleaney, Michael (1976). *Underconsumption Theories: A History and Critical Analysis*. New York: International Publishers.

Blix, Hans (2004). *Disarming Iraq*. New York: Pantheon Books.

Bloch, Hannah (2021). "A Look at Afghanistan's 40 Years of Crisis—From the Soviet War To Taliban Recapture," *NPR* August 31; retrieved: September 1, 2021: www.npr.org/2021/08/19/1028472005/afghanistan-conflict-timeline

Blum, William ([1986] 2003). *The CIA: A Forgotten History*, revised ed. Monroe, ME: Common Courage Press.

Bocock, Robert (1986). *Hegemony*. London: Tavistock Publications.

Bonneuil, Christophe and Jean-Baptiste Fressoz (2017). *The Shock of the Anthropocene*. London: Verso.

Borger, Julian (2022). "Joe Biden Arrives in Europe for Summits . . .," *The Guardian* March 23; retrieved: March 29: www.theguardian.com/us-news/2022/mar/23/joe-biden- europe-russia- ukraine-nato-g7-european-council

Brakman, S. and B. J. Heijdra (2004). *The Monopolistic Competition in Retrospect*. (eds.). Cambridge: Cambridge University Press.

Braverman, Harry ([1974] 1998). *Labor and Monopoly Capital*. New York: Monthly Review Press.

Brenner, Robert (1977). "The Origins of Capitalist Development: A Critique of Neo-Smithian Marxism," *New Left Review* 104 (July-August): 25–92.

Bromley, Simon (1991). *American Hegemony and World Oil*. University Park, PA: Pennsylvania State University Press.

Bryan, Dick (1990). "'Natural' and 'Improved' Land in Marx's Theory of Rent," *Land Economics* 66 (2): 176–180.

Bryan, Dick (1995). *The Chase Across the Globe: International Accumulation and the Contradictions for Nation States*. Boulder, CO: Westview Press.

Buckman, Greg (2004). *Globalization: Tame It or Scrap It?* New York: Zed Books.

Burns, William J. (2019). "How the U.S.-Russian Relationship Went Bad," *The Atlantic* April; retrieved: March 15, 2022: www.theatlantic.com/magazine/archive/2019/04/william-j-burns-putin-russia/583255/

Cable, James (1971). *Gunboat Diplomacy*. New York: Praeger.

Callinicos, Alex (2022). "Why the Ukraine Crisis has Dragged On," *Socialist Worker* February 21; retrieved: March 11, 2022: https://socialistworker.co.uk/alex-callinicos/why-the- ukraine-crisis-has-dragged-on/

Chamberlin, Edward H. (1933). *Theory of Monopolistic Competition*. Cambridge, MA: Harvard University Press.

Chamlee, Virginia (2021). "George W. Bush Says Afghanistan Withdrawal is a Mistake: 'Breaks My Heart'," *People* July 14; retrieved: August 20, 2021: https://people.com/politics/george-w-bush-says-afghanistan-withdrawal-is-a-mistake-unbelievably-bad/

Chandler, Alfred D., Jr. (1977). *The Visible Hand: The Managerial Revolution in American Business*. Cambridge, MA: Harvard University Press.

Chattopadhyay, Paresh ([2018] 2019). *Socialism and Commodity Production: Essays in Marx Revival*. Chicago, IL: Haymarket Books.

Chotiner, Isaac (2022). "Why John Mearsheimer Blames the U.S. for the Crisis in Ukraine" (an Interview), *The New Yorker* March 1; retrieved: March 15, 2022: www.newyorker.com/news/q-and-a/why-john-mearsheimer-blames-the-us-for-the-crisis-in- ukraine

Clarke, Richard A. (2004). *Against All Enemies: Inside America's War on Terror*. New York: Free Press.

Clifton, James (1977). "Competition and Evolution of the Capitalist Mode of Production," *Cambridge Journal of Economics* 1 (2): 137–151.

Cockburn, Andrew (2007). *Rumsfeld: His Rise, Fall, and Catastrophic Legacy*. New York: Scribner.

Cole, Juan (2022). "Ukraine: What the Libya War Tells Us About Why We Really Don't Want a NATO No-Fly Zone," *Informed Comment* March 9; retrieved: March 23, 2022: www.juancole.com/2022/03/ukraine-libya-really.html

Cox, Robert W. (1987). *Production, Power and World Order*. New York: Columbia University Press.

Cox, Robert W. and Michael G. Schechter (2002). *The Political Economy of a Plural World*. London: Routledge.

Cox, Robert W. and Timothy J. Sinclair (1991). *Approaches to Word Order*. Cambridge: Cambridge University Press.

Cypher, James (1979). "The Internationalization of Capital and the Transformation of Social Formations: A Critique of the Monthly Review School," *Review of Radical Political Economics* 11 (4): 33–49.

Daalder, Ivo H. and Janes M. Lindsay (2018). "The Committee to Save the World Order," *Foreign Affairs* November/December: 72–83.

Davis, Mike (2017). *Planet of Slums*. New York: Verso.

Desai, Radhika (2010). "The Absent Geopolitics of Pure Capitalism," *World Review of Political Economy* 1 (3), Fall: 463–484.

Desai, Radhika (2013). *Geopolitical Economy: After U.S Hegemony, Globalization and Empire*. London: Pluto Press.

Desai, Radhika (2015). "Introduction: The Materiality of Nations in Geopolitical Economy," *World Review of Political Economy* 6 (4), Winter: 449–458.

Digby Parton, Heather (2021). "No, George W. Bush doesn't Deserve a Pass on Afghanistan," *Salon* August 18; retrieved: August 20, 2021: www.salon.com/2021/08/18/no-george-w-bush-doesnt-deserve-a-pass-on-afghanistan/

DiSavino, Scott and Eileen Soreng (2020). "US Oil Rigs See Biggest Decline in a Week since February 2015," Baker Hughes," *Reuters* April 17: www.reuters.com/article/us-usa-rigs-baker-hughes/u-s-oil-rigs-see-biggest-decline-in-a-week-since-february-2015-baker-hughes-idUSKBN21Z2XO

Dixit, A. and J. Stiglitz (1977). "Monopolistic Competition and Optimum Product Diversity," *America Economic Review* 67 (3): 297–308.

Dorfman, Ariel and Armand Mattelart (2018 [1971]). *How to Read Donald Duck: Imperialist Ideology in the Disney Comic*. New York: OR Books.

Draper, Theodore (1991). "American Hubris," in *The Gulf War Reader*. M. L. Sifry and C. Cerf (eds.). New York: Random House.

Duménil, Gérard and Dominique Lévy (2018). *Managerial Capitalism: Ownership, Management and the Coming of New Mode of Production*. London: Pluto Press.

Durand, Cedric (2017). *Fictitious Capital*. New York: Verso.

Eagleton, Terry (2003). *After Theory*. New York: Basic Books.

Ellsberg, Daniel (1971). *The Pentagon Papers*. New York: Bantam Books.

Elm, Mustafa (1992). *Oil, Power, and Principle: Iran's Oil Nationalization and Its Aftermath*. New York: Syracuse University Press.

Elwell-Sutton, Laurence P. (1955). *Persian Oil: A Study of Power Politics*. London: Lawrence and Wishart.

Emmanuel, Arghiri (1972). *Unequal Exchange*. New York: Monthly Review Press.

Engler, Robert (1977). *The Brotherhood of Oil*. Chicago, IL: University of Chicago Press.

Fine, Ben (1978). "On the Origins of Capitalist Development Remarks," *New Left Review* 109 (May-June).

Fine, Ben (1979). "On Marx's Theory of Agricultural Rent," *Economy and Society* 8 (3): 241–278.

Fine, Ben (1982). "Landed Property and the Distinction between Royalty and Rent," *Land Economics* 58 (3): 338–350.

Fine, Ben (2006). "Debating the 'New' Imperialism," *Historical Materialism* 14 (4): 133–156.

Fine, Ben (2012). "Review Article: Revisiting Rosa Luxemburg's Political Economy," *Critique* 40 (3): 449–456.

Fine, Ben and Laurence Harris (1977). "Surveying the Foundations," in *The Socialist Register 1977*. Ralph Miliband and John Saville (eds.). New York: Monthly Review Press: 106–120.

Fine, Ben and Laurence Harris (1979). *Rereading Capital*. New York: Columbia University Press.

Fine, Ben and Laurence Harris (1985). *The Peculiarities of the British Economy*. London: Lawrence and Wishart.

Fine, Ben, Costas Lapavitsas, and Jonathan Pincus (2001). *Beyond the Post-Washington Consensus*. London: Routledge.
Fine, Ben and Dimitris Milonakis (2009). *From Economics Imperialism to Freakonomics: The Shifting Boundaries between Economics and Other Social Sciences*. London: Routledge.
Fine, Ben and Alfredo Saad-Filho (2014). "Politics of Neoliberal Development: Washington Consensus and the post-Washington Consensus," in *The Politics of Development: A Survey*. Heloise Weber (ed.). London: Routledge: 154–166.
Fine, Ben and Alfredo Saad-Filho (2016). "Thirteen Things You Need to Know About Neoliberalism," *Critical Sociology* 43 (4–5): 685–706.
Fine, Ben and Elsa Van Waeyenberge (2005). "Correcting Stiglitz: From Information to Power in the World of Development," in *Socialist Register 2006: Telling the Truth*. Leo Panitch and Colin Leys (eds.). London: The Merlin Press: 146–168.
Fleming, D. F. (1961). *The Cold War and Its Origin*, 2 vols. New York: Doubleday.
Forgey, Quint (2021). "Bush Slams Biden's Afghanistan Withdrawal," *Politico* July 14; retrieved: August 20, 2021: www.politico.com/news/2021/07/14/bush-bidens-afghanistan-withdrawal-499598
Frank, Andre Gunter (1969). *Capitalism and Underdevelopment in Latin America*. New York: Monthly Review Press.
Frankfurt, Harry G. (2005). *On Bullshit*. Princeton, NJ: Princeton University Press.
Freeman, Chas W. 2022. "The US fighting Russia 'to the last Ukrainian': Veteran US Diplomat," *The Grayzone* Pushback with Aaron Maté March 22; retrieved: March 2022: www.youtube.com/watch?v=0vxufUeqnuc
Freeman, Chris (1994). "Critical Survey: The Economics of Technical Change," *Cambridge Journal of Economics* 18 (5): 463–514.
Friel, Howard and Richard Falk (2004). *The Record of the Paper: How the New York Times Misreports US Foreign Policy*. New York: Verso.
Fromkin, David ([1989] 2009). *A Peace to End All Peace*. London: Macmillan.
FRONTLINE (2020). "The Virus: What Went Wrong?" (Virus-Documentary Film) *PBS* June 16: www.pbs.org/wgbh/frontline/film/the-virus/
FRONTLINE (2021). "America After 9/11," *PBS—A Two-Hour Documentary Special* September 7; YouTube; retrieved: September 7, 2021: www.youtube.com/watch?v=Q5iBxva_pm8
FRONTLINE (2022). "Plot to Overturn the Election," *PBS* (An Hour Documentary) March 29; retrieved: March 29, 2022: www.pbs.org/wgbh/frontline/film/plot-to-overturn-the-election/
Fukuyama, Francis (1992). *The End of History and the Last Man*. New York: Free Press.
Galbraith, James K. (2008). *The Predator State*. New York: The Free Press.
Galbraith, James K. (2012). *Inequality and Instability: A Study of the World Economy Just Before the Crisis*. New York: Oxford University Press.
Galbraith, James K. (2014). *The End of Normal: The Great Crisis and the Future Growth*. New York: Simon & Schuster.
Galbraith, John K. (1967). *The New Industrial State*. Boston, MA: Houghton Mifflin.
Galbraith, John K. ([1967] 2007). *The New Industrial State*, expended ed. Princeton, NJ: Princeton University Press.
Galeano, Eduardo ([1973] 1977). *Open Veins of Latin America*. New York: Monthly Review Press.
Geiger, Julianne (2020a). "Extreme Volatility in Oil Continues as WTI June Contract Tanks 65%," *Oilprice.com* April 21, 2020: https://oilprice.com/Energy/Oil-Prices/Extreme-Volatility-In-Oil-Continues-As-WTI-June-Contract-Tanks.html

Geiger, Julianne (2020b) "The Largest Rig Count Collapse in 5 Years," *Oilprice.com* April 3: https://oilprice.com/Energy/Energy-General/The-Largest-Rig-Count-Collapse-In-5-Years.html

Gendzier, Irene L. (2015). *Dying To Forget: Oil, Power, Palestine & the Foundation of U.S. Policy in the Middle East*. New York: Columbia University Press.

Ghizoni, Sandra K. (1971). "Nixon Ends Convertibility of U.S. Dollars to Gold and Announces Wage/Price Controls," *Federal Reserve History*; retrieved: January 7, 2022: www.federalreservehistory.org/essays/gold-convertibility-ends

Glazebrook, Dan (2014). "The Lessons of Libya", *CounterPunch* November 12: www.counterpunch.org/2014/11/12/the-lessons-of-libya/

Gleick, James. (1988). *Chaos: Making a New Science*. New York: Penguin.

Gramsci, Antonio (1971). *Selected from the Prison Notebooks*. New York: International Publishers.

Green, David (1971). *The Containment of Latin America*. Chicago: Quadrangle Books.

Grossman, S. and J. E. Stiglitz (1980). "On the Impossibility of Informationally Efficient Markets," *American Economic Review* 70 (3): 123–136.

The Guardian (2020a). "Oil Prices Deep Below Zero as Producers Forced to Pay to Dispose of Excess," April 20: www.theguardian.com/world/2020/apr/20/oil-prices-sink-to-20-year-low-as-un-sounds-alarm-on-to-covid-19-relief-fund

The Guardian (2020b). "Complacency to Chaos: How Covid-19 Sent the World's Markets into Freefall," March 28, 2020: www.theguardian.com/business/2020/mar/28/how-coronavirus-sent-global-markets-into-freefall

Hacking, Ian (1990). *The Taming of Chance*. Cambridge: Cambridge University Press.

Harding, Luke (2014). *The Snowden Files*. New York: Vintage.

Hardt, Michael and Antonio Negri (2000). *Empire*. Cambridge, MA: Harvard University Press.

Hardt, Michael and Antonio Negri (2004). *Multitude: War and Democracy in the Age of Empire*. New York: The Penguin Press.

Hardt, Michael and Antonio Negri (2019). "Empire, Twenty Years On," *New Left Review* 120, November/December: 67–92.

Harris, Laurence (1983). "Periodization of Capitalism," in *A Dictionary of Marxist Thought*. Tom Bottomore (ed.). Cambridge, MA: Harvard University Press: 365–368.

Harvey, David ([1982] 1999). *The Limits to Capital*. New York: Verso.

Harvey, David (2003). *The 'New' Imperialism*. Oxford: Oxford University Press.

Harvey, David (2004). "The 'New' Imperialism: Accumulation by Dispossession," *Socialist Register 2004: The New Imperial Challenge*, vol. 40. Leo Panitch and Colin Leys (eds.). London: The Merlin Press: 63–87.

Harvey, David (2005). *A Brief History of Neoliberalism*. Oxford University Press.

Harvey, David (2010). *The Enigma of Capital and the Crises of Capitalism*. New York: Oxford University Press.

Harvey, David (2011). "The Urban Roots of Financial Crises: Reclaiming the City for Anti-Capitalist Struggle," in *Socialist Register 2012*. Leo Panitch, Gregory Albo, and Vivek Chibber (eds.). London: Merlin Press: 1–35.

Harvey, David (2012). "The Urban Roots of Financial Crises: Reclaiming the City for Anti- Capitalist Struggle," in *Socialist Register*. Leo Panitch, Gregory Albo, and Vivek Chibber (eds.). London: Merlin Press.

Heath, Thomas (2020). "Oil Prices Extend Slide One Day after US Crude Drops below Zero; Dow Plunges more than 600 Points," *The Washington Post* April 21: www.washingtonpost.com/business/2020/04/21/oil-crash-stocks-today-coronavirus/

Heinrich, Michael (2014). *An Introduction to the Three Volumes of Karl Marx's Capital*. New York: Monthly Review Press.

Helpman, E. and Paul R. Krugman (1985). *Market Structure and Foreign Trade: Increasing Returns, Imperfect Competition and the International Economy* Cambridge, MA: MIT Press.

Hersh, Seymour (2004). *Chain of Command: The Road from 9/11 to Abu Ghraib*. New York: HarperCollins.

Hersh, Seymour M. (2013). "Whose Sarine?" *London Review of Books* 35 (24), December 19; retrieved: April 5, 2022: www.lrb.co.uk/the-paper/v35/n24/seymour-m.-hersh/whose-sarin

Hersh, Seymour M. (2014). "The Red Line and the Rat Line: Erdoğan and the Syrian Rebels," *London Review of Books* 36 (8), April 17; retrieved: April 5, 2022: www.lrb.co.uk/the-paper/v36/n08/seymour-m.-hersh/the-red-line-and-the-rat-line

Hilferding, Rudolf ([1910] 1981). *Finance Capital: A Study of Latest Phase of Capitalist Development*. London: Routledge & Kegan Paul.

Hirsh, Seymour M. (2015). "The Killing of Osama bin Laden," *London Review of Books* 37 (10), May 21; retrieved: April 5, 2022: www.lrb.co.uk/the-paper/v37/n10/seymour-m.-hersh/the-killing-of-osama-bin-laden

Hobson, John A. ([1902] 1961). *Imperialism: A Study*. London: George Allen & Unwin.

Hooglund, Eric (1991). "The Other Face of War," *MERIP* July/August; retrieved: February 20, 2022: https://merip.org/1991/07/the-other-face-of-war/

Huntington, Samuel (1993). "The Clash of Civilizations," *Foreign Affairs* 72 (3), Summer: 295–302.

Ikenberry, G. John, Michael Mastanduno, and William C. Wohlforth (2009). "Introduction: Unipolarity, State Behavior, and Systematic Consequences," *World Politics* 81 (1), January: 1–27.

Jeon, Heesang (2010). "Cognitive Capitalism or Cognition in Capitalism? A Critique of Cognitive Capitalism Theory," *Spectrum: Journal of Global Studies* 2 (3), Summer: 90–117.

Jevons, William Stanley ([1871] 1957). *The Theory of Political Economy*. New York: Kelley and Macmillan.

Kalecki, Michael (1939). *Essays in the Theory of Economic Fluctuations*. London: George Allen & Unwin.

Kalecki, Michael (1943). *Studies in Economic Dynamics*. London: George Allen & Unwin.

Kennan, George F. (1947). "The Sources of Soviet Conduct" [Well-Known Memo on Containment], *Foreign Affairs* 25 (4), July: 566–582.

Keynes, John M. (1920). *The Economic Consequence of the Peace*. New York: Harcourt, Brace and Howe.

Keynes, John M. ([1936] 1964). *The General Theory of Employment, Interest, and Money*. New York: Harcourt, Brace & World Inc.

Keysen, C. (1949). "Basing-Point Pricing and Public Policy," *Quarterly Journal of Economics* 62 (3): 289–314.

Khalidi, Rashid (2020). *A Hundred Years' War on Palestine: A History of Settler Colonialism and Resistance, 1917–2017*. New York: Metropolitan Books.

Khan, Nasir (1994). "US Abuse of UN in Gulf War," *Economic and Political Weekly* 29 (35), August 27: 2277–2282; retrieved: April 5, 2022: www.jstor.org/stable/4401680

Kinzer, Stephen (2003). *All the Shah's Men: An American Coup and the Roots of Middle East Terror*. Hoboken, NJ: John Wiley & Sons.

Kinzer, Stephen (2013). *The Brothers: John Foster Dulles, Allen Dulles, and Secret World of War*. New York: Henry Holt and Company.

Kissinger, Henry (2015). *World Order*. New York: Penguin.

Klare, Michael T. (2003). "It's the Oil, Stupid," *The Nation* April 24.

Klare, Michael T. (2004). *Blood and Oil: The Dangers and Consequences of America's Growing Dependency on Imported Petroleum*. New York: Metropolitan Books.

Knight, Frank H. (1921). *Risk, Uncertainty and Profit*. Boston: Houghton Mifflin Company.

Kolbert, Elizabeth (2014). *The Sixth Extinction: An Unnatural History*. New York: Henry Holt and Company.

Kool, Tom (2020). "A Massive Wave of Shut-Ins Fails to Halt Oil Price Crash," *Oilprice.com* April 21: https://oilprice.com/Energy/Energy-General/A-Massive-Wave-Of-Shut-Ins-Fails-To-Halt-Oil-Price-Crash.html

Kotz, David M. (2015). *The Rise and Fall of Neoliberal Capitalism*. Cambridge, MA: Harvard University Press.

Krauthammer, Charles (1990). "The Unipolar Moment," *Foreign Affairs* 70 (1): 23–33; retrieved: December 31, 2021: www.jstor.org/stable/20044692?origin=crossref

Krugman, Paul R. (1979). "Increasing Returns, Monopolistic Competition, and International Trade," *Journal of International Economics* 9 (4): 469–479.

Krugman, Paul R. (1995). *Development, Geography, and Economic Theory*. Cambridge, MA: MIT Press.

Kuruma, Samezõ ([2017] 2018). *Marx's Theory of the Genesis of Money: How Why, and Through What is a Commodity money?* Chicago, IL: Haymarket Books.

Lackner, Helen (2019). *Yemen in Crisis: The Road to War*. London: Verso.

Lange, Elena Louisa (2021). *Value without Fetish: Uno Kõzõ's Theory of 'Pure Capitalism' in Light of Marx's Critique of Political Economy*. Leiden: Brill.

Leffler, Melvyn P. (1984). "The American Conception of National Security and the Beginning of the Cold War, 1945–1948," *American Historical Review* 89: 346–381.

Lenin, Vladimir I. ([1916] 1970a). *Imperialism: The Highest Stage of Capitalism*. Peking: Foreign Language Press.

Lenin, Vladimir I. ([1916] 1970b). *The Proletarian Revolution and the Renegade Kautsky*. Peking: Foreign Language Press.

Lenin, Vladimir I. (1963). "Imperialism: The Highest Stage of Capitalism," in *Selected Works*, vol. 1. Moscow: Progress Publishers: www.marxists.org/archive/lenin/works/1916/imp-hsc/

Lenin, Vladimir I. ([1899] 1974). *The Development of Capitalism in Russia*. Moscow: Progress Publishers.

Levin, Murray B. (1971). *Political Hysteria in America: The Democratic Capacity for Repression*. New York: Basic books.

Lewis, Arthur (1954). "Economic Development with Unlimited Supplies of Labor," *The Manchester School* 22 (2): 139–191.

Liedman, Sven-Eric (2018). *A World to Win: The Life and Works of Karl Marx*. London: Verso.

Luxemburg, Rosa ([1913] 1951). *The Accumulation of Capital*. London: Routledge Kagan Paul Publishers.

Machlup, Fritz (1949). *The Basing-Point System*. Philadelphia, PA: Blackstone.

Macron, Emmanuel (2019). "French President Emmanuel Macron Lays Out France's Foreign Policy Priorities," *French Public Broadcast Service* (YouTube Video) August 27, 2019; retrieved: March 20, 2022: www.youtube.com/watch?v=4t75eVvLnn8

Mandel, Ernest (1978). *Late Capitalism*. London: Verso Press.

Marglin, Stephen A. and Juliet B. Schor (1992). *The Golden Age of Capitalism: Reinterpreting Postwar Experience* (eds.). New York: Oxford University Press.

Marshall, Alfred (1893). "On Rent," *Economic Journal*, 3 (9), March: 74–90.

Marx, Engels (1989). *Collected Works*, vol. 31. New York: International Publishers.

Marx, Karl ([1845] 1983). "Theses on Feuerbach," in *The Portable Karl Marx*. Eugene Kamenka (ed.). Harmondsworth, England: Penguin: 155–158.

Marx, Karl ([1847] 1969). *The Poverty of Philosophy*. New York: International Publishers.

Marx, Karl ([1847] 1973). *The Poverty of Philosophy*. Moscow: Progress Publishers.

Marx, Karl ([1852] 1963). *The Eighteenth Brumaire of Louis Bonaparte*. New York: International Publishers.

Marx, Karl ([1852] 1975). *The Eighteenth Brumaire of Louis Bonaparte*. New York: International Publishers.

Marx, Karl ([1859] 1970). *A Contribution to the Critique of Political Economy*. Moscow: Progress Publishers.

Marx, Karl ([1867] 1977). *Capital*, vol. 1. New York: Vintage.

Marx, Karl ([1885] 1981). *Capital*, vol. 2. New York: Vintage.

Marx, Karl ([1894] 1981). *Capital*, vol. 3. New York: Vintage.

Marx, Karl ([1939] 1973). *Grundrisse: Foundations of the Critique of Political Economy*. New York: Vintage.

Marx, Karl ([1939] 1993). *Grundrisse*. London: Penguin Edition.

Mavroudeas, Stavros D. 2006. "A History of Contemporary Political Economy and Postmodernism," *Review of Radical Political Economics* 38 (4), Fall: 499–518.

Mayer, Jane (2008). *The Dark Side*. New York: Doubleday.

Mearsheimer, John (2020). "Why Can't Ukraine Decide Its Own Future," *YouTube Channel* April 8; retrieved: April 9, 2022: www.youtube.com/watch?v=oR-yS6kULXw

Mearsheimer, John (2022). "Intervention d'un géopolitologue très apprécié d'Emmanuel Todd, John Mearsheimer, au sujet de la crise ukrainienne," *YouTube* March 13, 2022; retrieved: March 21, 2022: www.youtube.com/watch?v=w5qSO1BbXsU

Menger, Carl ([1871] 1950). *Principles of Economics*. Glencoe, IL: Free Press.

Michie, Jonathan (2017). *Advanced Introduction to Globalization*. Cheltenham, UK: Edward Elgar.

Mikdashi, Zuhayr (1966). *A Financial Analysis of Middle Eastern Oil Concessions: 1901–65*. New York: Praeger Publishers.

Milios, J. and D. Sotiropoulos (2009). *Rethinking Imperialism*. New York: Palgrave.

Milonakis, Dimitris and Ben Fine (2009). *From Political Economy to Economics*. New York: Routledge.

Moffatt, Mike (2020). "The Definition and Significance of the Walrasian Auctioneer," *ThoughtCo* February 11: www.thoughtco.com/overview-of-walrasian-auctioneers-1147333.

Mommer, B. (2002). *Global Oil and the Nation State*. Oxford: Oxford University Press.

Moudud, Jamee, Cyrus Bina, and Patrick Mason, eds. (2013). *Alternative Theories of Competition: Challenges to the Orthodoxy*. New York and London: Routledge.

Moudud, Jamee K. (2011). *Strategic Competition, Dynamics, and the Role of the State: A New Perspective*. Cheltenham, UK: Edward Elgar.

Murray, Robin (1977). "Value and Theory of Rent (Part 1)," *Capital and Class* 3: 100–122.

Nagel, Ernest and James R. Newman (1958). *Gödel's Proof*. New York: New York University Press.

National Archives, *The Pentagon Papers*; retrieved: August 20, 2021: www.archives.gov/research/pentagon-papers

Negri, Antonio (1991). *Marx Beyond Marx: Lessons on the Grundrisse*. London: Autonomedia/Pluto.

Nitzan, J. and S. Bichler (2009). *Capital as Power*. New York: Routledge.

Nwoke, Chibuzo (1987). *Third World Minerals and Global Pricing*. London: Zed Books.

Nye, Joseph (1991). *Bound to Lead: The Changing Nature of American Power*. New York: Basic Books.

Nye, Joseph (2004). *Soft Power: to Success in World Politics*. New York: Public Affairs.

NYMEX (2020). "Crude Oil WTI May," *NYMEX*, April 21: www.barchart.com/futures/quotes/CLK20

Orbie, J. and F. De Ville (2020). "Will the COVID-19 Crisis Herald the End of Neoliberal Globalization . . ." *United Nations University* (UNU-CRIS), April 30: http://cris.unu.edu/covid-19-end-of-neoliberal-globalisation

Palley, Thomas I. (2018). "Three Globalizations, Not Two: Rethinking the History and Economics of Trade and Globalization," in *Forum for Macroeconomics and Macroeconomic Policies*, no. 18. Berlin, Germany: Hans-Böckler-Stiftung.

Palloix, Christian (1975). "The Internationalization of Capital and the Circuit of Social Capital," in *International Firms and Modern Imperialism*. Hugo Radice (ed.). London: Penguin: 63–88.

Palloix, Christian (1977). "The Self-Expansion of Capital on a World Scale," *Review of Radical Political Economics* 9 (2): 1–28.

Panitch, Leo and Sam Gindin (2003). "Global Capitalism and American Empire," in *Socialist Register 2004*. Leo Panitch and Colin Leys (eds.). London: Merlin: 1–42.

Panitch, Leo and Sam Gindin (2012). *The Making of Global Capitalism: The Political Economy of American Empire*. New York: Verso.

Pass, Jonathan (2019). *American Hegemony in the 21st Century*. New York: Routledge.

Pettypiece, Shannon (2022). "Takeaways From Biden's Trip to Europe: Unity, Reassurance and a Memorable Gaffe," *NBC News* March 27; retrieved: March 29, 2022: www.nbcnews.com/politics/white-house/takeaways-bidens-trip-europe-rcna21718

Piketty, Thomas (2014). *Capital in the Twenty-First Century*. Cambridge, MA: Harvard University Press.

Polanyi, Karl ([1944] 1967). *The Great Transformation: The Political and Economic Origins of Our Time*. Boston, MA: Beacon Press.

Prashad, Vijay (2022). "'Open, Rank Hypocrisy' in Condemning War Crimes," *Democracy Now* April 15; retrieved: April 16, 2022: www.youtube.com/watch?v=TloP2RdHVPw

Predella, Lucia (2013). "Imperialism and Capitalist Development in Marx's Capital," *Historical Materialism* 21 (2): 117–147.

Putin, Vladimir (2007). "Speech at the Munich on Security Policy," February 10, Munich, Germany; retrieved: March 15, 2022: http://en.kremlin.ru/events/president/transcripts/24034/print

Putnam, Robert D. (2000). *Bowling Alone: The Collapse and Revival of American Community*. New York: Simon & Schuster.

Quinn, Andrew (2011). "Clinton says Gaddafi Must Go," *Reuters* February 27; retrieved: August 20, 2021: www.reuters.com/article/us-libya-usa-clinton/clinton-says-gaddafi-must-go-idUSTRE71Q1JA20110228

Radice, Hugo (1999). "Taking Globalization Seriously," in *Socialist Register 1999*, vol. 35. LeoPanitch and Colin Leys (eds.). London: The Merlin Press: 1–28.

Radice, Hugo (2015). *Global Capitalism: Selected Essays*. London: Routledge.

Reddy, Sanjay G. (2005). "Counting the Poor: The Truth About World Poverty Statistics," in *Socialist Register 2006: Telling the Truth*. Leo Panitch and Colin Leys (eds.). London: The Merlin Press: 169–178.

Reinsberg, Bernhard, Alexander Kentikelenis, and Thomas Stubbs (2021). "Creating Crony Capitalism: Neoliberal Globalization and the Fueling of Corruption," *Socio-Economic Review* 19 (2), April: 607–634.

Ricardo, David ([1817] 1911). *The Principles of Political Economy and Taxation*, 2nd ed. New York: J.M. Dent; E.P. Dutton.

Robinson, Joan ([1933] 1969). *The Economics of Imperfect Competition*. London: Macmillan.

Robinson, William I. (2014). "The Fetishism of Empire: A Critical Review of Panitch and Gindin's 'The Making of Global Capitalism'," *Studies in Political Economy* 93 (Spring): 155–173.

Rosdolsky, Roman (1977). *The Making of Marx's 'Capital'*. London: Pluto Press.

Rosenberg, Nathan ([1982] 1995). *Inside the Black Box: Technology and Economics*. Cambridge: Cambridge University Press.

Rosenberg, Paul (2020). "Does the Coronavirus Pandemic Mean the End of Globalization? Good!" *Salon* May 7: www.salon.com/2020/05/07/does-the-coronavirus-pandemic-mean- the-end-of-globalization-as-we-know-it/

Ryan, Maria (2018). "The Rise and Demise of American Unipolarism: Neoconservatives and Foreign Policy," *American Studies Journal* 65 (8); retrieved: December 31, 2021: www.asjournal.org/65-2018/the-rise-and-demise-of-american-unipolarism-neoconservatism-and-us-foreign- policy-1989–2009/

Saad-Filho, Alfredo (2020). "Coronavirus, Crisis, and the End of Neoliberalism," *The Bullet* April 17: https://socialistproject.ca/2020/04/coronavirus-crisis-and-the-end-of-neoliberalism/#more

Saad-Filho, Alfredo and Allison J. Ayers (2008). "Production, Class, and Power in the Neoliberal Tradition: A Critique of Coxian Eclecticism," in *Political Economy and International Relations Theory*. Allison J. Ayers (ed.). London: Palgrave Macmillan: 109–132.

Sachs, Jeffrey D. (2020). *The Ages of Globalization*. New York: Columbia University Press.

Sands, Philippe (2008). *Torture Team: Rumsfeld's Memo and the Betrayal of American Values*. New York: Palgrave Macmillan.

Sassoon, A. Showstack (1982). "Passive Revolution and the Politics of Reform," in *Approaches to Gramsci*. London: Writers and Readers.

Scahill, Jeremy (2007). *Blackwater: The Rise of the World's Most Powerful Mercenary Army*. New York: Nation Books.

Schumpeter, Joseph A. (1928). "The Instability of Capitalism," *Economic Journal* 38 (151): 361–386.

Schumpeter, Joseph A. (1942). *Capitalism, Socialism and Democracy*. New York: Harper and Row.

Schumpeter, Joseph A. (1954). *History of Economic Analysis*. New York: Oxford University Press.

Semmler, Willie (1984). *Competition, Monopoly and Differential Profit Rates*. New York: Columbia University Press.

Sen, A. K. (1977). "Rational Fools: A Critique of the Behavioral Foundations of Economic Theory," *Philosophy and Public Affairs* 6 (4): 317–344.

Sergent, Jim and Veronica Bravo (2020). "6 Charts Offer Lessons from Past Bear Markets," *USA Today* March 17: www.usatoday.com/in-depth/money/2020/03/17/coronavirus-how-stocks-moved- previous-bear-markets/5011397002/

Seymour, Richard (2022). "The Belligerati," *New Left Review* (Sidecar Blogpost—Politics) March 22; retrieved: March 25, 2022: https://newleftreview.org/sidecar/posts/the-belligerati?pc=1431

Shaiken, Harley (1986). *Work Transformed: Automation and Labor in the Computer Age*. Lexington, MA: Lexington Books.

Shaikh, Anwar (1974). "Laws of Production and Laws of Algebra: The Humbug Production Function," The *Review of Economics and Statistics* 56 (1), February: 115–120.

Shaikh, Anwar (1977). "Marx's Theory of Value and the Transformation Problem," in *The Subtle Anatomy of Capitalism*. J. Schwartz (ed.). Santa Monica, CA: Goodyear: 106–137.

Shaikh, Anwar (1980a). "Laws of Production and Laws of Algebra—Humbug II," in *Growth, Profits and Property*. Edward J. Nell (ed.). Cambridge, UK: Cambridge University Press: 80–95.

Shaikh, Anwar (1980b). "Marxian Competition versus Perfect Competition: Further Comments on the So- Called Choice of Techniques," *Cambridge Journal of Economics* 4 (1): 75–83.

Shaikh, Anwar (1982). "Neo-Ricardian Economics: A Wealth of Algebra, A Poverty of Theory," *Review of Radical Political Economics* 14 (2): 67–84.

Shaikh, Anwar (1983). "Centralization and Concentration of Capital," in *A Dictionary of Marxist Thought*. Bottomore, Tom, Lawrence Harris, V. G. Kiernan, and Ralph Miliband (eds.). Cambridge, MA: Harvard University Press: 68–69.

Shaikh, Anwar (2007). "Globalization and the Myth of Free Trade," in *Globalization and the Myth of Free Trade: History, Theory, and Empirical Evidence*, Ch. 3. Anwar Shaikh (ed.). New York: Routledge: 51–68.

Shaikh, Anwar (2016). *Capitalism: Competition, Conflict, Crises*. New York: Oxford University Press.

Shaikh, Anwar and Rania Antonopoulos (2013). "Explaining Long Term Exchange Rate Behavior in the United States and Japan," in *Alternative Theories of Competition: Challenges to the Orthodoxy*. J. Moudud, C. Bina, and P. Mason (eds.). New York: Routledge: 201–228.

Singh, Kavaljit (2005). *Questioning Globalization*. New York: Zed Books.

Skinner, Michael (2021). "Twenty Years of the Afghanistan Occupation Ends: A New Phase of Struggle Begins," *The Bullet* September 2; retrieved: September 2, 2021: https://socialistproject.ca/2021/09/twenty-year-afghanistan-occupation-ends/#more

Solow, Robert M. (1957). "Technical Change and the Aggregate Production Function," *The Review of Economics and Statistics* 39 (3), August: 312–320.

Sraffa, Piero (1960). *Production of Commodities by Means of Commodities*. Cambridge: Cambridge University Press.

Starkey, Sara (2022). "Putin Reminds Everyone that Ukraine Joining NATO Could Lead to Nuclear War," *Bulletin of the Atomic Scientists* February 11; retrieved: March 28, 2022: https://thebulletin.org/2022/02/putin-says-ukraine-membership-in-nato-would-make-nuclear-war-more- likely/

Steel, Ronald ([1967] 1970). *Pax Americana*. New York: The Viking Press.

Steindl, Josef (1952). *Maturity and Stagnation in American Capitalism*. Oxford: Basil Blackwell.

Stiglitz, Joseph E. (2002). *Globalization and Its Discontents*. New York: W.W. Norton & Company.

Suskind, Run (2006). *The One Percent Doctrine*. New York: Simon & Shuster.

Sweezy, Paul M. (1939). "Demand Under Conditions of Oligopoly," *The Journal of Political Economy* 47 (4), August: 568–573.

Sweezy, Paul M. (1946). *The Theory of Capitalist Development: Principles of Marxian Political Economy*, 2nd ed. London: D. Dobson.

Sweezy, Paul M. (1981). "Competition and Monopoly," *Monthly Review* 33 (1): 1–16.

Taylor, Alan (2014). "The Soviet War in Afghanistan, 1979–1989," *The Atlantic* August 4; retrieved: August 20, 2021: www.theatlantic.com/photo/2014/08/the-soviet-war-in-afghanistan-1979-1989/100786/

Telford, T. and T. Heath (2020). "Wall Street Seizes up as Pandemic-Fueled Volatility Sends Dow into a Deep Dive," *The Washington Post* March 18: www.washingtonpost.com/business/2020/03/18/markets-economy-live-updates-coronavirus/

The 9/11 Commission Report (2004). New York: W.W. Norton & Company.

Thomas, Peter D. (2009). *The Gramscian Moment*. Chicago, IL: Haymarket Books.

Thompson, Edward P. (1978). *The Poverty of Theory and Other Essays*. New York: Monthly Review.

Tomforde, Anna (1989). "The Fall of the Berlin Wall—Archive, November 1989," *The Guardian* November 10; retrieved: February 20, 2022: www.theguardian.com/world/from-the-archive-blog/2019/oct/30/the-fall-of-the-berlin-wall-archive-november-1989

Trotsky, Leon ([1917] 2008). *History of the Russian Revolution*. Chicago, IL: Haymarket Books.

Uno, Kõzõ ([1964]1980). *Principles of Political Economy*. Essex, UK: The Harvester Press.

US Congress, House Committee on Foreign Relations (1990). *Hearing before the Subcommittee on Europe and the Middle East, United States-Iraq Relations*. Washington, DC: US Government Printing Office, April 26.

US Congress, Senate Committee on Foreign Relations (1987). *War in the Persian Gulf: The US Takes Sides*. Washington, DC: US Government Printing Office, November.

Wallerstein, Emmanuel I. (2003.) *The Decline of American Power: The U.S. in a Chaotic World*. New York: New Press.

Wallerstein, Emmanuel I. (2004). *World-Systems Analysis: An Introduction*. Durham and London: Duke University Press.

Wallerstein, Immanuel I. (2002). "The Eagle Has Crash Landed," *Foreign Policy* July/August: www.foreignpolicy.com/issue_julyaug_2002/wallerstein.ht

Walras, Léon ([1871] 2014). *Elements of Theoretical Economics*. Cambridge: Cambridge University Press.

Walras, Léon ([1874] 1954). *Elements of Pure Economics*. Homewood, IL: Richard D. Irwin.

Weeks, John (1981a). *Capital and Exploitation*. Princeton, NJ: Princeton University Press.

Weeks, John (1981b). "The Differences between Materialist Theory and Dependency Theory and Why They Matter," *Latin American Perspectives* 8 (3–4): 118–123.

Weeks, John (2011). *Capital, Exploitation and Economic Crisis*. London: Routledge.

Weeks, John (2012). *The Irreconcilable Inconsistencies of Neoclassical Macroeconomics: A False Paradigm*. New York: Routledge.

Weeks, John (2013). "The Fallacy of Competition: Markets and Movement of Capital," in *Alternative Theories of Competition: Challenges to the Orthodoxy*. J. Moudud, C. Bina, and P. Mason (eds.). New York: Routledge: 13–26.

Weeks, John (2014). *Economics of the 1%: How Mainstream Economics Serves the Rich, Obscures Reality and Distorts Policy*. London: Anthem Press.

Westra, Richard (2021). *Economics, Science and Capitalism*. London: Routledge.

White House (2002). *The National Security Strategy of the United States of America*. Washington, DC: Government Printing Office, September 17.

Whitlock, Craig (2021). *The Afghanistan Papers*. New York: Simon & Shuster.

Wikan, Vilde Skorpen (2015). "What Is 'Neoliberalism', and How Does It Relate to Globalization," *E-International Relations?* May 21; retrieved: December 31, 2021.

Wolf, Zachary B., Curt Merrill, and Ji Min Lee (2022). "Zelensky's Address to Congress" (annotated), *CNN* March 16, 2022; retrieved: March 18, 2020: www.cnn.com/interactive/2022/03/politics/ukraine-zelensky-congress-speech-annotated/

Woodward, Bob (2018). *Fear: Trump in the White House*. New York: Simon & Schuster.

Woodward, Bob (2020). *Rage*. New York: Simon & Shuster.

Woodward, Bobb and Robert Costa (2021). *Peril*. New York: Simon & Shuster.

World Health Organization (WHO). 2020. "Coronavirus Disease (COVID-2019) Situation Reports." April 19. www.who.int/emergencies/diseases/novel-coronavirus-2019/situation-reports

World Health Organization (WHO) (2022). "Coronavirus Disease (COVID 2019) Situation Reports," April 19: www.who.int/emergencies/diseases/novel-coronavirus- 19:2019/situation-reports

World Statistics (2022). "Coronavirus Cases." April 19: www.worldometers.info/coronavirus/

Yergin, Daniel (1991). *The Prize*. New York: Simon and Schuster.

Yergin, Daniel (2011). *The Quest*. New York: Penguin.

Zevin, Alexander (2022). "The Normal War," *New Left Review* (Sidecar, NLR blogpost: Politics) March 31; retrieved: April 2, 2022: https://newleftreview.org/sidecar/posts/a-normal-war?pc=1432

Zinn, Howard (2015 [1999]). *A People's History of the United States*. New York: HarperCollins.

Zoninsein, Jonas (1990). *Monopoly Capital Theory: Hilferding and Twentieth-Century Capitalism*. New York: Greenwood Press.

Zuboff, Shoshana (2019). *The Age of Surveillance Capitalism: The Fight for Human Future at the New Frontier of Power*. New York: Public Affairs.

Index

Note: Page numbers in *italics* indicate a figure and page numbers in **bold** indicate a table on the corresponding page.